Going Broke

Going Broke

Why Americans (Still) Can't Hold On
to Their Money

UPDATED EDITION ■

STUART VYSE

OXFORD
UNIVERSITY PRESS

OXFORD
UNIVERSITY PRESS

Oxford University Press is a department of the University of Oxford. It furthers
the University's objective of excellence in research, scholarship, and education
by publishing worldwide. Oxford is a registered trade mark of Oxford University
Press in the UK and certain other countries.

Published in the United States of America by Oxford University Press
198 Madison Avenue, New York, NY 10016, United States of America.

Library of Congress Cataloging-in-Publication Data
Names: Vyse, Stuart A., author.
Title: Going broke : why Americans (still) can't hold on to their money / Stuart Vyse.
Description: Updated edition. | Oxford; New York : Oxford University Press, [2019] |
Includes bibliographical references and index.
Identifiers: LCCN 2018008296 | ISBN 9780190677848 (pbk.) |
ISBN 9780190677862 (epub)
Subjects: LCSH: Bankruptcy—United States—Case studies. |
Finance, Personal—United States. | Consumer education—United States.
Classification: LCC HG3766 .V97 2019 | DDC 339.4/70973—dc23
LC record available at https://lccn.loc.gov/2018008296

9 8 7 6 5 4 3 2 1

Printed by Sheridan Books, Inc., United States of America

For Emily and Graham

CONTENTS

When the first edition of this book was written, George W. Bush was president of the United States, the first iPhone had just been introduced, and Amazon. com was the twenty-fifth top retail company in the country—today it is the third. Most importantly, we were just beginning to feel the first signs of what would eventually be the biggest economic event since the Great Depression. After a long boom in the housing market, foreclosures were starting to increase, but it would be another year or more before we knew the full depth and breadth of the crisis, and longer still before our national economic headache would be memorialized with a name: the Great Recession of 2008.

As a result, the first edition of this book concentrated on the expansion of our consumer economy in the decades between the late 1970s and 2007. It chronicled how new technologies and banking methods fueled a kind of home invasion, making it possible for us to spend money whenever we were awake. For the first time, there was no refuge from the commercial marketplace, and although these innovations helped drive a long period of economic growth, they also created many new challenges for individual consumers hoping to keep their financial houses in order.

Despite the profound effects of the recession, many of the original themes of *Going Broke* carry through in this edition. In both old and new ways, the commercial invasion outlined in the first edition continues unabated today. A number of new technologies introduced since the first edition have made spending—anytime and anywhere—even easier than it was a decade ago, and although there was hope that the experience of 2008 would turn us into a nation of savers, that dream has failed to materialize. Nonetheless, there is some good news. Several of the worst abuses of the banking industry have been limited—at least for the time being—by new regulations, and for those struggling to keep their personal accounts in the black, there are a number of new tools available to help you balance your budget and manage your saving and spending.

As I write this, the economy appears to have almost completely recovered. The stock market has broken records, and unemployment is lower than it has been since the late 1990s. But it would be a mistake to say that consumers are substantially better off than they were in the prerecession period covered by the first edition. As we will see, there is overwhelming evidence that a substantial portion of the population is still hanging by a thread, just one financial shock away from disaster. Furthermore, today's economic problems span both the lower and middle economic classes. Only those in the higher income brackets can breathe freely.

Some features of the postrecession world are different. Many of us still have little or no savings and too much debt, but the shape of our indebtedness and the nature of our economic challenges have changed over the last decade. Furthermore, when people get into financial difficulty today, often the manner of their distress is not what it used to be. It is hard to imagine, but when I was writing the first edition of this book, real estate foreclosure seemed like a rare and distant phenomenon. A house that was "under water" was assumed to have been in a flood. Today this and many other new economic concepts are part of our standard vocabulary.

The time between the first and second editions of *Going Broke* has been one of great economic change, but this edition is not merely an update. The field of behavioral economics has continued its rapid development in the intervening years, and the importance of this research has continued to be recognized, most recently by the selection of Richard Thaler for the 2017 Nobel Prize in economics. For several years, I used portions of *Going Broke* as readings for a senior seminar in behavioral economics, and the responsibilities of teaching that class helped me keep up with many of the latest findings. As a result, this edition benefits from some of these new developments in behavioral economics.

It has been a rare privilege to be able to take a second plunge into a topic I visited ten years ago—to once again become immersed in an issue that touches so many lives. In doing so, I tried to approach the subject with new eyes. I conducted additional research, both in the library and in the real world. I went to many sessions of small claims court and housing court to get a glimpse of the faces behind the economic statistics, and I talked to people who had lost their homes to foreclosure. It is an undeniable fact that a very large proportion of adults in the richest nation on Earth are scraping by from day to day, or not scraping by at all, and I hope this book provides a more complete picture of how so many people have arrived at a place where they are unable to manage their financial affairs. The explanation is less about the individual people involved and more about the shape of our modern economy—an economy that is, to a great extent, dependent on individual consumers carrying large burdens of debt.

Finally, my greatest hope for *Going Broke* is that in revealing the psychological forces at play in the contemporary marketplace, readers will recognize things they can do to strengthen their standing and achieve a life free of financial stress. To that end, the final chapter is devoted to reflecting on the story that has gone before and applying the principles of behavioral economics to the project of avoiding debt and increasing savings. It is a great joy to live a life within one's means, a life where money is no longer a barrier. In the United States, such a life is possible for all but those at the very lowest income levels, and I hope the following pages will help more people reach that comfortable end.

Stuart Vyse
January 4, 2018

Going Broke

The Open Drain

At times he angrily wished the whole thing done with, wished some supernal referee would blow a whistle and declare him out, bankrupt. But he was beginning to learn that financial ruin, like death, is not a moment but a process, a slow, merciless grinding down. Sometimes not even an expert could say, in a given case, that ruin has now come, or ruin, though close at hand, has not yet arrived.

—JOHN GARDNER, *Mickelsson's Ghosts*

The poor have little, beggars none, the rich too much, *enough* not one.

—BENJAMIN FRANKLIN, *Poor Richard's Almanack 1733–1758*

I got my first real job in 1976, working at a school for autistic children for $6,000 a year. In those days, this was a reasonable entry-level salary, and for the first time in my life I had enough money to rent an apartment without need of roommates. After college and an aimless stint in graduate school, I had landed in Providence, Rhode Island, and life was good. I was in my mid-twenties and unattached, and thanks to generous parents, inexpensive state universities, and a string of student-work jobs and graduate assistantships, I was free of student loans. I entered the world of work unburdened by responsibility or debt.

For several years, I lived reasonably on a cash-and-carry basis. I drove a Ford Mustang handed down to me by my parents, and my only bills were rent and utilities. I was not living in luxury. My apartment was outfitted with yard sale furniture and bookcases made of planks stacked on piles of bricks. At that time, an annual income of $6,000 was below the poverty level for a family of five. But for a single person living alone, it was more than sufficient. I could go to the movies and eat out several times a week.

As a kid I had never picked up the habit of saving. I always worked—as a paperboy, as an ice cream jockey at the local Dairy Queen, and, in the summers, at a variety of factory jobs. I was not a financial wizard, but neither was I an idle youth. Money was coming in, but it went out just as fast. And when I arrived in Providence in the mid-1970s, I lived the same way. I was young and had no concept of the future or what my needs might be once it arrived. I was living in the moment, and for the moment, everything was fine.

I don't remember when I got my first credit card. It might have been a charge plate for the local Apex department store. In those days, many people began their borrowing careers with store credit cards, and I may have followed the same pattern. Apex was something of a Rhode Island institution offering reasonably priced clothes, appliances, and furniture. I know I shopped there regularly, but my credit report provides no evidence of an Apex charge plate at that time.[1] Accounts that have been inactive for more than ten years should not appear on the report, and although there are several old entries on mine, there is no mention of Apex.

My credit record does show that I got my first Visa card in April 1979 from Norwest Card Services of Des Moines, Iowa. That was a period of change in my life, five months before I got married. At approximately this time, my future wife and I moved into a more expensive apartment. My wife, who was a teacher at the school for autistic children where I worked, soon quit her job to attend graduate school, and eventually I, too, went back to graduate school to pursue a doctorate in psychology. So our combined earnings fell. I always worked, at least part-time, and we lived frugally enough that I don't recall any serious financial strain. We rarely ate out, and our vacations were camping trips within driving distance of home, but I don't recall feeling underprivileged. In many ways, this graduate school period was a very happy one.

During the 1980s, I took on $2,000 or $3,000 in student loan debt to cover graduate tuition payments, and despite having returned to very low levels of income, I seem not to have done much borrowing. At this time, my wife and I lived in a comfortable and inexpensive apartment in Providence, and we were busy with work and school. Looking back, life seemed remarkably uncomplicated in those days. But in the autumn of 1986 I began teaching at a college an hour away, and we took out an auto loan to pay for a new Dodge Colt. Having completed her degree, my wife started her first social work job. We both needed dependable transportation, and the new Colt would be added to a Honda Civic given to us by my wife's father.

Our first car loan did not represent much of a change in our financial profile. By then my wife was making a good salary, and my teaching position brought a significant increase in income over the part-time work that had sustained us through graduate school. But other events soon rocked our financial world.

First, we bought a house. To help cover the mortgage payment, we chose a two-family home in a middle-class neighborhood of Providence, but even with the help of rental income, the realities of homeownership neutralized my increase in salary. As renters, we had never had to shoulder the burdens of residential upkeep, and now we had tenants. Whenever anything broke in the renters' apartment, we were obligated to fix it right away, whereas nonessential repairs in our half of the house could be dealt with or not, as our current needs dictated. Meanwhile, I was an untenured professor learning how to teach and trying to publish enough research to pass my tenure review. It was nice to own a home in the city we loved, but life had suddenly become more complicated.

Then we had a child.

Our son was born in September 1989, and suddenly my wife and I needed more space. Our half of the house had been very comfortable for the two of us, but there were only two bedrooms and one would now be the baby's room. I took care of our son on days I didn't have to be on campus, but I also needed a place to work at home. The solution was to expand upward. Our apartment was on the second floor, and above it was an attic that you could stand up in if you stood near the peak of the rafters. So in the summer of 1989 we hired a contractor to install skylights and studs for the walls of an attic room that would serve as a combination home office and playroom. Between diaper changes and trips to the park, I would be able to work at a desk tucked under the sloped ceiling while my son napped or played.

The arrival of a child and the creation of this attic room marked the beginnings of a life beyond our means. I did most of the work of remodeling the attic myself, but we needed lumber, wallboard, insulation, paint, carpeting, electrical wiring, and fixtures. In addition, we began to pay for a babysitter on the days that neither my wife nor I could be at home, and my hour-long commute ate up cars at a rapid rate. In 1990, we were forced to buy a second Dodge Colt when the Honda threw a rod on Interstate 95, and now there were two car loans, school loans, a mortgage, and many other expenses. Our combined salaries were higher than ever before, but we seemed poorer than we ever had been.

Also during these early years of parenthood, I began to acquire more credit cards. Between 1985 and 1992, JCPenney, Sears, Macy's, Filene's, and American Express cards were added to my wallet, and although these accounts never had substantial balances, I discovered that plastic was an easy way to pay. For the first time, I was making minimum payments on several accounts without any real plan to pay down the balances. The mortgage, car loans, and school loans were always paid on time, but often it was hard to pay more than the minimum amount on the revolving store accounts or on my Visa.

Then came our second child.

In October 1992, our daughter was born, and now the house was really too small. I had been awarded tenure earlier that year, and although my successful review produced only a modest salary increase, I now had job security. As much as we loved Providence, our lives had changed with the coming of children, and now it was time to move on. My son would soon be school-age, and the commute to work was beginning to wear on me. So we put our house on the market and started the search for a new home in a suburban community closer to the college.

Our timing was not good. We had purchased our home when the market was high, and now we needed to sell when the market was low. After six months or so, we unloaded the house at only a modest loss, but when we found a suitable single-family home just twenty minutes from my office, we were forced to take out a second mortgage to make up for an inadequate down payment. However, in the new house, everybody had a bedroom, and there was even an office space for me. But the squeeze was on. Carrying two mortgages and other debts without any help from rental income, we quickly entered a period of real financial strain. We continued to eat out very rarely—in part because eating out required the added expense of paying a sitter. Like many couples with small children, we stayed home and watched rented movies. I brought bag lunches to work and tried to be very frugal, but between the heavier mortgage and paying for child care on the days we both had to be away from home, it was difficult to cover all our bills.

In the mid-to-late 1990s I had two bank credit cards. In March 1995 I transferred $3,000 from my Norwest card to a new People's Bank card, but by July 1997, I had worked the balance down to $2,099 and was able to pay it off completely with some of the early royalties from my first book. But I also had a First USA card that was now hovering close to its $5,000 limit, and I had a balance of $829 on my Sears account. My wife and I made good salaries, but with two car loans, school loans, childcare, and household expenses, I frequently found myself trying to decide which bills we could get away without paying each month. Utility bills were often the best choice, because it took several months of nonpayment before the electric or phone would be disconnected, and I had a sense that these delinquencies would do the least damage to our credit rating. Nonetheless, our phone was disconnected on one occasion, and during this period, my credit record also shows a number of late payments on my People's Bank and Sears accounts.

I was a college professor; my wife was a social worker. We lived in a modest house in a neighborhood that was a mixture of blue- and white-collar families. I rarely bought clothes, and our kids went to public schools. We thought of ourselves as solidly middle class—even upper middle class—but somehow we were sinking. Yes, we had a house and young children, but at this stage in our careers, life seemed much harder than it was supposed to be. Every decision we made was tinged with anxiety and worry about where the money was going to come from. We never felt comfortable.

Then came the divorce.

In January 1999, my wife and I began the process of dissolving our twenty-year marriage. Soon I moved out of the house and began paying child support, but there were also thousands of dollars in attorney's fees and other settlement expenses. Because we agreed that she would keep the house until our daughter, who was seven, entered middle school, I had to start over again in an apartment with few of the furnishings my new life would require. I entered this period with approximately $7,000 in unsecured credit card debt. I was driving a twelve-year-old Toyota Corolla I had purchased used. All my previous school and automobile loans had been paid off, but now I was forced to take out a $4,000 loan to cover mounting divorce costs. My credit card balance started to grow.

Four years later, in the summer of 2003, my world had regained some stability. The loan for divorce expenses was paid off, and I was paying all my bills on time. My children had adapted well to traveling between their mother's house and my apartment. By necessity, I was living rather frugally, but my children and I had what we needed. There was just one remaining problem: my MBNA MasterCard, the only bank card I was carrying at the time, had a balance of $12,000 (the equivalent of $16,000 in 2017). In relation to the funds I had available to support myself—after child support and taxes were taken out—this unsecured debt represented 30 percent of my net annual income. When I looked back, I knew my life had not been particularly lavish or undisciplined, but somehow I found myself among those Americans who are dragged down by the weight of substantial debt. Once the hole got to be this size, I could not imagine how I might fill it in, and so I just assumed it would always be there.

LIVING IN THE RED

The only thing remarkable about this story is that, at this point in history, it is completely ordinary. In fact, it is a dream compared to the dramas being lived out by millions of Americans whose phones never seem to stop ringing. With more bills than cash, they have fallen behind and are unable to make the payments on their credit cards, auto loans, school loans, rent, or mortgages. Collection people from doctors' offices, utility companies, banks, and stores call daily demanding payment, and to avoid these embarrassing conversations, many people let the calls go to voicemail. After longer periods of delinquency or nonpayment, some debts are sold to private collection agencies, whose callers are sometimes aggressive and threatening. Although there are laws against harassment by collection agencies, the laws are difficult to enforce, and as America's indebtedness has risen and the demand for debt collection agencies has grown, consumer complaints have skyrocketed. For several years debt collection has topped the list of complaints received by the Federal Trade Commission (FTC)—859,090 complaints in 2016, which is more than twelve times the number of complaints in 2005. Fully 28 percent of all complaints to the FTC are about debt collections, which was more than twice the rate of the next most common complaint, impostor scams.[2] Many of these complaints are about belligerent agents who call at all hours, often misrepresenting the size and nature of the debt. In violation of the law, callers sometimes contact the debtors' relatives, employers, and neighbors and threaten legal action.[3] Bills, often with pink paper showing through the envelope window to signal an overdue account, arrive daily, and when things get far enough out of control, there are letters from collection agencies and lawyers threatening lawsuits. After months or years of this kind of stressful existence, foreclosure or bankruptcy begin to look like attractive ways to stop the steady barrage of phone calls and bills.

The numbers tell us we continue to live in an era when people save very little and borrow a lot. As a result, problems with debt are widespread. In the United States, the average personal savings rate, which hovered between 10 and 12 percent throughout the 1960s, 1970s, and 1980s, dropped to a seventy-year low of 2 percent in 2005. In the years following the recession of 2008, savings edged back up to 6 percent levels, but it is currently on the decline again. By November of 2017, the personal savings rate had dropped to 2.9 percent, only 1 percent above the record low set in 2005.[4] Meanwhile, although some observers hoped the recession of 2008 would turn Americans away from debt, borrowing has continued to grow unabated. As Figure 1.1 shows, the dip in household indebtedness following the 2008 recession ended in 2013, and since then Americans have resumed a steady upward pursuit of debt. In the first quarter of 2017, aggregate household debt hit a new peak of $12.8 trillion, surpassing the previous prerecession peak from 2008, and our hunger for more debt shows no signs of tapering off. Although my credit card balance of $12,000 seemed high at the time, today it would be very typical. The current average balance held by people who carry credit card debt is over $16,000, a sum that is equivalent to my debt in 2003. Many of these people must feel—as I did—that their debt is an impossible mountain to climb.[5] Worse still, the

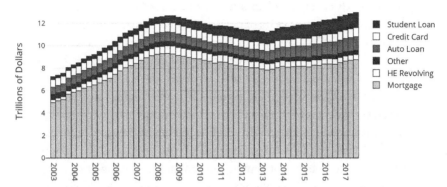

Figure 1.1 Total US household debt by type of loan from 2003 through the third quarter of 2017. Mortgage, revolving home equity (HE), and, to a lesser extent, credit card debt all declined after the 2008 Great Recession, but student loan debt and auto loan debt have grown substantially since 2008. In addition, mortgage debt resumed its climb in 2013, and by the end of the first quarter of 2017 total household debt once again topped the 2008 record level (nominal dollars).
SOURCE: Federal Reserve Bank of New York/Equifax.

financial landscape has changed in the years leading up to and following 2008, presenting new financial challenges.

THE VIEW FROM THIS SIDE OF THE CRASH

Economists now call it the Great Recession, a name that gives it a place in the pantheon of modern financial debacles just below the Great Depression of the 1930s. In 2007 the median cost of a new home fell for the first time in fifteen years, setting off a cascade of events that most of us who witnessed it will never forget: bank failures, bank bailouts, an economic stimulus package, 10 percent unemployment, foreclosures, personal bankruptcies, and a stock market plunge that lasted six years.

Now much of the dust has cleared, and we can see some things have changed and others have not. In many ways, we've remained remarkably loyal in our long-term love affair with borrowing, but the average household's debt profile is different today than it was when I was running up my credit cards in the 1990s and early 2000s. The Great Recession of 2008 did little to alter the overall picture, but the particulars of our indebtedness have changed.

THINGS THAT ARE THE SAME

- **Our Overall Level of Indebtedness Continues to Climb**. Figure 1.1 shows that after a few years of decline during the Great Recession, household debt has resumed its steady rise. Furthermore, a number of factors suggest it will continue its current pattern. First, for the last ten years, increases in the cost of living have outpaced the growth in wages, creating strain on family budgets. Furthermore, long before the crash, the fates of those on the top and bottom of the economic ladder were pulling apart. As a result, while income has risen for those in the upper half of the income curve, salaries of those at the bottom half of the curve have not kept up with inflation, making borrowing a tempting means of maintaining a standard of living. With most of the increase in wealth going to people at the top, borrowing remains a priority for those at the bottom.[6]
- **We Still Love Plastic**. Credit card use has hardly changed at all. There was a drop in credit card debt and a decrease in credit card delinquencies during the recession, but much of that came from "charge-offs." When everything went sour, banks closed many delinquent accounts and wrote off the unrecovered balances. In addition, the Credit Card Accountability Responsibility and Disclosure Act (CARD Act), which passed in May of 2009 in the wake of the financial crisis and President Barack Obama's election, went into effect in 2010, limiting lending to younger borrowers and placing restrictions on solicitations.[7]

Credit cards represent less than a trillion dollars of the nation's aggregate household debt burden, but of all the debt streams in Figure 1.1 credit cards and "other" varied the least during the recession. The "other" category includes some very similar forms of borrowing—store credit cards and gas cards, as well as miscellaneous forms of consumer loans. These convenient forms of household credit took only a modest hit during the recession and, in recent years, have resumed their prerecession growth.

- **We Still Don't Save Very Much**. As mentioned above, the United States savings rate rose slightly following The Great Recession and has since resumed a downward trend. Figure 1.2,[8] which is based on somewhat more favorable 2015 data, shows United States was merely average for this group of countries, all of which are considered developed and high-income relative to the rest of the world. Although being in the middle of this pack might not seem so bad, it is important to remember that the social safety net is much better in almost all of these countries than it is in the United States. Savings is what gets you through a rainy day, and if you have little savings and there is nothing else out there to keep you dry, you may drown.

Here are two examples of the weaknesses of the American social safety net. First, in only a handful of the countries shown in Figure 1.2 do fewer than 100 percent of the citizens have either public or private health insurance. The numbers at the base of each bar represent the percentage of citizens not covered, and, where no number appears, all the citizens are covered. Despite the progress made by the Affordable Care Act, as of 2016, 9 percent of US citizens lacked health insurance. Among the Organisation for Economic Co-operation and Development (OECD) nations in Figure 1.2, only Greece, a country that has long been in economic crisis, had fewer people covered. Furthermore, over 50 percent of US citizens were covered by private insurance—a much larger proportion than any other country on this chart—and as we all know, private insurance in the United States varies widely in what and how much it covers. For many people, an unexpected illness or injury can result in crushing medical expenses—even when they have insurance—and without savings, many people soon find themselves unable to make the payments. Unanticipated medical

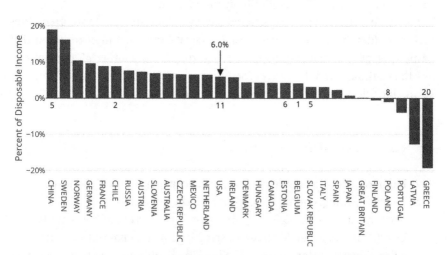

Figure 1.2 Average household savings rate for thirty countries of the Organisation for Economic Co-operation and Development and the percentage of the population of each country that is not covered by health insurance (numbers at the base of each bar). Where there is no number at the base of a bar, 100 percent of the population is covered. Both savings rates and health coverage data are from 2015.

expenses have long been cited as a common precipitating factor for declaring bankruptcy, and a 2016 Kaiser Family Foundation survey found that in 20 percent of households *with* medical insurance someone was experiencing problems paying medical bills.[9]

Second, the United States has no mandated paid family leave. Indeed, of 165 countries studied in a 2014 report by the International Labor Organization, only two countries failed to mandate paid family leave, the United States and Papua New Guinea. According to the US Bureau of Labor Statistics, only 13 percent of all private employees have access to paid family leave.[10] As a result, most people in the United States who have a child or get sick will have greater need for a rainy day fund than people in almost any other country. America may be the land of opportunity, but if life throws you a curve ball, you're on your own.

With the rise of Uber and Lyft, we have seen the promotion of a "gig economy," in which workers are recast as ambitious independent entrepreneurs. But as a practical matter, the gig economy is just an upbeat reformulation of an old business strategy: turn employees into independent contractors to avoid paying overtime, sick leave, and other benefits.[11] As I write this in 2017, the Republican Party controls the White House and both houses of Congress, and the administration hopes to eliminate the Affordable Care Act and further reduce worker benefits and entitlements. If they are successful, the country's social safety net will get smaller rather than larger.

Finally, other measures of personal savings paint an even more precarious picture hidden beneath the averages. A survey conducted in 2016 found that 34 percent of American adults had zero savings, and another 35 percent had less than a thousand dollars saved. So our current single-digit levels of personal saving include a large group of people who are not saving at all.[12]

THINGS THAT ARE DIFFERENT

- **Homeownership Is Down**. Always a central part of the American Dream, owning a home has gone decidedly out of fashion. After reaching an historic high of approximately 69 percent of households in 2006, homeownership began a steep decline that has only recently given signs of bottoming out. The housing bubble appears to have dampened the appeal of signing a mortgage, and homeownership is at its lowest level in three decades. In direct parallel with this trend, the stock of available apartments has plummeted. Of course, some of the drop in homeownership is due to the tsunami of foreclosures during the recession, but foreclosures alone cannot explain this trend. There are some signs of a recovery in the housing market, but the good news is primarily concentrated in the upper end. Prices have increased most for homes worth $500,000 and higher, but below this level, the effects of the recession have lingered.[13]

- **Student Loan Debt Is Growing Rapidly**. The aggregate student loan debt started to expand well before the Great Recession of 2008, but, as Figure 1.1 shows, it has accelerated in the years since. At 1.36 trillion dollars in the fall of 2017, aggregate debt on student loans is now the second-largest pile of household debt after mortgages, more than 1.6 times the amount owed on all bank credit card debt. As we will see, the student loan picture is complicated, but there is some evidence that the burden of college loan payments is increasing the time young people live with their parents and delaying the purchase of homes, a possible contributing factor to the decline in homeownership. It has been a long-standing trend that, young people with a history of student loan debt were more likely to purchase a home in the years following graduation—presumably because their education had improved their financial standing. That pattern has now reversed. Twenty-seven- to thirty-year-olds *without* student loan debt are now more likely to buy homes than those of the same age with a history of student loans.[14]

- **Auto Loans Are Also Growing Rapidly**. Along with student loans, auto loan debt has grown substantially since the Great Recession. At 1.2 trillion dollars in total outstanding debt, auto loans are third in line after mortgages and student loans. In a pattern that parallels the lead-up to the recession, much of the growth is in the area of subprime loans offered to higher-risk borrowers who generally have lower credit scores.[15] In addition, the amounts and lengths of auto loans have increased. According to the credit monitoring firm Experian, by June 2016, the average loan amount was over $30,000 and the average term of an auto loan had risen to 68 months. Seven-year loans are becoming more common, even when purchasing used cars.[16]

In 2011, the economists Annamaria Lusardi, Daniel Schneider, and Peter Tufano introduced a new way to measure the financial fragility of households. They simply asked survey respondents whether, if faced with an emergency, they could "come up with" $2,000 in thirty days. The language of the question was designed to leave the door open to a variety of means for amassing the needed funds, including savings, credit, borrowing from friends and family, working more, or selling something, and the $2,000 amount was thought to be comparable to an expensive car repair, an unexpected medical expense, or home maintenance emergency. Surprisingly, Lusardi and colleagues found that half of Americans said that they probably or certainly could not muster $2,000. Half. Furthermore, this level of financial precariousness was not limited to the poor. Almost a quarter of those with incomes between $100,000 and $150,000 per year said they could not produce this emergency amount in a month.[17]

In recent years the Federal Reserve has published an annual report on the economic well-being of households, and they have introduced a question about a considerably smaller emergency sum than in the Lusardi study: $400. In 2015, an astonishing 46 percent of American adults said they could not produce that amount of cash or, if they could, they would have to borrow the money or sell something.[18]

Why have Americans found themselves in this precarious situation? The United States has the highest gross domestic product of any nation.[19] Compared to many other places in the world, unemployment is low and wages are high. Immigrants from all over the world go to extraordinary lengths—often risking death—to come to this country in pursuit of economic advantage. Although many of the products that symbolize the American way of life are now made in other countries, the United States is the most highly sought-after of all markets, and American culture is exported throughout the world in television and film images. By any number of measures, most of us have everything we—and the rest of the world—could possibly want. But for all too many Americans, the good life is slipping through their fingers.

It often seems like we are living in a kind of anxious, foggy dream. Even if our own financial world is stable, on some semiconscious level we have a sense that for many people—perhaps even people we know—something is very wrong. Watching television late at night, after all the commercials for luxury cars and diamond necklaces have slipped away, advertisements appear offering to consolidate your debt into "one easy monthly payment," to "work with your creditors" to reduce your payments, or to arrange for you to get a new credit card "even if you have been denied credit in the past." Used car dealers offer to get you a set of wheels even if you have "bad credit or no credit." In today's high-tech world, people who are concerned about whether they can get a loan install apps on their smartphones that allow them to monitor their FICO credit score on an hourly basis. Credit dried up for a bit in the years just following the recession, but Visa, MasterCard, and Discovery Card solicitations have begun to fill our mailboxes again, and mortgage lenders on television and the Internet are back offering to refinance your home loan for the purposes of lowering your interest rates, consolidating your bills, and getting cash out of your home. Advertising on television—even at night—is expensive, so there must be a substantial market for these products aimed at the financially downtrodden.

For most Americans, it is still taboo to discuss matters of personal finance. Unless things get truly desperate, the details of our neighbors' household balance sheets are hidden from view, and we tend to assume things are going just fine. If our own economic house is in free fall, it is often possible to hide it from others almost indefinitely. Although finding myself $12,000 in the hole in the summer of 2003 was bad enough, it might have been much worse. Over the years, the credit limit on my MasterCard account gradually grew to $25,000. Furthermore, without my asking them to, Sears converted my store charge card into a Sears MasterCard account that, like any MasterCard, could be used wherever the card is accepted. The credit limit on this account was set at $15,000.[20] So without trying very hard, I could have spent another $28,000. In today's economy, that amount of credit would be harder to get, but it is easy to see how you might go on vacations or buy expensive items that would give your friends the impression you are doing fine, while at the same time, behind closed doors, you are rummaging under the sofa cushions in search of lunch money for the kids.

It helps if you have a good salary. The steady stream of paychecks makes it easier to make regular payments to your creditors. Before 2009, credit was available to those who wanted it, whether they had income or not. College students, most of whom were still a few years away from full-time work, were flooded with credit offers. But the CARD Act of 2009 limited the marketing of credit cards to teenagers and required that borrowers who were under 21 years old have a cosigner on their credit card account or have sufficient income or assets to justify getting a card.[21] Despite these changes, in many respects, we seem to be back to where we were before to bottom fell out.

For those who have both steady income and a good credit record, the solicitations come in a steady stream. My mailbox seems to produce a couple of credit card offers each week. Amazon.com tries to get me to adopt their credit card each time I make a purchase, and almost every department store I visit offers me a store credit card at check out. On television Samuel L. Jackson demands to know what I've got in my wallet. Credit—or, perhaps more accurately, debt—seems to be there for the asking. In the summer of 2003, I had a total of $40,000 available to me on the cards I had in my wallet, but if I had taken on the task of searching for credit and mailed in all the applications I received, there is no telling how much money I might have found. In recent years, the credit limits offered to most borrowers have come down from those heady prerecession days, but even for people with relatively low income, more credit than you can handle is easily available. If you set out to hang yourself, the banks and credit card companies are more than willing to give you the rope.

THE PARTICULARS OF FINANCIAL FAILURE

People who have money problems suffer privately in a number of ways, and for any individual person it is difficult to say what manner of torment is the worst. But there are few concrete indicators of failure that are perhaps the most objectively onerous: getting sued, declaring bankruptcy, losing your home through foreclosure, being evicted from a rental property, losing your car, and having your wages garnished.

Getting Sued

In August of 2017, the writer Dominique Matti published a revealing essay about her financial problems, admitting that she and her husband fought about money ("About not having enough. About whose fault it is"). She described being summoned to small claims court over a credit card bill she could not pay. While there, she met another woman who had been to court before:

> "They just call you in the back to talk to the lawyers, tell them what's goin' on. Sometimes they be nice, but sometimes they be mean, like you doin' it on purpose. I would pay it if I could," she said, "but I cant."[22]

You might be surprised to know that a large segment of the US court system is devoted to pursuing people who cannot pay their bills. A 2015 study of 960,000 non-domestic-relations civil cases in ten urban counties found that by far the largest number (64 percent) were contract dispute cases, and over half of these (37 percent overall) were debt collection cases. The next largest category was landlord/tenant disputes.[23] Civil court is one of the stops along the road for millions of people who are going broke in America.

A 2016 report by the National Center for State Courts described these debt collection cases in brutal terms. By definition, most defendants have very limited financial resources and most are unfamiliar with the court system. The attorneys for the banks, landlords, and collection agencies have enormous advantages over these debtors, and the results are as you might expect:

> Generally, unrepresented defendants face attorneys whose business model is based on processing huge numbers of cases with limited effort and whose insider knowledge often enables them to achieve one-sided outcomes through defaults or onerous settlements. After securing a judgment, plaintiffs' lawyers are able to evict, garnish wages, and seize assets.[24]

I have spent some time sitting in the benches in small claims court listening to cases. It is nothing like what you see on television. There are attorneys for auto financing companies, credit card companies, and debt-purchasing firms that buy up old debt from credit card or other commercial lending companies in return for the right to collect on it. There are also attorneys for hospitals seeking payment on medical bills and landlords suing for unpaid rent. On occasion a case involves a tenant trying to recover a security deposit that has not been returned.

These rooms are not happy places, but in my experience, the judges are remarkably kind and fair. For many defendants, going to court would entail lost wages or a search for childcare, and as a result, the debtors often do not appear. When they do go to court, debtors are sometimes required set aside the taboo of talking about money and testify about their financial circumstances in open court. Frequently the story involves unemployment, broken personal relationships, and health problems. When cases come to a successful settlement, the debtor agrees to make weekly payments directly to the plaintiff's attorney. If they fail to pay as agreed, the court can order wages garnished or property or bank accounts seized. According to a 2017 report by the Federal Reserve Bank of New York, 12 percent of American adults had debt that was owned by a collection agency.[25]

Bankruptcy

Declaring bankruptcy involves giving up control over some aspects of your life in exchange for a bit of peace. There are two forms of personal bankruptcy available to individual debtors in search of some financial breathing room: Chapter 7, liquidation, and Chapter 13, reorganization. Chapter 7 is the most popular, perhaps because it allows for a fresh start with the complete elimination of many debts. Chapter 13 provides protection from harassment by creditors, but requires the petitioner to repay most debts under an extended repayment scheme.[26] Changes in the bankruptcy law introduced in 2005 limited Chapter 7 bankruptcy to people whose income is less than the median in their area. Otherwise, debtors must choose a Chapter 13 repayment plan. However, because most people who declare bankruptcy are on the lower half of the income curve, this change had little effect on the eligibility of most debtors.

The process of filing begins with Form B101, a voluntary petition to the US Bankruptcy Court in the local district. With this form, the applicant officially acquires the label of "debtor," or "co-debtor" in the case of a married couple filing jointly, and is required to report any aliases used in the last eight years. Applicants summarize their financial lives with two simple questions asking for total assets and total liabilities. Additional forms must be attached to the B101 that give a more complete accounting of the debtor's financial circumstances, including lists of assets, lists of secured debts (such as a mortgage or car loan), and lists of unsecured debts (such as credit card balances). The debtor must also report all current income and expenses. The result is a full accounting of the manner and extent of the petitioner's financial failure.

The forms are filed with the local bankruptcy court, and an independent trustee is assigned to represent the court and administer the process. Bankruptcy creates an "estate" made up of the petitioner's assets and liabilities that is placed under the control of the court. The beginning of the process introduces a ceasefire in the war between debtor and creditor and assigns the trustee the job of determining whether there is anything in the asset column that could be used to satisfy creditors who are entitled to payment.

As soon as bankruptcy papers are filed, the court notifies the creditors that the debtor is pursuing bankruptcy and the phone stops ringing. All creditors are required to refrain from calling or writing in an effort to obtain payment. The debtor begins to feel some relief, but the outcome of the case will not be known for some time. Once a petition has been filed, the trustee will arrange for a meeting of the creditors. The person seeking bankruptcy must attend this meeting, and creditors may also appear. The purpose of this gathering is to allow creditors to confront the debtor and ask questions about his or her financial affairs. If a creditor objects to the bankruptcy application, the court may deny the debtor's petition. Alternatively, a Chapter 7 petition, which would have allowed for a complete elimination of the debtor's obligations, might be converted to a Chapter 13 case, in which debtor and creditor agree on a repayment plan. At the meeting of creditors, the trustee is required to question debtors to make sure they understand the implications of bankruptcy, including which responsibilities will be eliminated and which will not, as well as the effects of bankruptcy on the petitioner's ability to obtain credit.

If there are no complaints from creditors or other difficulties, the court will grant the bankruptcy two or three months after this meeting. Next, any property that is not exempt from seizure will be sold by the trustee, and the proceeds will be given to the creditor who is first in line under the bankruptcy rules. The assets exempt from liquidation vary from state to state, but often the petitioner is allowed to keep his or her car and home, depending on their value and the amount of equity accrued. For example, if the debtor owns a car but is still making payments on the loan, they may choose to "reaffirm" the debt and keep making payments to avoid losing the car. On the other hand, if the car is owned outright and has value that exceeds the amount allowed in the state, it may have to be sold so that the proceeds can be distributed to creditors. Similarly, as long as the equity in the debtor's home does not exceed the amount allowed by state law, the debtor may also be able to keep the home.[27]

Although Chapter 7 allows for the liquidation of a petitioner's assets, most people who file for bankruptcy have no assets to sell. The law allows the debtor to keep a certain amount of personal property, and for most who face this kind of financial failure, the value of their personal effects falls within the limits allowed. Thus, in most cases, bankruptcy makes for the kind of fresh start it was intended to provide. People whose financial lives have spun out of control can escape some—though not all—of the burdens they face and begin life again under simpler, more restricted terms. Important obligations, such as alimony and child support, cannot be avoided, but Chapter 7 bankruptcy can wipe away credit card debt and the burden of many other loans. The majority of debtors who make it through the gauntlet of bankruptcy emerge with all of their property intact and can begin the long process of rewriting their financial histories.

Foreclosure

Bankruptcy is perhaps the most concrete measure of financial failure, but losing your home to foreclosure probably comes in a close second. For many who struggle to achieve the classic symbol of the American dream—homeownership—it is particularly humiliating to have this most important possession slip through their fingers. One commonly used index of stressful life events, where death of a spouse rates 100 and the holiday season rates a 12, gives "foreclosure on a mortgage or loan" a score of 30.[28] In the 1960s, when this scale of stressful life events was created, foreclosure was thought to be more stressful than a major change in living conditions (25) but less stressful than a substantial change in the number of arguments with one's spouse (35). Today, it is difficult to judge where the loss of one's home should rank, but for the person who experiences it, foreclosure is probably just one of many stressors.

The typical foreclosure results from defaulting on a mortgage. For a variety of reasons—loss of a job, illness, or problems with other financial obligations—a homeowner fails to make mortgage payments. After several months of nonpayment, the mortgage lender begins the legal process of foreclosure, which eventually leads to an auction sale of the home. As a lien holder, the bank or mortgage company has a right to force a sale of the home in an effort to make back the money lent to the homeowner. In some cases the former owners can continue to live in their home as renters to the new owners, but often they must find a new place to live.[29] To make matters worse, with a foreclosure on your record—and perhaps other indicators of poor credit—finding a new place to live can be more difficult.

The first tremors of the economic earthquake were felt in 2007, when foreclosures rose sharply, setting off a chain of events that resulted in the largest financial crisis since the Great Depression. Furthermore, because the recession was centered in the housing industry, its effects have taken a long time to work themselves through the system. Foreclosures did not hit their peak until 2010, when almost three million homes in the United States were in foreclosure, and as of this writing, a decade later, foreclosure rates have still have not returned to pre-2007 levels. When housing prices fell, many homeowners found themselves "under water," tied to mortgage obligations that were much greater than the value of their homes. According to some estimates, by the end of 2010, 23 percent of all residential mortgages were underwater, and in Nevada, the worst hit state, fully 65 percent of all homes were underwater.[30] Many homeowners who could still make their payments chose "strategic default" as a way of getting out from under a bad financial investment. Other buyers fell victim to aggressively marketed subprime mortgages that included teaser rates and balloon payments. Of course, all of these foreclosures—whether they were deliberate investment decisions or due to a simple inability to pay—further depressed the housing market.

Buying a house involves a number of risks. In addition to the mortgage, homeowners are required to pay taxes on their property. Nonpayment of taxes, even when the mortgage payments are up to date, can lead the city or town to take legal action to force foreclosure and sale of the home. Furthermore, in recent decades many homeowners have taken out second mortgages or home equity loans to obtain cash for any number of uses. This kind of borrowing against equity produces two forms of additional risk. First, nonpayment or failure to adhere to the terms of the home equity loan can lead to foreclosure action, even if the first mortgage has been paid on time. In addition, if the borrower has eaten up all the equity in the home, there is no protection against falling home prices. Should the real estate market collapse, as it did in 2008, homeowners who have cashed out the equity in their homes are more likely to find themselves underwater. To make matters worse, many of those who lost their jobs in the recession soon found themselves in a kind financial checkmate: both incapable of keeping up the mortgage payments and unable to cover the mortgage debt by selling the house.[31]

Eviction

For some Americans, the dream of owning a home is not under consideration, because the more modest goal of simply keeping a roof over their heads is difficult enough. Evictions used to be rare events that sparked great outrage in the local community. In February of 1932 the *New York Times* reported that a protest of the eviction of three Bronx families had probably been limited to an estimated 1,000 people because of the cold temperatures.[32] Today millions of Americans are evicted each year, primarily in low-income urban neighborhoods, with little notice. According to recent estimates, there are sixteen evictions a day in Milwaukee, Wisconsin, and sixty a day in New York City. Matthew Desmond's 2017 Pulitzer Prize–winning book *Evicted: Poverty and Profit in the American City* exposed the brutal state of housing in the inner cities. Focusing on Milwaukee, Desmond described an interconnected system of landlords, courts, moving companies, and sheriffs that swept through Milwaukee's poorer neighborhoods, putting those who could no longer pay the rent out on the street.[33] Desmond persuasively argued that, as much as eviction is a product of poverty, it is also a cause. Families who lose their homes to eviction are forced to move into much poorer and more dangerous neighborhoods where they are disconnected from the schools and communities they know. Life quickly becomes even more difficult.

Automobile Repossession

It may not have come to your attention, but repo videos are a lively category on YouTube. There is an advanced science of auto repossession practiced by large, muscular people driving specially designed tow trucks, many of which appear to be outfitted with video cameras. As we will see in chapter 3, the auto financing industry of today bears some striking similarities to the mortgage industry of a decade ago, and one point of comparison is a rash of repossessions due to unmet loan or lease agreements.

Repossessions are an important source of used cars. Creditors who repossess cars typically sell them to cover as much of the loan as possible and bill the former owner for any remaining debt and fees. According to an industry report, there were 1.65 million auto repossessions in 2016. The rate of repossessions had been growing steadily since 2012 and was expected to continue to increase in 2017 and 2018.[34]

Much of the appeal of repossessions on YouTube seems to be the guilty pleasure of not being the sad shmuck whose car is being dragged away. But, as can be seen in many of these videos, the story on the other end of the towline is not a happy one. If you lose your car, you may still have a place to live. Perhaps you will even find some other way to get yourself to work. But repossession, like eviction, is a particularly public and humiliating form of financial failure.

Garnishment

Wage garnishment is yet another variety of financial tragedy. If you are in default on child support payments, student loans, taxes, or a commercial debt, your employer may be required to divert a percentage of your pay directly to your creditors. In the case of a commercial loan, the creditor must first get a court order, but child support, student loans, and taxes can be withheld without a court order. For example, if you are in default on a student loan, the US Department of Education or the company that holds your loan can contact your employer directly and request that up to 25 percent of your pay be diverted. Money in a savings account and federal and state tax refunds can also be seized.

A study by the payroll company ADP found that, in 2013, 7.2 percent of all US employees were having their wages garnished. The most common reason was for unpaid child support, but approximately 35 percent of all garnishments were for student or commercial loan debts and another 18 percent were for unpaid taxes. Fully 48 percent of all companies had at least one employee whose wages were being garnished.[35]

Loss of Professional or Driver's License

In order to encourage repayment of government-guaranteed student loans, twenty states have passed laws permitting the blocking or revoking of professional or driver's licenses for borrowers who have stopped paying their loans. Doctors, psychologists, nurses, teachers, and hairdressers have all lost their licenses—and, in many cases, also their jobs—for nonpayment of student loans. According to a November 2017 *New York Times* report, it is difficult to get good statistics on the number of people affected by these laws, and not all of the states where these policies exist have acted on them in recent years.[36] But over a two-year period, South Dakota barred nearly a thousand people from holding driver's licenses, and in the period between 2012 and 2017, 5,800 borrowers in Tennessee were reported to their licensing agencies. In recent years, Kentucky has blocked the licenses of 308 nurses and 223 teachers. So, in a modern twist on debtor's prison, if you fall behind on your student loan, you may lose the license you went to school to get—as well as your job.

Lawsuits, bankruptcy, foreclosure, eviction, repossession, loss of professional license, and garnishment are all very concrete examples of financial failure, but even for those who are able to avoid these endpoints, negotiating the troubling waters of money and debt can be a substantial strain. Money problems have long been among the most common sources of depression and marital conflict, and in the workplace, financial problems are linked to lowered productivity and increased risk of workplace violence.[37] It has been estimated that employees who are worried about their personal debt are four times as likely to threaten violence in the workplace than workers on average.[38] The concerns about workplace violence are considered serious enough that many employers offer financial management programs to their employees in an effort to keep problems at home from becoming problems at work. The median household income in the United States is rising again and is approaching the historic high reached in the late 1990s, yet, for many Americans, balancing personal finances—income, expenses, assets, and debts—has become an enormous problem.[39]

My story had a happy ending. This time, the sale of the family home produced a much better result. When my daughter reached middle school and we put the house on the market, it happened to be during the prerecession housing boom: mortgage interest rates were at a thirty-year low and real estate prices in our area had soared. The house sold the first day it was on the market, and my ex-wife and I split a handsome profit. Soon we were both comfortably ensconced in new homes, and in the years since the sale of our house, I have managed to live in the black.

But many Americans have not been so lucky. I had the advantages of an income that was well above average and the kind of job security that few people enjoy. But millions of less fortunate Americans are living my former life, or worse—buried beneath piles of bills and credit card debt with no real hope of getting out. Very few of them have a sense of living extravagantly. If asked, most would say they have done their best to live within their means. They have not been wasteful, nor have they made particularly risky decisions. They have lived their lives from day to day doing the same kinds of things they see their neighbors, relatives, and coworkers doing. But somehow, as the months and years have rolled out behind them, they have picked up a burden they may have to carry for the rest of their lives.

LOOKING AHEAD

This is not just another money management self-help book. My first and most important goal is to gain a better understanding of the problem. Why, in the context of such wealth, are so many Americans going broke? Where did all the money go? Then, at the end of the book, I offer some solutions based on this new understanding.

There are three overarching themes developed in the chapters that follow:

1. *The standard explanations for our epidemic of debt and financial failure are wrong—or at least in need of significant revision.* The most common

explanations blame either the banks or the poor judgment of the consumer, and while there is some truth to both these interpretations, the standard explanations ignore many other factors—social and, especially, technological developments—that have conspired to empty our pockets. Chapters 2 and 3 examine the traditional interpretations of financial failure and show why they come up short when applied to our current economic environment, and chapters 4 and 5 go on to outline an alternative interpretation.

2. *Something happened in the mid-1970s.* As we will see, lenders and debtors have been with us for millennia, but the current culture of debt—extending into millions of American households—is a relatively new phenomenon. As a result, much of what follows will be aimed at uncovering the events of last four decades—some obvious and some not—that have brought us to this point. For example, in chapter 6 I will outline the marketing techniques that make us desire the products laid out before us, but rather than look at these techniques in the abstract, I concentrate on the new methods that emerged in this period. Similarly, in chapter 7, I describe the many new products and services that were never imagined in 1970 but now compete for the consumer's attention and dollars.

3. *New developments in psychology and economics reveal many of the causes of our current epidemic of indebtedness—as well as some of the cures.* Over the past forty years, behavioral scientists working in a variety of settings—using research subjects as diverse as laboratory pigeons and Parent-Teacher Association members—have begun to identify many of the forces that drain our bank accounts. These new discoveries rarely have been applied to the problems of debt and financial failure, but they are well suited to the task. I summarize the important findings of this new body of research and show how they help to explain many of our problems with money. Finally, I turn to the question of how we might apply this new understanding to the task of achieving financial stability.

DAVID

On the day Arthur Miller died, I met David, a man who had spent much of his life as a salesman. He was initially reluctant to be interviewed. He called my office and wanted to talk before agreeing to meet with me, but after a few minutes on the phone he consented. I later learned that only two other people knew about his bankruptcy, and when he received my letter, it was "like a kick in the stomach." It never occurred to him that someone could find out, and he worried that somewhere on the Internet the words "bankrupt failure" were written next to his name for all to see. I assured him this was not the case.

David grew up in Peoria, Illinois, in a middle-class neighborhood where it was assumed that children would go to college. He attended Northern Illinois University, where he got a bachelor's degree in English and went on to get a master's degree in sociology. By then it was the late 1960s, and although he enjoyed school, he saw no career at the end of the line. So he quit graduate school and eventually started driving trucks. The pay was good, and before long he became the union representative for his company. But after five or six years, he wanted a more settled existence and a family, so when a college friend invited him to Rhode Island, he quit his job and drove east.

It took some time to find work, but his experience as a truck driver led to a job selling tools and other supplies to mechanics and machine shops. He started as a representative of someone else's company, then became an independent distributor. Like Willy Loman, he traveled New England, making stops at shops and garages, taking orders and delivering goods. Meanwhile, he began dating a woman his age, and they married and had a child. Coming east had paid off. He had a successful business, a nice home, and a family.

Then David's luck changed. He and his wife divorced. The breakup was amicable, and both parents remained involved with their son's life. His wife, who also ran her own business, made substantially more than David, so as part of the settlement agreement, he ended up with the house. David weathered the divorce as well as might be expected, but his financial picture was beginning to deteriorate. The tool and supply business had fared well until the late 1990s, when his income dropped off significantly. Customers could now order many items on the Internet, and some basic items could be found in local stores for less than he was charging. Although he had brought home between $70,000 and $80,000 annually during the good years, he reached the point where he was working very hard to bring in only $20,000—far less than he needed to cover his bills.

As his income began to fall, David did everything he could to trim his expenses. He had not gone on vacation in years, and he never went to movies. He drove a very old car and rarely bought clothes. But his mortgage was approximately $11,000 a year, and taxes were another $3,000. Because he was self-employed, he had to pay $5,000 a year for health insurance, and once utilities, food, gas, and other expenses were added in, David's obligations easily exceeded his income. So he began using his Visa card to fill in the gaps.

Meanwhile, David missed a number of mortgage payments on his house, prompting his bank to begin foreclosure proceedings. Intellectually, he knew what was happening to him. He could do the math, and he understood precisely why he was failing. But he was, as he said, "frozen." He could not reason out a solution, and he was stuck, unable to take action. By the time he was facing the possibility of losing his house, he had accrued $50,000 in credit card debt, fully two and a half times his annual income.

The end finally came when a friend saw the foreclosure notice for David's house in the local newspaper. The friend, a doctor who attended the same church, called David up and urged him to see a bankruptcy attorney in an effort to avoid foreclosure. Reluctant to do so, David nevertheless didn't want to lose the house, and so he took his friend's advice, sought an attorney, and eventually filed for the bankruptcy.

By the time I met him, a year had passed since the bankruptcy became final, and although he still had the house, David continued to feel very vulnerable and was scrambling just to get by. The credit card debt was gone, but his income still had not grown enough to reliably cover his expenses. Even after the bankruptcy, he had twice fallen behind on his mortgage payments, but in each case checks had come in that he was able to use to make up the missing payments. He was trying to sell the house, but because he had taken out a second mortgage to cover expenses back when his income began to fall, he needed to get his asking price to cover the mortgages. Despite a healthy housing market, so far he had been unable to sell the house. The good news was that David had begun a new job, selling health insurance. His old business was still bringing in some money, and if it worked out, the new job might get him back on his feet.

For David, bankruptcy had been a double-edged sword. The hardest part was admitting defeat. More than once in our interview he said, "I feel like a failure." He hated declaring bankruptcy but felt he had no other choice. On the positive side, going through the bankruptcy process had gotten him unfrozen. Before his friend called, David had been unable to move against the tide, and taking this action—even though it represented a formal statement of his financial downfall—was a step in the right direction. Even so, every day was uncertain, and the future was still a risky place. But bankruptcy had helped him move on toward making himself whole again.

Making Sense of Financial Failure

He bought the American dream but it put him in debt.

—Bob Dylan, *"Clean-cut Kid"*

In a May 2016 article in *The Atlantic*, author Neal Gabler broke the taboo of financial silence and admitted that, despite always earning at least a middle-class income and sometimes better than a middle-class income, he was just scraping by. In addition to a short stint as co-host of the PBS movie-review show *Sneak Previews*, Gabler had written hundreds of magazine articles and several successful books, including well-regarded biographies of Walt Disney, Walter Winchell, and Barbara Streisand. Nonetheless, he had been reduced to living for days on a diet of eggs, having creditors seize funds from his bank accounts, and being forced to ask his adult daughter for money when he and his wife ran out of heating oil. The inspiration for his confessional came when Gabler read about the Federal Reserve's annual financial fragility survey mentioned in the last chapter and realized that he was among the 47 percent of Americans who lacked $400 in cash to cover an emergency.[1]

Gabler described himself as a financial "ignoramus" and admitted he'd made many mistakes. He bought a co-op in Brooklyn to be near the center of the publishing world and continued to live in the city after he and his wife had two girls. Unsatisfied with the local public schools, they sent their daughters to private schools, and then, in an attempt to save on private school tuition, Gabler bought a modest house in East Hampton, Long Island. Unfortunately, having purchased the new home before unloading the old, he and his wife were stuck paying two mortgages for years because they couldn't sell the co-op in New York. With the move to Long Island, Gabler's wife stopped working to take care of the kids, which meant the elimination of private school tuition did not produce a net financial gain. Later, because they placed a high value on education, the couple paid for the girls to go to expensive private universities, and when their younger daughter got married, they used their small retirement savings to pay for the wedding.

Gabler's article attracted considerable attention. On *The Atlantic* website it soon collected over 3,500 comments, the majority of them negative. Journalists spanning the political landscape from *Huffington Post* and *Slate* to the *National Review* seized the opportunity to pile on Gabler. He was accused of representing a privileged male writer stereotype, failing to fully accept responsibility for his own bad choices, and being unrepresentative of people in the middle class and lower who face more pitiable struggles. Internet commenters accused him of having "champagne taste on a beer budget" and were more than happy to point out at all the things he had done wrong.

The world of Internet comments is a vicious place. Emboldened by anonymity, many people appear to take great joy in the downfall of others and are quick to heap more pain on those they see as hapless losers. In general, we are a judgmental lot. But is our outrage justified? In 2016, Americans suffered 770,000 personal bankruptcies, 1.65 million auto repossessions, and 933,000 homes lost to foreclosure. All these calamities happened in a single year, and, because married couples often hold mortgages jointly and file for bankruptcy together, the figures substantially understate the number of people directly affected. Countless others who have yet to hit one of these dismal milestones suffer quietly like Gabler.

Many social critics stress the importance of personal responsibility in the construction of a good life and blame the financially downtrodden for their own circumstances. Nobody forced them to put all that stuff on plastic. No one made them buy that nice car or refinance the house. These people are deserving of ridicule, not sympathy. We can help them best by letting them muddle through on their own and, perhaps, learn from their mistakes.

Our response to our neighbor's financial problem is, in many ways, determined by our general attitude toward human failure. What do we say when someone breaks the law, becomes an alcoholic, loses their job, or is unable to sustain important social relationships? We witness these events every day, and as observers, we are driven to find a way to make sense of them. Luck, either good or bad, plays a role in everyone's life, but when we stand in judgment of others we tend to say that people are responsible for things that happen to them—particularly their failures. We believe these failures tell us something about a person's essential nature.

Today there are two common ways of thinking about human failure. When we witness someone's life going wrong, either we say they are morally bad or suffering from a disease—often a mental disease. They are either bad or sick.

Evil or ill. These explanations have very different implications for the individual and produce divergent reactions from those around them. Yet most important human problems are framed in these terms.

INDEBTEDNESS DISEASE

The twentieth century saw a great expansion of medicine into the treatment of psychological problems. Before the 1960s, large state hospitals warehoused the mentally ill, caring for their inhabitants while separating them from the rest of society. But beginning in the second half of the century, two forces combined to empty out most of the mental hospitals.

First, the introduction of powerful psychotropic drugs made it possible for many people who suffered from schizophrenia and other serious disorders to leave the hospitals and live more typical lives. These drugs did not cure mental illnesses, and the early generation of drugs had serious side effects, such as Parkinson's-like tremors. But for many mental patients, the improvement from these new drugs, as well as from other new therapeutic strategies, was sufficient to make living in more normal housing possible.

In addition, the civil rights movement identified mental patients as a group whose individual rights had been unnecessarily restricted, and advocates began a movement to provide the mentally disabled with better educational programs and living spaces.

The result was a wholesale dismantling of many state institutions, often with very positive results. People who had rarely left the hospital grounds were now able to live in a variety of community settings.[2] Deinstitutionalization did not work for everyone. Even casual observation of the homeless who wander our cities provides evidence that the movement went too far, leaving many people with serious problems to fend for themselves.[3] But one important outcome was the growing belief that psychological problems were akin to physical diseases because both, after all, responded to drug treatment.

But the medical analogy doesn't always fit: for example, how are we to diagnose psychological problems—that is, mental illnesses? Physical diseases have physical symptoms, and the correct detection of the illness is aided by the use of tests. Temperatures are taken, heart rates are measured, and substances in the blood are identified. In most cases, illnesses present an identifiable set of symptoms, and once the illness has been diagnosed, a course of treatment can be recommended. The difficulty with psychological problems is the lack of physical symptoms that are a clear indication of a condition. Germ theory, which had been so successful in the treatment of physical disease, cannot be easily adapted to behavioral or emotional problems. There is no identifiable germ for depression, for example. Clinicians and researchers have often presumed an inward physical cause for the behavioral disorders they treat or study. In some cases this presumption has been justified, but often the evidence for a physical explanation has been lacking. Nonetheless, beginning in the mid-twentieth century, drugs were developed that appeared to have beneficial effects on patients with a variety of psychological problems, so a piece of the medical analogy seemed to hold.

The medicalization of mental illness also began to gain currency through the publication, in 1952, of the American Psychiatric Association's first edition of its *Diagnostic and Statistical Manual of Mental Disorders*, commonly called the DSM.[4] It was a catalog of mental disorders, and due to the absence of a physical cause that was separate from the symptoms, each disorder was categorized on the basis of a checklist of features. If your behavior matched enough of the listed criteria, your problem could be given a technical name. Now in its fifth edition, the DSM weighs in at just under a thousand pages and has added many new disorders, all with specific defining characteristics. The DSM-5 also includes a numerical coding system that facilitates billing for psychological services and gives the manual the flavor of a scientific instrument. For example, the diagnostic code for social anxiety disorder, which involves excessive anxiety provoked by exposure to certain types of social or performance situations, is 300.23.

In short, the explosion of pharmaceutical treatments and the expanding influence of the DSM helped the disease concept of psychological problems take hold, and it is now a commonly accepted belief. Alcoholism and drug addiction, once considered evidence of moral failure, are now popularly understood as diseases, and much effort has gone into the search for their presumed genetic origins. Those who are controlled by addictions often welcome the news that they have a disease: it removes a layer of stigma and turns them into victims of a condition largely out of their control. They are not responsible for their problems and, rather than being ridiculed, are deserving of sympathy and assistance.

But what about debt and financial failure? As of this moment, the American Psychiatric Association (APA) does not consider indebtedness alone to be a mental disorder. When the authors of the 2013 edition of the DSM revised the list of substance-related and addictive disorders, they included gambling disorder, a condition that often produces high levels of debt. Gambling disorders made it into the DSM in part because brain imaging data showed that gamblers' patterns of arousal were similar to those of substance users.[5] In contrast, compulsive buying disorder, for which there was limited brain imaging data, did not make the cut.[6] There are a number of other disorders (for example, bipolar disorder or what used to be called manic depression) that can result in high levels of financial debt, but the APA does not consider indebtedness itself to be a mental illness.[7] Debtors Anonymous (DA), a twelve-step program patterned after Alcoholics Anonymous, disagrees. The DA website clearly asserts, "compulsive debting is a disease."[8]

For a variety of reasons, I resist the current trend toward the medicalization of every human problem and argue that being over your head in debt does not mean you have a disease. The chapters that follow present a more natural, less pathological explanation for our current tendency to live beyond our means. We may have a metaphorical epidemic on our hands, but it is not a real plague of indebtedness disease.

The full case against the disease view of indebtedness and financial insolvency appears in subsequent chapters, but the foundation is laid here. At the edges, the APA's approach to the DSM appears to have redefined many of life's normal challenges as psychological problems. Despite evidence that the genetic influence on alcoholism and other substance use problems is dwarfed by the effects of adolescent environment, the disease view of addictions is by far the most popular, and the DSM includes criteria for alcohol use disorder (code 303.90), cocaine use disorder (304.20), and many other serious substance-related problems.[9] But how far can we stretch this concept? The DSM also includes tobacco use disorder (305.1) and nightmare disorder (307.47).

Although the popularity of smoking has decreased over the last few decades, according to recent global estimates, 30 percent of men and 10 percent of women use tobacco daily. Of course, not all of these people would meet the criteria for tobacco use disorder, but many would.[10] Similarly nightmare disorder is thought to occur in 19 percent of children and 2–6 percent of adults[11] Does it make sense that things as common as smoking and nightmares should be called mental disorders?

Critics of the DSM have challenged the basic idea that psychological problems are medical conditions. In addition, there are concerns about the motives of the APA. After all, each time the APA increases the number of approved mental disorders, the opportunities for billable hours for psychiatrists expand. Furthermore, unlike most psychologists, psychiatrists have the ability to prescribe drug therapies, and the DSM's list of mental illnesses has provided the motivation for marketing a large proportion of the drugs sold by pharmaceutical companies. Television commercials already hawk drugs to help us quit smoking, and researchers are working on medications for nightmare disorder and compulsive shopping, even though the APA has yet to give compulsive shopping its endorsement as a genuine mental disorder.[12]

There is a growing view that psychologists and other mental health professionals have spent too much time laboring in the fields of human weakness, abnormality, and failure. Positive psychology and humanistic psychology are movements aimed at human betterment through building strengths and virtues.[13] Rather than focusing on weaknesses, these approaches strive to identify the characteristics that will help people achieve their potential in life.

The picture of American indebtedness and financial failure that unfolds in the following pages is consistent with the philosophies of humanistic and positive psychology. When millions of people each year are faced with bankruptcy, foreclosure, or repossession, and almost half of the population cannot handle a $400 emergency, it seems wrong to call indebtedness a mental illness. As we will see, our economy is deliberately constructed to put consumers in this predicament. But there are habits and personal strategies that, if adopted, will protect us from these ends, and in coming chapters I present many of these methods. In the meantime, it seems more reasonable and realistic to assume that the great majority of people struggling with money problems are normal. Certainly there are psychological factors that may play a role in the financial failure of any particular person, but a problem that affects so many people must be bigger than mental illness. Its causes are more likely social than psychological, more likely cultural than personal. The same can probably be said for smoking and many behavior-related health problems. It may be convenient to think of the smoker or the overweight person as having a psychological problem—a mental or physical disease—but a more realistic assessment will recognize the powerful social and economic forces that encourage us to smoke and eat.

IMMORAL INDEBTEDNESS

Perhaps because it plays so central a role in our lives, we have always had an uncomfortable relationship with money. For many people, wealth is the yardstick by which their lives are measured, and yet the pursuit of wealth has often seemed a little unclean. Plato believed it was impossible for the rich to be virtuous, and in *The Republic*, his portrayal of a utopian state, he prohibited money lending and banished gold and silver.[14] Similarly, Aristotle thought the pursuit of wealth for its own sake was immoral and believed charging interest on loans was unnatural. Money was merely a sterile convention with no reality apart from that given to it by humans; therefore, the reproduction of money through the charging of interest violated natural law. These early Aristotelian ideas later gave birth to the medieval notion that "money does not beget money."[15] Nonetheless, money lending was common in ancient Greece and Rome, and borrowers who did not pay back their loans could be imprisoned by their creditors, sold as property, or even put to death.

The term *usury*, which today we associate with unreasonably high interest rates, originally referred to any interest charged for a loan, and at one time or another it has been strictly forbidden by all of the world's great religions. The earliest known religious objections to usury come from the Vedic texts of ancient India, dating to approximately 2000 BCE, and prohibitions against charging interest became part of Hindu and Buddhist religions.[16] In the West, most religious objections to money lending are derived from passages of the Old Testament that sternly condemn the charging of interest on loans. In *The Divine Comedy*, Dante placed usurers in the seventh circle of hell, alongside sodomites, suicides, and blasphemers. However, the biblical prohibition did not eliminate all usury, only that charged to a "brother," which was interpreted as meaning a member of the same religious faith. As a result, usury was allowed among those willing to cross religious boundaries. Christian groups, such as the Lombards and the Cahorsins, lent money for interest in Muslim communities, and Jews, who were prohibited from lending within their own community, lent money to European Christians. Shakespeare's dark portrayal of Shylock in *The Merchant of Venice* reflects both the anti-Semitism of the era and the stigma that adhered to usurers.

Beginning with the Protestant Reformation and moving into the Age of Enlightenment, traditional religious and moral attacks on trade and lending began to fall away in favor of economic arguments pro or con. In 1776 Scottish economist Adam Smith published his classic *An Inquiry into the Nature and Causes of the Wealth of Nations*, which strongly defended the free market principles that we now associate with capitalism. Smith was in favor of saving and opposed to reckless consumption, but he was not entirely against lending. His greater concern was for the intended use of the loan. Borrowing to provide funds for spending on consumable items was to be avoided because it squandered rather than created wealth, a view Smith expressed in this famous passage from *Wealth of Nations*:

> The man who borrows in order to spend will soon be ruined, and he who lends to him will generally have occasion to repent of his folly. To borrow or to lend for such a purpose, therefore, is in all cases, where gross usury is out of the question, contrary to the interest of both parties.[17]

Loans for the purchase of durable goods or investment in business or production, on the other hand, had the potential to produce wealth, so these forms of lending were acceptable. This separation of loans and spending into two categories, "productive" versus "consumptive," would persist well into the twentieth century, with a moral stain adhering to those who borrow money simply to spend it. But Smith understood that lending money at interest could not be eliminated. Any prohibition on the practice merely sent it underground, where there were no controls to protect the borrower. As a result, Adam Smith, otherwise known for his support of free markets and laissez-faire government policies, identified one market that he believed governments should regulate: the market for loans. This reasoning led him to advocate usury laws that set acceptable levels of interest.[18]

Islam is the only major religion that retains strong objections to usury, and with the modern growth of Islam worldwide, there has been a great expansion of banks that serve customers without breaking sharia law regarding the charging of *riba*, or interest.[19] The biggest centers of Islamic banking are in Saudi Arabia, Malaysia, and the United Arab Emirates, but the market is expanding to many other countries, including the United States and Britain. According to a recent estimate, there are approximately twenty-five institutions offering Islamic financing in the United States.[20]

Modern Islamic banks use a number of systems to provide loans that do not violate the sanctions against interest. For example, a mortgage from an Islamic bank might involve a kind of rent-to-own arrangement. In contrast to a conventional mortgage, the bank and the homebuyer both put up money to become co-owners of the home, dividing it into shares, of which the bank typically owns the majority. On a regular schedule, the homebuyer purchases shares from the bank, and because the buyer is using the house during this period of shared ownership, the bank also collects rent. As a result, the bank and the homebuyer become partners, with the homeowner gradually assuming full ownership. Rental income, which is allowed under Islamic law, is paid to the bank instead of interest.

With the growth of Protestantism in Europe and America, the traditional religious objections to wealth and lending subsided, but they were replaced by a different kind of morality. In the United States in particular, Protestantism turned the vice of wealth into a virtue. Success or failure in business was equated with success or failure in life. In the eighteenth and nineteenth centuries, America was a place of "go-aheadism," and whether you fared well or not, the outcome was your own responsibility. Ralph Waldo Emerson stated this viewpoint most clearly in 1842:

> The merchant evidently believes the State street proverb that nobody fails who ought not to fail. There is always a reason, *in the man*, for his good or bad fortune, and so in making money.[21]

The same American individualism that offered an optimistic economic picture to all placed a heavy moral burden on those who failed, and if you failed, it did not go unnoticed. For the first time, businesses sprang up whose sole purpose was to collect and sell information about the creditworthiness of merchants and businesspeople. In 1841, Lewis Tappan opened the Mercantile Agency, the forerunner of Dun & Bradstreet, in Manhattan. Long before the era of electronic credit reporting, Tappan employed thousands of informants who would report on business dealings they knew about to clerks who penned the details into large ledgers held at the Mercantile Agency's office. Prospective suppliers or investors could approach Tappan's agency as a way of determining whether a merchant or businessman was worthy of their trust.[22]

In nineteenth-century America, personal loans were also widely available, but a request for money was an admission of poverty. Thus, borrowed money came with a substantial measure of shame. Pawnbrokers, the bankers for the poor, began to emerge in the early 1800s. In cities where there were large numbers of working-class families, the three gold balls of the pawnbroker's sign hung in the poorer neighborhoods. The typical customer was a woman whose job it was to make her husband's salary stretch from payday to payday. When the money could go no further, she would—in the vernacular of the times—become a "furniture dealer" and visit her "uncle" the pawnbroker.[23] Clothing and household items could be handed over as security for a loan, and if the loan and the broker's fee were not paid off in the agreed-upon period, the pawnbroker was free to sell the item to recover the costs. Because there was shame associated with visiting the pawnbroker and because women often pawned items without telling their husbands, the typical shop was designed to accommodate the reluctant borrower. Some had side entrances for those who did not wish to be seen entering or exiting, and once inside the establishment, customers often stood in separate divided stalls that afforded a measure of privacy.

Small lending businesses were also common, particularly in the second half of the nineteenth century. In most states, usury laws prohibited charging more than 6 percent interest on a loan, which effectively restricted legal loans to larger banks that serviced businesses and the wealthy. But the great demand for small loans among the lower classes encouraged the establishment of illegal lending operations. Often housed in sparsely furnished second-floor offices, these small lenders advertised "ready cash" and used a number of methods to get around the usury laws and charge rates ranging from 20 to 300 percent.[24] These establishments typically used a form of payday lending. To qualify for a loan, the applicant had to be employed and was required to appear once a week, on his or her payday, to make a payment on the loan. A similar kind of lending has emerged since the 1990s. Most modern payday lenders operate much as their nineteenth-century counterparts did, in small storefronts offering "cash advances," but the terms of today's loans are substantially collapsed. Whereas the typical nineteenth-century small loan was extended over thirteen weeks of payday payments, today's cash advances average terms of only fourteen days. The borrowers give the lender a postdated check for the amount of the loan plus a fee, and if they don't return with the payment at the appointed time, the lender is free to cash the check. Despite charging fees that often exceed the equivalent of a 500 percent annual rate, payday lending is legal in thirty-six states, and the industry has seen particularly rapid growth in recent years.[25]

This brief history suggests that, with the notable exception of Islamic banking, money lending has gone from a moral vice and a violation of religious law to an acceptable form of financial transaction. Furthermore, in the contemporary world, much of the earlier disdain for money borrowed for nonproductive uses has been eliminated. According to their advertising appeals, credit cards seem particularly suited to the purchase of meals, gifts, and vacations. Usury has been transformed from a moral evil to a common feature of contemporary life and even, according to some, an essential ingredient of our economic success. However, as the moral stain was removed from the business of lending, it had not been completely removed from those who require its services. Borrowing is necessary, but for the individual, it is still an admission of failure. If you are able to manage your debt adequately, the failure is small and undetectable, but for those who struggle, their failure can become visible. Both lending and debt have lost much of their dishonorable taint, but even in today's world, money is still a measure of the person. In an interesting reversal of Plato's ideas about wealth, many people believe it is impossible to be both a financial failure and a good person.

In nineteenth-century cartoons and illustrations, debtors were depicted as thin, sickly-looking people and creditors appeared as portly, self-confident men.[26] The different social positions of the two types of people could be seen in their body shapes and posture. Today, the debtor—and particularly the delinquent debtor—is often described in similar moralistic terms. The negative responses to Neal Gabler's confession were remarkably bitter. A number of readers found his financial behavior reprehensible. "His piece was one big deflection from personal responsibility," wrote one anonymous Internet commenter.[27] Obviously, how we manage money can affect how others judge our character. But is that right? Should all those who fall behind on their bills be judged with the same harshness? As a general rule, people should honor their promises. Financial agreements are built on trust, and not living up to those agreements is a violation of that trust. But how should we judge the people who fail to pay their bills or merely carry a heavy load of debt? What should be the relationship between this kind of financial predicament and our moral assessment of the person?

People approach moral questions differently. For many, the borders between good and bad, right and wrong are sharply etched, unmoving lines of demarcation. They believe, as the philosopher Immanuel Kant did, that we are bound by categorical imperatives. If we want our world to be one in which people always tell the truth, then it is our duty to be honest without exception. Even if a ruthless murderer comes to our door and asks where their next victim is hiding, we must tell. Most of us would agree that honesty is a highly valued character trait, but we might relax our judgment when a lie is told with the purpose of protecting oneself or others from undeserved harm. Nonetheless, many people see questions of morality—particularly when we make judgments of others—in these stark, unflinching terms.

Aristotle's view of ethical behavior was quite different. He identified a number of important virtues, including honesty, generosity, modesty, and courage. Each of these virtues was acquired by practicing virtuous acts, but a virtue could become a vice if practiced too little or too much. For example, if, over the course of a lifetime, you developed the habit of being neither stingy nor extravagant, then you were said to possess the virtue of generosity. Furthermore, your average level of generosity was much more important than any individual act. Without going down the path to moral relativism, Aristotle understood that on a given occasion we might be weak. Or we might be faced with a moral dilemma that makes it impossible to be completely good. If the murderer's victim is your child, then you cannot be both an honest person and a good parent. So in a particular case we might fail to be completely virtuous, but if on average we are good, we are said to be virtuous. While for Kant moral action was aimed at universal standards of behavior—as you would wish everyone behaved—the purpose of Aristotle's morality was living well. For him, living ethically was the path to a satisfying life.

It is essential that we learn to live by moral principles. Much of life is a conflict between our self-interested desires (eating all the mashed potatoes) and the wish to benefit our larger social group (sharing with the others at the table), and by adopting codes of conduct we can balance these opposing forces. Living by the Golden Rule and other moral principles helps to keep our selfish selves in check. But whichever brand of moral philosophy you choose, whether Aristotle's, Kant's, or that promoted by some other authority, making moral judgments about the actions of others is not the same as explaining their behavior. It is tempting to say that Joe failed to pay his bills because he is a bad person or that Joan is careful with her money because she is virtuous. Such general descriptions of a person's goodness or badness are descriptions of the social end points these people have reached. Based on their histories, they are now seen in a favorable or unfavorable light. But without more information, we cannot say *how* they got there. Habitually violent people may be judged to be dangerous and bad, but this does not tell us *why* they are dangerous and bad.

Aristotle's moral system is consistent with the idea that ethical behavior is learned. His virtues are acquired through practice, and eventually good or bad behavior becomes typical of us. But the idea that moral behavior is learned has not achieved universal endorsement. The layperson's view of human behavior is typically a form of trait theory. The people we encounter in our daily lives are said to possess lasting dispositions that define the kind of person they are. Michael is outgoing and warm. Jeannette is withdrawn and acerbic. We may attribute parts of their current selves to the history of their lives. Michael comes from a large family where he had to speak up to get noticed. Jeannette has had a number of bad experiences that have made her wary of those around her. But often the core of an individual's personality is assumed to be a more permanent and essential part of his or her being, acquired at birth.

Psychology's most famous and lasting controversy is over the varying contributions of heredity ("nature") and environment ("nurture") to intelligence, personality, and success at life's challenges. Most modern scientists now agree that both nature and nurture play important roles in everything we do, but battles still rage over the relative credit that should be given to heredity or environment in any particular area of human achievement. Nativists, such as Richard Herrnstein and Charles Murray, the authors of *The Bell Curve*, argue that most of what we are is determined by our genes, and those on the nurture side of the divide, such as Stephen Jay Gould and Jared Diamond, suggest that the role of genetics has been overestimated.[28] Nonprofessionals come down on both sides of this debate, but many appear to be amateur nativists, attributing their behavior and the behavior of others to fixed traits of personality.

A good example of this kind of dispositional lay psychology is astrology. Although it is not supported by scientific evidence, astrology is probably the most popular everyday theory of personality worldwide.[29] The basic premise of astrology is that the arrangement of the stars and planets at the time of a person's birth assigns him or her a discernible set of traits, and these traits endure for the rest of the person's life.

Particularly at the extremes, human failure and achievement are likely to be attributed to biological causes. The genius, the exceptional athlete, the serial killer, and the habitual liar (the word *congenital* comes to mind) are assumed to have been dealt some gift or deficit, some exceptional capacity or some "bad seed," that defines who they are. Because we observe people at a given point in time and are rarely privy to the circumstances that have come before— circumstances that might provide a different kind of explanation—it is easy to make what psychologists call the *fundamental attribution error*.[30] We conclude that people—other people in particular—do the things they do because of the fixed dispositions they possess. He is aggressive. She is selfish. But when we turn our detective's eye on ourselves, the view is quite different. We are intimately familiar with the details of our past and how they have shaped us. In addition, we know—in a way outsiders never can—the external forces that press on us at the moment we act. The very same behavior viewed from the inside and from the outside will often be explained in very different terms. The student understands the late term paper as a natural result of various random and unique circumstances, but the professor believes she has uncovered a core feature of the student's personality.

Particularly in the case of unfortunate events, when we explain the misbehavior of others by appealing to inborn traits, we draw a line between them and ourselves. This is a natural self-protective impulse. We hear about someone who is stricken with a disease, and immediately our mind races to find lines of separation: He was overweight, and I am not. He drank too much, and I do not. He probably has some genetic risk factor that I do not. If we convince ourselves that a border can be drawn between this unfortunate individual and ourselves, we can go on with our lives, taking comfort in the belief that we will not come to the same fate.

But these lines of demarcation have other effects. They afford us the privilege of not caring. If we assume that the downtrodden are different, have little in common with us, and are lacking in some of the strengths of personality we possess, it is easier to turn away. It is a harsh reality of our social world that we assign greater value to people who seem similar to us than we do to people who seem different. In theory, all lives should be of equal worth, but in practice, we do not act as if they were. The murder of a person in our city or town is reported in great detail, whereas the slaughter of thousands in Africa or some other distant place can go all but unnoticed. Africans are people, too, but their kinds of lives don't stack up to ours.

Furthermore, there is a sense that even if we could bridge the gap of difference we have constructed between the unfortunates and ourselves, there is probably nothing we can do. Aristotle's moral system allows for a distinction between bad people and bad acts. Good people sometimes do bad things, and vice versa. But if we assume, as many psychologists and nonpsychologists do, that our behavior is produced by a collection of more or less permanent traits forged within us at the time of birth, then the die is cast. Individuals' goodness or badness is built in at the factory, and if they do bad things, we tend to think they are bad people. If they are bankrupt, then they must be lacking in the traits of thriftiness and moderation. Their basic nature is both different from ours and not subject to easy improvement, so we might as well turn our attention to things we can control.

When we make moral judgments about other people who fail, we face yet another obstacle in our effort to understand *why* they failed: our sense of justice. Psychologists have discovered that, consciously or not, many people live by the motto "You get what you deserve." They are followers of the "State street proverb," as Emerson called it: "Nobody fails who ought not to fail." This philosophy or value system has come to be called belief in a just world, and it is a widespread and powerful phenomenon. It manifests itself, for example, in the legend of the American dream, which tells us that anyone who works hard and follows the rules can succeed. The symbols of economic stability and comfort are achievable for all. The flip side of this optimistic maxim is the implication that failure is your own fault. You reap what you sow. Many people believe the world is a just place, while others are less convinced, seeing the evidence of randomness or even inherent injustice in the world they inhabit.[31] When those who believe in a just world encounter injustices, they are often motivated to correct them, and in this case, the justice motive can be a very positive force, leading to efforts to right wrongs and punish wrongdoing. But in our present case—problems of personal finance—belief in a just world tends to sap any sympathy we might have for the Neal Gablers among us. They have earned what they are getting.

Indeed, we often take pleasure in the downfall of others. The Germans call it *schadenfreude*. We watch from afar, secure in our belief that we stand above those poor schmucks: They screwed up, but they're not like us. How could they have been so stupid? The sense of moral superiority and righteous indignation are magnified when heroes fall. Cable television and Internet news sites feed on our sanctimonious impulses by parading a never-ending lineup of celebrity failures. We peer down our noses at the likes of Bill Cosby, Lindsay Lohan, Martha Stewart, and O. J. Simpson. These and similar media spectacles fill hours of daily program time and provide us the dual satisfaction of seeing the high and mighty knocked down a peg or two—down to the lowly plane where we reside or, better still, below—and knowing that they are bad and we are good. How could they have done it? They had everything, and they blew it. What idiots.

HOW FREE IS FREE WILL?

The belief in a just world, as well as both Aristotle's and Kant's views of moral behavior, are based on the idea of free will. Faced with the decision to buy something on credit or not, consumers get to decide. They can say yes, or they can say no. They can choose the virtuous path or the primrose path. This idea—that we all have a choice—is what allows us to hold people responsible for their actions. This is why we put so much emphasis on a person's intentions. When a child breaks a glass, she may say, "I didn't do it on purpose!" To have broken the glass deliberately would be a clearer reflection of her character and would make her eligible for punishment. This is also why our courts spend so much time determining whether defendants were aware of what they were doing and knew right from wrong. If it can be proven that the act was consciously willed, perhaps by showing evidence of premeditation, then conviction and punishment are more likely. Alternatively, if you kill someone but have no choice in the matter—it is an accident or someone holds your hand and forces you to pull the trigger—then it is not your fault. You are not responsible and, in a just world, you would not be punished.

The common dispositional view of human behavior stands in contrast to the ideas of free will and responsibility. If our personalities and behavior are the products of fixed traits acquired at birth, then our actions are locked in and not subject to choice. On the other hand, if we are free and can be held responsible for our actions, then a deterministic world of biological traits must not hold. Free will versus determinism is another of the great debates that have occupied philosophers and psychologists for centuries. But as different as these two views are, they produce a common effect. No matter which side you are on, each theory of human behavior provides an excuse for the neglect of other people's misery. If we are willful beings who make choices for which we are rightly assigned the praise or blame, then the Neal Gablers of the world have gotten their just deserts. If a person's character is fixed at birth, then there is little we can do for the bankrupt people around us. Their problems are a reflection of their true selves, and they are likely to make the same mistakes in the future that they have made in the past. Either way, these people seem alien to us, and attention need not be paid.

MAYBE THEY AREN'T SO DIFFERENT

This book approaches the problem of indebtedness and financial failure with a new set of assumptions. The traditional view of human failure as a reflection of either mental illness or moral weakness does not seem fitting to financial problems that are both so widespread and so characteristic of the modern age. The banking industry has a long history, and people have had problems with debt and bankruptcy from money lending's earliest beginnings.[32] But recent decades have produced both unprecedented levels of wealth and, paradoxically, record rates of financial failure. Therefore, to make sense of these modern phenomena, I adopt principles that seem more suited to the task:

1. *Financial failure is not caused by mental illness.* The current culture of disease would have us label those who live beyond their means as mentally ill. It may be tempting to say these people are shopaholics, stricken with the spending disease and powerless over their addiction. The disease approach may remove a layer of shame and make it easier for the stricken to get help, but this is not a good enough reason to create an indebtedness disease if it really isn't there. If millions

of people suffer from a mental disease each year, then it challenges our ideas about what is normal and what is not. Thus I start from the premise that the overwhelming majority of Americans who find themselves in serious financial difficulty are typical people. A small number may suffer from real psychological problems, and their difficulties with money and thrift may be part of a larger disorder. But they represent a very small minority.

2. *Our moral judgment obscures the root of the problem.* Societies must have moral standards and must hold people accountable to those standards, but if we really want to encourage virtuous behavior, we must go beyond standing in judgment and try to uncover the causes of moral failure. Our tendency to blame the failure of others on lasting character traits obscures the truth. We may make judgments about people who should have enough money yet manage to go broke anyway. We may find them lacking in moral fiber, or, at least, we may conclude that they have made some important mistakes. But if the argument of this book is correct, what we cannot say is that they are in any essential way different from the rest of us. People are not blank slates, but most of the numbers that make up our personal balance sheets are written by the hand of circumstance and experience, not by our genes. If the tables were turned, we might be in the debtors' spot and they in ours.

3. *The most important causes of financial success and failure are found in our social and economic environment.* The particulars of our lives, both current and past, have greater influence on how people come to succeed or fail than we recognize. Yes, we all have individual personalities and characteristics, but many of the things we think of as fixed traits are in fact more akin to habits—patterns of behavior— acquired over the course of a lifetime. This argument rests on an understanding of how lives are shaped by experience, and the following chapters draw on current developments in cognitive and behavioral psychology to make the case that good or bad economic behavior can be learned. This approach is substantially more optimistic than one based on disease or hardened personality traits, because it holds out hope for change. If our habits of getting and spending, buying and saving, have been acquired over the course of our lives, then new experiences can shape different patterns of behavior. If our wastefulness is more akin to an absent skill than a disposition, then maybe we can learn new skills.

This view of spending and debt will turn our attention outward, toward the effects of our current brand of free market economics delivered to our doors in ways that Adam Smith never anticipated. Beginning in the 1970s and continuing today, technological changes have altered our lives in many wonderful and bewildering ways. But the greater control over our lives that we enjoy today has, to our surprise, made it much more likely that our lives will spin out of control.

4. *Freedom of will is a bounded concept.*[33] Our Western culture places great emphasis on conscious action and individualism. Although Freud's particular theory of unconscious action is not widely supported by behavioral scientists today, in our everyday lives we often act without the assistance of conscious thought. For example, many of us arrive at our parking spots at work with no memory of the drive. Although we have completed a complex visual and motor activity, it was automatic, and our conscious minds were elsewhere. Nonetheless, as everyday psychologists and moral philosophers, we assume almost everything a person does is a conscious choice.

Furthermore, not all choices are equal. The patient whose doctor tells her that her breast is cancerous and must be removed has a choice: she can follow her doctor's advice and agree to the mastectomy, or she can say no and watch herself slowly die. In either case she makes a conscious decision. But is she really free to take one option or the other? When making judgments of blame and responsibility, we often place enormous weight on choices that are sometimes less free than they may seem. If a wife murders her abusive husband, we may blame her by saying she had other choices. She could have continued to take his beatings in the hope that he would change. Or she might have left him. But if she is without money, without a place to go, and without much hope of getting away safely, what kind of freedom does she have? We can imagine two options short of killing her husband, but this kind of freedom bears little resemblance to the choices we make when we decide what clothes to put on or what food to eat.

My goal in writing this book is to outline the causes of financial failure and propose some solutions. Determining the guilt or responsibility of the debtor in this episode is a different kind of task. In some cases, we—as members of the larger society—may wish to punish people who misuse their money, and when that misuse of money extends to breaking the law, punishment is justified. But my efforts are aimed at an earlier point in this drama. I am concerned with identifying the causes of financial failure and the remedies that might lead to avoiding failure altogether. Often this will involve an acknowledgment that freedom is a concept of degrees, and some choices are easier than others.

SUSAN

Susan was the youngest of six children. Her father was a police officer, and her mother was a legal secretary. They lived in a big house in West Hartford, Connecticut, and each of her older siblings got married or moved out, until Susan was the only one left. When she was in high school, her father died of stomach cancer, and soon the house was too big and too difficult for its remaining occupants to maintain. So Susan's mother sold the house and bought a condominium. Susan joined her mother in the condo and continued to live there when she entered nursing school and later when she got her first job. Then she moved into an apartment of her own, but she spent so much time at her mother's place that, after a couple of years, she moved back home. Meanwhile, she had landed a good nursing position at an assisted-living facility, and eventually became a nurse supervisor. When I met Susan, she had been working with the same facility for almost twenty years, and she was making a little over $30,000 a year.

After many years together, Susan and her mother had worked out a comfortable living arrangement. "We were like roommates," she said. Susan contributed financially, and each had her role in the upkeep of the house. Susan did all the grocery shopping and took care of ordering household repairs and maintenance. The women enjoyed each other's company, and sharing the condo worked quite well for both of them.

Then her mother died unexpectedly of a brain aneurysm. One day Susan's closest friend in the world was a healthy, active woman, and the next she was gone. A tremendous emotional shock, her mother's death also brought on a sudden change in her standard of living. The condominium represented the primary asset of her mother's estate, and there were six heirs. So the condo was put on the market and the proceeds divided, but this meant that Susan had to move.

Suddenly, her expenses doubled. Where before all the bills were split between the two women, now she was paying almost the same amount of money with no help from anyone else. She could just barely cover her basic living expenses—rent, a car payment, utilities—and had nowhere near enough money left over for the credit card bills she had incurred while her mother was still alive. She liked to shop, but she had always been responsible about her obligations. Even after her mother's death, she tried to keep up with the bills and paid a little each month. Unfortunately, because the amounts she sent were less than the minimum payments, the phone began to ring. Banks, stores, and credit card companies called every day and made her feel horrible. Eventually, she began to screen her calls and never answered the phone unless she recognized the number.

When she finally decided to declare bankruptcy, she owed $50,000, about one and a half times her annual salary. She had spent the money on a variety of things: clothes, furniture for the condo, vacations, and car repairs. She was working the balances down before her mother died, but once she was forced to move into her own place it was impossible to keep up. To make matters worse, for the first time ever, she was being charged late fees and higher penalty interest rates, and the balances on her cards began to mount even higher. She went to a credit counseling service, but because it seemed as though their best efforts would help only a little, she chose to continue going it alone.

"At first, I thought it would be wrong to declare bankruptcy. I didn't want to be irresponsible and just walk away from my debts, but I didn't know what else to do. I tried to manage for over a year before I gave up and called an attorney."

About six months after Susan declared bankruptcy, she got a solicitation to apply for a Visa card, and she sent it in. Surprisingly, she was approved with a credit limit of $700. So far she had used the card only once, to cover some car repairs, and immediately paid it off. When I met with her, Susan's only debt was her car loan. Still, in the years since filing for bankruptcy, life remained difficult. There was little money left after her bills were paid each month, and lately, to avoid incurring new debt, she had stopped carrying any credit cards in her wallet. Though she still enjoyed shopping—"If I had a lot of money, I'd be shopping right now," she said—she chose instead to stay home most nights watching the Yankees on TV. "And I am fine with that," she said. She also said that it had taken some time for her to feel better about herself and that her friends had been very helpful. She was doing her best now to move on.

Looking down at her hands, she said, "Just because I did this, it doesn't mean I am a bad person. I'm still me."

The Road to Ruin

There has been a decline, as we all know, in the stigma of filing for personal bankruptcy, and certainly we would agree that appropriate changes are necessary in order to ensure that bankruptcy not be considered a lifestyle choice.

—SENATOR JOHN KERRY

It all seems like a hazy fever dream. In October of 2007, the Dow Jones Industrial Average hit 14,164 and began a gradual descent, but if you weren't an insider, this seemed like background noise. You could be forgiven for not paying attention. Nine months earlier, Illinois Senator Barack Obama had declared his candidacy for President of the United States, and he was now locked in a battle with New York Senator Hillary Clinton for the Democratic nomination. On the Republican side Senator John McCain was one of several hopefuls fighting for the nomination. The first primaries were to be held the following January.

Little did we know that the stock market slide would continue for seventeen months, at which point the Dow would have lost over half its value. As of December of 2007, the country was officially in a recession, but there was much worse news ahead.

In March of 2008, the investment firm Bear Stearns failed, and, with the help of a $25 billion Federal Reserve bailout, JP Morgan acquired Bear Stearns at a fire-sale price. But many of us would not become fully conscious of the crisis until September 15, 2008, when the New York investment bank Lehman Brothers filed for bankruptcy. At that point, the stock market became unhinged, making 300- and 400-point swings in a single day. On September 24, President George W. Bush addressed the nation about his plan to keep the economy afloat by introducing a bill to lend money to troubled banks.

The dream gets fast and blurry at this point. The unemployment rate, which had hovered between 4.5 and 5.0 percent for all of 2007, would end 2008 at 7.3 percent. The country continued to lose jobs in the coming months, and unemployment finally peaked at 10 percent in October of 2009. As measured by the Gross Domestic Product, the economy shrank for four quarters in a row, and although the recession would be declared over in June of 2009, the unemployment rate did not return to pre-recession levels until 2016, and—as of this writing—the housing market, which led the crisis when prices plateaued at the end of 2006 and began falling in 2008, has yet to return to pre-crash levels.

Those who lived through the bad dream known as the Great Recession acquired new vocabulary words, including the adjective "sub-prime," the noun "mortgage-backed security," and the funny-sounding names, "Freddie Mac" and "Fannie Mae." But, as is often the case in highly charged circumstances, there was greater agreement about *what* had happened than there was about *why* it had happened. President Bush gave a partial explanation in his September 24th speech:

> Many mortgage lenders approved loans for borrowers without carefully examining their ability to pay. Many borrowers took out loans larger than they could afford, assuming that they could sell or refinance their homes at a higher price later on.
>
> Optimism about housing values also led to a boom in home construction. Eventually, the number of new houses exceeded the number of people willing to buy them. And with supply exceeding demand, housing prices fell, and this created a problem.
>
> Borrowers with adjustable-rate mortgages, who had been planning to sell or refinance their homes at a higher price, were stuck with homes worth less than expected, along with mortgage payments they could not afford.
>
> As a result, many mortgage-holders began to default. These widespread defaults had effects far beyond the housing market. (President George W. Bush, September 24, 2008)[1]

The effects "beyond the housing market" were caused, in part, by the manner of financing the mortgages. Rather than being held by local banks, like mortgages of old, these loans were originated by firms who then sold them off to be bundled together. Pieces of these bundles of mortgages where then sold to investors as mortgage-backed securities, and the investors were rewarded with the interest payments generated by the pooled mortgages. All of this went well for a time—in hindsight, a fairly brief time—until the housing bubble burst and a historic wave of residential foreclosures took off. When the mortgages on which they were based went south at much higher levels than anyone anticipated, the demand for mortgage-backed securities collapsed. Bear Stearns and Lehman Brothers failed because so much of their portfolios were in these new—and as it turned out—very risky securities. Once banks began to fail, investment and lending dried up in the banking world in general, but the most damaging effects were not felt in the banking world.

As the wave of foreclosures spread, real estate values fell sharply, and millions of homeowners watched the wealth they had tied up in their homes disappear. In many cases, people who had continued to pay their bills on time were suddenly "underwater," with negative equity in their homes, owing more on the mortgage than the house was worth. At the peak of the home equity crisis an estimated 29 percent of mortgaged homes in the United States were worth at least 25 percent less than the remaining balance on the loan.[2] As homeowners watched their personal wealth disappear, consumer spending fell, and the economy went south. Employees were laid off, and a big downward spiral gained steam. There are a few other details to the story, some of which we will get to in later on, but that's the nightmare of the Great Recession in a nutshell.

Who's Responsible for This Mess?

When the dust cleared and there was time to look around for someone to blame, the commentaries fell down on predictably political sides. Free market conservatives claimed government programs designed to bring the benefits of homeownership to lower income buyers had led to bad policies on the part of Fannie and Freddie.[3] Fannie Mae and Freddie Mac were government sponsored financial organizations that themselves bundled mortgages into securities. Conservatives also pointed to the Community Reinvestment Act, which encouraged banks to lend in underserved areas.

In contrast, liberals described an unfettered banking system that used arcane new bundling strategies in an ultimately failed attempt to protect investors from the risks of mortgage-backed securities. They also blamed mortgage originators who relaxed traditional banking standards and sold adjustable rate and no-interest mortgages with balloon payments to people who were not credit-worthy.[4] Finally, liberals pointed out that Fannie and Freddie began as government programs, but by the time the housing bubble was underway, they were fully private entities that eventually followed other banks into the riskier forms of securities.

Also predictably, conservatives thought the solution was to reduce banking regulations, whereas the liberals wanted to increase regulation. When it all came down, President Obama and the liberals were in power, and as a result, the Dodd–Frank Wall Street Reform and Consumer Protection Act was passed in July of 2010.

Our Dangerous Dance with Debt

These debates about the causes of The Great Recession were up at the level of policy and politics, but down at the level of households and individuals different things were going on. People were losing their jobs, losing their homes, and going bankrupt. As we shall see, the underlying problem in American households was too little savings and too much debt. Mortgage debt was a large part of the problem in 2008, but not the only source of difficulty. Furthermore, as the following chapters will make clear, the problems began decades ago.

Figure 3.1 lays out the sad tale. A lot of really bad stuff seems to be happening on the right-hand side of the graph, in the years surrounding the Great Recession, but the misery starts much earlier. The dotted line shows the number of personal bankruptcies, and the vertical line at 1978 marks a point where bankruptcies seemed to make a sharp upward turn. One of the major arguments of this book is that something got started in that period of the late 1970s that helped get us to where we are today. What precisely that something is will be the subject of subsequent chapters, but for now let's just follow the

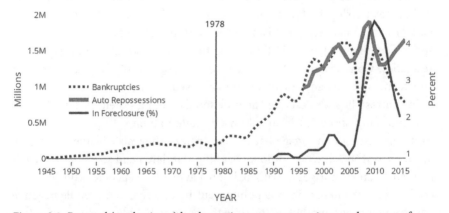

Figure 3.1 Personal (nonbusiness) bankruptcies, auto repossessions, and percent of residential mortgages in foreclosure (right-hand scale).
SOURCES: US Courts, Manheim Consulting, and the Mortgage Bankers Association.

dotted line up the hill. You can see that bankruptcies rose steeply, peaking in 2006, and made a sharp drop in 2007. All of this was before the Great Recession got underway, but the two may not be completely unrelated.

THE PARABLE OF BANKRUPTCY

In the spring of 2005, President George W. Bush signed the Bankruptcy Abuse Prevention and Consumer Protection Act of 2005, a bill strongly supported by the banking industry and by both Republicans and Democrats in the House and Senate, many of whom had received campaign contributions from credit card companies. In the 2004 election campaign, President Bush's largest contributors were banking and investment firms (contributing through political action committees), and MBNA, the Delaware credit card giant that is now part of Bank America, was his sixth-largest contributor.[5] Among other things, the bill introduced new income restrictions on bankruptcy relief and placed additional requirements on bankruptcy attorneys that would increase the cost of filing for bankruptcy.

Supporters of the bill claimed that too many people had abused bankruptcy. As President Bush said at the signing ceremony, "They've walked away from debts even when they had the ability to repay them."[6] Critics of the bill argued that it was a giveaway to the credit card companies, aimed at keeping their profits high by placing obstacles in the path of bankruptcy. The result, they argued, would be that many people who had fallen on hard times and might benefit from the fresh start bankruptcy was intended to provide would instead be trapped under mountains of debt without hope of escape from a life of indentured servitude, working for the bank.

Both sides of this debate agreed on one fact: personal bankruptcies had soared to record levels. Over the previous three decades there had been an unprecedented six-fold increase in bankruptcies. Financial failure was on the rise, but the explanations offered by the two sides could not have been more different.

The Parable of Bankruptcy, Version One: "It's Too Easy"

The pro-business story has the beauty of simplicity. Version One largely blames the problem on the Bankruptcy Reform Act of 1978, which made it too easy for debtors to walk away from their responsibilities. Under this law, Chapter 7 bankruptcy in particular allowed consumers who got into trouble to wipe away mountains of debt and, in many cases, retain their homes, cars, and other property. According to the supporters of Version One, in the years after 1978, Chapter 7 emerged as the chapter of choice in 70 percent of the cases precisely because it provided an easy out. The repayment requirements in Chapter 13 discouraged debtors from taking this option. Even though Chapter 13 allowed debtors to keep more of their assets, according to the supporters of Version One, the prospects of escaping any obligation to pay old debts while still being able to keep all future income attracted debtors to Chapter 7 in droves. According to the "it's too easy" account, the vertical line at the late 1970s in Figure 3.1 marks the introduction of the 1978 bankruptcy law. Without question, bankruptcies grew at an alarming rate after that point.

One of the popular subplots of Version One involves a Supreme Court decision one year prior to the 1978 bankruptcy reform bill. The Court found that advertising by attorneys and law firms was a form of free speech protected by the First Amendment.[7] According to Version One, in addition to dooming us all to a steady diet of commercials from personal-injury lawyers, this ruling had the effect of encouraging bankruptcy as a financial strategy. Ads for bankruptcy lawyers greatly helped to reduce the stigma previously associated with financial failure. This legal advertising subplot paints debtors with the same unsavory brush as the stereotypical malingering personal-injury plaintiff and reminds us that bankruptcy attorneys have a vested interest in convincing people to take the easy way out.

To give it more color, Version One is often buttressed with such memorable examples as the celebrity bankruptcies of Kim Basinger, Curt Schilling, Mike Tyson, Toni Braxton, and 50 Cent (Curtis Jackson).[8] Because these famous people squandered enormous sums of money prior to bankruptcy and, in some cases, went on to amass great wealth after bankruptcy, their stories highlight poor financial management and the strategic use of the law.[9]

Finally, although the authors of Version Two are the consumer advocates in this debate, the supporters of Version One insisted that weak bankruptcy laws were bad for consumers. According to this view, stricter bankruptcy laws could result in tens of billions of dollars in savings for the banking industry, making it possible for banks to lower interest rates and extend credit to people in lower-income and riskier demographic groups. The bankruptcies of the irresponsible few were being paid for by the responsible many.

The Parable of Bankruptcy, Version Two: "It's Not My Fault"

The alternative to Version One follows a David and Goliath plot, except Goliath wins. The underdog is the American consumer, and the villains are Citicorp,

Bank of America, MBNA, and the other companies that make up the highly profitable card industry.[10]

Once upon a time there were usury laws. Each state set a limit on the interest rates allowed on loans. Most states passed laws prohibiting usurious interest rates, and these laws protected citizens from being gouged on loans and placed a fair limit on the lender's profits. But then an important Supreme Court decision changed all that. In *Marquette National Bank of Minneapolis v. First National Bank of Omaha,* the Court held that credit card companies could charge the interest rate in the state where they had their offices to a cardholder in a different state. In effect, interest rates could now cross state lines. This allowed credit card companies to search out the states with the highest allowable interest rates and set up offices. Your credit card bills are sent from places such as South Dakota, Maryland, and Delaware because those states discovered that by relaxing their usury laws and allowing higher interest rates, they could attract jobs and tax revenues in the form of credit card companies and credit card divisions of existing banks. After the *Marquette* decision, Citicorp entered into negotiations with the state of South Dakota, and in return for a further loosening of the state's usury laws, the bank moved its credit card division and two thousand jobs to Sioux Falls. Other deals with competing card issuers followed in Delaware and Maryland.[11]

Suddenly credit cards were a much more profitable product, and according to Version Two, banks and credit card companies began to flood our mailboxes with card applications. Upbeat commercials by Visa ("It's everywhere you want to be"), MasterCard ("There are some things money can't buy, but for everything else there is MasterCard"), and American Express ("Don't leave home without it") became staples of our evening viewing. We were inundated with advertising and 0 percent APR introductory offers tempting us to apply for credit. Credit cards with generous limits were extended to almost anyone who sent in the form, regardless of whether the person had enough income to support the debt. Citicorp, an early aggressive marketer of bank credit cards, was soon able to turn around its business, building substantial profits in the 1990s, largely driven by its credit card division.[12]

Oh, and when did this all begin? The *Marquette* decision happened in the same year as the Bankruptcy Reform Act of 1978. So in Version Two, the relevant change takes place at the same point where the vertical line is drawn in Figure 3.1.

Soon after the banking industry got serious about credit cards, American consumers fell victim to a number of forces beyond their control, all of which made them more financially vulnerable. According to Version Two, in the decades following 1978 the United States continued a shift from good-paying manufacturing jobs to much lower-paying work in the service sector. In addition, more of the available positions were for part-time jobs that had both lower wages and fewer benefits than full-time work, and many workers were forced to take on multiple jobs to make ends meet.[13] Despite substantial income growth for wealthier Americans, wages for those in the middle-income bracket have remained stagnant for decades, and wages for the bottom income group are actually slightly lower than in the late 1970s.[14] What's more, as mentioned in chapter 1, despite being the wealthiest nation on earth, the United States does not have a universal healthcare system that provides coverage for all citizens. And in the 1980s and 1990s, prior to the Affordable Care Act, more Americans were without coverage than in the past. Employee health insurance contributions rose substantially, and many people either did not have the option of coverage or could not afford to subscribe.[15] This lack of security created by the risk of uncovered medical expenses—which, by their nature, are often unexpected—put larger numbers of people in economic jeopardy.[16]

As The Parable of Bankruptcy, Version Two, with its central theme of "It's not my fault," unfolded during the last two decades of the twentieth century, indebtedness exploded and saving all but disappeared—a recipe for disaster. When marriages broke up (as they did more often than in the past), health problems set in, or jobs were lost, credit cards became the safety net. But the revolving credit safety net is hard to crawl out of. Credit card company profits soared in the decades after the *Marquette* decision, but as banks thrived, they left behind them the wreckage of many of their customers.

WHICH VERSION IS RIGHT?

An honest evaluation would have to concede that there is some truth to both these stories, but these different accounts are tainted by the influence of business and consumer interests, political expediency, and differing moral philosophies. With millions of dollars at stake, it is easy for logic and common sense to be lost along the way. So let's take a look at the evidence.

Because they rarely do controlled laboratory experiments, economists must collect data and look for the best explanations for the trends they find.[17] In scientific terms, they are confined to a search for correlations, relationships between variables. And both versions of the story of bankruptcy show correlations. In Version One, the period immediately following the Bankruptcy Reform Act of 1978 is correlated with a steep rise in the number of bankruptcies, whereas in Version Two, something completely different, the *Marquette v. Omaha* decision, which made the credit card business much more profitable, is followed by the same steep rise in the number of bankruptcies. But as any beginning statistics student can tell you, correlation does not mean causation.

Since the sharp upturn in bankruptcies in the late 1970s is part of both versions, we might be tempted to simply choose the story we like best and be done with it. But what if both versions are false? And if so, how could we figure it out?

As it turns out, the answer is rather simple. A few studies have compared bankruptcy rates in Canada and the United States and found that the shapes of the two curves are remarkably similar.[18] The Canadian bankruptcy rate turns upward in the late 1970s and, like the US curve, rises at an increasing rate through the 1980s and 1990s. But neither of the events presumed to have created the epidemic in bankruptcies in the United States occurred in Canada. There was no change in the bankruptcy laws at that time that could explain the rise, and interest rates have been unregulated in Canada since 1886, making it possible for a lender to charge any rate the market will bear. There was no need for a *Marquette* decision to make credit cards more profitable, and as a result, Version Two of the Parable of Bankruptcy, which indicts the change in lending laws, cannot alone account for the increase in bankruptcies.

Although both versions of the story of bankruptcy are wounded by the Canadian experience, neither one is fatally injured. Version One, "It's too easy," is strengthened by the results of the bankruptcy bill of 2005. When the bankruptcy bill was signed into law and word got out that declaring bankruptcy was soon going to be much more difficult, there was a spike in the number of filings, but in the period immediately after the bill went into effect, the number of people filing was reduced to less than half the previous rate (see Figure 3.1). It is still unclear whether, as suggested by Version One, the 1978 bankruptcy law increased bankruptcies, but since there are no plausible alternative explanations, it is clear that the 2005 law *decreased* bankruptcies at least temporarily.[19]

In the case of Version Two, "It's not my fault," although there was no change in interest rate policy in Canada in 1978, some evidence suggests that interest rate deregulation, such as that produced by the *Marquette* decision—and such as that previously in effect in Canada—was a necessary condition for the bankruptcy boom that began in the United States in the 1980s. Although banking laws that made credit cards more profitable were not enough to bring about the exponential rise in financial tragedy, these laws were a necessary first step. The support for this conclusion comes from a closer look at the patterns produced in these two countries. Although interest rate deregulation was not introduced in the United States until 1978, universal bank credit cards were introduced in both countries at about the same time. Visa and MasterCard entered the United States in 1966 and Canada two years later. (We look more closely at the history of credit cards in chapter 5.)

North of the forty-ninth parallel, bankruptcies had always been lower than in the United States, but following the introduction of bank credit cards they began a gradual increase, eventually rising to rates equal to that of the United

States in 1978, the year of the *Marquette* decision. In contrast, bankruptcies below the forty-ninth parallel remained flat for more than ten years after the introduction of bank cards and began their precipitous climb only after deregulation. By the mid-1980s, the United States had reestablished the gap between American and Canadian bankruptcies, a gap that continued into the twenty-first century.[20]

So what might we conclude from this pattern of results? First, bank credit cards seem to be related to bankruptcy. Their introduction in Canada is correlated with an immediate—though rather gradual at first—increase in bankruptcies. In the United States, where prior to 1978 usury laws made bank cards less profitable, credit cards alone were not enough to get bankruptcies rolling. Only after the *Marquette* decision did bankruptcies begin to rise at a much more rapid rate, both in the United States and in Canada. So one conclusion that might be drawn from these results is that it was the combination of universal bank credit cards and bank deregulation (which made consumer credit a more profitable business) that produced the current bankruptcy crisis. Second, making bankruptcy more difficult decreases its use at least for a while.

At least two additional questions remain unanswered by this simple two-factor (credit cards and interest deregulation) answer. First, why are bankruptcies consistently higher in the United States than in Canada? Given the many ways these countries are different, it may be difficult to answer this question, but the presence of universal healthcare in Canada—and its absence in the United States—provides one possible explanation. Legal or cultural differences that make bankruptcy less appealing in Canada are another. Second, in the years following the *Marquette* decision, both countries experienced acceleration in bankruptcies. Given that the *Marquette* decision affected only the United States, why would bankruptcies turn upward in both countries? Although it is impossible to give definitive answers to these questions, the social and technological changes outlined in the following chapters give a possible explanation. But first, let's turn to one more factor thought to contribute to the Parable of Bankruptcy.

Version One of the story of bankruptcy rests heavily on the premise that the shame of bankruptcy is greatly diminished, and this theory has been promoted enough that many people (including then Senator John Kerry, quoted at the beginning of this chapter) have accepted it. But the evidence for this aspect of Version One is far from overwhelming. The first problem is that stigma is a presumed psychological variable: the shame and sense of moral irresponsibility that people feel when they admit they can no longer honor their obligations. Measuring this psychological concept would require administering questionnaires to people as they consider the option of bankruptcy. The results of these surveys would need to be compared to similar data from the past—if they existed. For obvious reasons, no one has done this. Instead, economists attempt to capture the idea of stigma by measuring other variables—proxies— that might show the effects of stigma on the bankruptcy decision. Unfortunately, the results have been muddy. Some economic studies have concluded that this stigma has decreased in recent years, but others show no evidence of diminished shame.[21]

OTHER WAYS OF SPRINGING A LEAK

The Parable of Bankruptcy accounts for most of Figure 3.1, but once the Great Recession arrives on the right-hand side of the graph all hell breaks loose. Bankruptcy was the most common way of springing a financial leak for several decades before 2008, but the recession was not caused by bankruptcies. Starting in 2007, hundreds of thousands of homeowners who had stopped paying their mortgages created a sharp spike in foreclosures that continued to rise until 2009, triggering the biggest banking crisis since 1930s and a deep recession. Despite the reforms of 2005, bankruptcies spiked again during the recession. Both bankruptcies and foreclosures have come down substantially in recent years, but two new forms of financial failure have come along to replace them.

As the far-right side of Figure 3.1 shows, automobile repossessions have spiked in recent years. This somewhat surprising development stems, in part, from some new developments in automobile financing. In a pattern similar to the pre-recession housing market, automobile financing allows buyers to borrow very large sums of money over longer periods of time. As we saw in chapter 1, large auto loans spread over six or seven years have become common.[22] In addition, following a cue from the housing mortgage industry, many auto loan companies now offer refinancing that provides consumers with extra cash.[23] Unlike homes, however, automobiles are an asset that can be easily seized if the borrower defaults on the loan. In many states, lenders can have a tow truck at your house as soon as you miss a payment, and with auto loan defaults soaring, the repo industry is booming.

Another trend in financial failure cannot be seen in Figure 3.1. As we saw in chapter 1, the amount of money Americans owe on student loans is now greater than any other type of loan other than mortgages, but student loans are a special case. Unlike car loans and mortgages, student loans are not backed by an asset that can be repossessed or foreclosed if the borrower stops paying, and, unlike credit card debt, student loans cannot be discharged in bankruptcy. Once you have a student loan, the only way out from under it is to qualify for a public service loan forgiveness program or pay it off. Nonetheless, increasing numbers of borrowers are not paying their bills. As Figure 3.2 shows, although

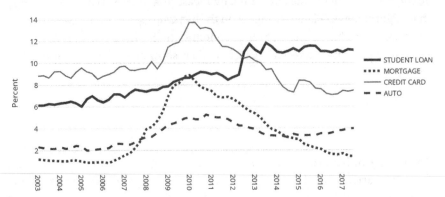

Figure 3.2 Seriously delinquent loans from 2003 through the second quarter of 2017 by type of loan. Seriously delinquent = 90+ days past due.
SOURCE: Federal Reserve Bank of New York/Equifax.

the serious delinquency rate on all other forms of loans rose and then fell as they passed through the Great Recession, student loan delinquencies are above 10 percent and remain high, but as concerning as this graph is, it greatly understates the problem with student loans.

The Federal Reserve Bank of New York, which is the source of these numbers, notes that approximately half of the student loans shown in Figure 3.2 were not in their payment cycle because they were either in deferment, a grace period, or forbearance. If the data considered just those loans where payments were expected, the delinquency rate would be roughly twice as high as the line in Figure 3.2.[24]

Many people consider college a necessity. Economic data consistently shows that higher education leads to higher income levels, and many American school children are under great pressure to perform well and get into the best possible colleges. But college costs have risen sharply. If, as is increasingly the case, parents cannot afford the price of sending their children to the colleges of their choice, schools typically offer financial aid packages that rely heavily on federal and private student loans. In this case, it is very difficult for either the borrower or lender to assess the student's future earning potential. Despite the enormous risks involved, it is now commonplace for young people—most of whom are several years away from being able to legally drink a beer—to make decisions that will affect their financial lives for decades.

Exploding levels of student debt have led to a rebellion on the part of many young people. One of the major themes of the Occupy Wall Street movement of 2011 was a push for student loan forgiveness.[25] During the 2016 presidential primary campaign, this issue was seized on by Democratic candidates Hillary Clinton and Bernie Sanders, who both offered student loan debt relief proposals.[26] Although neither of these candidates won the presidency, the student loan rebellion shows every indication of continuing on, and as Figure 3.2 shows, well after the official end of the Great Recession, student loan delinquencies continue to be a problem.[27]

One of the most respected interpretations of the Great Recession was presented by economists Atif Mian and Amir Sufi in their book *House of Debt*. Mian and Sufi argue that the Great Recession and recessions, in general, are created by too much household debt, which makes families vulnerable to an economic shock. In particular, constrained maxed-out families have a tendency to spend out of their household wealth, and they reduce spending when their wealth declines. This explains why the dot com bubble of 2001 had a relatively mild effect on the economy: the loss of wealth was concentrated in high-income stock-holding households that did not have the same tendency to spend their wealth. In contrast, during the Great Recession, losses were centered in home equity, and during the pre-2008 boom years, many homeowners took cash out of their homes by refinancing or taking out home equity loans. Once the housing bubble burst, millions of families saw their wealth wiped out and stopped spending, which, in turn, had a devastating effect on our consumer-driven economy.

When economists look at problems like debt, they often consider things on both the supply and the demand side of the transaction. Did households become dangerously leveraged because of factors related to the supply of credit or because of consumer demand? The following chapters take a very close look at the forces that create consumer demand for the products and services in our contemporary marketplace, but before we move on, it is worth taking a quick look at the role of supply side factors in the Great Recession.

As we know, during the housing boom years, an increased number of mortgages were offered to people who, in the past, would not have qualified for home loans. Housing prices were going up rapidly, and there was great investor demand for securities based on these mortgages. So for a time, there was considerable supply of credit going to consumers, encouraged, in part, by a demand for mortgage-backed securities. When the house of cards came tumbling down, these bundled investments became "toxic," and the investors went away.

Interestingly, as I write this, a similar phenomenon is underway in a different banking area. Recall that Figure 3.1 shows an ongoing surge in automobile repossessions. Demand for cars is always high because, for many people, having a set of wheels is considered a necessity, but there is also a credit supply angle to this picture. We are currently in the midst of a subprime auto loan boom, and similar to the mortgaged-backed securities boom of the early 2000s, many of these subprime auto loans are being bundled together—"securitized"—and sold to investors. Despite the obvious weaknesses of the underlying loans—many of which are offered to people with credit scores below 550—these asset-backed securities are thought to be less risky than the mortgage-backed securities of the pre-recession years because, relative to home mortgages, the market is much smaller and the loans are also smaller and of much shorter length.[28]

Finally, before we leave this long saga of financial ruin across the generations, I want to return to the Parable of Bankruptcy. Earlier I hinted that, although the Parable of Bankruptcy and the Great Recession seem to be two separate stories of financial ruin, they might be related. If there is a single message of Figures 3.1 and 3.2 it is that, since the early 1990s, large numbers of Americans—millions each year—have been springing financial leaks of one kind or another. For several decades they did so by declaring bankruptcy. In the mid-2000s, people switched over to not paying their mortgages, and today they are not making their student loan and car payments.

Of particular interest is the disastrous switch from bankruptcy to foreclosure. As a personal and economic event, bankruptcy is far less disruptive. For obvious reasons, people who file for bankruptcy often keep it private, and other than raising our credit card interest rates, bankruptcy has little effect on the overall economy. Indeed, the fresh start provided by bankruptcy allows borrowers to quickly return to rebuilding their financial lives.

In contrast, as we have seen, foreclosure has effects "far beyond the housing market." For each house that is lost to foreclosure, others nearby lose value. Homebuilders lay off workers, and fewer mortgages are signed. For all the reasons we have discussed, the effects of foreclosures on the economy are widespread and recovering from them is a very slow process. As of this moment, we are still not out of the woods.

Ironically, several studies have found that the Bankruptcy Abuse Prevention and Consumer Protection Act of 2005 was a contributing factor in the foreclosure crisis that launched the Great Recession. If you take a close look at Figure 3.1 you will notice that foreclosures take off in 2007, just as bankruptcies are falling. The bankruptcy reforms of 2005 made it more expensive and more onerous to file. For lower-income families without access to cash—the very people who were the most likely candidates for bankruptcy—it suddenly became easier to stop paying the mortgage than to go through the bankruptcy process. According to these studies, many foreclosures might have been avoided had the bankruptcy law remained unchanged. Financially stressed households might have been able to discharge their credit card bills and other consumer loans through bankruptcy and use the savings to make their mortgage payments.

If this analysis is correct, a policy that banks spent years lobbying for was a contributing factor in the biggest banking crisis since the Great Depression. A self-inflicted wound of enormous proportions.[29]

Versions One and Two of the Parable of Bankruptcy looked at the facts through different moral lenses. They were arguments created in service of different policy responses to debt and financial insolvency. Eventually, while George W. Bush was president, Version One, "It's Too Easy," won the battle of moral theories, and the Bankruptcy Abuse Prevention and Consumer Protection Act of 2005 became law. Unfortunately, the authors of the bill had not put themselves in the shoes of low-income homeowners saddled with debt. People who, like 47 percent of Americans, could not pull together $400 for an emergency without borrowing money or selling something. People who sat at the kitchen table knowing that the bills in front of them could not be covered by the money in the bank. Had the politicians put themselves into that kitchen table scene, they might have been able to predict what would happen next.

As tempting as it is to stand in judgment of Neal Gabler and others who cannot pay their bills, the Great Recession is a lesson in the interconnectedness of the economy. Whether we realize it or not, we all have a stake in each other's financial success. Your neighbor's foreclosure hurts you, too. Furthermore, Mian and Sufi make a compelling argument that the problem is debt. In the short term, spending on credit can fuel the economy. The housing boom financed by an abundance of mortgage credit was good while it lasted. But high levels of household debt make families vulnerable to economic shocks. Little or no savings combined with lots of debt is a recipe for disaster. An illness or the loss of a job are all it takes to send you into an economic tailspin, and as the graphs we have encountered thus far suggest, many Americans still have lots of debt and not very much savings.

Behavioral scientists approach financial ruin with a different set of goals. For the psychologist, too much debt is a behavioral problem, and an explanation of this modern phenomenon will come from an understanding of how people maneuver through their economic environments. Spending, borrowing, and saving are activities that involve both the body and the mind. On one level, we are financial animals trying to make our way through a maze of polarizing forces that draw us toward spending or push us away from it. But we are also thinking animals, and there are a multitude of chinks in our intellectual armor that cause us to make ill-considered money management decisions. We save the financial reasoning errors for chapter 8, but behavioral psychology provides us with a different way to look at the modern history of banking and spending— one that will soon lead us to a new perspective on the modern epidemic of debt and financial failure.

CAROLINE

Caroline met her husband, Tom, in college, and in the early years of their relationship he was very solicitous toward her. He gave her gifts, introduced her to all his friends, and took her out. Their happiness continued into the early years of their marriage. They had an active social life, primarily but not exclusively with his friends, and things were good at home.

After graduating from college, Caroline immediately got work in the accounting department of an insurance company. Tom also was hired right out of college, getting a very good position as a production planner at a toy manufacturing company. Before long they were able to buy a nice home in an upper-middle-class neighborhood of East Greenwich, Rhode Island. Caroline was laid off from her first job within a couple of years, but she wasn't unemployed for very long. Even when the couple started having children, she was able to find part-time accounting jobs that brought in money—sometimes quite a bit of money. Tom was adamant that she continue to work and contribute to the household income, even after the kids arrived.

Soon after their first son was born, the marriage began to go downhill. Tom never wanted to go out anymore, and their social life dried up. He was a very responsible husband, made a very good salary, paid the bills on time, and worked hard on the weekends to maintain the house. But he did all of this apart from Caroline and the kids. When he was home, he was either in the TV room by himself or in the basement or the garage working on a project.

Because neither Caroline's job nor her home life provided much in the way of adult social interaction, she would sometimes go out with friends on her own. Eventually she got a second job working a couple of nights a week at The Gap. Despite having to be responsible for the kids on the nights she worked, her husband put up with the second job because it brought in some extra money.

However, the job ended up being a net drain on the couple's income. For Caroline, evenings at the Gap were a little bit of freedom. She made friends with some of her coworkers, and using a MasterCard that her husband didn't know about, she would often pay for outings with her new friends during breaks and before work. Most of these activities—shopping, eating out—went on the card, but because she always got to the mail first, it was easy for Caroline to retrieve the bill before Tom saw it.

Then one day, Tom discovered one of the credit card statements and hit the roof. It was bad enough that she had a credit card he didn't know about, but that by the time he came across the bill she had an $8,000 balance on the card was much worse. Tom paid the card off out of their cash savings, but he was very angry. She apologized, cut up her card, and promised this would never happen again.

Relations between them got even worse after this credit card episode, with Caroline becoming increasingly angry over Tom's coldness toward her and their children. She got another credit card and started spending again. Once she got going, Caroline had some of the classic signs of a shopaholic. She loved clothes and shopping for bargains, but her closet was filled with outfits that still had the tags on them. She also shopped for other people—for friends and for charity fund-raising drives, often contributing brand-new items when other people donated things out of the attic.

Tom had primary control over the joint checking account, and he now paid all the bills. Caroline had her own checking account, into which her paychecks were automatically deposited. Their arrangement was that she would give him an amount equal to the pay from her daytime accounting job and she could keep the money from her part-time job at The Gap. But as her spending progressed, Caroline found she didn't have enough to cover her credit card bills. After two or three years, she had acquired about a dozen cards—three bank cards, Macy's, JCPenney, Talbots, and a number of other store cards—and most of them had balances on them. Even just the minimum payments got to be more than she could cover with the money from the Gap, so she had to hold back money from her daytime job to try to keep up with the payments. After a time, her deceptions and the burden of all her debt got to be too stressful to handle. This was her second time building up credit card balances behind her husband's back, and now she owed much more: a total of $40,000. So finally she confessed.

Tom was outraged and threatened to divorce her. They went to a consumer credit counseling service, but when the counselors offered to take over the payment of the couple's bills, Caroline and Tom decided to tackle the problem on their own. Once again they went through the ritual of cutting up the cards, and at her husband's insistence Caroline cashed in $8,000 from her retirement account. He borrowed another $20,000 against his retirement, and the rest they paid off in installments. It took some time to get rid of the debt, but they did it.

This last debt crisis happened about six years before I met Caroline, and she had been debt-free ever since. Furthermore, she was happier and more self-confident than she had been in the past. Some of her success came from a new financial structure she had worked out with her husband, and some of it came from counseling. After the last credit card incident, Caroline had all her paychecks automatically deposited into the joint checking account, which Tom still controlled. Caroline was still responsible for household shopping, for which he would give her a regular sum of money. She still had her personal checking account, but a Mobil Oil gas card was the only credit card she carried. She paid cash for everything and found this a liberating experience. There was no worry about being able to cover the expense or about building up debt. If she needed more money for an unusual expense, her husband usually would give it to her.

Counseling did a number of things for Caroline. During her spending days, Caroline had developed friendships with very needy people and had gotten trapped into helping them—often by giving them money or buying things for them. With the help of her counselor, she learned how to set limits on her generosity. Sometimes that meant the friends got angry and cut her off, but she learned to recognize these breakups as evidence of a bad friendship.

Perhaps most helpful was a counseling group for people with spending problems. These sessions provided lots of practical information about budgeting (the irony of an accountant needing budgeting advice was not lost on her) and about the importance of finding other, more positive activities. Based on this advice, Caroline joined a health club and eventually started jogging with a local runners' group. She lost weight and got into better shape than she had been in for years. Furthermore, the runners' group had many regular activities together, providing her with a new, much more positive social life.

Tom had not changed. They still lived together like strangers, and Caroline assumed that eventually she would get a divorce. But at the moment, that wasn't practical: she was working only part time, and at eight years old, her youngest child was still too young for her to make full-time work as a single adult a good option. And at least now she was free of debt. Life was not perfect, but Caroline had the sense that she was on the right track and things would work out in time.

Self-Control and Money

I'm living so far beyond my income that we may almost be said to be living apart.

—H. H. Munro (Saki), *The Unbearable Bassington*

So how did all this happen? Why are so many people strapped? Why doesn't anybody save? And, what happened in the 1970s? Before we can answer these questions, we need to take a closer look at the psychology of self-control. One of the most important contributions to our understanding of money problems, as well as all other problems involving what the Greeks called *akrasia*, or weakness of will, was made by a medical student pursuing a research project in his spare time. It is a story involving competing mathematical curves, pigeons, and the seductive effects of time on the better judgment of reasonable people.

THE MATHEMATICS OF DESIRE

When I speak to audiences I sometimes give them the following problem to solve. Imagine that I have two envelopes. One contains $10, and the other contains $12. If you could have only one, which envelope would you choose? At this point most people say they would like to have the $12 envelope, thank you very much. The two options differ only in the amount of money you get, so barring any additional conditions (such as that I will give the envelope you don't choose to charity), the choice should be obvious. $12 is more than $10, and more money is better than less. But the problem doesn't stop here.

Next I offer a choice between the $10 envelope right now and the $12 envelope a week from now. This makes the decision a little more difficult. Instead of just differing in amount, the choices differ on two dimensions: time and amount. Nonetheless, most people still say they want the $12 envelope, even though they have to wait to get it. But then I extend the larger reward further into the future. What about two weeks from now? Three weeks from now? Eventually, often when the larger amount is pushed somewhere between two and three weeks into the future, most people change their minds and say they want the $10 now.

This exercise demonstrates that time has value. Assuming the immediate $10 envelope is preferred over a $12 envelope two weeks from now, then many people are willing to pay $2 for an immediate reward. And why shouldn't they? Given the $10 now, if they have an entrepreneurial impulse, they might use the money to buy some raw material, produce a product, and sell it at a profit. If they are very lucky, they might make up the lost $2 or even exceed it. Alternatively, they might buy some item of lasting value—a book, for example—and be able to use it in the intervening weeks. Furthermore, there is the risk that something will happen during the waiting period and they will not get their money.[1] Stated another way, the two-week delay has the effect of diminishing the value of the $12 envelope. But we still are not finished with this problem.

Once I have established the crossover point—where the delayed, larger reward is less attractive than the immediate, smaller one—I freeze the gap between the two envelopes and move them both out into the murky future. What about when the choices are between $10 four weeks from now and $12 six weeks from now? Or $10 in twenty-eight weeks and $12 in thirty weeks? At some point in this process, as both envelopes recede into the future, people generally return to a preference for the larger, $12 envelope. Both rewards are far away, unable to help us with our immediate spending needs, and thus, once again, $12 looks like the better choice.

This is a remarkably simple narrative: 12-10-12. Swayed by the effects of time, our choices shift from the larger amount to the smaller and back to the larger again. But within this tiny three-act play lies the key to a multitude of human tragedies.

When they think about the three versions of this problem, most people have the sense that if the $12 envelope is the right choice in the long run, it should be the right choice in the short run, too. Why should playing around with the delays to these little windfalls change our opinion of which envelope is better? When neither is delayed, it is easy to choose, and when both envelopes are off in the future, it is easy, too. We know we will have to wait a bit longer for the larger reward, but from our vantage point here in the present, it takes little effort to do the right thing and pick the larger reward. The problem arises when one of the rewards is immediate and the other is delayed. If we think about it, we have a sense that choosing $12 in two weeks is still the right choice. If some rich uncle were to give us this choice every few days, it is clear that we would be far better off in the long run if we always chose $12 in two weeks. But the immediacy of $10 now is hard to walk away from.

Economists have long known that money in the future is worth less than money right now. They call this *present value discounting*. The value in the present of money in the future is discounted—worth less—relative to money right now. In the two-envelope example, $12 two weeks in the future is discounted by more than $2, making it less valuable than $10 now. Alternatively, present value discounting—or what psychologists call *delay discounting*—implies that immediate rewards have much higher value than delayed rewards. When, in act two of our little drama, people choose the $10 envelope now over $12 in two weeks, in effect they are paying a $2 fee to get the money right away. It is this strong attraction to having things now that explains why people are willing to pay interest on loans rather than save money for the things they need. If you are a young person approaching the purchase of your first car, you could decide to rely on other means of transportation until you can put aside enough money to buy one. But, more often than not, having the car now is worth paying a higher price for it. If the young person can obtain a loan, they will pay the price of the car plus the interest charges in return for having wheels right now. Immediacy is worth paying for, and for centuries moneylenders have made a healthy profit by providing immediacy at a price.

But the most interesting aspect of the two-envelope problem is not the simple fact that delayed money is valued less. It is that we choose inconsistently. Ever since the classical economist Adam Smith outlined his philosophy of the market, most economists have assumed that we are all rational actors strutting across an economic stage. Given adequate information and free choice, each player will do what is best for themselves. The invisible hand of the market supposedly guides us to transactions that benefit both the buyer and the seller. But if we are such sensible participants, then why do we choose inconsistently? Why is $12 worth more than $10 in acts one and three but less than $10 in act two? Part of the answer to this question came when a young medical student discovered a wrinkle in the mathematics of desire.

In the early 1960s, George Ainslie was an undergraduate at Yale University, and in an introductory psychology course a professor suggested that the value of a reward could be expressed as a curve. If a rat was running through a maze to get a piece of food, a larger piece would produce faster running. Increasing the size of the piece of food would make the rat run faster, but the effect would gradually taper off as the rat reached the limit of its athletic prowess. Ainslie was intrigued by the idea that the relationship between the size of the reward and its value—how hard the rat would work for it—could be described by a mathematical function, a curve. But he was also interested in questions of self-control and conflicting motivations. He noticed that people are often at war with themselves (Should I have dessert or not? Should I study or go out with friends?), and even at this young age, Ainslie was searching for a way to investigate these conflicting desires.

Ainslie wanted to become a psychiatrist, so after graduating from Yale, he entered Harvard Medical School. The demands of his medical training were such that for a couple of years Ainslie was far too busy studying to think about research, but eventually he approached a scientist at Harvard who put him in touch with Richard Herrnstein in the Psychology Department. Herrnstein had studied with the famed behaviorist B. F. Skinner, and by the time Ainslie knocked on his door, Herrnstein had assumed leadership of the Harvard pigeon laboratory from his mentor.

At that time, there was uncertainty about the shape of the drop-off in a reward's attractiveness as it became more delayed. Prior to 1955, the assumption was that the weakening force of future rewards followed a smooth path, sometimes called an exponential decay function. This is a pattern often found in nature, and it represents a constant percentage drop in value over time. Furthermore, the idea that money is exponentially discounted is reflected in the calculation of compound interest. If you put $1,000 into a savings account at a 5 percent annual interest rate, the interest is often calculated (compounded) on a daily basis, and the tiny amount of interest earned on the first day is added to the principal. On day two, the interest is calculated again, based on the new, slightly larger principal amount, and added to the principal, and so on. As this pattern is repeated every day, your growing wealth follows an exponential curve such that after a year, an initial investment of $1,000 at 5 percent has grown to $1,051.27 instead of just $1,050.[2] Not a dramatic difference, but the exponential nature of interest calculation was another reason why exponential discounting curves seemed plausible.

The mathematics of exponential functions are not important enough for us to get into here, but when this curve is applied to decay processes, such as the diminishing pull of money or possessions in the future, it has one very important characteristic: it makes us more rational—or at least more consistent.[3] Why? Because exponential curves do not cross, and therefore the exponential person does not waffle. The top panel of Figure 4.1 shows one version of a consistent exponential person. At the far right-hand side of the graph, $12 is being offered right now—at zero delay—and, as a result, the line representing the value of this choice is at full height and tapers off to the left as the delay gets longer. Money deferred is worth less. The arrow at the right of the graph shows the introduction of a choice between $10 right now and $12 in two weeks. For this particular person, the delayed $12 is still worth more than $10 now. By itself this is not very remarkable, but as the delay to both amounts is extended to the

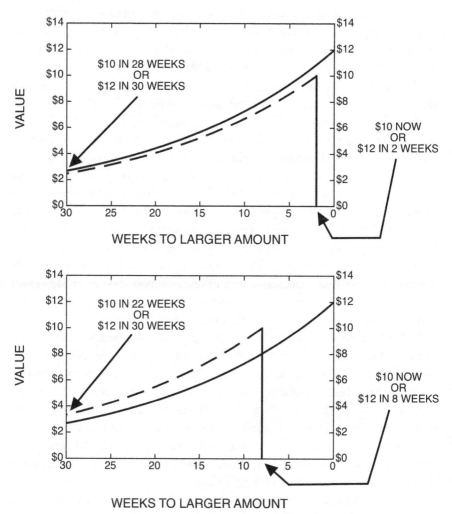

Figure 4.1 Exponential delay discounting. In these graphs, time moves from left to right. The solid and broken lines show the present value of $12 and $10 amounts, respectively. Because the curves never cross, the exponential person makes more consistent and rational choices.

left, our exponential person remains consistent. Rather than choosing 12-10-12, they choose 12-12-12.

The lower panel of Figure 4.1 shows how even the exponential person can reverse choices. In this case, the $10 right now is worth more than $12 in eight weeks (right-hand arrow). Money in the future is worth less. But the exponential person holds firm when the delays to both choices are extended. At the left-hand side of the graph, $10 in twenty-two weeks is still preferred over $12 in thirty weeks. The beauty of the exponential curve is that when summoned to describe our devaluing of money over time, it makes us more consistent and rational because the lines never cross. Once we decide which choice is preferable, we stick with that decision as waiting time is added or subtracted.

The only problem with this model is that it almost never happens. Once both the amounts of money are far off in the future, almost everyone chooses $12. It's as if we reason that neither choice gets us any money soon, so we might as well wait for the larger amount. By the 1960s some economists and psychologists were beginning to understand that the exponential person was a fiction.

Unknown to Ainslie, about ten years before he became interested in the problem of self-control, the economist Robert Strotz had proposed the heretical idea that time discounting might not be exponential.[4] Instead he suggested that the effect of time on the value of money might better fit a curve that dropped off far more steeply with short delays and leveled out as delays got longer. Such a curve would give great weight to the immediacy of a reward and would produce the kind of inconsistent decisions seen in most people's choices of $12 versus $10. Strotz did not perform any experiments; he simply proposed an alternative theory that seemed to fit many of our common experiences.

In 1967, Herrnstein and Shin-Ho Chung published a study on the effect of delayed reinforcement on the key-pecking behavior of pigeons, and after reading their article, Ainslie realized it suggested that a different kind of curve—a hyperbola—might best describe the weakened effects of delayed reinforcement. In their previous work, Herrnstein and his colleagues had discovered that several basic reinforcement processes followed the shape of a hyperbola, a far more angular curve than the gentle exponential function— one closer to what Strotz had proposed. Ainslie soon saw that when applied to the question of time discounting, the hyperbola would produce the kind of motivational conflict and inconsistent decisions people make when attempting to exert self-control.

Herrnstein generously offered to let Ainslie conduct research on self-control in the Harvard pigeon laboratory, and he soon showed that pigeons would regularly choose a small immediate reward over a larger delayed one—even when doing so meant they lost out in the long run. Based on these results and those of other researchers, Ainslie proposed a theory of self-control based on the idea of hyperbolic discounting, a theory that, among other things, explains why most people choose $10 now over $12 in two weeks.

As Figure 4.2 demonstrates, the hyperbolic person gives inordinate weight to immediate rewards and strikingly less weight to rewards that are delayed even briefly. Unlike the exponential curves in Figure 4.1, hyperbolic curves cross and, as a result, mirror our typically inconsistent behavior perfectly. Once again, at the far right of Figure 4.2, $12 is given its full value because there is no delay, but as delays are added going left, the value drops off sharply. In this case,

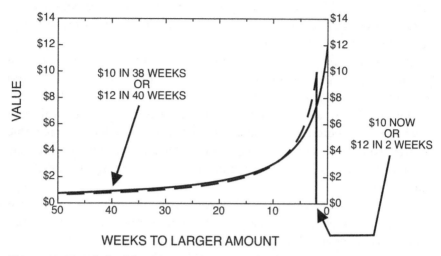

Figure 4.2 Hyperbolic delay discounting. As in Figure 4.1, time moves from left to right, and the solid and broken lines show the present value of $12 and $10 amounts, respectively. Because the curves cross, the hyperbolic model duplicates the inconsistent decisions typical of self-control problems.

given the choice between $10 now and $12 in two weeks (right-hand arrow), $10 now is more attractive. But as we move left and additional delays are added to both amounts, the value of the $10 option drops off quickly, and the $12 reemerges as the preferred option.[5] Finally, although Ainslie's research was done on pigeons, many subsequent studies with humans using money rewards have supported the hyperbolic model.

This capricious three-act play is sometimes called the double reversal effect. When delays of the right lengths are added to simple decisions about $10 versus $12, our preferences make two reversals: 12-10-12.

Problems involving different amounts of money are commonly used in decision-making research because it is so simple to compare the different options, but other commodities also obey the double reversal effect. Another example that I often use is a corollary of the two-envelope problem: the two-car problem. I ask my audience to imagine that I am going to give them a present, one of two cars: a Lexus sedan (a luxury car) or a Toyota Corolla (a standard, more moderately priced sedan). Usually the audience has already been through the two-envelope problem, so they have an idea where I am headed. Nonetheless, given a choice between these two options, almost everyone picks the Lexus. Now, I tell them that I am not really that rich, and as a result, the Corolla is a new car but the Lexus is used. Similar to the previous problem, I gradually age the Lexus, and somewhere around the point where the Lexus is ten or twelve years old, most people switch over to the brand-new Corolla. Finally, I begin to age both cars equally, maintaining the difference in age I have established. Eventually, once both cars are quite old—perhaps a twenty-two-year-old Lexus and a twelve-year-old Toyota Corolla—most people switch back to the Lexus.[6]

These examples tell us something else about the double reversal phenomenon: it is not always bad. At some point, an old Lexus has less value than a brand-new Corolla. The comfort and status it provides will be diminished by wear and tear, and the brand-new Corolla will beam with solid reliability. Once both cars are old and not expected to perform like new, the relative luxury of the Lexus will begin to speak to us again. This seems entirely rational. But choices between something now and something later are often a different matter.

Time changes everything. This elusive fourth dimension has fascinated scientists, philosophers, poets, and novelists almost from the moment human beings became aware of its passage. Without it there is no change. Ainslie's discovery of the shape of time's curve helped to reveal how it alters our motivations and desires in remarkably predictable ways. Self-control, once a topic whose moral overtones made it almost the exclusive purview of parents, priests, and philosophers, could now be studied experimentally by behavioral scientists and appeared to be at least partly tied to the way we are wired to respond to the choices we encounter. Immediate things are very powerful, and this intense value of things right in front of us often creates conflict with our long-term desires. Ainslie's work had a profound effect on the fields of both economics and psychology, and time-discounting theories of self-control have become an important area of study in both fields.

It is not entirely clear why we are so myopic in our decisions. Given our great powers of reasoning and prediction, why are we slaves to immediacy? One theory suggests that it is a vestige of our ancient, preagricultural past.[7] As hunter-gatherers, humans faced important moment-to-moment decisions. When food was plentiful, life was good, but when food became scarce, we had to decide whether to continue foraging in a particular spot or travel to a new area. Travel required effort and involved the risks that no food would be found or that unknown predators might be encountered, but it also held the promise of more plentiful feeding grounds. Staying put meant little expenditure of energy but also relatively small amounts of food. Given the risks of starving as a result of travel that does not produce the desired result, natural selection may have favored the choice of small amounts of relatively immediate food over potentially more plentiful amounts farther away. Though we may never be certain whether this explanation is valid, it is consistent with our understanding of evolution, and since the same hyperbolic curves and preference reversals are seen in pigeons and rats, we know that this strong impulsivity is not unique to humans.

In the everyday world of managing money, it is easy to see how our natural impulsivity can cause problems. We all have long-term goals that are important to us: a place to live that feels like home and that we and our families will enjoy, being in a position to retire without having to lower our standard of living, college for our children, enough money so that daily life is not a constant worry. But competing against these distant goals are the many objects and temptations of the moment: iPads, eating out, vacations, laptops, jewelry, fine wines, flatscreen TVs, designer clothes, boats, sports equipment, collectables, and all-electric cars with GPS, rearview video, and satellite radio. We are hyperbolic people. Although most of us would say our long-term financial goals are very important to us, the influence they exert on us right now is quite weak. Meanwhile, the products that pass by us every day—particularly those that could be obtained quickly—are riding high on the curve of desire. Under these circumstances, our priorities are likely to get reversed.

Much of our contemporary struggle with personal finance has been produced by changes in our economic landscape that have removed the barriers to impulsive consumption. When you live in a world where you can always buy something—either with your own money or with borrowed money—then every potential purchase lives at the steep end of the hyperbolic curve. You are always in act two of the play, where the purchase of the moment looms large and you are likely to forget your greater true desires. In the following chapters we examine the many ways that modern life encourages impulsivity, but first we need to consider some other aspects of the psychology of self-control.

THE MURKY FUTURE

The two-envelope problem has been deliberately pared down to the simplest kind of decision. No matter which envelope you go for, you are choosing between two clearly defined options: a fixed amount of money that is either delayed or immediate. But in his book *The Science of Self-Control*, Howard Rachlin points out that many everyday decisions—particularly the ones that lead us into temptation—are not of this kind. Consider, for example, a young man who wants to buy a $500 iPad. He has an entry-level job that pays an adequate salary, but he finds it difficult to save money. He generally lives within his means, but at the end of the month he has very little—sometimes nothing—left in his bank account. He knows the iPad is a luxury that may create a problem, but there have been other months when he splurged on something extra and managed to get by. And he really wants the iPad.

This is a much more common dilemma from everyday life. We are forced to choose between something very tangible and immediate, a new iPad, and something that is delayed and rather vague. Standing in the store gazing at the iPad display, our young man would find it hard to imagine exactly what piece of his future he will forfeit by making this one purchase. In addition to being diminished in value by delay, the downside of this decision is much less certain than the upside. Our young man knows with 100 percent certainty that he can walk out of the store with a new iPad, but it is not as clear that at the end of the month he will be faced with unpaid bills or lack of cash. He might get into trouble, but perhaps if he budgets a little better for the remainder of the month he will be able to get by. He has done it before.

Although our technology lover may not be considering this point, buying the iPad would probably mean he could not save any money this month, but the consequences of this are even more vague. He is young, and retirement seems very far away. There is time. His salary will go up. Things will work out. There will undoubtedly be unexpected expenses for which he should be saving, but the influence of these future emergencies is weakened both because they are off in the discounted future and because they are far from certain. Maybe his car will work just fine for many years without need of substantial repairs. Maybe he will never marry and never have children. Who knows? All the potential negatives that are balanced against this purchase are much more ambiguous than the neat little tablet on the shelf in front of him.

We have little difficulty choosing between an iPad now and an iPad in a year, or between an iPad now and a good retirement income fifty years from now. But we never encounter choices like these. No individual $500 purchase will prevent our young man from having a comfortable retirement or any of the other things he is likely to want in the future. But some piece of his future is lost each month he does not save. As Rachlin points out, the inner conflict we all face becomes clear when we consider the choice between longer and shorter segments of our lives. If our young man were to choose between individual months isolated in time, he would probably choose a splurge month over a saving month. Splurge months are always more fun. But if forced to consider a string of ten years of consistent splurging versus ten years of uninterrupted saving, he might make a different choice. Ten years' worth of savings could add up. Furthermore, once he splurges, our protagonist sometimes finds the object that was once so attractive soon loses its shine. Now that he thinks about it, ten years of splurging might not have as much value as ten years of saving. When forced to choose between two individual months of splurge or save and ten years of consistent splurge or save, the dilemma becomes clear: any splurging month beats any saving month, but any ten-year period of saving beats any ten-year period of splurging.

The beauty of this reconfigured iPad problem is that the ten-year commitment forces us to think about our long-term goals in a way that we almost never do when strolling the aisles of the store or browsing a retailer's website. In addition, thinking in a ten-year block makes the potential money saved much more tangible and makes all the yet unencountered temptations of the future more vague. The myopia of the human condition is such that we know there will be temptations in the future, but at the moment we can tell you only about the ones that preoccupy us right now. This turning of the tables places our two selves in direct competition.

I am not suggesting that merely thinking about decisions in the long term is the cure for overspending. If it were that easy to solve our financial problems, a book such as this would not be necessary. No, one of the most important messages of contemporary research on self-control is that very smart, rational people fall prey to the steep slope of the hyperbola. If we could simply put together a sensible budget and will ourselves to stick to it, few of us would have financial problems.

HABITS AND THE RELATIVITY OF REWARD

One of the important contributions of Richard Herrnstein's research in the pigeon lab at Harvard was the concept of *melioration*, which suggests the reason you like a particular activity may have less to do with the activity itself than with the rest of your life. The idea of melioration—doing a thing because it improves our present circumstances—implies that if things are bad enough, we may be attracted to something we would never consider otherwise.[8] One of the most dramatic examples of this was the pattern of drug use among American soldiers who went to Vietnam.[9] As the war progressed, many GIs began to use heroin, which was plentiful and cheap in Southeast Asia, and there was concern back home that when these addicted service members returned to the United States they would bring their drug problems with them. Funds were allocated to study drug use among discharged veterans in an effort to avoid a new domestic drug problem fueled by addicts returning from the war.

To the surprise of most professionals, the results of these studies showed that the great majority of heroin users—including those who reported being addicted—did not continue their drug use. Furthermore, surveys of these service members showed that there was no problem getting the drug: most reported that they knew where to find heroin at home, and indeed, some had used briefly after coming home without returning to habitual use.[10] Rather, it appears that when placed in their normal environments—which were substantially more rewarding than the jungles of Vietnam during a raging war—they no longer needed the drug. Normal life provided many rewards that were more satisfying than drug use, such as family, home, and work. Furthermore, in many cases, continued drug use after the war would have meant risking the loss of these more valued pleasures.

It appears that a similar story of melioration is being played out today—with a far less happy ending. In 2015 economists Anne Case and Angus Deaton published research showing a surprising rise in mortality for middle-aged non-Hispanic white men and women.[11] For the last two decades, the United States has suffered an epidemic of opioid use, but initially it was unclear why this particular demographic group should be experiencing an increase of deaths. In subsequent analyses, Case and Deaton attributed their results to an increase in "deaths of despair" caused by opioid and alcohol poisoning, suicide, and alcoholic liver disease. However, they did not point to the availability of opioids as the primary explanation for this phenomenon. Rather they identified worsening circumstances for people with less than a college degree, including decreasing real wages, lower labor-force participation, and lower marriage rates. If life looked more hopeful for this demographic group, drugs and alcohol might not have been so attractive.

Everything is relative. Caroline, the woman whose profile precedes this chapter, is another example of the relative nature of reward. She got very little pleasure from her marriage, and shopping in the evenings provided some melioration of that unpleasant circumstance. Later on we will meet Frank, a man who reversed the Vietnam pattern. His life was happier during a long military career, and after retirement, during a time when he felt less comfortable and fulfilled, he took on activities that got him into financial difficulty. For both these people, their self-destructive money problems were, at least in part, due to a sense of unhappiness in other areas of their lives.

The good news is that rewarding activities can substitute for each other. Ideally, if Caroline's marriage and Frank's return to civilian life had been happier, their more expensive activities might have been unnecessary. But in Caroline's case, with the help of her counselor, she discovered that the running club had both physical and social benefits that provided adequate melioration. Substituting another kind of rewarding activity helped her avoid debt and feel better about herself. Much of Herrnstein's research suggests that many things we consider addictions—even heroin use—are often more accurately described as habits. The concept of a habit is a rather old-fashioned psychological principle that is now experiencing a renaissance. William James, the founder of American psychology, called habits "the great flywheel of society," referring to the heavy wheel in an internal combustion engine that provides momentum to keep the contraption going.[12] Based in part on James and Herrnstein, contemporary researchers have begun to recognize that many problem behaviors are habits—initially taken on because they are *relatively* rewarding—that gain momentum through repetition. There are many useful ways to get rid of bad habits, but as we have seen, the substitution of one activity for another can be particularly effective.

CHOOSING NOT TO CHOOSE

Economist Thomas Schelling has a rather poignant way of thinking about our struggles with self-control. First, he labels them with the same phrase used three centuries ago by Adam Smith: *self-command*.[13] According to Smith, people who have self-command are able to control their appetites and desires. In addition, Schelling sees problems of self-command as struggles with the different personalities that emerge within a single individual over time. To illustrate this problem, he gives the following example:

> A man gave up smoking three months ago. For the first six or eight weeks he was regularly tormented by a desire to smoke, but the last three or four weeks have been less uncomfortable and he is becoming optimistic that he has left cigarettes behind for good. One afternoon a friend drops in for a business chat. The business done, our reformed smoker sees his friend to the door; returning to the living room he finds, on the coffee table, an open pack of cigarettes. He snatches up the pack and hurries to the door, only to see his friend's car disappear around the corner. As he will see his friend in the morning and can return the cigarettes, he puts the pack in his jacket pocket and hangs the jacket in the closet. He settles in front of the television with a before-dinner drink to watch the network news. Twenty minutes in to the news he walks to the closet where his jacket hangs and takes the cigarettes out of the pocket, studies the pack for a minute, and walks into the bathroom, where he empties the cigarettes into the toilet and flushes it. He returns to his drink and his news.[14]

Schelling's interpretation of this story is that at five o'clock, while he is watching the news, the man does not want to smoke, either now or later in the evening. But he knows that as he has his drink and the evening progresses, he may change his mind. The person who is watching the news does not want to smoke, but the person he will be a few minutes or hours later may want to smoke. In an effort to achieve self-command, the man treats his later self as a different person and throws the cigarettes away.

Schelling's story also demonstrates an important strategy for overcoming struggles with self-control. Knowing that his future self might be weak, the reformed smoker takes an action in the present that commits him to being good. This is an example of *commitment*, an important strategy for avoiding impulsive decisions.[15] The classic case of commitment is the story of the Sirens from Homer's *The Odyssey*. The Sirens were birds with the heads of women whose singing was so enchanting that all sailors who heard it were uncontrollably attracted and crashed their boats on the rocks of the Sirens' island. In an effort to safely hear the Sirens' music, Odysseus ordered his men to place wax in their ears and continue rowing past the island no matter what. In addition, Odysseus had the crew lash him to the mast, and he ordered them to ignore his pleas to be untied (Figure 4.3).

Odysseus wanted both to hear the Sirens and to stay in the boat, but he also knew—like Schelling's reformed smoker—that his future self might fall prey to temptation. Thus, while standing a healthy distance away from the moment of potential weakness with their long-term goals firmly in mind, both men committed to a course of action. In effect, they chose to restrict their future choices.

Economist Robert Strotz was the first to identify the strategy of commitment, as well as the Sirens example, in his early article on myopic choice, and in the six decades since, extensive research has shown that commitment strategies of various kinds can be very useful in avoiding short-term thinking and impulsive decisions. Using ideas based in the work of Strotz and Ainslie, psychologists Howard Rachlin and Leonard Green conducted an early study showing that under the right conditions pigeons would commit to a better, long-term choice, and in so doing earn larger rewards overall.[16] If, well ahead of time, they were given a choice to peck a key that would lock in the larger, more delayed reward,

Figure 4.3 John William Waterhouse (English, 1849–1917), *Ulysses and the Sirens*, 1891, oil on canvas, 100.6 × 202.0 cm. Purchased, 1891. National Gallery of Victoria, Melbourne, Australia. Used with permission. (Ulysses is the Roman equivalent of the Greek name Odysseus.)

many pigeons would learn to do so and avoid the myopic behavior they typically showed.

The irony of the commitment strategy is that it represents a voluntary restriction of choice and personal autonomy. The dieter who wants to avoid inner conflict over food chooses not to keep ice cream in the house. Yes, it might be possible to have a pint of mocha mint chip in the freezer and still show the resolve to avoid eating it, but the careful dieter knows that the immediacy of the dessert is likely to pose a problem when hunger strikes late at night. Americans generally think more choices are better, and we value freedom and a sense of individual responsibility. But as psychologist Barry Schwartz suggested in his book *The Paradox of Choice*, we are often happier in situations that involve fewer choices.[17] In the United States, the daunting array of products and services can leave the typical consumer bleary-eyed and exhausted. Flushing the cigarettes down the toilet or choosing not to keep desserts in the house can be paradoxically liberating. In the final chapters of this book, I offer a number of suggestions for maintaining financial balance, and several of these involve commitment strategies.

The discovery of hyperbolic discounting tends to equate us all and portray us as primordial animals foraging in a complicated contemporary environment, but people do vary in their degree of impulsiveness. For example, an investigation of cultural differences discovered that Japanese, Chinese, and American students all show a similar hyperbolic discounting effect, but that for Japanese students, delayed money retains its value more than for either Chinese or American students.[18] In addition, people of different ages place different values on money in the future. In one experiment, psychologist Leonard Green and colleagues compared how people of different ages discounted a hypothetical $1,000 that was delayed up to twenty-five years. As might be expected, they found that twelve-year-old children were very impulsive, devaluing the money severely if it was delayed by even a small amount of time. Young adults who averaged approximately twenty years of age were slightly less impulsive than twelve-year-olds, but somewhat surprisingly, older adults, who—due to their average age of approximately seventy—might not have had twenty-five years to wait for $1,000, discounted the delayed reward substantially less than either of the younger groups. For older adults, waiting for the full $1,000 was much more attractive than it was for the younger groups. Perhaps it is easier to imagine waiting for twenty-five years if you have lived almost three times that long. As I get older, I have become acutely aware of time's different meanings. For millennials, being forty years old sounds like a death sentence, whereas for me it sounds like a dream. Since the different groups in Green's study were of different generations, it is also possible that the results he and his colleagues saw were due to the contrasting generational values of the eras in which each group was raised. Whatever the reason, Green and colleagues showed that for the older adults he studied, money retained its value much better over time than it did for younger age groups.

The capacity to wait for rewards in the future has many benefits. In the 1960s and 1970s, psychologist Walter Mischel conducted his famous marshmallow experiments in which he told young children that they could have one small reward (a marshmallow or a cookie) now or, if they waited, they could have two rewards. In subsequent follow-up studies he found the children who were better at delaying gratification had better SAT scores and better health.[19] More recent results show that steeply discounting future rewards is correlated with a variety of negative outcomes. Several researchers have examined the discounting of addicts, and in each case, those addicted to cocaine, heroin, alcohol, gambling, and cigarettes (yes, cigarettes) all devalued delayed money more severely than their nonaddicted counterparts.[20] Another study found that people who devalued future rewards more had lower credit scores than those who did not.[21]

So, as we might expect, people differ in the degree of their impulsiveness. Furthermore, rewards of different sizes are devalued differently. In particular, smaller rewards, such as the $10 and $12 envelopes of my example, are more rapidly discounted. Larger rewards, such as $1,000 or more, tend to retain their value. For example, although many people might accept $8 now over $12 in thirty days, many fewer people would accept $800 now over $1,200 in thirty days. This is known as the *magnitude effect*.[22] Delayed rewards are devalued, but smaller amounts are devalued more rapidly than larger ones.

Some hyperbolas are steeper than others. Our problems with self-control vary depending on how old we are and other characteristics, but the studies that reveal these differences leave one question unanswered: why? Is, for example, the much greater impulsiveness of heroin addicts caused by a trait that was with them at birth, or is it something they acquired—in effect, learned—through the course of their lives? Run as they might, behavioral scientists can never completely escape questions of nature versus nurture, and I can offer no easy answer here. We all feel the pull of the peak of the curve, but for whatever reasons, some people feel it more strongly than others. Even if we never discover how these differences develop, knowing about them helps to fill in part of the picture.

Although we each have our own level of impulsiveness, it is important to understand that all the studies point to one unifying force. We each have a unique hyperbola that, for any given commodity, is ours and ours alone, but we are all faced with the challenges of the steeply dropping curve. We all are prone to changing our minds, and we are all strongly susceptible to the power of immediacy. Although we may want to save money and plan for financial emergencies, we often forget these goals in favor of a dinner at a nice restaurant or a pair of expensive shoes. The many small choices we make on a daily basis are often in direct conflict with the relatively few big things we want in the future.

FREEDOM FROM CHOICE

All the self-control dilemmas we have been talking about have one thing in common: conflict is created, at least in part, by the presence at a given time of two or more choices. In our everyday financial environment, the choices are often simply between spending or not spending some amount of money. It is important to recognize that there is no conflict when you don't have the choice. Let's take a moment to think about the requirements of a monetary transaction. First, there must be a seller. The thing we want must be available for sale, and it helps if the seller is able to deliver the product or service quickly, with little effort required of the buyer. This will keep the buyer's level of interest at the high end of the hyperbola. Second, there must be a buyer. The buyer is not a buyer if they don't want the product or service being offered, and the buyer is not really in the game if they don't have the wherewithal—cash or credit—to complete the transaction. If any link in this chain is missing, then the buyer's psychic struggle is reduced.

Consider our young iPad-desiring professional. Let's call him George, and for the moment let's assume he does not have the cash to buy this nifty little tablet, but he has a valid credit card with enough juice to cover the purchase. On the other hand, Jill, another imaginary young professional, has exactly the same financial circumstances as George and would be very interested in an iPad except that she has no credit cards. No cash, no credit cards, no iPad. But Jill is much less likely to be sweating about this decision. She knows she cannot make the purchase, so she moves on to other things. Actually, if she really wanted to get the iPad, Jill could probably find a way. She could hit up her friends and family members for a loan, she could go to her bank and apply for a loan, or she could apply for a credit card. If she was really desperate, she could mug someone on the street, hold up a liquor store, or simply attempt to steal the iPad.

These options are all possible, but they involve effort, time delays, and in some cases the threat of jail time. As a result, Jill is much less likely to pursue or even consider these actions, and she probably won't end up with an iPad anytime soon. But paradoxically, she may also be somewhat happier than George—at least during the moment of decision. George knows he can have the iPad, and to some degree, that is the source of his trepidation. His two personalities—the impulsive splurger and the sensible saver—are locked in conflict because the credit card makes it possible. We consider the workings of credit cards in detail in the next chapter, but suffice it to say that at $500 this purchase is hardly going to put a dent in George's Visa card. He has the credit available, and the additional minimum monthly payment created by the iPad will be almost nothing—less than lunch money.

Once the purchase is made, it is too late. George's myopic personality will be enjoying its favorite apps, and the debt he acquired in exchange for the privilege will be a fact—a new feature of George's financial portfolio that his more prudent personality will have to worry about at some point in the future. But at the moment of decision, when there is still hope that the distant end of the hyperbola will win out, George might experience a bit of agony that Jill never feels. The impulsive part of George will be arguing its case with the sensible part; at the same moment, Jill is calmly living a simpler life. She is stuck reading books and surfing the web in more conventional ways, but she is resigned to her fate and thinking about something else.

Similarly, I experience not a whit of trepidation about whether I should buy a Porsche Panamara 4S Sport Turismo with optional heated fourteen-way memory seats, LED headlights, and surround sound audio system. If pressed, I might confess that I would like to own such a machine, and there are dealers in my area standing ready to deliver it. But with such a car costing approximately $110,000, I cannot begin to imagine how I would finance it. Even robbing a liquor store would not do the trick. So I rest easy about this particular decision and reserve my inner conflict for purchases that are within reach.

At this moment in history, the dominant political philosophy in United States holds that—at least in the economic world—freedom is an unqualified good. More choice is better, and almost all barriers to trade and commerce should be systematically eliminated. Without question, free market economics has produced great strength in Europe, Japan, the United States, and now increasingly Asia and Latin America. But current research on self-control argues that as consumers struggling to negotiate our economic environments, we are often better off with less choice. When we use commitment strategies to help us avoid myopic decisions in favor of our more distant goals, we are voluntarily relinquishing choice. Many of our common resolutions—to forgo dessert tonight, to exercise, to save more money—can be reversed at almost any point. As a result, when the chocolate mousse is sitting in front of us or the time to exercise approaches, it is easy for us to forget the distant end of the curve and discard our resolution. We will undoubtedly experience regret and hope to do better another day, but much of this agony is caused by our freedom to choose at any moment. In the modern world of personal finance, more choice is not always better.

TIME AND MONEY

So what does this new approach to self-control tell us about the causes of financial failure? We examine several of these things in more depth later, but let us pause for a moment and think about the role of the hyperbola in everyday life.

1. *Any purchase that can be made more quickly, with less effort and greater convenience, will be harder to resist.* When I was in college and wanted to buy a new album—in those days it was a vinyl LP record—by the Who or the Rolling Stones, I had to get up, put on my clothes, get downtown to the store, and either fork over cash or write a check that was backed up by cash. Not a huge effort, but time-consuming enough that any number of distractions (an invitation to lunch, for example) might intercede to take me off course. Not to mention that if the store did not have the album in stock or I did not have the cash on hand, I was out of luck. Today, almost all these barriers have been removed. While still in their pajamas, today's college students can purchase practically any album ever recorded from an online store that is never out of stock, whether they have the money or not.

   The impulse that began for both me and today's students while sitting in our dorm rooms can now be satisfied in an instant with one-click shopping. The same purchase could also be accomplished while speeding down the highway—preferably not by the person driving—or walking on the beach. In subsequent chapters we examine the new marketplace in detail, but to the extent that our modern world provides for more and easier access to purchasing, the hyperbola will help make those choices more appealing.

2. *Quicker and easier purchasing leads to conflict between our different personalities.* Sitting at my desk, it is easy to say that I would prefer to eat less ice cream and fewer fatty foods, but when my future self happens to be walking past the local gourmet ice cream shop or finds himself gazing at a menu that includes barbecued ribs or lamb chops, he may have a different idea. All of us have a person inside us who wants to be frugal, save money, and achieve our financial goals, but the person on the outside likes gadgets, hates to cook, wants to go on vacation, and is a very snappy dresser. People differ in their ability to handle these conflicts, but the latest science tells us everyone is built to splurge and, because our modern world provides more opportunities than ever, we frequently choose the smaller immediate reward when on some other level we are completely and tragically aware that what we really want is the big reward off in the future.

3. *With commitment there is hope.* Once many people were members
   of holiday or vacation clubs at their local banks. They would
   voluntarily agree to deposit a regular amount of money into a
   savings account each month (now it can be deducted automatically
   from your checking account), and if they saved regularly and did
   not take out any money before Halloween or some other agreed-
   upon deadline, they would receive a bit of interest on their savings
   and avoid an early-withdrawal penalty. In the age of plastic money,
   this savings mechanism seems rather quaint, but it is still offered
   by some smaller banks and credit unions. A savings club is a simple
   commitment device that helps people hold out for more distant
   rewards. To survive in today's economic environment, it will take
   much more than savings clubs to keep us on an even keel, but
   commitment strategies will be an important part of the solution to
   our financial predicament.

4. *Freedom isn't free.* Often choice is a burden, and ironically, we find
   we have a greater sense of freedom and autonomy in a life with fewer
   options. When I really need to get some work done—say, catch up on
   an overdue writing assignment or read a professional article I have
   been putting off—it is much easier to do so if I hide myself away
   somewhere far from radios, televisions, magazines, the Internet, the
   refrigerator, and the phone. I find I am often exceedingly productive
   while stuck on a train or an airplane. Why? Because many of the
   freedoms that lurk in everyday places, trying to distract me from my
   long-term goals, are not in attendance. If asked, I might say I wish
   I could cruise the Internet and check my e-mail while on an airplane.
   But it will usually cost me money to have those privileges, and if what
   I really want is to get some work done, I am better off without them.
   The contemporary world has forced us to consider financial choices in
   places and times that were once blissfully free of such decisions. As the
   Sirens invade our every waking moment, we must labor heroically to
   remain fastened to the mast.

The study of self-control is part of the larger field of behavioral economics,
which is one of the most vigorous areas of research for both psychologists
and economists. In chapter 8 we will see how several other principles
derived from behavioral economics influence our ability to manage our
personal finances. But the problems we have with self-control are made
more serious in an environment of easy credit, so next we will turn to the
changes in our banking and economic environment that have so challenged
our self-control.

SYLVIA

When I met Sylvia, she was fifty years old and had $50,000 in debt. She had not been fully employed for the past four months, finding only short-term jobs here and there, and she had no immediate prospects for regular work despite trying hard to find it. Her unemployment benefits had long since run out. Her parents were both dead, and she had never married. She owned a condominium apartment and a car, but she had so little money that it was hard for me to imagine how she held on to them. Collection people called regularly and threatened her for payment on various debts. She had become so desperate that to get by she withdrew funds from the retirement account she had built up at her previous job and sold much of her furniture.

Sylvia would have been an excellent candidate for bankruptcy except that she had already declared bankruptcy. Her remaining debt was all in federal and state education loans taken on when she went to law school, and since student loans cannot be forgiven through bankruptcy, there was no escape from her $50,000 obligation.

Sylvia had always been a good student. In college she pursued a double major in history and anthropology, and she went on to get a master's degree in library science. After graduation she began to work for a small historical museum in Rhode Island, but when it closed, she moved to another museum in Connecticut. During these years, Sylvia made a very modest income, but she was able to get by. Museum jobs were scarce, and she felt lucky to be working in her chosen field, even though she wasn't paid very well. Then after many years at the same museum, long-standing staff conflicts began to wear on her. That combined with the poor salary prompted Sylvia to think about how she might better her circumstances. While still working forty hours per week, she entered law school at night.

Up to this point, Sylvia's credit card debt had been at manageable levels—a few hundred dollars spread over a handful of cards. But without any savings other than her retirement account, she had to get educational loans to pay her tuition during the regular school year. She put the tuition for the summer courses that her law school program also required on her Visa, MasterCard, and Discover cards.

Unfortunately, law school did not go well. For the first time in her life, she struggled in an academic setting. In part this was because her mother had died shortly after Sylvia started law school, and a therapist later diagnosed her as suffering from depression. She did well enough in most of her classes, but civil procedure was her Waterloo. She got a D in the course and now was in trouble. Eventually Sylvia was asked to leave school. Unwilling to give up, she found another law school program within a two-hour drive from home that would accept her. Her performance in civil procedure still did not improve, and again she was unable to complete the degree. Three years into the law school episode, she found herself $70,000 in debt and out of school without a degree. When she began this project, it never occurred to her that she might not succeed. She already had bachelor's and master's degrees, and she had always done well in school. But things had not turned out as she expected, and now she was deeply in debt. The loans had run out, and her dreams of a law degree and a better-paying job had slipped away.

A few years after her frustrating experience in law school, Sylvia found she could no longer take the political problems at the museum. She quit and found a job at a bookstore. Unfortunately, the new job did not pay as well, and Sylvia began to fall behind on her bills. To make matters worse, the bookstore ultimately failed, and Sylvia was out of work.

A friend told her that the only way out of her financial misery was to declare bankruptcy, whereupon, ironically, Sylvia's final indignity came at the hands of a lawyer. She understood that bankruptcy would not provide an escape from the burden of her educational loans, but the attorney she sought said her personal problems might be adequate justification for the discharge of these loans as well as her credit card debt. It was not until after the court proceeding was over that Sylvia realized only her $20,000 in credit card debt was being released. In the hallway of the court building, she confronted her lawyer and asked him about the school loans. Apparently he had forgotten their earlier conversation and so had failed to make the case for the discharge of these loans. He then said that if she provided documentation of her psychological problems, he would file an appeal on her behalf. However, an appeal would cost her more money— money she didn't have. Although Sylvia produced documentation in the form of a letter from her therapist, in the end the appeal was never filed. Sylvia had gone through the embarrassment of bankruptcy and had assumed its negative consequences, including the limits on her ability to obtain loans or credit cards, but she was denied the relief bankruptcy was designed to provide.

At the time I talked to her, Sylvia was hoping to get another job in a bookstore. In addition, she had been studying horticulture, and she was hoping to find a partner who would help her open her own plant store. Although she had become acquainted with many people in the local gardening community, there were no prospects. She also considered selling her condo—real estate values had gone up dramatically in recent years, and she knew that with the proceeds from the sale she could pay off most or all of her debt. But she also worried that her bankruptcy status would make it difficult to ever own a home again and that with no job and bad credit, most landlords would not rent to her. So she held on to her home, kept looking for work, and hoped her luck would change.

A Different Road to Ruin

Technology makes it possible for people to gain control over everything, except over technology.

—John Tudor

We can now begin to sketch an alternative story of our contemporary problems with debt and financial fragility, one that improves on the parables described in chapter 3. Indeed, the theory of self-control just discussed points us in an unexpected direction when we consider the events of the late-1970s. Rather than initiating an era of social collapse and moral irresponsibility, the 1970s began a long period of economic and technological innovation, and the central argument of this book is that these changes are responsible for much of today's personal finance crisis. Rather than peering inward in search of a disease or character flaw that could explain our great indebtedness, we should be looking outward, toward the brave new world we have created for ourselves. Research on self-control tells us that, given the right set of choices, we are all prone to irrational, impulsive decisions, and a close examination of our recent history reveals that we have designed the world in such a way that we can always have the smaller reward right now instead of the larger one later on. We have allowed the hyperbola to haunt our every waking moment, and often the immediate choice speaks to us very persuasively. Credit cards and the banking industry in general have helped to create this new, more challenging environment, and, of course, the banks have profited greatly from the current debt crisis. But the credit card and lending companies don't deserve all the blame. They did their part, but many other factors have helped to turn our personal balance sheets from black to red. At the end of this chapter I give a more even accounting of how we got to where we are today, focusing on how changes in our social and economic environment have affected our behavior.

We begin by taking a closer look at spending. Continuing the behavioral perspective presented in the previous chapter, I outline the "physics of spending" by examining the psychological variables that conspire to draw money out of our pockets. Hyperbolic discounting gives us a piece of the puzzle—in particular, the powerful effects of immediate gratification—but there are additional features of our economic environment that help to complete the picture. Then I go on to apply these psychological principles to a brief history of banking, credit, and debt, with particular attention to the period since the 1970s, concentrating on how a variety of innovations affected the physics of spending and, in turn, our behavior and our bottom line.

THE PHYSICS OF SPENDING

At the most basic level, spending money is a physical act. We spend when the necessary prerequisites are in place and the surroundings are conducive. We are economic animals, and there are a number of forces that conspire to pull money out of our pockets. Let's examine five variables that facilitate the spending response and consider how they have affected our relationship with money over the last forty years.

Variable 1: Availability of the Spending Response

The mere availability of the product or the option to spend is an extremely powerful variable. We cannot buy things that do not exist or that exist somewhere but not where we can get at them. If the invisible hand is to do its work, buyers must be paired up with sellers. Years ago, many products could be obtained only in cities or by mail order, but today that is no longer the case. Americans can purchase almost anything under the sun that can be shipped by UPS. Furthermore, on a daily basis, new products are being introduced that compete for our attention with all the older products that are still on the market. The effects of product innovation are considered in much greater detail in chapter 6, but it is safe to say that our list of wants is expanding at a rapid pace. If we can imagine an object we wish to possess, the modern world can almost always provide it.

An issue related to product or service availability is the likelihood of a successful search. Though it sounds like ancient history now, shopping for a specific item once meant traveling from store to store hoping to find the sought-after object. After the telephone became a universal and casually used device, we were able to "let our fingers do the walking" and call each store in turn. But these blind searches often ended in frustration before a purchase could be made. Furthermore, a history of failure often led us to give up before we started. Today the physical and information barriers to a successful search are far less substantial. Some items must still be purchased in the old-fashioned way. In most cases, to find a doctor who will accept you as a patient, you must get names of local physicians and call each one in turn to see whether they are accepting new patients. But many items that were once hit or miss can now be very reliably obtained by Internet or telephone purchase.

Variable 2: The Wherewithal

In addition to a seller who is offering the object of desire, any transaction requires a buyer with something to offer in exchange. Cash was once the universal medium of the marketplace. Even as credit cards have expanded their reach, landlords often require cash, as do some restaurants and service providers, such as babysitters and plumbers. But as plastic has become more ubiquitous, the reverse is also true: a few places have emerged where cash is not accepted—some hotels and airlines in-flight purchases require a card.[1] So, although you can buy almost anything with plastic, to be covered in all environments you have to have access to both cash and a card.

Economists highlight the different uses of credit and cash in their effort to solve an interesting puzzle. It is a peculiar fact that many people carry substantial balances on their credit cards even though they have enough cash on hand to pay the cards off. These people are losing money because, in most cases, the interest they pay on the cards far exceeds what they can earn in a savings account. One of the explanations for this apparently paradoxical behavior is the relative universality of cash. It can be applied to almost any purchase, whereas—even now—credit cards have greater limitations. If paying off the credit cards required wiping out your savings and eliminating your liquid assets, then any future expense that exceeds your regular budget would be limited to things you can get with a credit card. As universal as credit cards have become—you can even buy a $2 cup of coffee with one—cash is still more widely accepted in the most common consumer settings. For example, my barber still wants cash. Furthermore, for people who are living very close to the edge, the typical problems that pop up unexpectedly—illness, burst pipes, car breakdowns—often require cash.[2]

But most people walk around with the wherewithal to make any number of purchases, whether they have any cash on hand or not. As we will see, the role of credit in our modern society has exploded in two directions. First, credit has been extended to millions of people who, in an earlier era, would have had difficulty getting the option to pay in installments. Loans have been offered throughout history, even before there was money, and merchants have long allowed those without cash to put items on a tab. But the general and purposeless extension of credit to large numbers of people happened for the first time at the end of the twentieth century—during the same period as the Parable of Bankruptcy. This easy access to credit has had undeniable benefits for many people, allowing them to pay for large purchases over time and making it possible to weather many unexpected expenses. But with this purchasing power come new money management challenges.

The second explosion of credit purchasing has been its attachment to almost any kind of good or service. When credit cards were first introduced, they were designed to allow businesspeople to purchase meals and cover travel-related expenses without using cash. Today, the list of goods and services that cannot be purchased with plastic is small and shrinking.

When you can have anything, not going into debt requires greater self-control than when transactions required cash. Before our wallets were full of plastic, we may have longed for things we could not have, but they were out of reach and, as such, posed no burden for our good judgment. In contrast, a world where credit can be exchanged for anything under the sun makes life both easier and more difficult.

Once the means of making purchases is in place, the game is under way. The economic animal is loosed on the world, and other variables increase or decrease the likelihood of a purchase. These variables are equally as effective whether you are buying with your own money (cash) or the bank's (credit).

Variable 3: Time

In chapter 4 we learned the importance of immediacy and the power of the high end of the hyperbolic curve. Things that can be had now are given inordinate psychological weight, often provoking short-run behavior that is in conflict with our long-run goals. If we apply this view of self-control to modern history, we can point to a number of innovations that have made it easier to act on impulse. Internet purchasing is the most obvious example, but since the 1970s, many technological advances have served to speed the pace of transactions and shorten the interval between the decision to buy and the act of buying. Our descent into debt has been greatly accelerated by the expanded potential for immediate gratification in today's high-tech marketplace.

Variable 4: Effort

Another important variable involves the effort required to make the purchase. Back in the 1930s, B. F. Skinner discovered that when he trained rats to press a lever for food, they pressed less often if he added a weight to the lever, requiring the rats to exert more force.[3] As we navigate our daily environments, we are a little like rats, factoring in the amount of work involved in the choices we make. Whether it be mowing the lawn, exercising, doing the dishes, or doing homework, things that are hard are done less often. In ways we hardly notice, the modern world has been smoothed to minimize any friction that might slow our path toward purchases. The effort of travel has been reduced, the work of spending has been eliminated, and losing one's money can be accomplished with the flick of a wrist. When shopping required more effort, the environment provided a natural aid to self-control. Where an expenditure of energy is required, temptation looms less large. As a result, today's shopping experience has been engineered to remove as much of the work as possible.

Variable 5: The Social Barriers to Spending

When the spending response involves contact with other people, that social interaction can either jam or grease the wheels of commerce. Some purchases are easier to make when a salesperson says, "That looks great on you," or when a clerk tells you about their own experiences with the cellular phone you are thinking about buying. Sometimes there are questions we need to ask before we can decide. But social contact can also be an obstacle to spending. Some social situations are intimidating, and the shopper who doesn't want to look stupid will sometimes shy away from clerks or other customers they imagine are thinking negative thoughts about them. In these cases, it may be easier to go without. But the contemporary marketplace is adapted to the problem of social barriers. Today we live in a self-service world where we buy many more things without the assistance of a salesperson or clerk than ever before. In addition, we can now spend money on things in the privacy of our homes that we would be reluctant to purchase at a store or in some other public space. By removing many of the social obstacles to spending, today's consumer economy has smoothed the path to temptation and made it much easier to fall into a financial hole.

All five of these variables play an important role in any act of spending, and an analysis of our recent history with these variables in mind produces a more detailed account of the Parable of Bankruptcy than either Version One or Version Two.

THE NEW ROAD TO RUIN

The end of World War II brought a period of economic growth in the United States. The expansion of suburban communities that began in the 1950s created a movement that ultimately would leave most cities relatively bereft of middle-class citizens and, as suburban shopping centers emerged, with downtown areas emptied of department stores and other retail businesses. Consumer loans were common in the decades after the war. The home mortgage industry had expanded and become more standardized with the introduction of the Federal Housing Administration (FHA) in the 1930s, and most automobiles had been purchased with installment loans since the 1920s, an era of great credit expansion. Many large department stores and other businesses offered store credit accounts and "easy payment plans." Finally, banks offered consumer loans to white-collar professionals, and personal finance agencies and credit unions extended loans to blue-collar workers. Much of the social stigma associated with borrowing and lending was removed in the 1920s, and after the interruptions of the Great Depression and World War II, lending and credit became a common part of postwar life. The writer William Whyte introduced the term *budgetism* to describe the phenomenon of middle-class families struggling to make ends meet. According to Whyte, monthly bills and loan payments provided the external structure required to keep 1950s families striving to live within their means and perhaps eventually to get ahead.[4]

This was the backdrop for a period of rapid change that started in the late 1960s and early 1970s. The great influx of women into the workforce had not yet begun. Personal computers would not become part of our lives for several decades. Whyte's ideas about the budgetism of the 1950s did not anticipate the enormous expansion of personal debt, bankruptcy, and home foreclosure that would emerge at the end of the twentieth century and the beginning of the twenty-first. The image of middle-class families working hard to stay within their budgets gave way to the normalcy of a tightwire life beyond one's means. Paradoxically, the rise of our current indebted society took place during a period of great economic growth. Many events contributed to the construction of our contemporary economic world, but the most important behavior-altering events fall into three broad categories: banking, telecommunications, and transportation.

The Birth of the Card

According to legend, the modern credit card grew out of a lunch at Major's Cabin Grill in midtown Manhattan in 1949. Alfred Bloomingdale, grandson of the founder of Bloomingdale's department store, was eating with two other men, one of whom was Francis McNamara, the owner of a small consumer finance company. At the lunch, McNamara told the story of one of his clients, a businessman from the Bronx who had gotten into trouble by virtue of his own generosity. The client would lend out his own credit to friends who were short on cash. For example, if a neighbor needed a prescription filled, the businessman would send the neighbor to a pharmacy where he had an account and have the neighbor charge the item to his account. To authorize the purchase, the druggist was instructed to call McNamara's client for approval. Later the businessman would collect the money from the neighbor over time, plus interest. The problem arose when the Bronx businessman's creditors—the stores where he had accounts—wanted payment before he was able to collect from his friends and neighbors. At the time of the lunch, McNamara's company had lent the Bronx man $3,000 to cover these shortfalls, and it looked as though this loan might never be repaid.[5]

Aside from McNamara's collection problem, the men were fascinated by the concept of a third-party lender. The most common lending arrangements involved just two parties: the lender and the borrower. Small loans were made directly to a borrower who later made payments back to the lender to eliminate the debt. Similarly, stores that offered credit lent money directly to the purchaser (or agreed to defer payment). What the unlucky Bronx businessman had done was to lend credit to a consumer, who then used it to obtain goods from a third person. The fly in the ointment, according to the three men at the luncheon, was that the Bronx businessman had lent his good name to the wrong people. Rather than marketing credit to the poor, the men agreed, credit should be offered to the business class. Furthermore, as they ate in Manhattan, they could quickly see that credit extended for the purpose of buying meals at restaurants might be a very attractive proposition for both the businesspeople and the restaurants of New York City.

So was born Diners Club, the first third-party credit card. Metal charge plates fashioned after the dog tags worn by soldiers in World War II were already in use at many stores. The plates served both as customer identification and, where credit was extended, as charge cards. The three founders of Diners Club proposed to make a similar card that would be accepted at any restaurant that joined the program. In return for the business attracted by the card, restaurants would pay 7 percent of the total charge back to Diners Club. This figure was determined when the three original founders called the owner of Major's Cabin Grill to their table to ask how much he would pay to attract cardholders to the restaurant. Mr. Major's answer became the discount charged on the original card.

The first credit cards were status symbols offered only to those who were able to pay. Diners Club was soon followed by Carte Blanche and American Express, both of which marketed their cards to people with good incomes for use in dining and travel. Thus the first credit cards differed from today's Visa and MasterCard in three important ways: they were used by a limited segment of the population, they could be used only for specific kinds of purchases, and, most importantly, they did not revolve—balances could not be carried from month to month. Our current predicament of millions of Americans each carrying thousands of dollars in credit card debt is made possible by the option of making small payments over time. Diners Club was simply meant to be a replacement for cash. Restaurants required cash payment, and in the years before automated teller machines, most cash was obtained during banking hours from a live teller. Diners Club members were expected to pay off their accounts at the end of the month (most did), and the three partners had only thirty days to pay the restaurants that accepted the card. Thus timing was tight, and profits came largely from the restaurants' 7 percent fee.

The history of the truly universal revolving credit card begins in 1958, when Bank of America introduced BankAmericard in California. Easy payment and installment buying had been common in the United States for a long time. In the mid-nineteenth century, pianos and pieces of large farm equipment, such as reaping machines, were often sold on an installment basis, but paying on time became a much more popular practice when in 1856 I. M. Singer & Co. began offering installment loans for the purchase of sewing machines. At the time, most sewing machines were sold primarily to garment manufacturers, because even the less expensive models cost too much for most families to afford. When Singer began to offer machines on an installment basis, private sales took off.[6] These early chattel loans—loans tied to the purchase of a specific movable object—helped to popularize installment buying.

Commercial credit took another small step toward greater universality when department stores began issuing revolving charge accounts that could be used for anything in the store. The older system of running a tab or a personal account at a store was built around social relationships. People who were dependent on local merchants and were known in the community could be trusted to pay off their bills because they had few alternatives.[7] As Americans became more mobile, particularly after World War II, the relationship between customer and merchant grew distant, and there was need for a more systematic way to manage credit. By the time Diners Club was introduced, gas credit cards had been in existence for some time, and department stores such as Montgomery Ward, Sears, Saks, Gimbel's, and Bloomingdale's offered charge accounts that could be used to purchase anything in the store on a revolving credit basis. But BankAmericard went a step beyond both Diners Club and previous merchant accounts. As a true bank credit card, it offered the holder credit that was not tied to any one store and, unlike the travel and entertainment cards, was not limited to a particular kind of product or service.[8] The first cards typically carried a credit limit of $300–$500, and holders were charged 18 percent interest on unpaid balances.

The early years of the bank credit card were rather rocky, with banks struggling to make a profit and some, such as Chase Manhattan, dropping out of the credit card business because they could not generate enough income.[9] Much of the problem stemmed from a mere lack of saturation. To be successful, businesses had to sign up to accept the card and consumers had to open accounts. To jump-start the use of credit cards, Bank of America orchestrated an unsolicited "drop" of BankAmericards by sending out a mass mailing of cards to sixty thousand Californians. These drops got cards into the hands of the public quickly, but each mailing was followed by enormous bursts of fraud and misuse of the cards. As a result, Congress ended the practice in 1970. To further expand the usefulness of the card, Bank of America began to franchise the BankAmericard system—later known as Visa—to banks in other states. This brought in additional income for Bank of America, but more importantly, it created a nationwide network of businesses that would accept the card. Competition with Bank of America soon appeared when a group of East Coast banks created a rival card that eventually became known as MasterCard. By the mid-1970s, revolving-credit universal bank cards had become a common way to spend. For a time, some retailers with competing cards, notably Sears and the gas companies, refused to accept bank credit cards. But by the time the *Marquette* Supreme Court decision made credit cards a more profitable business, much of the work of saturating the market had been accomplished.

Getting the card accepted at businesses and getting it into the hands of as many people as possible were necessary prerequisites for today's indebted society. Whereas the original travel and entertainment cards were designed for white-collar executives and the wealthy, the history of the credit card is one of expansion out and down. Today MasterCard, Visa, and Discover are offered to the poor and to people with no income at all. Credit card drops are a thing of the past, but millions of credit card applications are mailed out each year offering introductory 0 percent APR and other inducements to attract customers. In the boom years before the Great Recession, college students fresh out of high school, many of whom had little or no income, were aggressively solicited,[10] and lenders penetrated deeper and deeper into the subprime market of high-risk borrowers.[11] If the stigma previously associated with declaring bankruptcy has waned, the banking and credit card industry itself is partially to blame. Some of the stigma of bankruptcy came from the knowledge that your credit would be seriously damaged, making it very difficult to borrow money.

As many people who have recently declared bankruptcy will tell you, that is not the case. Although the personal shame of bankruptcy stays on your credit record for ten years, it is often possible to get a new credit card or a car loan immediately after bankruptcy. As mentioned in chapter 1, the subprime auto loan market has been particularly active in recent years, offering to keep people on the road no matter what their credit status. The terms of these loans may not be as favorable as for someone with a credit score in the 700s, but those in the banking industry who decry the misuse of bankruptcy might look to their colleagues who advertise "Bad credit or no credit OK." Much of the incentive to avoid a life without credit after bankruptcy has been eliminated by lenders who pursue people who are desperate to get their credit back.

The universality of purchasing with credit cards helped encourage their use. Prior to the card, most things that cost more than the monthly budget could absorb were purchased with savings or were out of reach. Now there was a third way, and each temptation to buy—or each unexpected expense—was a potential reality. Instead of saying "I don't have the money" and walking away, people found that new desires became true dilemmas. With cards in their pockets, consumers had the power to act on impulse. An aura of possibility hung over anything that did not exceed the card's limit, and many heads began to swim.

Finally, once a customer has made the transition to being a "revolver"— someone who carries a balance from month to month—there are banking policies that can affect the likelihood of paying the card off. Interest, late fees, and annual fees are a major source of income for the credit card companies, so the banks have an incentive to encourage customers to maintain high balances without defaulting. Andrew Kahr, a consultant to the credit card and banking industry, convinced one lender to reduce the minimum payment on outstanding balances from 5 percent of the total to 2 percent.[12] This allowed many customers to maintain balances that were two and a half times as large as they had been in the past. The innovation, which was quickly adopted by other card issuers, was highly profitable. From a psychological point of view, the size of the minimum payment is an important variable. Since payment is required on a regular monthly basis, your credit card payment must fall within the bounds of the monthly budget. This is an inescapable limitation on borrowing. The monthly payment is an immediate loss, and as a result, its psychological impact is very strong. In contrast, the endpoint of the loan—the day the credit card is paid off—is somewhere in the cloudy future, presenting a classic self-control dilemma. Prior to the Great Recession most consumers had no idea how long it would take to pay off the balance by making minimum payments. The Credit Card Accountability Responsibility and Disclosure Act (CARD Act) signed by President Obama in the wake of the 2008 crisis now requires banks to provide information on the monthly bill about how long it will take to pay off the balance on the card with minimum payments and the total cost in interest and principle of doing so.[13] It is unclear how many people look at that disclosure on their bills. Consumers know that larger payments now will pay off the card sooner, but because the monthly payment is an immediate loss, it has a more powerful influence than savings in the distant future. Paying less now is an attractive feature, both for the banks and for many consumers, but it can lead to much larger levels of indebtedness.

Telecommunications

The expansion of easy and universal credit throughout the land was an essential prerequisite for the growth of our current indebted society. Its primary effect on the physics of spending was to provide the wherewithal to millions of people. But much of our debt problem stems from technological changes that were quite apart from—or at least only indirectly associated with—the banking industry. It is hard to overestimate the impact the telephone—in all its variations—has had on our economic environment. The voice-carrying machine invented by Antonio Meucci (*not* by Alexander Graham Bell, as is commonly believed) is only the most familiar form, but telecommunications also includes computer networks and the Internet, all of which have transformed our world. To see how technology has affected shopping, consider a simple example. Imagine that a man named Bill is watching television at home in 1965 when he sees an advertisement for a set of pruning shears available at a local hardware store. The bushes around his house are getting unruly, and he is tired of borrowing his neighbor's shears a couple of times a summer. He decides that he will go ahead and buy the advertised pair of shears.

I should point out that as powerful a cultural force as it is, television alone cannot explain the surge in household indebtedness that was to begin in the years after Bill buys his pruning shears. Indeed, the great invasion of television into our homes happened during the 1950s. By 1965, 93 percent of American households owned a television set, and the number has increased by only a few percentage points since.[14] Other advances in telecommunications have had more powerful effects.

The top panel of Figure 5.1 shows a simple timeline for Bill's purchase. Bill works a regular nine-to-five job, and he does not have time to go to the hardware store after work the next day. Therefore his first opportunity to buy the shears is on Tuesday after work. The store is a couple of miles out of his normal path from work to home. So, after work, he drives to the store, locates the shears, and proceeds to the cash register.

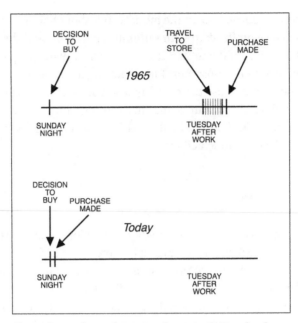

Figure 5.1 Timeline of a purchase of pruning shears in 1965 and today.

This uncomplicated scenario still holds. Today we often make purchases just this way, by going out to the store, bagging our prize, and dragging it home. But psychologically speaking, the time between the decision to buy and the transfer of funds is a crucial interval. There are many obstacles that could block Bill's path to the cash register. Having the wherewithal—be it cash in the bank or a credit card—is an important necessity, but even when money is available, many other things can prevent us from closing the deal. Once the money has changed hands, the buyer is committed. If the product or service is not delivered immediately, it is sometimes possible to reverse the commitment to buy, but very few transactions are reversed once the funds have been committed.

So the interval between decision and purchase is a perilous one for Bill. The television commercial on Sunday night was very appealing, but at any point between Sunday night and Tuesday afternoon, Bill might decide that the shears just aren't worth it. Other demands on his money might come to mind, making the purchase begin to look like a luxury. He doesn't need to trim the hedge that often. He could go on borrowing from his neighbor a little while longer. Alternatively, Bill might simply forget. On Sunday night the plan to buy the shears was clear, but he is a busy guy. At work on Tuesday, he might make plans to go out for a drink with a coworker and forget that he intended to go to the hardware store. His car might break down on Monday, making it both physically more difficult (effort variable) to get to the hardware store and financially unwise to spend money on the pruning shears. There are any number of ways the plan to buy the shears might go awry.

To understand how modern telecommunications alters this scenario, imagine Bill is making his decision to purchase today (see the bottom panel of Figure 5.1). As in the previous case, he sees an advertisement for pruning shears on television on Sunday night and decides to buy. However, now Bill is able to act on his decision immediately. If the commercial for the shears provides a toll-free number, Bill can pick up the phone and buy the product within minutes. He can give the operator a credit or debit card number over the phone, his account will be charged immediately, and the product will be mailed to his home. If instead Bill sees the shears online, rather than on TV, the sale can be completed even quicker. On Amazon.com his purchase is made with a credit card in just a few clicks, shortening the twenty-first-century interval between the decision to buy and the transfer of funds by two days.

There is a certain convenience in the modern version of the pruning shears purchase. The travel to the store has been completely eliminated. With an Amazon Prime membership, Bill will still get the shears on Tuesday, but in this case they will be delivered to his door at no extra charge. Even without Amazon Prime, many people are willing to accept the trade-off of no travel and less effort for slower and more expensive delivery. After all, he does not need the shears right this minute. Later in the week will be fine. But in the contemporary world, *convenience* is a deceiving and potentially dangerous word. As we have seen, it is a simple law of behavior that responses that require less effort happen more often. As a result, when the spending response is made more convenient, it is more likely to occur.

It is also important to note that if we extend these scenarios to a million Bills in 1965 and a million Bills today, there will be many more pruning shears purchased today. Even if on average the Bills in both eras are equally thrifty, intelligent, and self-disciplined, the twenty-first-century Bills will buy more, because quicker and easier responses are made more often. Furthermore, by diminishing the time between the decision to buy and the completed transaction, the modern world makes it more difficult for us to reconsider or be interrupted. Thus the probability of completing the transaction is much higher. It is impossible to say which world makes us happier, but it is clear that the modern world provides more temptation than in the past. Much of this additional challenge to our self-control is created by recent advances in telecommunications.

As the pruning shears scenario demonstrates, direct marketing, in all its various forms, plays a much greater role in our lives today than ever before. We tend to think of direct marketing as junk mail, junk e-mail, and calls from telemarketers, but direct marketing is any kind of advertising that seeks a direct response from the recipient. It is contrasted with general or image advertising that promotes a product or service but does not seek an immediate response.[15] The roots of American direct marketing are in the earliest catalogs, first printed in fifteenth-century Europe, and in the Yankee peddlers of the eighteenth and nineteenth centuries who traveled the countryside selling a variety of wares. Montgomery Ward and Sears began the modern era of direct marketing with the popularization of mail order sales, an innovation that greatly expanded the list of products available to rural families.[16] But today we are confronted with a plethora of appeals too numerous to list. The contemporary explosion of direct marketing was made possible by several technological advances that had profound effects on our behavior.

The telephone was the beginning. As the technology of the telephone developed in the era after World War II, home telephone use became very popular. By 1960, approximately 80 percent of US homes had telephone service, and in that year AT&T offered businesses an important new product: wide-area telecommunications service, commonly know as WATS lines.[17] WATS lines offered businesses discounted high-volume long-distance calling. Outward WATS lines made it more affordable for companies to engage in direct sales calls, what we now think of as telemarketing. Inward WATS lines allowed customers to initiate calls to businesses without charge to the customer, ushering in the era of 800 numbers and television commercials telling us that "operators are standing by." Because most people had a phone, direct telephone sales largely replaced the door-to-door salesman. But it was not until the mid-1970s, when credit cards became much more widespread, that the phone and the credit card combined to make impulsive (convenient) purchasing easier.[18] For example, in 1976 L.L. Bean began accepting credit card sales. The company had been in business for sixty years, selling sporting goods and outdoor wear by mail order, but five years after L.L. Bean began accepting credit card purchases, the company experienced its largest-ever growth in sales.[19]

The effect of the toll-free number combined with the credit card was substantial. Now purchases could be made at home, in many cases twenty-four hours a day, seven days a week. Variable 1, the mere availability of the spending response, had been greatly expanded. The hyperbola extended into our living rooms. The desire to buy could be stimulated by a colorful catalog, a television or radio commercial, or a telemarketer's call, and we could now be separated from our money in just a few minutes—no time to reconsider, no physical effort involved in the transaction. Shopping had come home.

Television contributed to the direct marketing revolution in the late twentieth century. It was a medium that allowed advertisers to present beautiful images, emotional music, and voices extolling the virtues of the product. Furthermore, toll-free numbers could be presented both verbally and in text on the screen, making it much more likely that the customer would be able to remember or write down the digits. But the expansion of cable television and the introduction of cable channels had another effect. In addition to providing more choices and greater opportunity for advertisers to target appeals to particular kinds of viewers (think beer and sports), twenty-four-hour cable programming lengthened the shopping day. The ultimate endpoint of television marketing was the combination of cable television, telephone, and credit card to bring shopping to the living room couch. QVC and the Home Shopping Network are channels that represent stores on the screen. As we will see in chapter 7, products can be viewed, demonstrated, and praised by a live host. The price of the object can be displayed on the screen, along with a toll-free number and an Internet address. Anything you buy must be purchased during a short time window, so impulsivity is the order of the day.

The introduction of Internet shopping simply makes the shopper more active. If the idea of buying anything comes to mind while I am at home—be it pruning shears or a new shirt—I can go to the computer and buy without getting dressed or leaving the house. The credit card is also an essential ingredient in this kind of purchase, but telecommunications—this time over the Internet— makes it possible to act quickly (the time variable). Finally, the likelihood of satisfying one's desires is greatly enhanced by the Internet. If, for example, you are a fan (as I am) of Pears original transparent soap, a British product that is rarely available in stores in the United States, it is quite easy to satisfy your desire on the Internet. It might be cheaper (factoring in shipping) to settle for whatever bath soap is available at the local grocery store, as we did in the pre-Internet days, but powerful searching capabilities combined with a growing number of Internet retailers make it very likely you will find almost anything your heart desires on the Web. The availability of the spending response has been expanded enormously. But convenience and shopping success have their costs. The brief interval from idea to purchase—which can now be satisfied at any hour—makes it much harder to hold on to your money.

Advances in telecommunications created a home shopping revolution at the end of the twentieth century, but telecommunications also had important effects on spending away from home. The first automated teller machine (ATM) was introduced in 1965. These early machines used a special ATM card and a personal identification number (PIN). The original purpose of this invention was to reduce labor costs by providing many of the most popular banking transactions without human intervention, but soon the full potential of the machines became clear. If the ATM of one bank could connect with an account at a different bank, then customers could get cash and perform other transactions wherever they happened to be. Banks began to understand that an electronic funds transfer (EFT) system was needed, and in the late 1960s and early 1970s the industry worked its way toward standardized encoding systems for bank information, allowing ATMs manufactured by different companies to communicate. Gradually a system of nationwide networks for the transfer of banking information emerged.[20] The eventual impact of the EFT on our daily lives was enormous, because in addition to providing for ATMs, this telecommunications backbone makes it possible for us to make debit card purchases, bank by phone and on the Internet, pay bills online, and have our paychecks electronically deposited into our bank accounts.

ATMs add convenience because live human tellers work banker's hours. Like the police, they are rarely around when you need them. Some of us are old enough to remember the days when most financial transactions required cash or a check. Many a transaction was deferred for want of a sawbuck. Nowadays, you may have to trek a mile or two to find an ATM, but if you have money in the bank, you can always have money in your pocket. Even if you don't have money in the bank, you can use an ATM to get a cash advance on your Visa card. Yes, the ATM adds convenience, but every added convenience transfers more of the burden of self-control onto our shoulders.

In the early 1970s, when credit cards were still in their developing stages, it became clear that a similar network would be needed to link the merchant— actually the clerk at the cash register—with the bank that issued the customer's card. In the early days of universal bank credit cards, the clerk authorized a MasterCard purchase by making a paper imprint of the customer's charge plate and placing a phone call that eventually reached someone who could say that the card in question had available credit that would cover the purchase. In 1973, National BankAmericard Incorporated introduced an electronic authorization system that lowered the average point-of-sale transaction time from five minutes to fifty-six seconds.[21] Additional advances, principally clerk- or customer-operated terminals that read a magnetic strip or a chip on the credit or debit card, have lowered the transaction time even further.

Why is transaction time important? From the merchant's point of view there are a number of reasons. First, quicker handling of customer checkout means lower labor costs. A single clerk can process more purchases per minute, and the introduction of self-checkout machines has further reduced the need for expensive staff. But in the fast-paced modern world, quick transactions are also more likely to be completed than slower ones. Just as in the pruning shears example, shortening the time to the transfer of funds promotes sales. As anyone who has shopped at a busy store knows, the checkout process is one of great psychological conflict. If we are in a hurry and the store is busy, we are of two minds, trying to decide between fight and flight. The checkout is often near the store exit, and if the line is long and the item in our hands is not essential, then we are likely to ditch it and head for the car. Our contemporary impatience with the purchasing process is so refined that merely discovering that the person ahead of you in the grocery store checkout is about to pay with a check can create considerable frustration and a strong urge to flee.

In addition, for merchants, banks, and credit card companies that want to encourage the use of plastic, reducing the time involved in a card transaction is essential. People buy more when paying with a credit card, and handing over real cash carries the additional cost of the labor involved in going to the bank, an ATM, or a store that offers "cash back" to obtain it.[22] So easy payment with a card is good for business, but cash transactions are very quick. In most cases, even with the most efficient point-of-sale card-reading devices and electronic authorization procedures, the age-old process of handing over bills and counting out change can be accomplished in fewer seconds.

Much effort has gone into developing technologies that will keep transaction times short. As I write this, the US market has recently made a transition from magnetic strip swiping system to a chip reading system known as the EMV chip (for Europay, MasterCard, & Visa). The EMV chip system has been promoted to increase the security of the transactions and make it more difficult for counterfeiters to use stolen card data, but merchants were quick to notice that the card approval time associated with the chip reader is generally longer than with the old swipe system. As a result, industry groups have responded with a number of strategies for speeding the process.[23] Finally, even under the old swipe system many businesses further decreased transaction times by eliminating the requirement of a signature or a PIN for card purchases less than a set amount. The customer swipes the card or inserts the chip at a point-of-sale terminal in the normal way, but as soon as the charge is approved, a receipt is automatically printed. Quicker transactions are a convenience for the customer, but they are much more than that for the business. Former McDonald's CEO Jack Greenberg claimed that unit sales went up 1 percent for every six seconds shaved from drive-thru transactions.[24] So time is money, and when it comes to paying with plastic, time is often debt. Quicker transactions lead to fewer interrupted purchases, greater impulsivity, and more money spent.

Transportation and the Large-Muscle Hierarchy

As we have seen, the simple lesson of the effort variable involved in the physics of spending is that easy responses are made more frequently. Often the variables of time and effort are correlated. The quickness of shopping by phone or on the Internet is complemented by the minimal effort involved. But when spending takes us out of the home, both time and effort are required. In these instances, the effort variable has a powerful influence on our shopping and spending.

The largest muscles of the human body are the gluteus maximus (buttocks) and the quadriceps (upper thigh), and both are used when moving from a seated position to standing and in climbing stairs. These are activities that require much energy, and therefore anything that diminishes the need for standing up and climbing will produce a substantial decrease in the effort variable. As a result, when it comes to shopping outside the home, a simple hierarchy applies: sitting is better than walking, and walking is better than climbing stairs. Gradually, through a number of innovations in transportation and retail design, the modern shopping experience has been engineered with this hierarchy in mind.

Whether or not Americans love their cars is a debatable question, but studies show that compared to Canadians and Europeans, Americans own more cars, travel more miles, and, for any given urban trip, are several times more likely to drive than use public transportation. In 2013, 76 percent of American commuters traveled to work alone in their cars.[25] Comparisons with other countries demonstrate that it didn't have to be this way. We might have structured our transportation systems differently. But the peculiarities of American history—and, in particular, some important government programs— helped to create a society that is dependent on the automobile.

Our modern life behind the wheel is in large part a function of the suburban world we inhabit. Until the first half of the twentieth century, cities were places where people lived, worked, and shopped. In 1934, Franklin Roosevelt introduced the FHA as one of his New Deal programs designed to encourage employment in the housing industry and to help create a new stock of homes.[26] The FHA did not lend money directly. Rather, it provided insurance—mortgage guarantees—to commercial lenders in an effort to encourage them to underwrite home purchases and new construction. The program worked well, particularly after World War II, when FHA and Veterans Administration (VA) mortgages spurred a substantial real estate boom.[27]

One of the consequences of the FHA and VA mortgage programs was the creation of new single-family homes at the expense of other kinds of residential properties. Because these programs often made it cheaper to buy than to rent, there was little incentive for the renovation of existing multifamily buildings or for the construction of row-house-style multifamily structures. Rather, housing policies encouraged the establishment of Levittowns, large developments of single-family homes complete with ample parking for the family cars. The zoning philosophy of these new suburban communities dictated that buildings of different uses should be segregated into separate areas of town. Large tracts of land were zoned exclusively residential, commercial, or industrial. This kind of planning stands in stark contrast to the philosophy of mixed-use neighborhoods—combining residential and commercial or entertainment spaces in the same area—advocated by Jane Jacobs in her 1961 book *The Death and Life of Great American Cities*.[28] Although there may have been some advantages to single-use zoning, one clear effect was to increase the need for automobile transportation and decrease the practicality of pedestrian travel. Development in all three major zones, residential, commercial, and industrial, had to provide substantial space for parking.

Automobiles took another step forward when President Eisenhower signed the Interstate Highway Act of 1956, which created the network of interstate highways that we use today. The existence of these high-volume, high-speed corridors further enhanced the possibilities for commuting from home to work. For a time, people moved to new developments in the suburbs but continued to work and shop in the city. Eventually, however, shopping followed the commuters to the suburbs. As early as the 1920s, when the automobile became a popular feature of American life, there were serious traffic and parking problems in most large cities. Department stores went to great lengths to provide easy downtown shopping for their customers, buying empty lots and constructing multilevel garages, but a great conflict had begun between the demands of the automobile-driving consumer and the restricted confines of the central city. From the 1920s forward, all city planning and building construction would take the automobile into account.[29] But particularly in the post–World War II era, most of the commercial construction was going on away from the city.

Shopping centers and malls, surrounded by huge parking lots, sprouted up in suburban locations zoned for the purpose. The great central city department stores that once helped define the identity of downtown began to close one by one—a process that continues to this day. Macy's survives, both as a chain store at the mall and as the famous department store in Manhattan, but Boston's Filene's and Chicago's Marshall Field's both closed in 2006, just the latest victims in a long line of fallen giants. Today relatively few people live within walking distance of stores. Beginning in the 1990s and continuing to today, mixed use development of the kind promoted by Jane Jacobs has become fashionable again, and a number of US cities have made their downtowns attractive places to live and work; however, much of this revitalization has come in the form of gentrification, making life in the central city a rich person's game.[30] The large American middle class remains predominantly suburban, and for these people, almost anything they want outside the house that cannot be ordered online will require wheels.

The automobile provides access to all three of the major bricks-and-mortar shopping destinations: regional malls, strip malls, and big-box stores. The driver remains seated while operating the vehicle, covering great distances with relatively tiny expenditures of physical energy. Thus the typical shopping trip involves a short walk from the house or apartment to the car and possibly a somewhat longer walk from the parking lot to the store. In addition, automobiles protect you from the weather, keeping the amount of time spent outdoors to a minimum.

On occasion we do still shop outside the home without using the car. Even today in large cities, people walk from their apartments or take public transportation to shop at retail stores. Commuting into the city to shop was much more popular in the early days of suburban flight, but some people still take public transportation into cities to shop or spend money on entertainment. Finally, in many revitalized urban centers residents are able to walk from their homes to local shops. But each of these non-auto-dependent methods of shopping suffers in comparison to the car on several variables of the physics of spending. Even when public transportation is available, the trip is likely to require more walking and perhaps stairs—if, for example, a city subway is used. Often where there is more walking involved, the trip is likely to take longer, so the variable of time also argues in favor of the car. Furthermore, if you walk, purchases must be hauled back home by hand instead of in the trunk (effort). Finally, as we have seen, there is the weather. For all these reasons, even when there are other ways to shop outside the home, the convenience of the car is often very persuasive.

For a time I lived approximately two city blocks from a small shopping area where many of life's necessities could be found. I enjoyed walking into town for any number of errands, but having a car parked in the driveway often created substantial ambivalence at the crucial choice point. If the weather was bad or if I'd constructed my day in such a way that I was rushed when it came time to do the errand, I often took the car. The trip was embarrassingly short, but collectively my two-block automobile rides—four blocks round trip—ate up a substantial quantity of fossil fuel. This is a classic problem of self-control. The immediate convenience of a quick, comfortable trip into town combined with some delayed costs, such as the burned gasoline and some immeasurable contribution to environmental pollution, is contrasted with walking, which provides all its drawbacks up front, in the walk itself. As the self-control research presented in chapter 4 suggests, we are likely to choose immediate benefits and delayed costs over immediate costs.

We should probably recognize that the automobile and the physics of spending have much to do with our current problems with obesity and health. Food is a necessity. We must have it to survive, but today we have many food choices. Often the foods that are both economical and healthy are the ones we buy at the grocery store and prepare at home. On the other hand, grocery shopping and cooking draw fairly substantially on the variables of time and effort. It takes both of these to acquire and assemble the ingredients of a home-cooked meal, and our contemporary world always provides many opportunities to remove these obstacles. Food that is delivered to your door eliminates physical effort almost completely. You must wait for the food to arrive, but often the wait is shorter than the time required to prepare a meal. Thus home-delivered pizza and Chinese food are staples throughout the country, and in large cities, where take-out and home-delivery menus arrive under your door on a daily basis, many people eat a varied and inexpensive diet without ever having to cook.

In the suburban world, it is the automobile that provides the difficult food choices. As we drive back and forth among our different single-use zones, we have many opportunities to eliminate time and effort from the food gathering and preparation process. Drive-thru windows beckon with fully prepared fast-food meals that can be obtained and paid for in approximately five minutes while remaining seated in the car at all times. Other take-out venues require a short walk from the parking lot to the restaurant for Chinese food or Subway sandwiches. The effects of these choices have been profound. We eat more and more of our meals outside the home. For the first time in 2015, Americans spent more at restaurants and bars than at grocery stores.[31] Furthermore, foods prepared outside the home tend to be higher in calories and fat and generally less nutritious than foods prepared at home.[32] There is little doubt that the variables of effort and time, as employed by the restaurant and fast-food industries, have served to make us less healthy and less wealthy.

BEYOND SPENDING

In chapter 7 we look more closely at the psychology of shopping, but before we complete our psychological history it is important to return to the wherewithal and another way we have been affected by easy credit.

Up to now, our discussion of banking, telecommunications, and transportation has been in the context of using credit to acquire goods and services. But there is another role that credit cards play in our national indebtedness. First, recall that Americans save very little. The US personal savings rate began a long slow drop in—you guessed it—the mid-1970s, hitting bottom at 2 percent in the years just before the Great Recession. It crept up slightly after the recession, but it has dropped to very low levels again.[33] Furthermore, we also know that approximately 47 percent of Americans, including author Neal Gabler, do not have $400 in emergency cash on hand. Life without savings presents another kind of risk.

It is interesting to note that when the savings rate hit its low mark in 2006, many of the economic writers who commented on it either questioned the numbers or argued that a minimal savings rate was not necessarily a bad thing.[34] Part of the support for this idea comes from the paradox of thrift, a theory introduced by economist John Maynard Keynes.[35] Keynes proposed that people who save take money out of the economy, which has a depressive effect overall. In contrast, people who spend their savings produce increased demand for goods and services, create more jobs, and help to keep wages high. Paradoxically, spending would create more income, which would then be available to be either saved or spent. In some respects, this spend-save quandary represents a classic prisoner's dilemma—a conflict between one's individual welfare and that of the larger economy. It would be better for me personally if I held on to more of my money, but it would not benefit the economy as a whole. It is now accepted economic dogma that America's consumer economy is largely driven by the spending of its citizens and that saving depresses the economy.[36] But it is possible to have too much of a good thing.

For several decades, Americans have lived with little savings and much debt, and in the years leading up to the Great Recession, many consumers used their homes as a substitute for savings. During the early years of the twenty-first century, real estate prices rose sharply, largely on the strength of low interest rates, but for many households, this was also a period of declining incomes, As a result, many Americans who had maxed out their credit and had insufficient income to continue buying took advantage of rising real estate values to refinance and cash out some of the equity in their homes. Others took out second mortgages or lines of credit guaranteed by equity. Much of this newfound cash was used to pay off their credit cards, buy cars, or support other kinds of spending.[37] As a result, despite increasing home values during this period, the amount of equity Americans had in their homes actually decreased and the ratio of household debt to income reached unprecedented levels.[38] In addition, the promotion of riskier adjustable-rate mortgages and interest-only mortgages allowed buyers to finance a larger house (take on more debt) than would be the case with a conventional mortgage. All of this made many people extremely vulnerable to the shock that eventually came in 2008. The absence of savings may grease the wheels of the economy, but for many people it is the first step on the road to ruin. Faced with a bump in the road—an unexpected expense, being laid off from your job—the consumer who has no savings stares at their credit card. Often it seems there is no good option. The roof is leaking, doing damage to the house. If, like almost half of Americans, a $400 expense is out of reach, our unhappy consumer has no choice but to put the repair on a credit card. In a previous era, before the advent of credit cards, people were forced to cope in some other way—find some way to fix the leak or find the money somewhere else. And, of course, in that previous era consumers were more likely to have savings. But today people use credit cards in place of savings accounts. Rather than saving for a rainy day, we put our rainy days on plastic.

During real estate boom years in the run-up to the recession, if the plastic ran dry, the search for wherewithal came home. For many people, the last source of wealth was the house, and while the housing market was strong, refinancing made that wealth available for use. Thus, many meals purchased with a credit card and long ago forgotten were converted into mortgage debt and amortized over the course of a thirty-year loan. All of which might have been fine if, as many people had hoped, their incomes had grown and the economy had sailed on without significant bumps. Unfortunately, for millions of people, a very different scenario played out.

LOOKING AHEAD

The parable of financial ruin that emerges from Version Three of the Parable of Bankruptcy is not quite as simple as the other two. Version Two's condemnation of the credit card industry is probably closer to the truth than Version One, but it is clear that easy credit alone is not responsible for our great contemporary indebtedness. Many other changes in our economic environment—quite separate from the banking industry—have played a part. Furthermore, although some things have improved since the Great Recession, others have remained the same or gotten worse. Financial regulations passed since the recession, such as the Dodd–Frank Wall Street Reform and Consumer Protection Act and the CARD Act provide additional protections for consumers, but they do not address all the pitfalls that await us. After a brief improvement, the savings rate is again very low, and 34 percent of Americans have no savings at all. For many of us, our cash on hand remains woefully inadequate to avert future disasters, and, if anything, the current economic environment is more difficult to navigate than the one experienced in the lead-up to the crash.

Version Three of the Parable of Bankruptcy cannot be a shallow caricature. There are many features of the modern world that conspire to draw down our bank accounts, and they defy a simple liberal or conservative, pro-business or pro-consumer stereotype. But much of the story of our indebtedness is subtler than cars, credit cards, and toll-free telephone numbers. Several other questions are waiting to be answered: When we think about money, why do we often choose badly? Where does the longing for things come from? How has the explosion of products, services, and entertainments affected our personal bottom lines? It is to these and other questions that we turn in the following chapters.

KATHY

Although Kathy declared bankruptcy in her early forties, she could not be faulted for lack of industriousness. "I've worked my whole life, often two jobs," she told me. And yet she had never made much money and never had a job with healthcare or dental coverage. Fortunately, with minor exceptions, she had always been healthy.

Kathy grew up in rural Massachusetts, and soon after high school she married a young man who worked as a stonemason. Six years later, after the birth of their third child, Kathy divorced her husband. She managed to establish a modest but good home for her little family. Using money from her settlement, she was able to buy a small house, and she paid off the mortgage in fifteen years. From that time forward, she had owned the house free and clear, and she never borrowed against it. In addition, she received child support from her ex-husband for approximately twenty years, until her youngest child was twenty-one. Her most dependable source of income came from bartending jobs. It was nighttime work, and the tips were good. She always had cash on hand whenever expenses came up between child support payments or paychecks from her other jobs.

Kathy also had an interest in biology and science, and during the day she worked at a local nature center and later at a children's museum. She loved this kind of work, even if it paid very little and it was difficult managing two jobs and the kids. Furthermore, these daytime positions were seasonal, which meant she was often laid off during the winter without any guarantee she would be hired back the following year.

Eventually, despite the good money, tending bar began to tire her out, and Kathy quit. She continued to work at the nature center when possible, but now money was more of a problem. She had a Sears credit card that she often used to pay for repairs or new tires for the car. Without health insurance or a regular physician, she had been forced to use the emergency room on a couple of occasions, and she owed the hospital $800.

Soon after her divorce, Kathy's oldest child was struck and killed by a pickup truck while walking to a friend's house. He was ten years old. Her other two children grew up and attended college, her daughter enrolling out of state and her younger son attending college locally while living at home. By this time the child support payments had ended, so her son helped out with bills when he could. His only income was his pay for service in the Army Reserve, and he was also paying tuition and had his own expenses.

Kathy's life was already unstable when two events knocked her for a loop within a few months of each other. First, the war in Iraq broke out in the spring of 2003, and her son was among the very first reservists called up. Then the news came that her daughter had been sideswiped by a car while riding her bicycle off campus. Her injuries were quite serious, and she remained hospitalized for several months. For Kathy this began a period when she believed she might have been "mildly depressed." The bicycle accident brought back memories of her older son's death, and she was having more severe money problems. Her credit card balances never seemed to go away, and once she had missed a few payments, her interest rates soared and exorbitant late fees were tacked on to her bills. Creditors began to call almost every day, especially Sears, and she finally unplugged the phone to avoid having to talk to them. In this pre-cellphone era it meant that none of her friends or family could reach her, but it was worth it to have a little peace. The creditors who called her were often belligerent and unsympathetic. She had done her best to meet her obligations, and being treated this way was humiliating. She managed to pay off one credit card entirely, partly because of the bank's willingness to work with her to set up a payment plan that was realistic. But being bullied by collection agencies made her angry and less willing to cooperate.

Still, in an effort to get her finances under control, Kathy went to a credit counseling service, and they set up a payment plan for her. She would give the credit counselors a certain amount of money each month, and for a small fee, they would pay her bills. Kathy followed this plan for a year and a half, but her balances never seemed to go down. Every once in a while she would get a windfall and make a payment directly to one of her credit cards, but these extra payments seemed to have no effect.

"It was like they disappeared. I followed the credit counselors' plan, but nothing ever changed. Between the interest rates and late fees, the balances never went away." Eventually the stress was too much to take. Between her unpaid hospital bills, the Sears account, a couple of other store cards, and her Visa bill, she had accumulated less than $10,000 in total debt, but in the year prior to declaring bankruptcy she had made only $15,000. Even though by some standards her debts were not that large, it seemed unlikely she would be able to pay them off anytime soon—especially given the interest rates she was paying. So she picked a bankruptcy attorney out of the yellow pages and called.

Soon after her bankruptcy was finalized, Kathy's son returned safely from Iraq, and he got a good job with an engineering firm and moved out of the house. Her daughter, having by now made a full recovery from her bicycle accident, completed college and got a teaching position. Things were looking brighter, and Kathy realized she was entering a new phase of her life. Her children did not need her anymore, and she was no longer tied to Massachusetts and the life she had been living for so many years. Cruising the Internet, she found a job listing at a resort in Alaska, and she applied. Kathy had always wanted to travel, and the position included room and board. "They paid for everything," she said. "They even picked you up at the airport."

Moving to Alaska was a huge risk, but she loved it. At the resort, she did accounting and office work, and she had a real sense of freedom. It seemed ironic to her that, after declaring bankruptcy, she got a job handling money, but she did. And she did it quite well. In her time off, she was able to travel much of this huge state and enjoyed it immensely. Part of her happiness stemmed from her financial freedom. Within weeks of declaring bankruptcy she had received credit card offers in the mail, but she didn't get a new card for over a year. She didn't really need one. When I met her during one of her visits to her house in Massachusetts, it had been two years since her bankruptcy; she had a balance of $500 on her MasterCard, the only credit card she had, and she was up to date on her payments. Her kids were doing well, and so was she. It was as if she had been through a long ordeal and finally earned the freedom she deserved.

New Ways of Wanting

Another possible source of guidance for teenagers is television, but television's message has always been that the need for truth, wisdom and world peace pales by comparison with the need for a toothpaste that offers whiter teeth *and* fresher breath.

—DAVE BARRY

One of the great mysteries of the marketplace is the origin of desire. Before we make the spending response, there must be some motivation to do so, but where does that motivation come from? Psychologist Abraham Maslow proposed what is perhaps the most famous theory of human motivation. Maslow was born in Brooklyn, New York, in 1908, the first of seven children of Russian Jewish immigrants.[1] His father was a successful small-business owner, and Maslow's life and career as a psychologist would intersect with the world of management and business at several points. He attended graduate school at the University of Wisconsin, studying with psychologist Harry Harlow, who became famous for his experiments with rhesus monkeys on tactile and emotional needs in infancy. When he returned to New York to take a teaching position at Brooklyn College, Maslow became friends with anthropologists Margaret Mead and Ruth Benedict and came into contact with the writings of other prominent psychologists, including Alfred Adler, Erich Fromm, and Karen Horney. His interests were eclectic, and in the 1950s and 1960s he emerged as an important figure in the new field of humanistic psychology. He was an early advocate of massage therapy and sensitivity groups and is associated with the beginnings of the human potential movement. Although he was never really a counterculture figure, he knew some of the most colorful figures of the era: Timothy Leary was a friend, and Abbie Hoffman was his student.[2]

Table 6.1 MASLOW'S HIERARCHY OF NEEDS

1. *Physiological:*   food, water, oxygen, sleep, temperature
2. *Safety:*   physical safety, security, stability
3. *Belongingness:*   love, friendship, affiliation
4. *Esteem:*   status, self-respect, prestige
5. *Self-actualization:*   self-fulfillment

Maslow's theory of motivation is based on a hierarchy of human needs (see Table 6.1).[3] He proposed that we all have needs of varying levels of importance. Typically, physiological needs are the most basic and must be satisfied before other, higher-order needs can be addressed. You can't be concerned about whether anyone will ever love you if you are about to starve to death. Similarly, self-actualization is normally a need that only the very well-off can afford to pursue. Those whose biological, safety, belongingness, and esteem needs are already under control will have the psychological foundation to support the drive for human fulfillment implicit in the fifth stage of Maslow's hierarchy.

Maslow was quick to point out that for some this hierarchy was less fixed than for others. For example, some people seem to pursue status and esteem to the detriment of love and family. Others value the sense of self-actualization they derive from art and creativity more than other needs. But the basic hierarchy has great intuitive appeal and, as a result, has been taught in introductory psychology courses for generations. Furthermore, Maslow's humanism has found new champions in the positive psychology movement.[4] In his most famous book, *Motivation and Personality*, he wrote:

> The science of psychology has been far more successful on the negative than on the positive side; it has revealed to us much about man's shortcomings, his illnesses, his sins, but little about his potentialities, his virtues, his achievable aspirations, or his psychological height. It is as if psychology had voluntarily restricted itself to only half its rightful jurisdiction, and that the darker, meaner half.[5]

This was precisely the philosophy that would be adapted by positive psychology fifty years later. Picking up where Maslow left off, positive psychologists are today working to turn the field away from its traditional dark preoccupation with mental illness and toward the brighter goal of helping people enhance their positive traits and virtues.

Maslow's ideas about human motivation emerged in the postwar and Cold War periods of the late 1940s and 1950s, and their relevance to business and industrial management was quickly recognized. His theory of human motivation could be applied to the world of work in an effort to help employees achieve satisfaction through the higher-level needs of esteem and self-actualization. Maslow's basic optimism about human nature translated into a benevolent management style that could serve both the individual and the organization, leading one writer to call him the "Father of Enlightened Management."[6]

Maslow's work was also warmly received in the world of commerce. Marketers recognized that many products and services could be made more attractive by directing them toward the human needs of Maslow's hierarchy.[7] Any given product can satisfy a variety of needs. Some products, such as toothpaste, are primarily *utilitarian*. They perform a basic practical function: cleaning your teeth. Other products and services, such as movies, Ben & Jerry's ice cream, and vacations at the beach, are *hedonic*—purchased for the pleasure they bring the consumer. But most products have a mixture of utilitarian and hedonic qualities. Maslow's ideas about human motivation have particular relevance for hedonic items. In most cases, a utilitarian purchase will go forward or not on the basis of the product's ability to satisfy a specific function. In general, shopping for toothpaste, laundry detergent, lawn care equipment, or aluminum foil involves rather simple judgments of usefulness and value. Houses, cars, clothes, and computers represent more complicated mixtures of attributes. The basic transportation function of an automobile is very important, but all cars include features that are more about pleasure than function. A new Lexus RX sedan has the ability to both get you to work and afford you a sense of accomplishment and esteem.[8]

The very act of shopping is also thought to satisfy a variety of hedonic needs. In a line of thinking that descends directly from Maslow, contemporary retail research has identified six hedonic motivations for shopping. These have nothing to do with the utilitarian goals of buying the stuff you need; nonetheless, they are important reasons people give for shopping (see Table 6.2).[9] For example, a trip to IKEA or the mall often satisfies the urge for adventure and stimulation by providing a new and rather electric environment that stands in contrast to the customer's usual places. Similarly, many shoppers can play out social roles and gain a feeling of personal gratification by finding the perfect book for a child or spouse or a great sweater for a close friend. Understanding these kinds of motivations can help retailers think about how to design their advertising, store environments, and websites to meet the hedonic preferences of their customers. Bookstores can emphasize the social aspects of shopping by adding a coffee shop, children's story hours, and book signings, and retail Internet sites can strive to make online shopping pleasant by designing stimulating and informative pages that will appeal to adventure and idea shoppers.[10]

Table 6.2 MOTIVATIONS FOR SHOPPING

Adventure shopping	Stimulation, adventure, and the feeling of being in another world
Social shopping	Time with friends, family, and bonding with others
Gratification shopping	Stress relief, therapeutic, treating oneself
Idea shopping	Keeping up with trends, new products, innovations
Role shopping	Shopping for others, as an expression of family or social roles
Value shopping	Bargain hunting, shopping for price as a competition

SOURCE: M. J. Arnold and K. E. Reynolds, "Hedonic Shopping Motivations," *Journal of Retailing* 79 (2003): 77–95.

ADVERTISING

As we have seen, spenders have different motives. Often there is a utilitarian motive: I need a new pair of sneakers. But the simple purchase of a pair of sneakers can also be influenced by other urges and desires. For any producer or retailer, the job is to connect the product with the motivations of their customers. Making a great line of sneakers is only half the battle. If no one knows about your shoes, then no one will want them, and in many cases, even when people know about them, the urge to buy does not automatically follow. So the manufacturer—or the manufacturer's advertising firm—must sell the virtues of the sneakers and convince potential buyers these shoes are an important purchase.

Surprisingly, there is little agreement about how advertising works. Millions are spent on developing and testing various ad campaigns, so advertising firms often have some understanding of how a specific product can be best pitched to the unsuspecting public. But to date, no unified theory of advertising has emerged. Economists cannot even agree on the question of whether advertising changes consumers' preferences for one product or brand over another.[11] Nonetheless, one early economic theory suggested that advertising's primary function is to grease the wheels of commerce by providing information to the consumer.[12] According to this view, products and services can be divided into *search goods* and *experience goods*.[13] The distinction between them is somewhat fuzzy, but search goods are those for which most of the relevant information can be discovered before the purchase is made. If you are looking for a replacement charger for your phone, your primary task is to find a compatible charger at a good price. Here you have great control over the situation, and if either of the crucial pieces of the transaction—the price or the type of charger—is wrong, you will not complete the purchase. A similar up-front approach to consumer choice is characteristic of other search goods, such as clothing, furniture, and kitchen tools.

In contrast, when you buy experience goods, you often don't know how well you have chosen until it's too late. Once you have taken a bite of mango, it's too late to say, "Come to think of it, I don't like mangos. Can I have my money back?" Of course, if the mango is rotten or otherwise defective, you may have a case for a refund, but if not, you will be out of luck. A similar problem exists for novels, movies, or restaurant meals. Since you have already handed over your money—or are obligated to pay—by the time you get to the bottom of the situation, the news—bad or good—can affect only the likelihood of making a repeat purchase of an experience good: from now on, mangos are off the list. Repeat purchases are important, so manufacturers have a vested interest in making the product as satisfying as possible. But given the much more matter-of-fact nature of consumer decision-making for search goods, producers tend to spend considerably more money on the advertising of experience goods. These can be either durable items (e.g., a Subaru Impreza) or nondurable items (e.g., Bud Light beer); in both cases, the uncertainty about the relevant information and the possibility of being burned by a car you don't like or a beer that tastes bad makes advertising aimed at these concerns an important aspect of boosting sales. Whenever possible, retailers attempt to let the buyer try out experience goods before purchase. Music lovers can often listen to samples of songs in the store or online before purchase, and the test drive is an essential part of the automobile-buying process.

The information view of advertising leads to different predictions about ads we are trapped into hearing or seeing versus ads we can choose to examine or not. When you watch a television program, listen to commercial radio, or are forced to watch a web ad before reading an article or watching a video, it is difficult to avoid the advertisements. Television commercial breaks are designed to be short so that people won't drift away from the tube for long periods of time or switch channels. Not many competing activities can be scheduled in the few minutes available. As a result, unless we are watching on a commercial-free streaming service, such as Netflix or Amazon Prime, or have recorded the program and can TiVo past the commercials, we tend to submit ourselves to advertising we often would choose not to see. (Of course, the mute button is helpful here.) In similar ways, we are trapped by advertisements of one sort or another at the movies, on the subway, while listening to the radio or podcasts, or while flipping through a magazine. Other forms of advertisement afford us the choice to look or not. For example, we have greater control over the circulars that come in the local newspaper, as well as catalogs and other advertising that comes in the mail. The trashcan is always near at hand.

According to the advertising-as-information view, the trapped consumer represents an opportunity for plugging experience goods. Here the difficult job of touting the quality and value of the product can be done while the consumer is a captive audience. As a result, the billboard ads above your head on the commuter train often seek to enhance your impression of a TV show or a brand of vodka. There will be some search good ads, too, telling you where to find cheap legal services, for example, but experience goods are there in abundance. In contrast, the common direct mail catalog or newspaper circular is designed for the consumer who is already in search mode. It would be a waste to send a beautifully photographed flyer about the latest Bourne movie through the mail, because most often it would be very quickly discarded. This kind of advertising is better suited to the entertainment section of the newspaper or the Internet Movie Database website (IMDb.com), places people go when they are in movie search mode. But, like newspaper ads for movies, grocery store circulars—packed with as many products, brands, and prices as possible—are often used by the motivated shopper. Similarly, at holiday time, many consumers will voluntarily choose to study the piles of catalogs from Lands' End, L.L. Bean, and Pottery Barn, and advertisements for other stores that appear in the local newspaper. Shopping is considered a necessity at this time of year, and catalogs provide very useful information about where products are available and at what cost.[14]

One of advertising's big jobs is simply to get us to remember the product. Producers assume we are rational decision makers, and when it comes time to consider our purchasing options, it will be helpful if we can recall something about their wares. Thus, marketers hope it is their brand of TV you remember when it is time to buy a new one. "Mad men" and women in expensive advertising firms spend considerable effort developing product names, logos, and color schemes to establish an iconic brand that they hope will bubble up out of memory whenever the relevant product category comes to mind. Much research has gone into how best to establish a brand. Is it better to reveal the brand early or late in a commercial? (Early.)[15] Do creative commercials help or hinder the recall of the brand? (Help in some situations, hinder in others.)[16] Of course, in many shopping contexts the product choices are arrayed in front of us, and the memory task is made much easier. In this case, even if you could not tell someone what kind of dishwashing liquid you usually use, you would probably be able to pick it out on the shelf, and familiarity with a brand makes us more likely to choose it.[17] But no matter what the context, establishing a brand firmly in memory will help sales.

Finally, one of advertising's most important jobs is to favorably dispose the shopper toward the items offered. As the consumer is learning about the product or service, it is helpful if he or she is also building a positive attitude that will

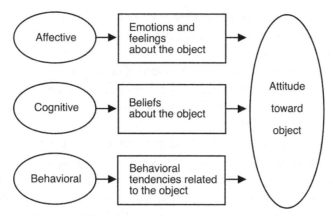

Figure 6.1 The ACB theory of attitudes. Each component contributes to our overall attitude with respect to a particular person, action, or object.

make buying more likely.[18] In psychology, the topic of attitudes and their effects on behavior has a research history that is broad and deep. Some personality researchers have suggested that our various attitudes about everything in the world combine to make an important contribution to our sense of self, and social psychologists have spent considerable time studying how we form attitudes about social groups and the actions of others.[19] A common view of attitudes suggests that they are general evaluative responses—good versus bad, love it or hate it—that are based on three components, labeled A, C, and B.[20] According to this theory, attitudes involve affective or emotional reactions (A), cognitions (C; ideas or beliefs), and behavioral tendencies (B) connected to the thing in question (see Figure 6.1). In the case of a product—for example, a particular brand of cough syrup—we may have a negative affective response based our past experience with its taste and the uncomfortable circumstances in which we have had to use it. At the same time, we are likely to believe the syrup helps eliminate or reduce common coughs—and perhaps even that its bad taste is evidence of its effectiveness—and as a result, our behavioral tendency may be to buy the syrup and take it at those times when we have an annoying cough. The affective, cognitive, and behavioral reactions to this product are decidedly mixed, but they combine to make an overall positive attitude that is enough to get us to make the purchase.

THE WAY WE WANT NOW

Most of this has been with us for a very long time. The basic principles of advertising are unchanged, so how can advertising contribute to our current indebtedness? The answer is not a change in the way advertising works. It works the way it always has. What is different now is where, how, and how often we encounter it. Advertising has been an important part of our lives since the introduction of mass production and mass marketing in the nineteenth century, but today it is almost ubiquitous. In ways both subtle and overpowering, the commercial message is with us from the moment we wake until we close our eyes again at night.

Before an advertisement can have any effect, we must perceive it. The psychological study of perception begins with raw sensation. We cannot be influenced by an advertisement unless we both are exposed to it and recognize it for what it is. Needing to be exposed seems like a trivial point, but it turns out to be quite important. There is evidence that mere repeated exposure to a person, an object, or a product or brand can breed a positive attitude, even when we are unaware of the exposure and have no memory of it later.[21] We tend to like products that are familiar, and sometimes they can become familiar without our knowing it.[22] But if an advertisement hopes to go beyond this rather weak emotional response to a thing that is vaguely familiar, it must capture our attention. Often we think of attention as something that we bring to the situation. We freely choose to focus our attention on a book or a television program. But marketers can't count on us to do the right thing. Advertisements must use color, sound, and images to grab our attention, to pull us away from our idle pursuits and compel us to focus our substantial powers of concentration on something really important—such as Honey Nut Cheerios. Once we are pulled in, the advertisement has a chance to be memorable and build a positive attitude toward this yummy breakfast food. The degree of attention the consumer is able to bring to the situation also affects the nature of the advertising appeal. If the customer is highly involved and attentive—either an expert in the product area or someone who is about to make a big purchase, such as an automobile or a flat-screen TV—the advertising appeal can be high on information value and can aggressively pursue a strategy of convincing the customer to buy. On the other hand, if the product is less central to the consumer's life, the advertisement is unlikely to capture much attention. Breakfast may be the most important meal of the day, but a television advertisement for Honey Nut Cheerios is not going to be particularly newsworthy or educational for anyone who is over five years old. As a result, the advertising strategy for this product is lighter and has more modest goals. The successful commercial for Honey Nut Cheerios will get the viewer's attention and encourage a positive emotional reaction to the product through a simple classical conditioning process, pairing attractive characters, images, and sounds with the product.[23]

Since the 1970s, parallel technological, media, and social revolutions have helped to commercialize our lives. It is much easier to draw our attention to advertising in part because of a gradual trend that has increased our use of electronic devices—devices that in some cases are trying to sell us things.

Screen Life and Hidden Algorithms

In a simpler time only a few decades ago, parents worried about how much time their children spent watching television, but now we are festooned with an expanding array of audio and video devices, all of which beg for our attention. A 2016 Nielsen Company report determined that Americans spent an average of 10 hours and 39 minutes a day consuming media, up over an hour from the 2014 estimate. Live television and radio were still the winners at 4.5 hours and 1.8 hours a day respectively, but smartphones had seized third place at 1.65 hours. By 2016, 94 percent of homes had HDTV and half of all homes had streaming video on demand services, such as Netflix, Hulu, or Amazon Prime.[24]

Our devices are incredibly addictive, so much so that social scientists routinely warn us about possible harms. We are all urged to limit our daily screen time, and the tempting pull of our phones has become a serious highway safety problem.[25] Given the amount of time we spend engaged with these electronic gizmos, it is not surprising that they have emerged as a major conduit for advertising.

The field of "digital marketing" is still quite young. Our devices and their capabilities change rapidly, and marketers are still figuring out how to "monetize" digital content and tempt us with products we never knew we wanted. What is quite clear, however, is that all those hours of screen time provide an almost limitless opportunity for exposure to advertising, and as of early 2017, it was estimated that marketers spent $72 billion in digital advertising.[26] There are a few spaces where ads do not penetrate. When we buy subscriptions to Netflix we pay to watch movies and television programs without commercials. Similarly, most applications used on computers—such as Microsoft Office and Adobe Illustrator—provide an ad-free workspace. But digital advertising's tentacle-like penetration of our screen life surges ahead at a dizzying pace. Free smartphone apps often include annoying "pre-roll" videos or banner adds. Web pages are cluttered with banner ads and auto-play videos that require us to hunt around for the elusive "x" that will close the window or stop the commercial before we can read an article or see a video. App and hardware developers can also use the desire to avoid advertising as an income stream by offering ad-free versions of smartphone apps, podcasts, and Kindles at a higher price. But on cable television, commercial radio, and most websites, we are bombarded with banner ads and commercials. Even when you pay a monthly fee to read a newspaper online, it is not uncommon to open the front page in the morning and discover that over half the screen is taken up with advertisements.

In this new digital world, many of the basics of advertising are unchanged from the halcyon *Mad Men* days of the 1960s. Catchy advertising copy and attractive images are still important, especially in the traditional or "legacy" media of television, radio, and print advertising. But as we have adopted new technologies and moved our lives online, new advertising technologies have come along to tempt us in ways Don Draper never imagined.

Google has been a pioneer in finding ways to target advertising to the unique whims of consumers. Google is by far the most popular search engine in the world, handling an estimated 64 percent of all searches. That means Google knows what we're investigating and what we desire. Furthermore, Gmail, Google's e-mail app, has topped 1 billion users, which means Google knows what we talk about when we send e-mails to our mothers.[27] In addition, whether you are at your computer at home or on your cellphone out in the world, Google often knows your location and can use Google Maps data to customize the advertising that it shows you. All of this means that when we search Google, the list of results and accompanying advertisements we see are determined by an algorithm that takes into account what they know about us. The shoes you checked out on your iPhone or mentioned in an e-mail to your friend haunt you in banner ads on all of your devices for days after, hoping you will be tempted to click and buy. The result is often so uncanny it makes you think Google is reading your mind—and in a very real sense that is exactly what the company is doing. It is no wonder that privacy issues are a continual concern.[28]

But Google's reach goes far beyond the Internet. In 2017, Google announced that it had established connections with bricks-and-mortar businesses, making it possible to track the credit card transactions Google users make when they leave home and buy things at traditional stores. Working with undisclosed partner companies, Google claimed to have access to 70 percent of all credit card transactions, which, when combined with their own user data, gives the Internet company enormous potential to assess the effectiveness of its ad campaigns.[29]

Facebook, the highly addictive social media platform, is the other giant of the digital advertising world. In May of 2017, the web-based program Mark Zuckerberg created in his Harvard dorm room had topped 1.28 billion daily users—or approximately 17 percent of the world's population.[30] Naturally, if you are using the service that much, then Facebook knows a lot about the things you like. As a result, the ads that appear in your news feed or in the spaces around your news feed, are geared to your age, gender, location, and tastes. Other social media platforms, such as Twitter and Instagram, use similar approaches, blending paid advertisements into the regular content. As of this writing, some of the newer platforms, such as the phone-based picture- and video-sharing program Snapchat and the Internet messaging and phone application Whatsapp have not yet solved the monetizing puzzle, but if the usual pattern holds, these companies will wait until they have a large, devoted base of users before introducing ways to present advertising or other sources of revenue.

It has all happened so quickly. Today we are never far from a screen. Many of us have one in our pocket that is connected to both a cellular phone network and the Internet. We gaze at our screens while cooking, eating, and doing the laundry. We look at them upon waking and just before sleep. If we are honest, some of us even check in the middle of the night. And if by chance, we don't carry a screen around with us, the modern world is here to provide. Televisions can be found almost anywhere. Today, any professional office or business waiting area is likely to have a television running. There are TVs at the doctor's office, the hairdresser's, the car repair shop, airport waiting areas, and the fitness room of the local gym. For years, televisions have been a common feature of bars, but the introduction of flat-panel sets has made it possible for TVs to come into the dining room of many restaurants without using up valuable floor space.

Screens everywhere means commercials everywhere. There are a few places—buses and cars—where it is possible to have a screen but technical problems have as yet prohibited the presentation of cable programming. As a result, movies without commercials are more likely entertainment for the bus passenger or the child in the backseat of the minivan. Everywhere else—including on airlines that offer it—live television programming comes with commercials. But the ubiquity of advertising is only one aspect of television's effect. It also projects images that teach us about beauty, style, and technology. People in sitcoms and dramas tend to be just a bit better off than we are. Their clothes are nicer, and their homes are more appealing. So as we watch, we absorb information about a kind of life we would like to have. Eventually TV lives begin to look typical. We may not have all the things the people on TV have, but the world on the screen convinces us that it is normal to want to have them. Television and movies hold up a kind of mirror to our material worlds. Reality may not be exactly like what we see in the mirror, but the face in the screen is one we are justified in wanting.

The media revolution of the last few decades has resulted in a concentration of most of our media outlets in a very few corporations. In 1983, fifty companies controlled over half of all media outlets; by 2016, just six corporations controlled over 90 percent of outlets.[31] The radio giant iHeart Communications, Inc. (formerly Clear Channel Communications) owns 858 radio stations in 150 US markets and boasts 250 million monthly listeners.[32] By 2011, The Big Six media companies controlled 70 percent of cable programming. There continues to be a very spirited debate about the effects of media concentration on our democracy, but whatever the sociopolitical impact, it is clear that the concentration of media in a few corporations has changed our consumer culture. Later in this chapter I have more to say about cultural trends that affect our desire for products. For now, I want to emphasize that in a world where media companies are able to construct enormous interconnected groups—stacking media outlets vertically on top of each other—there are many new ways to create the kind of buzz that energizes the spending public. For example, in May of 2017, during the ongoing investigation of Russian influence on the previous year's presidential election, CNN ran a story about the cover of *Time* magazine, which featured an image of the White House decorated with Russian onion domes. Both CNN and *Time* are owned by the Time Warner Corporation. The ABC News program *20/20* has been known to use a segment to promote a new Disney movie release.[33] Disney owns ABC. There are many other examples of this kind of cross-promotion.[34] With a little coordinated programming, a media conglomerate can easily create tremendous exposure for a product offered by one of its companies. In addition, it can offer similar cross-platform exposure to its advertising customers.[35]

Interestingly, at the same time this corporate consolidation has helped to turn us into clone-like buyers of the latest must-have item, the new media revolution has also been splitting us into many separate groups. Most dramatically apparent in the algorithm-driven world of the Internet, this splitting is also clearly visible in cable television. The Internet is a very rapidly growing segment of the advertising market. In 2006, it represented less than 3 percent of all US advertising dollars, but by 2016 digital advertising had reached a 38 percent share of the ad market, far outpacing radio with 9 percent and just behind television's 42 percent.[36]

For the moment, television still leads the advertising field, and historically TV has played an important role in the move to targeting product pitches to receptive audiences. In the 1970s, the great majority of households had a television set, but fewer than 10 percent had cable television. That meant that everyone, regardless of personal taste and demographic niche was watching the same three commercial networks. The expansion of cable television was once considered a very controversial issue. I have a vague memory of being asked to sign a petition opposing deregulation of cable at a movie theater, but in the 1980s deregulation passed. Cable soon spread throughout the country, and before we knew it anyone could watch Animal Planet or the World Fishing Network.[37] With diverse viewing choices came better-targeted advertising. Commercials for toys and diapers could be scheduled for Nickelodeon and the Cartoon Network; ads for Mercedes-Benz and Zales diamonds appeared on CNBC; Budweiser and Nike ads were shown on ESPN1 and ESPN2. Later, Google and Facebook developed much more effective targeting methods, hacking into our brains to monitor and control the neurons of our every desire, and soon digital advertising may have the biggest impact on our lives. But, for now at least, television is still the most popular screen of all.[38]

Television commercials and web videos have remarkable power to shape attitudes with images, motion, and sound. This kind of advertising has tremendous flexibility, and its creative potential is limited only by the imaginations of the ad people who use it. But TV advertising is very expensive, and despite its proven effectiveness, it has its problems. For example, new, more advanced television sets allow viewers to avoid commercials. Mute buttons have been around for some time, and many TV watchers use them religiously. More recently, TiVo and other digital video recorders (DVRs) make it easy to fast-forward past commercials, and as previously mentioned, there is a growing trend toward watching movies and TV series through commercial-free subscription services. Technology has opened up new ways to present advertising, but it has also threatened many old ones. As a result, marketers have begun to explore new methods of keeping their products in our faces.

At the Movies

I am old enough to remember a different kind of movie experience than is usually found today. As a child who was sometimes lucky enough to be deposited at the local theater on Saturday afternoon while my mother went off to shop, I enjoyed the short films that were shown before the main feature. For me, the *Flash Gordon* serials starring Buster Crabbe were the most memorable. Well into my college and adult years, movies were preceded by a *Road Runner* cartoon or some other short amusement. There has long been movie advertising in the form of previews of coming attractions, but provided they don't go on too long, audiences seem to have a high tolerance for previews viewed in the movie theater. Somewhere along the line the cartoons and short features disappeared and we began to be subjected to advertisements for Coke or jewelry or the local mall. Movie patrons are a captive audience that is fairly attentive to what is being presented on the screen. As a result, they are a good target for advertising. However, in contrast to television, where we understand that commercials are the price we pay for an otherwise low-cost form of entertainment, most moviegoers believe that ticket prices of $13+ should insulate them from the onslaught of commercialism. So there is a limit to what advertisers can hope to accomplish with traditional commercials at movie theaters.

Nonetheless, because today's television viewer has a greater ability to avoid commercials by TiVo-ing or by purchasing commercial-free forms of programming, marketers are increasingly using the content itself, the movie or television program, to sell products through the relatively subtle art of product placement. The placement of identifiable products in movies and television programs has been a serious form of marketing for a long time, with MGM maintaining an office for the solicitation of product placements as early as the 1930s.[39] Steven Spielberg's 1982 Oscar-winning hit *E.T.* was a modern advertising breakthrough. Reese's Pieces were featured in the story line, and according to Hershey, sales of the candy shot up 65 percent in the months following the film's release.[40] This marketing effect impressed the advertising industry, which began to exploit the power of product placement much more deliberately.

The beauty of product placement or product integration is that it is less disruptive than other forms of advertising and can even enhance the effect of the movie or television program by creating greater realism. We live in a highly branded world, and when an actor picks up a generic can of soda or uses a computer whose origins have obviously been obscured, this lack of verisimilitude serves as a subtle reminder that we are looking into a false world. On the other hand, once we know about product placement, heavy-handed display of brands and identifiable products can also be a distraction.

Today there are product placement agents who read scripts and meet with set designers to determine where products might be displayed on the screen.[41] Apple has been particularly effective in getting its products placed in both television programs and movies. It was one of the first technology companies to hire a representative in Los Angeles whose job it was to secure product placements.[42] The major studios also have their own departments for soliciting placements and working with product placement agents, and in recent years, this has become a big business. In the pre-*E.T.* days, product placements were often done on a barter basis, with placements exchanged for services, but now advertisers pay dearly. Heineken reportedly paid $45 million to have James Bond slake his thirst with their brew in the 2012 movie *Skyfall*, and the 2011 film *Transformers: The Dark of the Moon*, displayed seventy-one recognizable brands.[43]

Because product placement cannot be avoided without missing some of the story, its use will likely continue, and industry experts expect placements on television to increase.[44] Furthermore, digital technologies are quickly making product placement a more flexible and targeted strategy. Sports fans know that first-down lines can be digitally superimposed onto the football field during live broadcasts, and this technology is also used to project a rotating series of billboard ads behind home plate in televised baseball games.[45] The cutting edge of product placement is the digital insertion of products into prerecorded television programs and movies, making it possible for Jennifer Aniston to hold a Starbucks iced coffee in a rerun of *Friends* shown in the New York City market and a Dunkin Donuts iced coffee in the Boston market.[46]

There are a number of ethical concerns about the use of this form of advertising, particularly with respect to the marketing of cigarettes, and certain heavy-handed forms of product placement can backfire. For example, Netflix was quickly panned for ham-handed displays of Ford Fusion cars and other products,[47] But product placement is on the rise, and it has begun to move from the screen to other media. For example, British writer Carole Matthews admitted to accepting money from the Ford Motor Company to write a red Ford Fiesta into one of her novels, and Fay Weldon was paid a promotional fee by the Bulgari jewelry company for her novel *The Bulgari Connection*.[48] In addition, although magazine and print journalists are not supposed to accept money from advertisers, the standards seem to be slipping—particularly in the areas of food and fashion, where the boundaries between content and advertisement are very blurry.[49] Finally, besides networks promoting their own products in newsmagazine programs, many morning news programs demonstrate or promote specific products in "lifestyle" segments, and, unknown to many viewers, some of these segments are paid for by marketers. Although the atmosphere is often breezy and casual, that food segment you are watching may be nothing more than an embedded commercial pitch paid for by the cooking oil producer.[50]

The Leading Edge of Exposure

If all this were not enough, advertising is appearing in places we have never seen it before. For example, conventional two-dimensional ads have begun to appear on airplane tray tables (Microsoft), on subway turnstiles (Geico), on the insides of elevator doors (CBS), on the shells of supermarket eggs (CBS), and on the disposable paper linens of a doctor's examination room (Children's Tylenol). Huge digital billboards have updated a traditional form of outside advertising. Now computer control makes it possible to change the content of the billboard frequently and match content to the time of day. Smaller screens providing news and advertisements are being installed in taxicabs and office building elevators. Finally, the billboard genre has gone to new heights with the projection of advertising on skyscrapers. Toyota has projected advertisements on buildings in Chicago, Atlanta, and Dallas. For the consumer, there is little hope of a commercial-free space; and for the advertiser, the challenge is to fill every tiny hole with a message. In the words of one advertising executive, "We never know where the consumer is going to be at any point in time, so we have to find a way to be everywhere. Ubiquity is the new exclusivity."[51]

As the foregoing suggests, much of the culture of selling and spending that we now endure has come on the backs of new technologies that we have so readily adopted. This culture of commercialism may be less a reflection of the superficiality of our modern values and more a function of marketers' clever use of the many screens and headphones we have become so enamored of. These devices have wonderful qualities, making them hard not to love, but in our free market society, they also represent new avenues for advertising, new windows on desire.

NEW TRENDS IN THE MANUFACTURING OF DESIRE

Although much of this book is aimed at how our new economic environment affects our relationship with money—the physics of wanting and spending—several broad cultural trends have also affected our behavior in the marketplace. Yes, we are exposed to more advertising than ever before, but the content of that advertising has changed as well. Old appeals are being used more extensively or in new ways, and new techniques have emerged to make us reach for our wallets more often.

Shopping as a Leisure-Time Activity

Shopping has long been promoted as something to do for fun or to pass the time. In particular, the golden age of department stores from 1880 to 1920 popularized the image of the strolling shopper. The great downtown emporia were sumptuous palaces that made shopping an experience akin to visiting a foreign land. The spectacle of merchandise displayed in enormous quantities and in daunting varieties made the mundane chore of shopping into an adventure.[52] In addition, window displays were more meaningful in an era when more people lived in the center cities. Before television and the Internet, brightly decorated shop windows attracted the attention of passersby and kindled the flame of desire. If the shop was open, the stroller could step inside and make a purchase, but because window-shopping could take place at any time of day, it also became a popular after-dinner amusement. The brightly lit windows provided something of a show and were often compared to movies, a relatively new form of evening entertainment.[53]

Although they have suffered substantial declines in recent years, shopping malls and other bricks and mortar retail settings retain some of this function.[54] Families with young children use the mall as a replacement for the city parks that were left behind in the migration to the green lawns of suburbia. Often there is a play area, a train ride, or some other children's amusement, and the bathrooms are always equipped with changing tables. Mall movie complexes bring crowds, particularly in the evening. The food court has a variety of fast-food options for children and adults, and the whole environment is climate-controlled. It never rains at the mall. You have to drive to get to there, but once you are inside, the environment is even more conducive to recreation and relaxed shopping than the central cities of a century ago. When he created the original concept of the suburban shopping mall, the architect Victor Gruen had very lofty civic goals for this new commercial structure. He believed that in addition to providing citizens with their "physical living requirements," the mall could serve their "civic, cultural, and social community needs."[55] Not all these goals have been realized, but for a segment of the population, the shopping mall is a popular place to spend leisure time and money. Similarly, IKEA is designed as a shopping and entertainment destination, complete with a supervised play area for children and a cafeteria featuring inexpensive Swedish delights.

At home, the blurring of entertainment and shopping continues on the tube. Television is largely an entertainment medium. Even television news and educational programming now seem to survive largely on their entertainment value. Advertising and commercials are a necessary evil, but sometimes they become the programming itself. During off-peak hours, many cable channels fill out the schedule with "infomercials," lasting thirty minutes to an hour devoted to selling a single product: a juicer, exercise machine, or rotisserie oven. Similarly, cable channels such as QVC and the Home Shopping Network make home shopping into a new form of window-shopping.

It is a short step from cable shopping channels to the curious phenomenon of YouTube haul and unboxing videos—recent developments that show the democratizing effect of the Internet. With YouTube, anyone can become a star. YouTubers make money from pre-roll ads that run just before their content appears, but some people have taken it to the next level by becoming amateur hucksters. For example, haul videos typically feature young women who display and describe purchases made on recent shopping trips. Often the host of the video sits next to a large shopping bag, and clothing, cosmetics, and other items are revealed one at a time. The YouTuber (aka "vlogger") spends some time talking about each item, explaining everything she likes about it. In the case of clothing items, she may also model the purchase in the video.[56]

The more male equivalent of haul videos is unboxing videos. In this case, the items displayed are often technology products or sports equipment. There are some women who make unboxing videos, and going against gender stereotype, YouTuber Jason Robert Keef specializes in unboxing toys and dolls.[57] Unboxing videos are shot either over the shoulder of the host, so only their hands and the product can be seen, or in a frontal shot with the YouTuber becoming the star of their own little advertising show. These videos often start with a very affectionate examination of the packaging itself ("I love the design of this box!"), which serves to build suspense.[58] Apple products are known for their beautifully designed packaging and have long been popular subjects of unboxing videos. After the package is finally opened, the host typically goes over the features of the product in great detail.

In the case of both haul and unboxing videos the descriptions of the products are almost entirely positive. The hosts appear to be enthralled with the items, and as a result, YouTubers who are able to attract large numbers of subscribers to their channels also attract lucrative deals from product marketers. It is estimated that YouTube haul and unboxing videos achieve billions of views each month, and these videos are easily shared through social media. Some of the most successful video hosts have over a million subscribers, and some apparel companies attribute as much as 10 percent of their revenues to these Internet stars.[59]

The picture-sharing smartphone app Instagram is also filling up with advertisements. Instagram users periodically come across actual paid advertisements in their feeds, but amateur Instagramers regularly post photos of clothing or other products in the hope of becoming paid "influencers" or spokespersons.[60] In a trend that will undoubtedly continue, cyberspace is being invaded by a wide array of professional and amateur marketers.

The Branded World

Our possessions say a lot about us. Our houses, automobiles, clothing, and many other objects are clearly visible to others and tell the wise observer about our tastes, interests, and status. Historically, many societies have placed a special emphasis on clothing, making it a kind of uniform of social class, and laws were enacted to enforce the social hierarchy. In ancient Egypt, only people holding important positions could wear sandals, and in medieval and Renaissance Europe, special sumptuary laws strictly regulated the kinds of dress of each social class. For example, in 1510 the parliament under Henry VIII passed "an Act agaynst wearing of costly Apparrell."[61]

> No man under the degree of lord is to wear any cloth of gold or silver, sables, or wollen cloth made out of England, Wales, Ireland, or Calais. Velvet of crimson or blue is prohibited to any one under the degree of a knight of the garter; no person under a knight (except sons of lords, judges, those of the king's council, and the mayor of London) is to wear velvet in his gown and doublet, or satin or damask in his gown or coat.[62]

The restrictions on cloth made outside of England show that economic protectionism was an additional goal of the sumptuary laws, but the primary objective of these regulations on dress appeared to be to keep the underlings in line. Social status was communicated in an easy-to-understand dress code.

Today the ability to pay is the only restriction on the kinds of clothing or other status objects we can buy, and because everyone has a credit card, even this restriction is often blurred. A poor, unemployed person can quite often charge—and wear for all to see—an Armani suit. Still, credit cards cannot bridge the gap between a poor person's desires and a new Ferrari sports car. We associate such luxury items with the wealthy classes because usually it is impossible for the rest of us to legally possess them. So without the formality of sumptuary laws, five centuries after Henry VIII's parliament, we can often tell the haves from the have-nots—if not from their clothes, then from their zip codes and automobiles.

But the communication value of material possessions goes well beyond social class. How often have we heard a friend utter something like "Elyse, you should buy that dress—it's so *you*"? It is often said that clothing is the most personal and expressive of all material goods.[63] Because we wear our clothes on the outside, everyone else's extended self is visible to us. In a culture that places great value on appearance and image, being able to see everyone else's stuff creates the potential for desire. We see people we envy or admire and we make note of their clothes and possessions. Social psychologists call this *social comparison*, and depending up where we see ourselves in relation to our reference group— the people with whom we would like to be associated—we can feel good or bad about ourselves. For example, studies have shown that smart students at less selective colleges feel better about their abilities than equally smart students at a more selective college, a phenomenon known as the *big-fish-little-pond-effect*.[64] Because they fare better in relation to their reference groups, the students from less selective schools are happier.

We all want to be happier, and often our possessions make us so. But in today's world, it is hard to avoid social comparisons about material possessions, and in addition, our reference group has expanded greatly. No longer do we judge ourselves in relation to our neighbors and coworkers. Today, we are much more likely to see reference groups and desirable material extensions of identities on television and in magazines. Our fascination with celebrity and image tends to create a constant motivation for upward mobility—often displayed in clothes or other socially expressive material possessions. Products have images and evoke judgments about the people who buy them. As a result, marketers have come to understand that by making social comparison easier, they can often sell a product. When I was in college in the late 1960s and early 1970s, jeans were the rage, much as they are today. Levi's seemed to enjoy a kind of dominance over other brands, and although bell-bottoms (!) and other styles could be found, jeans did not come in the many variations they do today. Neither did they make the kind of fashion statement they do now. But in the late 1970s and early 1980s, the designer jean phenomenon was launched by companies including Jordache, Calvin Klein, Gloria Vanderbilt, Sasson, and Guess.[65] Designer jeans were substantially more expensive than Levi's, yet people were willing to pay for the name. Today many new designers have come into this highly competitive market, and what was once a fairly simple, almost meaningless purchase is now laden with great social significance. For example, today at Macy's I could buy a pair of True Religion Men's Super T Geno Slim-Fit Jeans for $329. Below this are many well-known name brands. Levi's, which now come in many different cuts and styles, are at the high end of the name-brand nondesigner category. Lee and Wrangler are also in this category but do not command the same prices as Levi's. Below this are the more generic store brands, such as JCPenney's Arizona and Kohl's Sonoma, and at the very bottom are a number of budget no-name brands.

What makes all this brand information about jeans important is that it is so visible. The Lee jeans I am wearing as I write this section have the word *Lee* in large letters on a leather patch on the back. This patch is obscured whenever I wear a belt, but on the front a small embroidered label is clearly visible, sewn into the seam of the coin pocket. Both of these brand labels are so firmly attached that most people would be reluctant to remove them for fear of damaging the pants. Other manufactures stitch the designer name or logo on a rear pocket. Similar brand information is attached to almost every visible piece of clothing we wear. Especially in the area of sportswear and casual clothing, the person who sets out to buy a generic T-shirt, sweatshirt, or pair of sneakers, shorts, or pants will have a very difficult time. Marketers have discovered that the use of company logos and visible brand labels is a very important part of advertising, and as consumers, we have come to accept that many of the things we own will force us to become walking billboards for the companies whose wares we have purchased. Meanwhile, if wealth and style are not the arenas you want to compete in, the marketing world will provide others. For example, the success of the Prius hybrid car has been partly attributed to Toyota's decision to give it a distinctive design. Other car manufacturers who entered the hybrid market by creating hybrid versions of existing models did not fare as well because driving a Prius provided a visible badge of environmental virtue.[66]

This is not a book primarily about the commercialization of America. Rather, it is about the new physics of spending and wanting. But commercialization plays an important part in our desire for new stuff. By teaching us all of this brand information, marketers have given the smallest aspects of our lives social and economic meaning. Everything is a product, and not just a product but a branded product with a certain status or cachet. As a result, our wants are often tied to specific brands that capture our attention, and they capture our attention because they communicate something about us or about some reference group we wish to be associated with.

There have been many periods of commercialization in our history. Perhaps the first important one came in the nineteenth century with the rise of mass-produced goods and central-city department stores, when shopping became an entertainment—an activity separated from its purely utilitarian function. But the 1980s and 1990s were also a time of growing commercialization. Several books have documented our contemporary consumer society, but perhaps the best of these have been written by the economist Juliet Schor.[67] In *The Overspent American*, Schor documents how branding and social comparison have created an environment of competition among consumers for the latest desirable objects of the day. In *Born to Buy*, Schor shows how children are being taught brand information at a very early age and are becoming the commercial conduit into the household. For example, marketers have gained access to children during the school day through Channel One, a news broadcast for teens that, according to company documents, is shown in eleven thousand high schools and junior high schools nationwide and is seen by more than six million children a day.[68] Since 1990, Channel One News has offered programming free to schools, which get the twelve-minute daily news broadcast in return for two minutes of commercials. It turns out there are limits to the level of commercialism communities will tolerate. In 2004, a company called BusRadio found a way to take advantage of the time children spend riding the bus. Bus Radio installed free radio equipment on school buses and provided free music, news, and public service programming, as well as eight minutes of commercials per hour. As compensation for this marketing scheme, school districts received a cut of the advertising revenues. But BusRadio was highly controversial from the beginning, with many parents objecting to the further encroachment of advertising and programming into the lives of their children. The less intrusive, 12-minutes-a-day approach of One Channel News has survived for over 25 years, but in September of 2009, BusRadio signed off for good.[69]

When Wants Become Needs

In our heavily branded world, advertising is everywhere, and the desire to buy can build gradually and strike at almost any time. We compare ourselves to others, to the faces that stare back at us from newspapers and magazines, and to the people on TV, in the movies, and on the Internet, and these comparisons often leave us wanting—wanting what we see but do not have. But sometimes we are moved to spend not because we want to but because we must. The popular image of the indebted American is often one of people who have frittered away their financial resources on needless items even they no longer value. But, as we have learned, this popular image is often wrong. The majority of debtors are not mindless chargers and spenders. Furthermore, many people get into money trouble not because they spend too much on luxuries but because they spend too much on necessities—or at least what they believe to be necessities.

One of the points Juliet Schor makes so effectively in *The Overspent American* is that many things once thought of as luxuries are now considered necessities. With some exceptions, the general trend is in the direction of greater need. For example, in 1973 home air-conditioning was considered a necessity by 26 percent of Americans, but by 1996 that number had risen to 51 percent. Furthermore, the trend has continued in the same direction in the intervening years. In 2006, fully 70 percent of respondents said that home air-conditioning was a necessity, not a luxury (see Figure 6.2).

In 2006 and 2010, the Pew Research Center surveyed Americans about what they considered to be necessities, and the results are a good indication of the effects of changes in technology and a recession on American's needs and wants.[70] Cellular telephones, which in 1991 were considered necessary by only 5 percent of Americans, were considered a need by 49 percent of us in 2006. They dropped only slightly, to 47 percent in 2010, when unemployment was at its highest rate in decades.[71] Clothes driers, home air conditioning, microwave

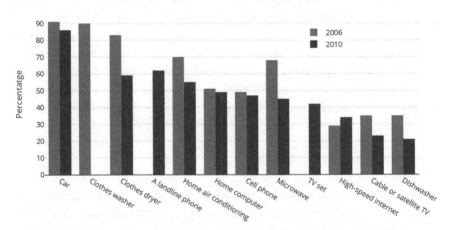

Figure 6.2 Percentage of respondents rating each item as a necessity based on surveys conducted by the Pew Research Center in 2006 and 2010. A single bar appears when one question was not asked in both years.

ovens, and dishwashers were all judged to be less necessary in the recession-era 2010 survey than they had been in 2006. The drop in cable or satellite TV, combined with the increased necessity of high speed Internet, probably reflects the ongoing shift of our attention to online media. Pew has not conducted a recent follow-up of this poll, but it is likely that as we move back into better economic times and credit becomes increasingly available, many of these items—or new ones we have yet to imagine—will once again be perceived as necessities.[72]

What's going on here? One interpretation is that in good times we get spoiled. Once we got along with much less and were happy as clams, but now we have become needy, narcissistic couch potatoes. But before we blame the victim entirely, we should recognize that many of the items listed in these surveys are new. They have not always been with us. As the authors of the 2006 Pew study put it:

> The old adage proclaims that "necessity is the mother of invention." These findings serve as a reminder that the opposite is also true: invention is the mother of necessity. Throughout human history, from the wheel to the computer, previously unimaginable inventions have created their own demand, and eventually their own need.[73]

Who is to say where the line between a need and a want should be drawn? How about between a necessity and a luxury? One could argue that most of the items in Figure 6.2 are really not needs. Though it would be difficult to work in some professions without a personal computer, life will go on quite well for most people without a microwave oven or a dishwasher. Indeed, in much of the world it does. There are ways to get your clothes clean without owning your own washer and dryer. Despite our sprawling suburban lifestyle, even not having a car can often be managed. But when an invention is really good, when it makes a big difference in your life, it is easy to think of it as a need and not a want. Furthermore, once a new invention is widely adopted, the social pressures begin to kick in: everyone I know has a smartphone, so I guess I'd better get one. Depending on your reference group, the list of necessities can be quite long.

To say the period since the 1970s has been one of incredible technological development seems more than obvious. So many aspects of our lives are different now. But new innovations create new demand. They ratchet up our needs, often without substituting for the old needs. For example, two 2015 Pew Research Center studies showed that 64 percent of Americans owned a smartphone, and that 67 percent of households had broadband Internet at home. Lower-income individuals are more likely to rely on their smartphones for Internet access, undoubtedly due to the cost of home Internet service. But it is clear that for most people, smartphones have come as an addition to—rather than a replacement for—home Internet.[74] So thanks to the ratcheting up of our needs, many of us are now paying separate streams of money for cellular phone service, smartphone Internet access, and household Internet access.

Product innovation creates desire and costs us money. But some of the largest dents in our budgets have come from innovation in health and medicine. The most profitable drug in 2016 was Humira, a treatment for a number of disorders, including arthritis and Crohn's disease, that brought in $16 billion for its maker, AbbVie.[75] Humira was first introduced in 2003 as a treatment for rheumatoid arthritis, and acquired FDA approval for other uses in subsequent years.[76] For the patients suffering from these painful diseases, the introduction of Humira is something of a mixed blessing. It brings the hope of substantial improvement in symptoms, but if your insurance doesn't cover it, Humira can cost as much as $6,660 per year.[77] This is just one example of a product that, once introduced, must somehow be absorbed into the budgets of millions of people. Health is the trump card. Humira does not appear on the Pew survey list of necessities because no one would question whether it was a necessity or not. If prescribed by a physician, Humira is not a luxury. The cell phone has been around longer, but Humira easily beats it out on the want-versus-need dimension.

The rapid rise of Humira is a dramatic example of medical innovation, but it is not the only one. Today there are new medicines being produced at a rapid pace, and their manufacturers are marketing them directly to consumers every day. If we just restrict ourselves to the drugs we have encountered in television commercials, then most of us know there are new prescription medicines for heartburn, impotence, insomnia, allergies, arthritis, asthma, diabetes, depression, irritable bowel syndrome, opioid-induced constipation, overactive bladder, restless leg syndrome, toenail fungus, and many other conditions, and narrators urge us to "Ask your doctor about whether (name of drug) is right for you."[78] Research, funded both by the biomedical industry and by the government, continues to produce rapid innovation in medical diagnostics, therapeutics, and devices, but pharmaceutical costs are rising at a greater pace than medical costs as a whole.[79] Not all Americans are covered by health insurance, and those who do have coverage are paying higher premiums and co-payments to cover the rising costs. So for many people, particularly those on the lower half of the income curve, the new healthcare necessities are a substantial strain on the budget. Yes, the benefits produced by these new medical technologies are often immeasurable: five of the most profitable drugs in 2016 were treatments for cancer.[80] But the great value of these innovations is precisely what makes them the economic trump card. When faced with a medical emergency, most people will do anything to get a lifesaving treatment—including taking on enormous debt. Can we really blame them?[81]

Medical product innovation is perhaps the most dramatic case of the rising cost of necessities, but there are many others that come close. For example, according to the Pew survey, 86 percent of Americans believe that owning a car is a necessity, and because America has largely rejected public transportation in favor of highways and suburban sprawl, many people would find this an easy purchase to justify. But cars need fuel, and the cost of fuel is not under the consumer's control. Gasoline prices have been relatively low in recent years, and automobile sales have recovered from the lean recession years.[82] But global events could easily bring back $4 per gallon prices, putting a strain on many household budgets. The problem of unexpected car repairs is even more troubling. A 2017 AAA study found that one in three US drivers could not manage an unexpected repair without going into debt, a statistic that is a restatement of the $400 financial fragility measure we encountered in chapter 2.[83] In the coming chapters we meet several people who encountered financial problems, and car repairs come up again. Gas and car repairs do not show up in the Pew survey, but because Americans have made cars an almost universal necessity, gas and repairs are necessities, too. Similarly, heat and shelter were not covered in the Pew report, because they are assumed to be necessities. But when the furnace goes out, or the price of fuel oil or housing goes up, consumers must absorb these costs—not out of want but out of need.

The discussion of luxuries versus necessities has led us into the territory of larger economic issues that bring uncertainty and strain to household budgets. Without question, the shape of our economy, with its particular network of jobs and social services, plays a large role in the contemporary epidemic of debt, foreclosure, and bankruptcy. I have more to say about these issues in the final chapter, but for now it is clear that modern America provides its citizens with many reasons to spend. Whether they are the subtler wants produced by our branded world and the expanded role of advertising or the more insistent demands of a growing list of necessities, most of us have no shortage of pressures on the family budget. Now we turn to the many ways these pressures turn into spending: how desire becomes action and want becomes an exchange of money.

FRANK

Frank's voice was a soft baritone with the remnants of a southern accent. There was no evidence of twang or rural colloquialism in his speech, just the lengthened vowels and meandering tones befitting an educated gentleman who had lived away from the South for several years. He was a tall man who might be an imposing figure were it not for his curly brown hair and gentle manner. At age fifty-six, he was a retired army officer currently employed as a business manager for a nonprofit agency, and he had $60,000 in credit card debt.

Frank grew up in rural Mississippi. His father dropped out of school after the sixth grade and went to work at the local textile mill. Frank's mother, who did not finish school, either, married his father when she was sixteen years old. There were four boys, spaced approximately three years apart, of whom Frank was "the baby."

Frank's parents were strict Baptists and instilled in their children a strong work ethic. "Everything was a sin. Smoking, drinking, dancing. We were not allowed to have cards or games in the house. Anything that might be fun was a sin."

When he was a senior in high school, Frank joined his father on the second shift at the mill, but he soon escaped to the army. Military life suited him. After basic training, he worked as a military police officer, and he was good at his job. After his first tour of duty, he went home and back to the mill, only to reenlist a few months later. When he came home the second time, he brought his young wife, whom he had married while stationed in Texas. Carol had grown up in a big city and had a college degree, and rural Mississippi life did not appeal to her. Frank was back in the mill. Neither of them was happy.

Between Frank, his father, and his three brothers, someone from Frank's family was in the mill twenty-four hours a day. As one brother ended his shift, another began, and by now Frank's father had been working in the mill for twenty-five years. He was a weaver on the day shift. Also on the day shift, Frank could look across the room and see his father toiling at his loom, and he saw a future for himself that he did not want. So for the third time, Frank quit the mill and looked for more satisfying work. He tried selling insurance and serving as a "chaser" for a bank, hunting down people who were behind on their bills. A year and a half later, he reenlisted.

Frank's return to the military was the beginning of a much happier period in his life. Carol gave birth to a baby boy, and eventually they were transferred to Germany, where they found a life they both enjoyed. When their son was old enough, he attended an American school on the base, and the couple became very active in the community. Frank was elected to the council of their local church, and he and Carol established a youth club for the children of the base.

Their work in the community was so outstanding that Frank and Carol won a commendation from the base commander.

In Germany, Frank encountered slot machines for the first time, and he liked them. As a boy in Mississippi, pinball machines had been one of the sinful activities he discovered in town away from his parents' supervision. The machines he had played in Mississippi were very simple devices with few lights and no bumpers or flippers. The object was simply to shoot the balls so that they fell into holes on the playing surface. But in Germany, casino-style one-armed bandits that paid out cash prizes were legal, and these machines could be found in the officers' clubs and the sergeants' mess. Frank noticed that once he started playing one of these machines, he wanted to go on and on, but he was able to control his play. The slot machines were a casual entertainment for him, not an obsession.

Except for an eighteen-month stint in New York State, Frank was able to secure assignments in Germany from 1969 until his retirement from the military in 1985. By this time their son had finished high school, and Frank and Carol were ready to enter a new phase of their lives. In the kind of sweet, self-sacrificing agreement that couples sometimes strike, Frank had promised his wife that if she followed him through his years in the military, he would follow her in the years thereafter. And Carol had plans. She had earned a nursing degree in college and had been a part-time nurse in Germany, but now she wanted to pursue a career in public health administration. She was accepted to a number of graduate programs in public health and chose to enter one in Connecticut. She received her master's degree three years later. In the interim, Frank's military pension enabled him to forestall looking for work and to return to school himself, in time earning a BA in business administration.

The couple both found jobs after graduation, with Carol landing a position as an administrator in a health maintenance organization and Frank finding work in the business office of a nonprofit agency. But he was not entirely happy. The changes in their lives left him somewhat unfulfilled. Carol's job kept her very busy, and as a result, he had more time on his hands than when they were in Germany. He was committed to the agreement he had made with Carol and genuinely felt she deserved the success she was enjoying in her new career. But their son was now on his own, and Frank was not involved with the community the way he had been in Germany. Because his job required that he drive around to different agencies and community centers, he was expected to be out of the office and unavailable much of the day, and he used this freedom to develop new pastimes. One of them was playing the lottery.

Connecticut, like many states, had a game called Lotto with a top prize that increased after each drawing until someone won. When he picked his own numbers, Frank used to play variations on his wife's birthday and other meaningful dates, but he often bought quick-pick tickets. One of his quick-pick tickets "hit" on five of the six numbers, the odds of which were 1 in 30,961. If he had been correct on all six numbers (odds of 1 in 7,059,052), he would have won millions of dollars, but five numbers still earned him the substantial prize of $4,050. Naturally, a win of this size was very exciting, and when he happened to mention it at the store where he bought the ticket, the owner said, "Now you're in trouble."

Recounting this to me, Frank added, "I didn't understand what he meant at the time, but later I did."

Winning a big prize fueled Frank's play. He began to spend more money on the lottery, sometimes buying as much as $50 worth of tickets for each twice-weekly drawing. He also bought scratch-off (instant-win) tickets that had relatively small, fixed-amount prizes. In Connecticut, prizes of over $600 had to be collected at a state lottery office, but smaller prizes could be obtained right away by redeeming the ticket for cash at the same place it was purchased. As a result, players often scratched off their tickets in the store or just outside. Frank quickly accelerated his involvement in gambling, and instant tickets allowed him to have the excitement of playing every day. At the peak of his involvement, he was buying between $20 and $30 worth of tickets a day.

Then an accidental encounter brought a different kind of gambling back into his life. When he bought lottery tickets, he tended to spread his business around to many different convenience stores and gas stations. He spent much of his time in the car, either making his rounds at work or commuting from home, and one day he discovered an illegal slot machine in a local convenience store. He began to play it on a regular basis, and this particular store became one of his daily stops. He applied for several credit cards, taking cash advances to pay for his gambling, and was frequently borrowing money from one to pay the bill on another. For a time he managed to hide his gambling from his wife, intercepting the credit card bills before she saw them. Eventually he could not live with his deception any longer, and he told his wife what he had been doing.

When I met him, Frank had joined Gamblers Anonymous and had not gambled for several years. In today's world, lottery tickets are everywhere, including at gas stations, but Frank did his best to avoid places where they were in evidence, for example, paying for his gas at the pump rather than going into a station. He was still married, still working, and still attending church regularly. When I asked him about the debt, he said, "We're knocking it down. It takes a while, but we're knocking it down."

New Ways of Spending

Eventually we began to figure gambling out: they take your money and
you go home.

—Frederick and Steven Barthelme

Tell me why I need another pet rock.
Tell me why I got that Alf alarm clock.
Tell me why I bid on Shatner's old toupee.
They had it on eBay.

—"Weird Al" Yankovic, *"eBay"*

Igor Ansoff was born in Vladivostok, Russia, in 1918; in the 1930s, he
emigrated with his family to New York City and entered Stuyvesant High
School.[1] He studied engineering in college and went on to receive a master's
degree in applied mathematics at Brown University. During World War II
Ansoff served in the US Naval Reserve, where he was both a liaison with the
Russian navy and an instructor in physics at the US Naval Academy. But after
the war Ansoff became involved in the world of business. He was hired by the
Rand Corporation and later as a planning specialist for Lockheed Aircraft
Corporation. He soon became one of the founding figures in the emerging
field of strategic management, promoting the view that by analyzing the market
environment and recognizing how it was changing, managers could increase
the growth and profitability of their companies. Ansoff went on to teach at
universities in the United States and Europe, publish several books and more
than 120 papers and articles, and found a successful consulting firm.

One of Ansoff's most important contributions was the product–market
growth matrix, which he introduced in 1965.[2] This table provided a simple

guide to manufacturers who were looking for ways to increase profits. The basic idea was that both the products or services a company sold and the markets or customers they sold them to could be either current or new. The various combinations of current and new markets and products are represented on the 2×2 table in Figure 7.1. For example, one strategy, known as *market penetration*, is simply to sell more of a current product to current customers. Once upon a time, one television per household was enough, but according to a recent survey, the average American household now has 2.3 working television sets.[3] But the modern strategy of television sales is not simply market penetration; many consumers discard working television sets in favor of newly purchased high-definition flat-screen TVs or Internet-ready smart TVs. Thus, new product development is another way for a company to sell more to its current customer base.

Ansoff's matrix was created for the benefit of marketers and producers who wanted to approach profit making strategically. Given a company's capabilities, the current business environment, and the likely changes in that environment, marketers could determine which of the four quadrants contained their best opportunities. During the period from the 1970s to the present, corporations have aggressively pursued all of these methods of achieving growth.

Several of the quadrants of Ansoff's matrix have produced rapid innovation in our social and economic environment, and some of these changes have made it much more difficult for us to balance our checkbooks. As outlined in chapter 5, the modern problem of financial self-control stems from the action of five variables: availability of the spending response, wherewithal, time, effort, and social barriers. The many technological innovations since the 1970s have

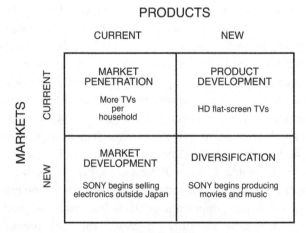

Figure 7.1 Igor Ansoff's product–market growth matrix.

produced new financial challenges involving each of these variables. Many more purchases are available than ever before, and spending is infinitely quicker, easier, and less embarrassing than it was in the past.

In the last chapter we saw how the development of new products can create new desires and needs. Technologies, once introduced into the marketplace, can—in the most successful instances—move from being fascinations to being necessities, and in this unprecedented period of rapid innovation, new product development has thrived. But much of what troubles us the most is not merely the result of changing wants and needs. The three variables of availability, time, and effort have been manipulated in ways that were impossible in previous eras. For example, as we will see, the Internet and other innovations have done much to capitalize on Ansoff's lower-left-hand square by bringing existing products to many more customers. Gambling, pornography, and large-scale auctions, once available to only a small segment of the population, can now be delivered to a much larger customer base. Furthermore, the time and effort involved in pursuing these activities have been greatly reduced.

What follows is a brief menu of modern temptation. Our world is changing rapidly, and therefore this list can never be complete and exhaustive. But I briefly outline some of the most important challenges to our self-control that have entered the marketplace since the 1970s. One of the most basic differences between today's world and the one that existed five decades ago is that we now do much of our spending at home. A generation ago, prior to the introduction of universal credit cards and toll-free lines, our homes were a relatively safe haven from commerce. Yes, we sat at the bill-paying desk and wrote out checks to the phone, electric, and gas companies, as well as to the local department stores where we had accounts. In addition, door-to-door salesmen were more common than they are now. But neither of these methods of spending at home comes close to the free and open marketplace that exists under our roofs today. Back then, you needed to visit a seller's establishment to spend in any serious way, and that physical restriction created a protection against financial demise. Today, thanks to the Internet and the mobile devices we carry at all times, there are no temptation-free environments. But before we enter the new world of spending in the virtual world, we take a look at how things have changed in the traditional marketplace outside our homes.

SPENDING IN THE PHYSICAL WORLD

Once we have a want, a desire for some object or service, there are a number of barriers that must be surmounted to complete the deal. As we learned in chapter 5, conquering the obstacles of time and effort are essential to the spending response, and another variable, social barriers, can be an important factor—particularly when spending in the physical world outside our homes.

Conquering social barriers has long been an important aspect of the growth of the consumer economy. Before the 1970s, relatively few women worked outside the home. Merchants understood that if married women could be convinced to devote their days to spending the money their husbands were earning, business would thrive. But the problem was that social constraints often kept women from venturing out. During the golden age of department stores, from 1880 to 1920, these establishments went to great lengths to make women feel comfortable in an era when many were reluctant to go out in public alone. Tearooms and large rest rooms, complete with comfortable furniture, helped to make women shoppers feel both pampered and safe.[4]

Another important obstacle is information. Many purchases are easy. When we buy generic items such as gasoline, butter, and pencils, there is little mystery. Of course, we pay attention to the price of the item, but we have no problem assessing whether it is a good buy or not, or in determining whether it will meet its intended purpose. Other purchases are more complicated. Cars, laptop computers, and insurance policies are multifaceted products. A car might get good gas mileage but be uncomfortable to drive and too small to haul much cargo. A laptop might be priced right and look great, but will it be powerful enough to play your favorite computer games? Furthermore, if you are already in search mode, you may need the assistance of a salesperson to explain certain features or even teach you how to use the product. In these cases, spending involves a direct social relationship with a salesperson. Even when the customer is motivated to buy and the seller has a product that will meet the customer's needs, the sale will go through only if the salesperson can help the buyer negotiate their information needs. The cellular telephone plan may be outlined in a brochure available in the store, but customers often need to ask questions before being convinced that the plan is right for them.

Once upon a time, the activities of buying and selling were much more social than they are today. For much of American history, particularly in the eastern cities, daily food purchases were made in outdoor markets or in large public market buildings, such as Quincy Market in Boston. This kind of shopping involved much conversation between sellers and potential buyers, and bargaining for a mutually acceptable price was common.[5] Of course, millions of people still shop this way in many parts of the world. Grocery stores were an outgrowth of the general stores that emerged in larger American cities during the seventeenth and eighteenth centuries, and service and bargaining were the norm. Even when stores specializing in groceries began to spread in the nineteenth and early twentieth centuries, shopping at the grocery store involved much contact with store personnel. The most common arrangement

Figure 7.2 Undated photograph of Weinhauer and Harm's Grocers in Wellsville, New York. The store demonstrates the common counter-and-wall service system. Used with permission of Darren Fleeger.

for grocery stores—and for most retail businesses—was the counter-and-wall service system (see Figure 7.2).[6] Merchandise was displayed in glass cases lining the perimeter of the store and on the shelves that covered the walls. Customers ranged freely in the center area of the store, while the shopkeeper or clerk stood in the alleyway between the counters and the wall. In most cases, customers were obliged to ask the clerk to hand over the counter each item they wanted.

Today, certain purchases are still conducted with substantial contact between the potential buyer and a representative of the seller. If you are shopping for a suit from Men's Wearhouse or for a Thomasville couch, the salesperson who is "up"—whose turn it is to take the next customer through the door—will greet you as you enter, and begin asking you a few questions: "How can I help you? What are you looking for?" In these stores, sales are often on a commission basis, and the salesperson lives or dies on the ability to determine a customer's needs and meet them. But this kind of highly personal, relationship-oriented shopping has been on the decline for a long time. For almost a century, the United States has undergone a self-service revolution in the consumer world. Social, informational, and physical barriers have been stripped away, making it possible for each individual consumer to do more without help. Unfortunately, the ease of self-service shopping also brings with it challenges to our self-control.

It All Began with Piggly Wiggly

Clarence Saunders was one of America's most innovative and unusual entrepreneurs. In 1916 he opened the first Piggly Wiggly grocery store in Memphis, Tennessee, and a mere seven years later there were twenty-five hundred Piggly Wiggly stores in operation. The success of these stores—despite the funny name—grew out of a number of innovations that changed grocery shopping and many other retail operations forever. Piggly Wiggly was the first self-service grocery store. Prior to 1916, the counter-and-wall service system was still the standard, and many items were stored in bulk behind the counter, which meant customers had to ask for their pound of beans and wait while a salesperson weighed out the correct amount and packaged it. Shoppers were completely dependent on the store's staff as they collected their provisions, and going to the grocer did not mean zipping in and out. Furthermore, prices often were neither displayed nor fixed, and customers were expected to bargain with the clerk.

Saunders changed all this. By 1916 many manufacturers were beginning to exploit branding and packaging to advertise their products. They realized that if customers began to request not just soap but Ivory soap, the manufacturer (in this case Procter & Gamble) would have an edge against the competition. Retailers would have to stock Ivory if they wanted to satisfy their customers.[7] This encouraged the use of paper wrappers and cardboard containers displaying the product name, and the use of uniform sizes and amounts that were designed for sale directly to the consumer (see Figure 7.3). All of this made shopping much more convenient, which increased sales.[8] Saunders went the extra step of advertising all his products and their prices in the local newspapers with the goal of "pre-selling" customers on his merchandise. Shoppers would enter the store already knowing what they wanted and would be able to find it on the shelf without the help of a clerk. In contrast to most other grocery stores, at Piggly Wiggly prices were clearly displayed, and bargaining was eliminated. As a result, the shopper had all the information required to make a purchase.

The Piggly Wiggly system, which was soon adopted by many other stores, cut through many of the social and informational barriers to buying food, and self-service shopping had come to stay. We tend to think of grocery shopping—buying our weekly supplies—as a simple utilitarian activity. Of course, this is not really true. The modern supermarket is filled with tempting luxury items,

Figure 7.3 Products as they appeared in the original 1916 Piggly Wiggly store. Prices were displayed on the tags hanging from each shelf, and products were clearly identifiable. Photo courtesy of the Memphis Pink Palace Museum.

from Ben & Jerry's New York Super Fudge Chunk ice cream to $20 bottles of balsamic vinegar, and impulse purchases can have a profound effect on how much we pay in the checkout line. Clarence Saunders's Piggly Wiggly was a great advance that benefited both grocery store owners and grocery shoppers, but it also placed new demands on the shopper's self-control. Furthermore, when the principles of self-service shopping pioneered in the grocery store were applied to other retail settings, the possibility of impulse spending spread to every corner of the market. Today, self-service shopping has advanced in ways that even the visionary Saunders could not have anticipated, and the hyperbola stalks us from big-box stores and over the Internet.

From approximately 1953—when I was three years old—through the end of the decade, my family and I lived in a suburb of Chicago, Illinois, and one of the more memorable events of that time was the arrival of our very first television set. Although by today's standards the screen was fairly modest, perhaps eighteen inches, the bulky picture tube—which displayed rather fuzzy black-and-white images—was surrounded by a wooden cabinet whose polished construction made it clear it was intended to be a piece of furniture. I also remember when we got our first stereo music system. This was a large wooden unit the size of a buffet table—an even more substantial and attractive piece of furniture, meant to be the centerpiece of the suburban living room. It had a walnut finish and contained two large speakers facing front, separated by a section of wood paneling. The turntable and AM/FM tuner were accessed through the top of the cabinet, and once the stereo was playing, these electronic components could be hidden behind sliding horizontal doors. In the first weeks after it arrived, the family spent hours lying in front of it on the carpet of our three-bedroom ranch house listening to specially produced LP records designed to demonstrate the wonders of stereophonic sound.

Today most American households have television sets—several of them— and stereo systems, but some things have changed. In the case of our 1950s electronic appliances, both pieces were brought to the house by deliverymen, and sometimes television sets were installed by the deliveryman or another serviceman from the store. These early TVs were often somewhat temperamental beasts, connected to large roof-mounted wire antennas that took on whimsical airplane or butterfly shapes. Both the television and the stereo must have been classic full-service store purchases. My parents would have gone to the local Marshall Field's, Sears, or Polk Bros. store, consulted a salesperson, and paid for an item that would arrive some days later.[9] This rather methodical process would have involved much consultation and interaction with store personnel.

The contemporary equivalent of these purchases is almost entirely self-service. Most television sets and stereo systems are purchased in big-box stores and brought home in the car or ordered online and shipped to your door. Stereo systems are dramatically smaller today than the one we purchased in the 1950s. My family's TV and stereo were powered by large vacuum tubes, but the invention of transistors and tiny integrated circuit boards has produced much more compact electrical devices. Today, most televisions and music systems are no longer considered furniture in the same way ours were in the 1950s, unless you want your flat screen TV mounted on the wall, most TVs and sound systems no longer require special delivery or setup. IKEA has been a leader in pushing the self-service envelope. Larger furniture items, such as couches, dining room tables, and bedroom sets have traditionally been the exclusive jurisdiction of the local full-service furniture store or large department store. By combining low prices and bit of do-it-yourself assembly, IKEA has made buying furniture a self-service same-day operation.

As these examples illustrate, self-service shopping is not just for groceries anymore. The style of self-directed shopping experience that Clarence Saunders introduced at Piggly Wiggly—which once stood in direct contrast to department store shopping with its highly personalized service—today is the dominant method of shopping in the physical world. Walmart, the world's biggest retailer and the United States' largest private employer, is a department store in the shape of a big box.[10] Most of the same departments and products one might find at Macy's or Sears—and many more—are represented, but all the merchandise appears in no-frills shelf displays. Plenty of shopping carts are available, and at many Walmart locations there are full-size discount grocery stores in addition to the usual departments. What were once two very different styles of shopping—department store and self-service grocery—have come together under one highly discounted, self-service, big-box roof. Something vaguely resembling the classic department store experience still can be found, most often at your local Macy's, Kohl's, Sears, Nordstroms, or JCPenney, but, until Amazon eventually surpasses it, Walmart will rule the world.

The Discount Store Movement

As soon as the great central-city department stores emerged at the end of the nineteenth century, an important competitive movement rose up to challenge these new behemoths. The grand scale and lavish displays of department stores offered a sense of luxury to shoppers who were primarily from the middle classes or above. In an effort to take advantage of the department store's class-consciousness, Frank W. Woolworth opened a store in 1870 that welcomed people from all social groups. The same rail transportation system and mass production manufacturing methods that made the department stores possible provided Woolworth with many inexpensive household items to sell. Initially, nothing in the store was priced higher than five cents, and bargaining was eliminated, all of which made the stores particularly inviting for the budget-minded shopper. In the 1910s, Woolworth's adopted the self-service methods popularized by Clarence Saunders and placed all the merchandise out on tables where it could be touched and handled by customers without need of a clerk. With their emphasis on low prices and a no-frills environment, Woolworth's "five- and ten-cent stores" were the beginning of the discount shopping movement, which even today stands as an alternative to full-price department stores.[11]

During the Depression, populist sentiment created a backlash against large chain stores, and legislation was passed that controlled the prices offered by discount stores in an effort to level the playing field and promote "fair trade."[12] But in 1948, the first E. J. Korvette store opened in New York City, specializing in appliances, and because its customers had to obtain a membership to shop, Korvette managed to evade the anti-chain-store laws. Korvette extended the concept of the large no-frills discount store, and by 1960, the company had opened forty-five stores in nine metropolitan areas.

When middle-class families began moving to the suburbs in the 1950s and 1960s, the discounting movement followed them. S. S. Kresge, a five-and-ten competitor to Woolworth's, became Kmart. Kresge stores, like Woolworth's, were typically located in downtown areas, but Kmart was designed as a large suburban discount store equipped with a parking lot. Kmart offered a wide variety of items so that shoppers could take care of many of their needs in a single stop. Zayre, Walmart, Bradlees, Caldor, Shopper's World, W. T. Grant, and many other discounters would soon follow. The basic approach was to offer brand-name goods in a bare-bones self-service environment designed to enhance the impression that the customer was getting a bargain. The message was "We're watching our costs so that we can give you the best possible price." Because of their large number of stores, discounters had considerable buying power and, as a result, offered 10 to 25 percent off standard retail prices.[13] Like Woolworth's, Kmart was designed to compete with the full-service, full-price department and chain stores, such as Sears and JCPenney, but now the competition had moved to the suburbs.

The next stage in the history of discounting involved compartmentalization. Some discounters chose to specialize in one category of product, hoping to corner the market in that area. Toys R Us, which has recently fallen to completion from Amazon, Walmart and Target, was the first of these focused discounters.[14] This was the beginning of the big-box system we see today. Best Buy; Bed, Bath, and Beyond; and Home Depot have become "category killers," leading sellers in a particular product area, however, even they have been challenged by Walmart and Amazon.com. If the big-box approach is to work, shoppers in need of electronics will automatically think of Best Buy, and dog owners in need of supplies will naturally end up at Petco. Traditional department stores have not completely disappeared, but many have been forced to adapt to the discount challenge, and in some cases (e.g., Sears and JCPenney) their long-term futures remain uncertain. Furthermore, today almost all the bricks and mortar retailers—traditional department stores and big box stores—are being threatened by the growth of Amazon.[15]

Self-Service, Discounting, and Self-Control

The self-service and discount movements in shopping emerged gradually over more than a century of American retail history, so these developments alone cannot explain why Americans are going broke, but self-service discount shopping has become much more pervasive in the last few decades. Combined with other factors, such as the increased availability of credit, the way we shop today is a powerful influence on our indebtedness. Furthermore, several important social trends have encouraged our obsession with discount goods. The most important of these involve women's changing roles, declining wages, and modern transportation.

In the 1970s, American women began to enter the workforce in large numbers. Today, the traditional *Leave It to Beaver* image of the stay-at-home mother and working father has all but disappeared.[16] Increasing numbers of adults are choosing to go solo, with over 28 percent of households being either a man or woman living alone by 2012. In the case of couples with at least one member in the workforce both people working is by far the most popular arrangement. Based on 2012 census results, this group represented 57 percent of male-female couples and 66 percent among same-sex couples.[17]

Looking back, there is a tendency to attribute this dramatic change to the women's movement. In the late 1960s and early 1970s, a burst of feminist activism encouraged women to take on roles that previously were reserved for men. Without question feminism was—and continues to be—a powerful social force. But in the 1970s and particularly the 1980s, inflation-adjusted wages for male workers at the median income level and below began to fall.[18] Many one-paycheck families discovered that the same level of income did not stretch as far as it once did, and as a result, many women entered the workforce in an attempt to maintain the family's standard of living or achieve the American dream of a rising standard of living. One effect of this phenomenon was to break down the previous role of the homemaker-consumer. As women began to work outside the home, there were much greater demands on their time. As a result, the classic form of department store shopping, in which married women ventured into the city for a leisurely, somewhat pampered experience, began to fade away. As we have seen, shopping as a leisure activity has not disappeared, but today most shopping in the physical world is increasingly directed to evenings or weekends.[19]

The decline in real wages had another effect on the American consumer: it created greater demand for low-cost items. As better-paying manufacturing jobs have dwindled, the United States has become a service economy. Except during periods of recession, employment has generally been high, but declining purchasing power has placed a much greater premium on low prices. Many people began to seek out deeply discounted items in an effort to keep their heads above water. Like earlier chain stores, large discount retailers are able to capitalize on economies of scale, negotiating very low prices from manufacturers in return for the prospect of huge orders. Computerized distribution and inventory management systems, combined with self-service shopping and low-wage labor, help to further control prices.[20] The result is discounting on a level that F. W. Woolworth never could have imagined. In the era of the $40 Walmart Blu-ray player, customers are willing to drive substantial distances in pursuit of savings. Which brings us to cars.

As we have seen, the automobile is still an integral part of the American way of life. We drive more than people in other countries, and we have more cars per household now than in the past. But the cars we drive have also gotten larger, and this trend has been a boon to self-service discount shopping.

The largest car my family ever owned was a 1959 Ford Ranch Wagon station wagon. It was one of the biggest cars available in the late 1950s and early 1960s, but it was tiny by today's standards. Now the roads are filled with minivans and sport utility vehicles that would dwarf our station wagon—vehicles that can't be squeezed into normal-sized parking spaces and that guzzle gas at alarming rates. Where did all these tank-sized cars come from?

The soaring popularity of very large family vehicles was prompted by a number of factors. Part of the trend was product diversification. The original station wagons were simply sedans with modified trunk areas. The 1956 Ford Parklane station wagon was a Ford Fairlane sedan in the shape of a wagon.[21] Minivans were designed from the ground up to be vans on car frames. They handled like cars, got relatively good gas mileage, and—because of their height—could carry much more cargo than station wagons. Sport utility vehicles (SUVs) were created by putting bodies that were reminiscent of station wagons on truck frames—producing a station wagon that rode higher and was not a variation on a sedan theme.[22]

The success of minivans and SUVs in the 1980s and 1990s was encouraged, in part, by favorable emissions standards. Most SUVs and passenger vans are classified as light trucks rather than cars, allowing manufacturers to dodge more stringent automobile emissions standards.[23] In addition, during the last decades of the twentieth century, the members of the baby boom generation were raising their own children, and many of them adopted the view that a larger car was safer than a smaller one. Finally, minivans and SUVs were designed to meet the transportation demands of soccer, Little League, and band.

But larger cars can carry much more than just kids and their backpacks. Big cars can hold big purchases. If you are anywhere in the United States and stand in the parking lot of a Walmart or any big-box store and squint a bit, you can easily imagine you are planted among a fleet of delivery vehicles. Much of the contemporary retail success story has been accomplished by maximizing the market penetration box of Ansoff's product–market growth matrix—that is, by selling more of the same stuff to the same people. Yet somehow consumers have to get all this stuff home. It is a hassle to arrange for a delivery and a disappointment not to be able to take immediate possession of your new treasure. All of this fuss is eliminated when you have an Escalade or a Grand Caravan in the garage. Removable or foldaway seats make it possible to transport stoves, refrigerators, and riding mowers. Wide-screen televisions are a snap. Thus, typical suburban dwellers are fully equipped to drive to IKEA with the confidence that if they find a suitable love seat or chest of drawers, they will be able to get it home in the same trip. Part of this confidence comes from the knowledge that the new piece of furniture will be unassembled and compactly packaged in a plain cardboard box, but much of it comes from having a vehicle with ample cargo space.

Ode to the Shopping Cart

And how do we get the stuff to the car? The shopping cart is an essential yet often overlooked piece of the twenty-first-century discount success story, and the use of carts has skyrocketed as self-service discount shopping has gained in popularity. This time the credit goes to Sylvan Goldman, owner—with his brother Albert—of the Standard Food Store chain in Oklahoma. In an effort to survive during the Depression, the Goldmans had converted their stores from traditional counter-and-wall full-service outlets to self-service groceries patterned after Piggly Wiggly. Wire hand baskets like the plastic versions found in grocery stores today were widely used, but Sylvan observed, "Customers had a tendency to stop shopping when the baskets became too full or too heavy."[24] To remove this barrier to buying more, Goldman mounted two hand baskets— one above the other—on a flimsy wheeled metal frame that was a variation of a folding chair. The result was the "folding carrier" depicted in the *Saturday Evening Post* cover in Figure 7.4. Eventually the shopping cart caught on, and future versions were designed to hold even more merchandise and to be nested together to simplify storage.[25]

It is difficult to exaggerate the contribution of the car-plus-shopping- cart nexus to the modern retail experience. Consider the place where it all began: the grocery store. Once upon a time, the trip to the open-air market or small neighborhood grocer was a daily ritual. Prior to the 1930s, refrigeration was not as common as it is today, and most urban shoppers had to carry their purchases home by hand, often lugging their packages up several flights to a walk-up apartment. But by the late 1930s refrigerators became larger and more affordable and supermarkets became more abundant. Soon the suburban housewife could substitute a single weekly visit to the discount self-service grocery store in place of daily trips to the local market.[26] Today weekly grocery shopping is the norm.

The big-box discount system also depends on shopping carts. In order to reduce labor costs and extend self-service to as many product categories as possible, big-box stores are all on one level. Increasingly, the stores are built without a curb separating the door from the parking lot, so a cart can be rolled smoothly from any point in the store to any point in the parking lot. Ideally the parking lot slopes slightly away from the store, so gravity aids the shopper in moving heavy items to the car. Clerks or "associates" must work a little harder to get the carts back up the hill, but the baskets are empty on the return trip. Today's carts are much larger than Goldman's original version because they must accommodate larger items, and most big-box stores have replaced the heavy wire construction of the early supermarket carts with plastic mesh models that are relatively light. Another advantage of the plastic design is that

Figure 7.4 Cover of the August 31, 1940, issue of the *Saturday Evening Post*, showing an example of the original Sylvan Goldman design of a folding carrier shopping cart. The illustration also depicts some of the temptations of self-service shopping. © 1940 SEPS: Licensed by Curtis Publishing, Indianapolis, IN. All rights reserved. www. curtispublishing.com.

the carts can easily be produced in the store colors: red for Target, orange for Home Depot, and green for Dick's Sporting Goods further strengthen brand recognition.

It is worth noting that, despite their growing importance in the American retail scene, shopping carts are not suited to all settings. The obvious example is the traditional regional shopping mall. It often has two or more levels, and stairways, elevators, and escalators—both inside the anchoring department stores and in the central areas of the mall—provide the means of moving between levels. Wheelchair users and others with mobility problems find Walmart a much more inviting environment. Furthermore, the mall is not a single store. It is a large collection of separately owned businesses, each of which has a different brand and different needs. Shopping carts would be out of proportion—not to mention totally uncool—at Gap, and they would not fit on the escalators at Macy's. In addition, a communal system of shopping carts to be shared by all the retailers in the mall would present a substantial management problem. From the point of view of the storeowner, it is simpler to deposit the customers' items in a shopping bag and send them on their way. Target, a Walmart competitor, depends on the use of shopping carts, and several deals aimed at making a Target one of the anchoring stores for regional malls have fallen through over the shopping cart issue. The mall didn't want them, and Target couldn't do without.[27]

Unlike the mall, the big-box store is designed to be as thoroughly self-service as possible. Most are like large storage facilities in which the customer assumes the role of shipping clerk in return for highly discounted prices. At Sears or another department store, most customers buying a large item such as a television would not be able to carry it directly out of the store. Instead, payment would be accepted in the electronics department, and the TV would be obtained a few moments later at a pickup window situated near the parking lot. This system is a great improvement over waiting for delivery several days later, as must have been the case when my parents bought our first set, but it represents a bit more hassle and delay than a typical big-box transaction. Compact packaging, convenient shelving, and a careful consideration of the physics of shopping carts and parking lots make it possible for customers to quickly take possession of even very large products. At Best Buy, it is even possible to get a washing machine or a full-sized refrigerator rolled out into the parking lot and put in the bed of your pickup truck.[28] The self-service shopping revolution has taken advantage of efficient packaging, shopping carts, and large cars to greatly extend the range of products the customer can take home in the family vehicle.

The Ballad of the Bottle

There is another technological development that demonstrates the importance of effort in the completion of an economic transaction. Up to now, much of our attention has been on the large muscles used in standing, walking, and climbing stairs, but consumer effort sometimes involves the smaller muscles of the upper body. For example, once you are a self-service consumer, equipped with a shopping cart, you must gather the items you want into your cart. If the product in view is heavy or ungainly, you are likely to leave it on the shelf for someone else to buy.

Consider the soda bottle. Prior to the 1970s, soda purchased for home use was sold in returnable glass bottles or in metal cans. Soda cans had advantages. They were relatively lightweight and could be tossed after use, but there were complaints about the taste of soda in cans, as well as safety concerns in the years before a workable pop-top system was introduced.[29] As a result, most soda was purchased in heavy glass returnable bottles. In hindsight, the reuse of soda bottles kept tons of materials out of the landfill, but even when sold in easier-to-carry six-packs, buying and consuming soda required much effort. Furthermore, store owners complained about collecting and storing the empties for return to bottling companies.

Back in 1941, two chemists working at the Calico Printers Association in England patented a new kind of plastic, polyethylene terephthalate (PET), that was considered safe to hold soft drinks and other fluids, but it was not until 1973 that Nathaniel Wyeth, brother of the American painter Andrew Wyeth, patented a PET bottle. Soon, single-use plastic soda bottles took over the market.[30] Aluminum cans with safe pop-tops remain popular, particularly for single-serving sizes, but PET plastic bottles have several advantages: they are strong enough to hold larger two-and-three-liter quantities; they don't break when dropped, making them both safer and less wasteful; and they are lighter.

For our purposes, it is this last characteristic that plays into the physics of spending. Imagine that you tip the scales at about a hundred pounds and are by no means a body builder. You're having a party soon, and you would like to buy enough Dr. Pepper and 7-Up to give your gathering a festive flair. Reason tells you that a few two-liter bottles would be a wise purchase, but you have to get them into your cart and out to the car. If the bottles were glass, this would be a more difficult and potentially riskier operation. You might ask for help, but many potential buyers would be reluctant to initiate social interaction. This is supposed to be self-service shopping. In 1970, Pepsi did introduce two-liter returnable glass bottles with a thick lip on the neck to help keep it from sliding through your fingers, but this form of container soon disappeared once Wyeth's plastic bottles hit the scene.[31]

In the science of spending, the important time period is from the idea to buy to the completion of the sale. In many respects buying soda is like the traditional 1965 purchase of Bill's new pruning shears encountered in chapter 5: you have to go to the grocery or convenience store to buy the beverages you want. But once there, you must still overcome the variables of effort and time to get your purchases from the aisle to the cash register. If the circumstances are too frustrating—unwieldy items, long lines at the cashier—you are likely to flee. Sylvan Goldman's shopping cart is a big help, and lighter, safer packaging—such as PET plastic bottles—also makes the job easier. Added convenience and lower effort in the shopping environment translates to higher sales. What happens after the transaction is less important to the merchant. Many of the conveniences consumers enjoy before they check out are paid for later on. The cardboard Amazon boxes and plastic soda bottles must all be organized and in some cases cleaned before we put them out in the recycling bins each week. (A friend once complained that modern life now compels us to wash our trash before we throw it away.) But by the time all these after-purchase inconveniences crop up, our money is long gone. The power of the hyperbola in our economic lives is all on the front end, pulling us toward quick and easy spending.

Information and Self-Service

For the nineteenth-century American, information was often a natural barrier to spending. The customer outside the store was often blind to what was being offered inside the store. Newspaper advertising was much less sophisticated, so buyers often discovered what was for sale when they saw it in the store window or walked in the door. Prices were not displayed and bargaining was often the accepted method of establishing a price, which meant that the shopping experience could be intimidating if you were not a member of the wealthier classes. Finally, shoppers were often completely dependent on the salesperson or clerk for information about the product under consideration. Together, the various obstacles of this heavily service-oriented system of selling produced a rather unwelcoming environment for the customer.[32]

One key to the success of the self-service shopping system was the breakdown of information barriers. Standardized, mass-produced, brand-name products took much of the mystery out of shopping. Once you had eaten a Uneeda biscuit, you knew what to expect the next time around. Shop windows became important vehicles for displaying both the products for sale inside and the prices the shopper could expect to pay. Clarence Saunders understood that if the self-service system was to work, the shopper had to have the information necessary to make a purchase possible, and he used newspaper advertisements as a way to pre-sell many items.

Today's consumer is pre-sold in ways Saunders could not have anticipated. It is sometimes difficult to separate the many ways we are enticed to want a product from the ways we learn about it. Greater knowledge and familiarity are important ingredients in a consumer's desire. But for many categories of products American shoppers have more information at their disposal today than ever before. As we saw in chapter 6, television was an important advertising vehicle from the beginning, and with the great expansion of stations made possible by cable television, the targeting of advertising to a particular audience became much easier. How-to programs have long been a source of information for consumers. These shows have the dual function of informing viewers about—and thereby creating demand for—new products and providing important support for the self-service do-it-yourself movement. PBS has long offered weekend how-to shows, and it has been joined by the Food Network, HGTV, and many other channels.

For consumers who are actively seeking product information, there are many more resources available. This kind of deliberate hunt for product information is most likely to occur when the item you are buying is expensive—making the consequences of a bad decision more costly. *Consumer Reports* magazine, founded in 1936, has long provided a relatively unbiased source of product information, and although the magazine frequently publishes the results of its tests of the most mundane products, such as peanut butter and oven cleaners, special attention is given to automobiles, appliances, digital cameras, financial products, and other items that often mystify the consumer. Similar types of product information are also provided by all the media discussed in the last chapter and in other specialty magazines. Finally, YouTube has become a limitless resource for do-it-yourselfers and those trying to decide what to purchase. In addition to the haul and unboxing videos we encountered in chapter 6, there are thousands of volunteer reviewers and instructors on YouTube waiting to teach you how to replace the bulb in your Honda's headlight or tell you what they like about their new Dahon folding bicycle. Recently I wanted to increase the memory in my laptop computer, but was confused as to how to proceed. After watching several YouTube videos, I was convinced I could preform the operation myself. Furthermore, my Internet instructors recommended the best kind of memory to buy and told me exactly what tools I needed to get the job done.

Even when you visit a big-box store, today's version of self-service shopping provides much more information for the consumer. For example, vacuum cleaners were once a full-service sales item. They were sold door-to-door or in department stores, where you would find an area of carpet and a box of sand (or some other dirt stand-in) ready for a customer demonstration. The shopper would be approached by a salesperson who answered questions and attempted to close a deal in the traditional manner. At today's a big-box stores, the self-service approach applies. Vacuum cleaners are displayed on the shelf; if necessary, it is often possible to find a salesperson to help you. But there is no test area provided, and the customer rarely gets a true sales pitch. Instead, as much information as possible is provided in the display. Typically an information card lists the product's main features (see Figure 7.5), and customers can easily move up and down the aisle comparing the costs and benefits of each model. Furthermore, most category-killer stores are big enough to provide many

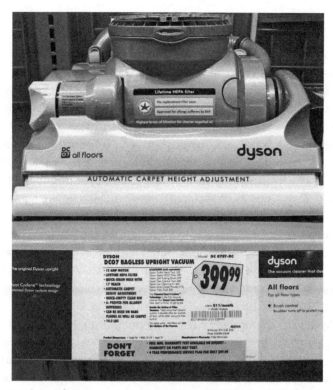

Figure 7.5 Product information card typical of big-box self-service discount stores. Photo by author.

choices, which tends to give customers the sense that they have considered many options before buying. When buying some products, such as computers and digital cameras, customers may want to consult a salesperson, but the big-box store is designed to provide as much information as possible to the buyer as a means of keeping labor costs down.

With all of this information at their fingertips, today's shoppers are much more knowledgeable and independent than their pre-1970s counterparts. Certain products and services will always require personal attention and the help of a salesperson, but today's marketplace has few dark corners. In addition, many services that previously required a professional, such as simple legal and real estate transactions, today have entered the realm of do-it-yourself tasks, and somewhere there is an entrepreneur who is waiting to sell you the tools you need for the job. Unlike pre–World War II America, today's economy is greased by a highly distributed sales force armed with remarkable levels of knowledge—the consumers. Today's customers sell themselves.

Drive-Thrus Redux

We last encountered drive-thru windows in chapter 5 as part of the discussion of the large-muscle hierarchy. The drive-thru window saves effort and time, and this kind of cruising for food has become a large part of the American diet. A 2013 US Department of Agriculture study found that, for the first time, meals purchased outside the home had reach 50 percent of all household food expenditures and that 37 percent of away from home spending was at "limited service restaurants," which includes fast-food restaurants, among other outlets.[33] Furthermore, in a 2016 press release in honor of National Drive-Thru Day (July 24, #NationalDriveThruDay), McDonald's reported that 70 percent of their total sales are earned at the drive-thru window.[34] The convenience of being served in your car has transformed the fast-food industry. Even Subway, the fast-food outlet with the largest number of stores, had drive-thrus at 10 percent of their shops as of 2017—despite the fact that ordering a subway sandwich typically requires considerable conversation between customer and staff.[35]

The physics of take-out and drive-thru purchasing have much to do with the popularity of fast food. Drive-thru windows are not truly self-service, but shouting at a disembodied speaker outside a Burger King is as close to self-service as you can get without having to use your large muscles. Perhaps buffet restaurants are the true equivalent of Piggly Wiggly self-service, but eating at most buffets involves getting out of your car and sitting in the restaurant—more effort, more time. The ease of drive-thrus is a powerful variable. At lunchtime, it is common to see a line of cars snaked around a Taco Bell or a Wendy's, waiting to make drive-thru orders while the dining room inside the store is empty. Furthermore, if you are on your way home from the beach and your swimsuit is still dripping wet, you might be reluctant to enter a restaurant, but the dress code is much more relaxed in the confines of your own car. Indeed, the social barriers are so penetrable at the drive-thru window that many people believe pajamas are acceptable attire for a late-night run for fries.[36]

DISCOUNTING YOUR WAY INTO DEBT

What's wrong with all this low-cost merchandise and self-service shopping convenience? In one sense, there is nothing wrong with it. Walmart, Target, and other big-box stores bring us more freedom of choice and shopping autonomy than were enjoyed by any previous generation. Most often we think of freedom of choice as an unqualifiedly good thing, but as we have seen, more choice

"What I don't like about these self-service stores is I'm always overselling myself."

Figure 7.6 Cartoon showing an example of Goldman's original shopping cart design. Reprinted from the *Saturday Evening Post* © Saturday Evening Post Society.

can sometimes be a burden. The discount store and self-service shopping movements have created new challenges to our self-control. As the cartoon from the *Saturday Evening Post* in Figure 7.6 shows, from the beginning the temptations of self-service shopping were clear: those who serve themselves are at risk of being overserved. Today's big-box stores have concentrated on three of the five variables involved in the spending response in an effort to make spending more likely.

The availability of the spending response is maximized by large category-killer stores that stock great quantities of goods and many choices of models.

It is still possible to go to Home Depot with a very specific brand and model of circular saw in mind and not find what you are looking for, but the sheer size of the place makes consumer disappointment much less likely. There will be lots of other circular saws on display, increasing the chances you will drop your specific demands and choose one of the others Home Depot offers. Big-box stores use their buying power to stock many more models than your neighborhood hardware store or even the tool section of Sears, making the profitable combination of product availability and buyer need more likely.

Two other variables, time and effort, have also been eased by the discount self-service movement. There is time involved in driving to a large regional store, particularly one such as IKEA, but compared to home delivery the operation is quick. The idea of obtaining the shiny new thing the same day has a powerful appeal, even if some assembly is required. Furthermore, because we drive to the store in a seated position, our large muscles don't have to work very hard, and we get to spend our travel time in a temperature-controlled environment with a radio and music included. IKEA knows that people often drive long distances to visit its stores, so the company makes the environment as kid-friendly as possible by offering Småland, a supervised play area, and a cafeteria featuring both Swedish and American foods.

Once we arrive at a big-box store, effort is minimized by the flat design of the store and parking lot, lightweight packaging, and the judicious use of shopping baskets, carts, and trolleys. As anyone who has waited in line at a department store checkout knows, the points in your shopping adventure that require the intervention of a store employee are the points where time is likely to stand still. In most cases, things are done more quickly when you do them yourself, and an important part of the true cost of a purchase is the time and effort involved in making it. But purchases that are easier and quicker to make—as in today's self-service big-box stores—are much more likely to happen. The hyperbola makes rapid purchases more attractive, and when we are spending the bank's money instead of our own, it is quicker and easier to go into debt.

If you are not convinced that the modern big-box version of self-service discount shopping is a powerful economic force, you need only look at the list of top retailers. Of the Forbes list of top retail companies in 2017, Walmart was easily the world's largest retailer with profits that are over twice that of second-place company, CVS Health. These big-box behemoths were joined by Amazon. com (third place), Walgreen Boots Alliance (fourth place), Home Depot (fifth place), Costco (seventh place), Lowes (eighth place), and Target (ninth place). To find a traditional full-service department story, you have to drop down to the Chilean store S.A.C.I. Falabella at eleven. Macy's, the largest US traditional department store, did not make the top-twenty-five list in 2017.[37]

WAGERING NATION

Throughout history, people have played games of chance for money or other rewards. The Hittites wagered on horse races four thousand years before the Christian era. The Chinese have gambled for more than four thousand years, and in Crete, Egypt, and India archeologists have discovered evidence of dice and gaming boards used between 1800 and 1000 BCE.[38] In an early example of sports betting, the Roman Colosseum provided the general public with the opportunity to wager on chariot races and combatant gladiators.

Gambling was so common among the troops during the Crusades that Richard I prohibited it among soldiers below the rank of knight.[39] After the Crusades, gambling was labeled a "Christian vice" and outlawed throughout the Islamic world, but it gained popularity elsewhere. The introduction of currency-based economies made gambling easier, and by the Renaissance, peasants and artisans gambled frequently in taverns and even in churches. Both Queen Elizabeth in the sixteenth century and Queen Anne in the seventeenth century used state lotteries to help finance public works projects and to support the colonization of America, and in eighteenth-century America, state-sponsored lotteries were again a common method of raising funds for government initiatives. The American Revolution was financed in part by lottery proceeds, and lotteries paid for the rebuilding of Faneuil Hall, the famous public market and meeting hall in Boston, and the construction of buildings on the campuses of Harvard, Yale, Princeton, and Columbia.[40]

Throughout eighteenth-century America, lotteries remained a popular fundraising tool used by both government and charitable organizations, and in the first half of the nineteenth century they spurred a new kind of private enterprise.[41] Brokerage firms opened shops in large cities offering lottery tickets at a commission. In 1831 Philadelphia had 177 lottery dealers, and comparable numbers were found in other cities. These businesses made it possible for players to participate in lotteries conducted in other states and served as exchanges for the different forms of currency in use at the time. Games were advertised in newspapers, and shops had names such as Kidder's Lucky Lottery and Dean's Real Fortune. But with the proliferation of lotteries also came corruption. In some cases operators either gave fewer prizes than advertised or failed to give prizes at all, and the prevalence of unscrupulous lottery operators gave ammunition to crusaders who had long opposed gambling on moral grounds. In the 1830s, states began to make lotteries illegal, and in the 1890s federal restrictions on use of the mails and on interstate commerce effectively ended the era of legal lotteries. From 1894 to 1964, churches and charitable organizations could operate bingo games and raffles, but there were no legal lotteries in the United States. Nonetheless, participation in foreign lotteries, such as the

Irish Sweepstakes, was allowed, and a survey conducted in 1938 revealed that 13 percent of those interviewed had purchased a sweepstakes ticket.

The reforms of the late nineteenth century merely drove gambling underground. The absence of legal lotteries led to a variety of illegal numbers-based games, and by the 1920s and 1930s, these illegal lotteries were very popular in America's cities. In New York and other areas of the Northeast, bookies offered a daily numbers game very similar to the ones run by many state governments today. For a small investment, players chose a three-digit number to play. Random winning numbers were determined by a variety of means; in New York the daily number was based on the win, place, and show results from local racetracks.[42] During the Great Depression, gambling declined, but from the 1930s through the present day, the promise of economic gain has been an important motivation for the legalization of gambling. Prohibition was repealed in the early years of the Depression because it had been widely violated and the government hoped a legal liquor industry would aid the nation's failing economy. A similar argument was used in 1931, when the governor of Nevada signed legislation to make all forms of gambling legal in that state. Further legalization of gambling would take decades, but similar economic development arguments would be used in each case.

Following the reforms of the nineteenth century, gambling on horse races was legal in only three states: Maryland, Kentucky, and New York.[43] But as pari-mutuel betting systems became more popular, other states began to allow this form of gambling. Prior to the advent of pari-mutuel betting, wagers at the track were made through bookies, who were notoriously unscrupulous. Racetrack bookies were independent of the track management, and for additional sums they would sell information about the horses that was often false. In some cases they fixed the races. Tracks that introduced pari-mutuel betting eliminated bookies by installing machines that sold tickets and set the odds for the races. Odds were determined by the betting patterns of the players, and the track merely took a percentage of the betting pool. Because the bettors were essentially playing against each other, the track had no financial interest in the outcome of the races, and the image of the sport improved.[44] By 1911, gambling at racetracks was legal in six states, and by 1963, twenty-six states allowed pari-mutuel betting on horse races.

The expansion of racetrack wagering in the earlier years of the twentieth century and the legalization of casino gambling in Nevada began the modern expansion of gambling in the United States, but gambling's great invasion during the decades since 1970 came in two parallel waves: state-sponsored lotteries and casinos.[45] In 1964, the state of New Hampshire, which has never raised revenues through income taxes, introduced the first state-sponsored lottery of the modern era. Other states saw the potential of this "voluntary tax" and soon followed suit. Today, forty-four states and the District of Columbia operate lotteries, and collectively, the states' gambling operations are comparable in size to the gaming industry. In 2015, total state lottery sales were $67 billion.[46] The adoption of lotteries as a means of generating revenue for state governments has given many more people access to this form of gambling, but perhaps even more troubling—given the enormously bad odds involved in this form of wagering—people are spending more money on the lottery. In 2005, the average adult living in a state where lotteries were legal spent approximately $198 on tickets over the course of the year. By 2014, that number had grown to $300.[47] According to Derek Thompson, writing in *The Atlantic,* 2014 sales in states that run lotteries exceeded the amount spent on sports tickets, books, video games, movie tickets, and recorded music sales in all fifty states combined.[48] It is clear that a lot of people are spending a lot of money on Powerball.

The second wave of gambling's invasion has been the dramatic proliferation of casinos, and "limited stakes" games found in bars, restaurants, and other establishments. Before 1990, casinos were limited to Nevada and New Jersey, but today there are over a thousand bricks-and-mortar casinos spread across forty states. In addition, there are fifteen thousand bars, restaurants, and other venues offering limited-stakes gambling across six states, and there are nine firms offering legal online gambling to residents of Nevada, New Jersey, and Delaware.[49] A 2016 Gallup poll found that 26 percent of adults had visited a casino in the last year, and 49 percent had played the lottery.[50]

Over the last fifty years, gambling has become as American as apple pie.[51] Pari-mutuel forms of betting, such as on horse racing, dog racing, and jai alai, have declined in popularity, but the twin powerhouse money machines of commercial gambling and government-sponsored lotteries have become almost ubiquitous. As I write this in 2017, much of the recent growth in commercial gambling has come from the introduction of limited stakes games in the state of Illinois and Internet gambling in Nevada and New Jersey. In 2016, fully 64 percent of American adults reported placing some kind of a bet in the past year.[52] Furthermore, Figure 7.7 indicates that demand for wagering appears to be relatively recession-proof. Gaming industry and state lottery data show that overall revenue for both commercial gambling and lotteries barely flinched in 2008, maintaining their gradual upward paths. In contrast, the number of automobiles sold dropped by over 35 percent from 2006 to 2008. It is often easy to put off the purchase of a new car in hard times, and growth in the lottery and gaming industries benefited from the ongoing expansion of new games to new markets. But in good times and bad, gambling has its pull. Unless you are a gambler yourself, you are likely to underestimate the impact of this form of entertainment on the American economy.

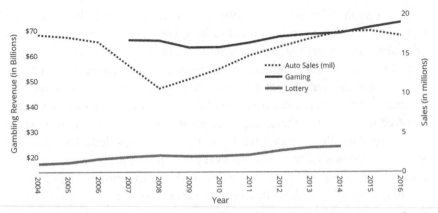

Figure 7.7 The growth in gambling revenue appears to be relatively recession-proof. Revenue for the US gaming industry is shown as total sales, whereas revenue for state lotteries is shown as total revenue minus prize money.
sources: RubinBrown LLP, "Gaming Statistics '17" http://www.rubinbrown.com/ Gaming_Stats.pdf; Federal Reserve Bank of St. Louis [auto sales] https://fred.stlouisfed. org; and the US Census Bureau.

Americans are spending much more on gambling than we were before the 1970s, but what role does gambling play in the parable of bankruptcy and our contemporary indebtedness? Research in this area is difficult to do, and the results have been inconsistent. But a recent large-scale study showed that areas where the types of gambling available expanded show increased levels of high-frequency gambling (over one hundred times per year).[53] Other studies have found that, compared to people elsewhere, those who live near a casino have higher than average levels of indebtedness and bankruptcy.[54]

Whether proximity to a casino is a risk factor or not, one thing is clear: gambling is a bad bet. The odds are stacked against the player, and in the long run, the more often you play, the more you will lose. There is a reason the casinos are so luxurious and state legislators are so enamored of the lottery. Some people make a living as professional gamblers, but they are a very exclusive group. Most are either poker players, card-counting blackjack players, or sports bettors who are successful handicappers. Poker is a game based on both skill and luck, and very skilled players can make a living at it. However, working as a professional poker player is not an easy life. Most must work long hours to make enough money to get by. Counting cards in blackjack can theoretically give the player an advantage over the house, but because most casinos use four or five decks of cards at a time, this strategy places extraordinary demands on the player's memory and concentration. Few players are able to master the skills required, and if they do, they risk being ejected from casinos if they are suspected of using a counting strategy. Finally, some very skilled handicappers can make a living gambling, but very few people fall into this category. One study found that only twenty-one career horseplayers in the entire United States could verify that they made their living at the track.[55] Thus for the overwhelming number of long-term players, gambling is a losing proposition. The house comes out ahead.

Despite the odds, Americans continue to gamble more and more, even as their attitudes seem to be changing. The gambling industry may deny a relationship between wagering and financial problems, but the betting public sees it differently. Recent surveys show that approximately two-thirds of Americans believe gambling is morally acceptable, but 70 percent of respondents in a 2006 Pew poll agreed with the statement "Legalized gambling encourages people to gamble more than they can afford."[56] Before 1972, when the state of Connecticut introduced the lottery, Frank, the man who was profiled before the start of this chapter, would not have encountered legal forms of gambling on his return to the United States.[57] It is difficult to say how much America's new romance with gambling contributes to our national indebtedness, but it seems clear that, combined with many other financial obstacles, gambling—a pastime that is particularly efficient at draining your bank account—does its part to help break our personal banks.

SPENDING IN THE VIRTUAL WORLD

The expansion of legal gambling in recent decades is a clear example of a previously unavailable spending response being made available for the first time, a form of what Ansoff would call market development. There were raffles, church Bingo games, and casinos in the world, but prior to the 1970s, most people in the United States did not have nearby legal opportunities to play. That is no longer the case. But the greatest expansion of spending opportunities has come in the wake of a telecommunications explosion, most notably in the last twenty years but beginning long before that. There has been a revolutionary change in the economic landscape, but it did not happen smoothly. The encroachment of the marketplace has come in a number of stages, as new technological advances were introduced. In addition, a number of social barriers had to be overcome before people felt comfortable being consumers in the new virtual world.

Stage One—Phoning Away Dollars

The first step in the process was a home invasion. In the 1960s home was a quiet sanctuary from the world of commerce When I was a child, a door-to-door salesman sold us a World Book encyclopedia set that helped me research many a school assignment, but door-to-door sales were extremely rare and never presented a serious challenge to self-control. We were free to think about other things and not be confronted with decisions about whether to buy or not. All that changed with the introduction of wide-area telecommunications service (WATS lines) in 1960 and the subsequent adoption of toll-free numbers by many businesses in the 1970s and beyond. Toll-free numbers made catalog ordering free and quick, and the trifecta of product desire, consumer credit, and toll-free numbers brought impulse shopping into our homes. In 1976, the L.L. Bean catalog arrived in the mail, and for the first time, you could go directly from the catalog to the phone to make a purchase. For most people, prior to 1976 L.L. Bean products could be ordered only by mail. The introduction of credit card orders taken by phone had the benefit of both greater convenience and a shortening of the delivery time. The delay involved in sending your order to Maine was eliminated, as was the hassle of writing out checks, filling out order forms, licking envelopes and stamps, and putting the order in the mail. The introduction of credit card orders taken by phone had a powerful effect on the mail order business. By 2006 only 2 percent of L.L. Bean's orders were received by traditional "snail mail."[58] The rest were received either by phone or over the Internet via the company's website.

Catalog mailings declined sharply following the Great Recession, but in the last few years, mailings have begun to recover. Even JC Penney, a traditional department store chain that is currently struggling to survive has reintroduced its catalog after discontinuing it in 2010.[59] It is tempting to browse through an attractive catalog that comes in the mail, and if the catalog does its job, you are moved to make the purchase based simply on the images and text you see on the page. This form of quick and convenient at-home shopping continues to be very popular.

Stage Two—TV Shopping

The second stage was the same as the first with the addition of a more effective catalog. Long before Amazon.com was the dominant mode of home shopping, television became a moving catalog that allowed us to order stuff from the couch. It all started in 1977 when an advertiser could not pay what he owed a Clearwater, Florida, radio station. According to legend, the radio station accepted 112 electric can openers in lieu of cash and auctioned them off over the airwaves.[60] The can openers sold out quickly, and the station soon initiated a radio shopping program, offering a variety of products that could be ordered by calling in. In 1981, the Home Shopping Channel was launched on a Tampa Bay–area local cable access channel, and by 1985 the company had gone nationwide, carried on cable systems throughout the country twenty-four hours a day. In the following year, a second shopping channel was introduced, called QVC (Quality, Value, Convenience).[61] QVC is the cable channel portrayed in the 2015 biopic *Joy*, starring Jennifer Lawrence as Joy Mangano, the inventor of the Miracle Mop. When Mangano was allowed to go on the air and sell the mop herself, she sold 18 thousand mops in a half hour.[62] As the number of channels offered on cable and satellite systems expanded, these two home shopping powerhouses spurred a diverse group of offerings, including the Evine, Jewelry Television, Shop LC, and others.

Shopping by television has a certain appeal. In an era of anonymous self-service shopping, QVC and HSN provide a return to service and attention to the shopper all blended with an easygoing form of entertainment. Attractive hosts and celebrities prattle on about the item of the moment, making an old-fashioned but relatively low-key pitch. The great majority of home shopping customers are women, and much of the programming is devoted to jewelry, clothing, and cosmetics. Generally, these are luxury items—nonnecessities— which shoppers would not be automatically drawn to purchase, so the salesperson must provide information about the product and its manifold features to kindle the motivation to buy.

But the success of television home shopping is not just a question of companionship and successful pitch making. The home shopping format is a well-honed system designed to encourage impulse buying. The physics of this environment make it remarkably easy to be separated from your money. In the beginning days of home shopping networks, the only things that might force you to leave the living room couch were the searches for your credit card and the phone. Now many people complete their orders using a smartphone app, tablet, or computer, where credit card and order information can be stored. Purchase time is just as quick or quicker than with catalog shopping, but these channels encourage impulsive purchases by selling in real time, with limited quantities. As the orders come in, the screen displays a decreasing number of units still available, and viewers are urged to move quickly or miss out. Everything is sold at a discount, and many items—whether they are expensive or not—can be purchased under an "easy payment plan" that spreads the charges to your credit card across several months. All of this has the effect of hurrying the customer to the phone or device to order before the segment ends.

By definition, this is impulse buying. Most people who have a particular item in mind would take a more direct approach and seek out specific stores or Internet sites where the thing is likely to be found. If you were looking for a gift for your mother and knew that she likes jewelry but you had no specific piece in mind, an HSN program might be a means of getting ideas. But this is a fairly passive way to go about solving your gift-giving problem. The typical home shopping viewer is probably watching both for entertainment and in search of a possible shopping experience. As we have seen, the lines between shopping and leisure have been blurred. Just as product placement turns a movie into a commercial, home shopping turns shopping into home entertainment. If they are not careful, today's home shoppers discover that the hyperbola comes into the house through the cable wire and pulls money out through the phone or Internet line at a remarkably rapid clip. Recently, the home shopping channels have suffered some decreased profits due to both the recession and the expansion of Internet commerce, but the remaining networks have adapted to the new environment by offering online streaming of their programming and online ordering. QVC, the most successful shopping network, had $8.7 billion in revenue in 2016, with $4 billion coming from Internet ordering. As a result, thirty years after their introduction, home shopping channels remain a unique but viable feature of the commercial landscape.[63]

Stage Three—Where's My Money?

The Internet launched the largest commercial invasion of our lives, intruding on our every waking moment. We can now buy anything the Internet has to offer at any time and in any location where a cellphone or wifi signal is available. But a number of challenges had to be overcome before we got to where we are today. The first of these was the money part, and the solution came from an unusual quarter: the pornography industry.

Sometime in the 1970s, while in graduate school, I attended a party that included a pornographic movie, a twenty-minute black-and-white feature that came on Super 8 film in a metal container. It was the kind of scratchy contraband that, in those days, was passed from hand to hand because very few people knew where to purchase it. There was *Playboy* magazine, which was fairly easy to find, but real pornography was hidden away in seedy adult bookstores in the bad parts of town. With few exceptions, sexually explicit films were universally deplored, and the reputation of the pornography industry was such that the few adult movie theaters that existed were considered places only the truly depraved would consider visiting. Except for *Playboy* magazine, pornographic material was encircled by social barriers so impenetrable that products of this nature represented a self-control problem for only a very tiny—and rather unsympathetic—segment of the population.

Today things are very different. It is estimated that Americans spend between $10 billion and $12 billion a year on pornography.[64] Pornography is distributed over the Internet, on cell phones, and on cable systems, both as subscription channels and pay-per-view. As a result, the industry has achieved such respectability that some of the largest corporations in the country make substantial profits by distributing adult content. Comcast, the largest US cable provider, offers adult programming to any subscriber who is willing to pay, as does Time Warner Cable. DirecTV, the largest satellite TV provider, features several adult subscription channels, as does the DISH Network. Not that long ago, hotel rooms provided a private environment for watching pornography on the room TV, but the Internet has destroyed that business. LodgeNet Entertainment, once the leading hotel cable system provider of on-demand adult movies filed for bankruptcy in 2011.[65]

Pornography is a product with special requirements. Because even now it carries a stigma, people usually want to be alone when they consume it. They also would like to have as little contact with other people as possible during the act of purchasing or renting adult material. When it comes to the physics of spending on pornography, the social barrier variable looms large. It is this need for privacy that made the invention of the videocassette recorder an important breakthrough in the modern expansion of pornography. The Sony Betamax was introduced in 1975, and by 1977 the first adult movie was put on videocassette.[66] The sexual revolution of the 1970s had made pornographic material much more acceptable, but with the introduction of a convenient—and increasingly affordable—method of watching this material at home, people who would never go to a movie theater to see *Deep Throat* or *Behind the Green Door* were buying or renting copies of X-rated movies on tape.[67] In the early days of video recording and playback systems, pornography was a major driving force, with X-rated videocassettes representing half of all sales in the United States by the end of the 1970s, and in 1980, German and British distributors reported that adult material represented 60 to 80 percent of sales.[68] The popularity of VCRs expanded rapidly in the 1980s, with more than 60 percent of households owning one by 1989, and as a direct consequence, adult movie theaters began to fail.[69] In 1980 there were an estimated 1,500 adult movie theaters in the United States, and nine years later that number had dropped to 250.[70]

When the Internet arrived it represented a tremendous opportunity for selling stuff, but first there were a number of social and technological problems to solve. As in the case of the VCR, pornography was the tail that wagged the dog. Long before Amazon.com or many other Internet-based businesses were making a profit, Internet pornography was in the black. The industry succeeded by pioneering secure methods of payment online.[71]

The growing popularity of the Internet provided the complete elimination of the social barriers associated with obtaining X-rated material and also allowed the customer a much wider array of choices. In the 1970s, pornographic material was rather generic and undifferentiated, but in today's much wider market, inexpensive video production methods make it possible to produce niche products. As a result, the customers can shop for their preferred flavor of porn, pay for it, and consume it without ever having any contact with a live person. This is the perfect marketing environment for a product that requires privacy. The primary problem was payment. Catalog and home shopping channel customers were comfortable giving their credit card information over the phone, but the Internet was a new and somewhat worrisome technology. In those early days, customers were reluctant to enter credit card information online and, due to the very real problem of credit card fraud, vendors did not want to accept credit card payments without a system of immediate verification. Because they recognized the unique potential of ecommerce for their industry, pornographers were the first to pioneer the secure payment methods we use today. For a humorous and somewhat fictionalized account of this bit of technological and financial history, see the 2009 film *Middle Men*, starring Luke Wilson.

Stage Four—I Don't Know You

Solving the payment problem made Internet commerce possible, but to realize the full potential of the online marketplace, a few other obstacles had to be overcome. As described in the modern-day version of Bill buying the pruning shears, ordering a product over the phone or the Internet means we must wait longer to hold the item in our hands, but for many people, the trade-off of delayed possession in return for greater shopping convenience—and often a substantially lower price—is worth it. The other great advantage of Internet commerce is a dramatic expansion of another variable in the physics of spending: the availability of the spending response.

Amazon.com began with books first, but after establishing a strong base in that market (and reshaping the bricks-and-mortar bookstore business in the process), the company began to move into other product areas and to sign up affiliate companies to sell their wares through the Amazon website. Today almost any nonperishable item that can be shipped to your house is available through the Amazon.com portal. And, because Amazon already has your credit card and shipping information stored, it is very convenient to take advantage of their patented one-click ordering technology.[72] Maybe there are other bargains hiding elsewhere on the web, but once you know how the Amazon system works, it's very tempting to start your search there. Other websites will probably require that you set up an account by entering your credit card information and shipping method and address. They might start sending you annoying e-mails. Why bother? Amazon's got you covered.

eBay has produced a similar expansion of the marketplace for individual sellers. If one day you get the bizarre urge to own a copy of a rare LP by the Fugs, a 1960s Greenwich Village rock band, there is a good chance you will be able to satisfy that urge with remarkable ease and speed. If anywhere on the face of the planet a seller exists who has been carefully storing old Fugs albums in the attic for just this kind of occasion, you are likely to find them on eBay. Once upon a time, it would have been pure fantasy to imagine that our every material whim could be satisfied at any moment with a few keystrokes and mouse clicks. Today that fantasy is quite often reality.

Auctions were once distinctly local affairs, and when the items in question are fine artwork or antiques, they often still are. But for most things that can be packed in bubble wrap and sent by UPS, auctioning has become a global enterprise. Here the Internet's ability to connect people has had a dramatic effect, creating a new cottage industry. If while cleaning out the garage you come across a vintage 1960s tin dollhouse in good condition, you are likely to find a buyer for it even if you live in the most rural area of Wyoming. Prior to eBay, the chances of finding a buyer probably would have been so remote as to make it a waste even to place a classified ad in the local paper. If you no longer wanted the dollhouse, you would probably decide that it was junk and put it out with the trash. But on eBay junk can be turned into cash. Someone will always buy that Alf alarm clock.

Today eBay is one of the Web's biggest success stories. In 2016, the company had 167 million "active buyers" and had facilitated the sale of $84 billion in merchandise.[73] According to the *Forbes* magazine 2017 list, eBay was the second largest Internet retail company behind Amazon. (Incidentally, number four on the Forbes list was Liberty Interactive, owner of QVC, among other companies.)[74]

Amazon brought an enormous self-service retail store to our computer screens, and eBay made auctions for hard-to-find items easily accessible. Both used secure payment methods to give users confidence in their financial transactions, but both still suffered an important weakness in comparison to traditional retail commerce: a lack of information, both about the product and about the seller. In Amazon's case, it was a wise move to begin with books. Even in a traditional bookstore, customers don't know how much they will value the transaction until after they go home and read the book. Amazon could supply potential readers with almost all the same information that preceded the sale of a book in a physical store: published reviews of the book, the number of pages, the price, and in some cases, sample chapters, so that buyers could get a taste of the work. For those who judged books by their covers, an image of the cover was provided. So books were a good choice because they could be easily shipped and deeply discounted based on high-volume sales, but books were also an excellent first product because the information disadvantage of online shopping was relatively low.

eBay faced a more challenging obstacle. The company was simply a kind of auction club, bringing together random buyers and sellers. Sellers needed confidence in the auctioning and payment systems, but buyers needed confidence in the far-flung sellers. "I don't know you. How do I know I'll get my stuff?" Interestingly, Craigslist, which has overtaken classified advertising for local goods and services, did not face this problem. Craigslist puts the two parties together, but typically the users meet face-to-face to make the exchange. If the potential renter is not happy with the apartment after seeing it in person, the deal may not go through. This conventional aspect of buying and selling is absent when the transaction takes place through the mail. As a result, eBay launched and sold its first item—a broken laser pointer—in 1995, and by the following year—recognizing the need for greater buyer confidence—the company introduced seller ratings.[75] For the first time, buyers and sellers could rate each other and create a community that allowed members to establish reputations and foster trust.

Amazon.com also launched in 1995, and by the time it began to expand beyond books, customer reviews had become an important part of its success.[76] There have always been worries about the accuracy of Amazon's five-star rating system. Each reviewer has a set of preferences and biases that may or may not line up with yours, making the value their opinions unclear. Worse yet, a substantial number of customer reviews are thought to be fraudulent, written for pay by unscrupulous entrepreneurs. Because customer ratings are such an integral part of online commerce, Amazon reportedly sued a thousand people for writing fake reviews on its site in 2016, and Yelp also makes an effort to weed out phony restaurant reviews.[77] Despite the concerns, there is good evidence that many people trust customer reviews and use them to decide on purchases.[78]

Today we have entered the "gig economy," where many people are freelancing as minihotel owners, cab drivers, home fix-it professionals, or other service providers, and this transition was made possible by the same system of customer and vendor ratings. It is somewhat ironic that hitchhiking, a venerable mode of transportation when I was younger, has almost completely disappeared. Today the thought of getting into a stranger's car—or, alternatively, letting a stranger into your car—evokes fear in most people. Similarly, the notion of a random person sleeping in your spare room conjures up any number of horror film scenarios. Nonetheless, in a very few years, entire industries have sprung up around just these kinds of encounters. Airbnb, Uber, and Lyft have used the mutual rating systems pioneered by eBay and Amazon to provide a sense of comfort about doing business with strangers. Participants in this web-based enterprise become public figures with ratings that anyone can check before considering a deal. Photos of riders, drivers, cars, apartments, and hosts are provided. As much information as possible is made available on the website or app, and, because everyone wants to continue using the service or operating their side business, maintaining a good rating matters. Amazon, eBay, Uber, Airbnb and other online retailers always had the advantages of convenience and expansive choice, and as Internet commerce has evolved, they have made great strides in overcoming the social and information barriers they face.

Stage Five—A Mall in My Pocket

The ride-sharing businesses Uber and Lyft are dependent on the wide use of smartphones. Most people who need a ride are out in the world, and the companies rely on the phone's ability to pinpoint your location on a map and display images of the rider, driver, and the driver's car. In addition, the apps are capable of offering various vehicle options that are not usually available in traditional cab services. The ride-sharing business is particularly wedded to the smartphone, but almost any online business can be operated on the fly, using a mobile device connected to the Internet or cellphone service. For example, both Amazon and eBay have phone apps that give users access to their enormous inventories. So if the urge for an antique Fugs album strikes while you are riding the bus to work, you can satisfy it instantly, as long as your cellphone signal holds out.

Most of the spending options on your cellphone are built into the app already. Stored credit card information allows you to buy something through Amazon or download a new album from iTunes. But mobile banking systems also help. Cell phone payment systems are widely used in developing countries, such as Kenya and Uganda, but have yet to gain wide use in the United States. In the meantime, various banking apps make it easier to check your balance, pay a bill, or deposit a check. In addition, those concerned about their credit score can monitor it as often as they like. Finally, when you need to split the cost of concert tickets or a meal, the money-sharing apps Venmo, Google Wallet, and Square Cash allow users to transfer money to one another. All of which provides more financial certainty for consumers. When you are out in the marketplace considering the purchase of a new tennis racket, uncertainty about whether you have enough money in the bank or credit left on your card is no longer a deterrent.

Amazon.com has become the largest single Internet shopping portal and, according to the 2017 *Forbes* magazine list, the third-largest US retailer behind Walmart and CVS Health.[79] Today we order all manner of stuff from Amazon.com, and in the future we are likely to order more. Furthermore, it is hard to anticipate what the next big thing in Internet commerce will be and how it will affect our pocketbooks. But we can be certain that there will be a next big thing and that the challenges to our self-control produced by virtual spending are here to stay.

THE TWENTY-FOUR-HOUR MARKETPLACE

These are just some examples of the how our economic environment has changed since the mid-1970s, and I am sure that you can think of many others. In the interest of brevity, my discussion of spending in the virtual world has entirely skipped over videogames, online dating services (Match. com, OKCupid.com, Tinder, and Grinder), counseling services (Talkspace, BetterHelp, Breakthrough), food-delivery services (Amazon Fresh, Blue Apron, and PeaPod), and the Internet's many specialty sites, such as Etsy. com for handmade and vintage items and Wondermade.com for gourmet marshmallows.

It would be impossible to list all the ways the spending response has been greased in the last four decades. Nonetheless, the picture that emerges is one of a world where it takes much greater effort to hold on to your money than it did a generation ago. The virtues of saving money never come to mind, and wherever the physics of spending has placed barriers in the way of the invisible hand of the marketplace, our commercial and technological innovators have risen to the challenge. The wheels of commerce spin freely on well-oiled axles. From the businessperson's viewpoint, the result has been a series of great successes in all four quadrants of Ansoff's product–market growth matrix. Yet for many of us out in the workaday world, life has become both easier and more difficult. Every convenience—drive-thru windows, self-service shopping, buying in the virtual world—makes spending more likely, and our places of quiet refuge—at home and out in the world—have become twenty-four-hour annexes to the mall. Of course, people vary in their degree of self-discipline and their ability to control the urge to spend, but it is also much easier to avoid eating chocolates if there are none in the house. While no one wants to have fewer choices, sometimes too much of a good thing is bad.

MARCIA AND JOEL

At the time we met, Marcia was just finishing up a master's degree in urban planning, and she was looking forward to getting a job. Her life was stable and good, and she seemed happy. But it had not always been that way.

Marcia's parents divorced when she was ten years old, and she lived with her mother, a dentist, in Springfield, Massachusetts. In her elementary years, Marcia was in a gifted program at a private school, but when it came time for high school her parents enrolled her in Catholic school. She soon became bored and rebellious and began to skip school, drink, and take drugs. "So they kicked me out of school, and I never went back," she said.

Instead, she studied for and took the high school equivalency exam, completing her degree before the other members of her high school class had graduated. After a year of community college work, she transferred to a local branch of the state college system. She worked part-time while in school and shared an apartment with three other girls, and life was generally good. But then she became pregnant, and things started to slip.

Several months earlier she had met Joel, who was to become her boyfriend, at a club, and when Marcia became pregnant, the couple decided it was time to get an apartment together. Although he was also a very intelligent young man, Joel had a number of health problems that made it difficult for him to sustain employment for very long, and as a result, he took on most of the childcare duties. Nonetheless, they both continued to look for work and took whatever they could get. Despite being a full-time student, Marcia was more successful than Joel at finding work, but her jobs tended to be secretarial or call center positions, most of which ended in layoffs.

When there were gaps in their income, they began to use credit cards to fill them in. They sometimes charged groceries and gas, but there were also bigger expenses that quickly built up their Visa and MasterCard balances. Unfortunately, over a period of just a few years, they had been in five car accidents, which cost them both in repairs and in increased insurance premiums. Without any other resources to draw on, they paid most of these expenses with plastic. They got to the point where they were juggling. There were only small balances on a couple of store credit cards, but over the years they had acquired several bank cards and owed money on all of them. Fortunately, Marcia's tuition was relatively inexpensive, and she arrived at her senior year of college having built up only $3,000 in student loan debt.

When their daughter was two years old, the couple got married. Just days before the ceremony, they discovered that Marcia was pregnant with their second child. To save money, they moved in with Marcia's mother and sister in a small condominium apartment. It was a ridiculous arrangement, with far too many people living in too small a space. No one had any privacy, and they bickered constantly. To make matters worse, they began to receive calls demanding payment on the $10,000 balance they had built up on their Visa account. One caller said that if they could just make a payment of $1,000, they would avoid being taken to court. So with great difficulty, Marcia and Joel scraped together the money, only to have someone else call a few weeks later to threaten them again. The $1,000 payment had been very difficult to make, but it seemed not to have helped.

Marcia was trying to finish her last year of college and waiting to hear whether she would be accepted into a master's program, but she would be able to go to graduate school only if she was offered financial aid. The future looked very uncertain, and the present was almost impossible to bear.

Finally, Marcia called a bankruptcy attorney. There seemed to be no other way to get out from under their bills. In the last year, their total income had been only $15,000, and they now owed twice that amount in credit card debt.

When I asked if there was anything else that contributed to their bankruptcy, they were remarkably forthcoming.

"My parents had money," said Marcia. "As a kid, I got used to being able to go out to restaurants without having to think much about it. Once I was on my own, it was hard to make the switch to a different standard of living."

She paused for a moment.

"And, of course, I got my first credit card when I was only nineteen years old. I had no idea what I was doing."

By the time I met them, it had been a year and a half since Marcia and Joel had declared bankruptcy. Marcia had been awarded a research assistantship that paid her graduate tuition and a small salary, and Joel was working part time at a nursing home. They had managed to find an inexpensive apartment, and having paid off their used Toyota Corolla, they had gotten a loan for a second car. They had no credit cards and were managing to live frugally in a cash world.

Thinking about Money

I should point out that I don't normally use the word "amortize" unless I'm trying to prove that something I can't really afford is not just a bargain but practically free. This usually involves dividing the cost of the item I can't afford by the number of years I'm planning to use it, or, if that doesn't work, by the number of days or hours or minutes, until I get a number that is less than the cost of a cappuccino.

—Nora Ephron

At a conference a couple of years ago, I explained the difference between my models and Robert Barro's by saying that he assumes the agents in his model are as smart as he is, while I portray people as being as dumb as I am. Barro agreed with this assessment.

—Economist Richard Thaler

We rarely look forward as far and as often as we should. We are busy people. We have to get the kids to school and get to work, and it seldom occurs to us that it might be a good idea to stop for a moment to think about how our lives might play out in the long run. Economists, on the other hand, place great value on rationality and order, and they are looking ahead all the time. All this diligent forward thinking has led to the development of something called the *life-cycle theory*, which attempts to summarize the relationship between earning and spending over the course of a lifetime.[1]

The life-cycle theory is quite simple, but it has important implications for everyday behavior. First, it assumes that income varies over the course of a life. When we are young and just beginning our careers, we make less money, but as we reach middle age, we enter our peak earning years. Finally, at the end of life, presumably during a relaxed period of dotage, earning drops off precipitously. This steep arch is depicted in Figure 8.1. Another assumption of the life-cycle theory is that consumption is tied to our total lifetime income and not to current income. According to this view, at any point in time we are calculating what our lifetime earning potential is likely to be and spending accordingly. It is as if we imagine that the sum total of our life's acquired wealth has been deposited in a bank or with an insurance company and is being doled out in even monthly payments throughout our lives. This approach to income and consumption tends to smooth spending, making it relatively flat and consistent across the years. As time passes, things might happen that force us to reevaluate our predictions about our lifetime wealth, and we may have to adjust our spending up or down accordingly. But the model assumes we will have a greater need to borrow in our youth and that as we hit our stride in middle age we will pull ourselves out of debt and into the black, as depicted in Figure 8.1.

Of course, the life-cycle theory assumes that we have a clear view of the future and that we have some interest in our ability to consume in the future rather than just spending everything we have right now. In the United States, the assumption of a rising income is often justified. If you go to school, make good choices, and work hard, your earnings will often mirror the rising arc of Figure 8.1. But critics have pointed out that a number of factors could disrupt the pattern predicted by the theory. For example, for many people the expectation of rising income has not been realized. As we have seen, real wages

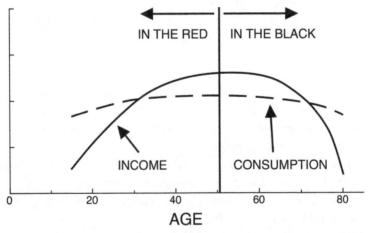

Figure 8.1 The life-cycle theory. Although an individual's income rises and falls over the life span, consumption is based on a more even allotment of total lifetime earnings. As a result, the theory assumes that early in life, when earning potential is still low, borrowing will be necessary, but during the peak earning years debts will be repaid and savings will be possible.

for most Americans have been flat or declining over the last three decades. In addition, job security has diminished, and, apart from some progress due to the Affordable Care Act, the social safety net has shrunk.[2] Many people have acquired debts early in life only to be indefinitely saddled with them because the dream of rising earnings has not been realized. This is particularly common now that eighteen-year-olds with very limited information about the future routinely choose to assume many tens of thousands of dollars in debt to pay for college. Similarly, uncertainty about the future can alter the way we consume. For example, if you are from an unstable part of the world where there is an ongoing war, you might choose to live like there is no tomorrow, consuming all your income as soon as you get it.[3] Nonetheless, the life-cycle theory has survived as a useful description of how many people earn and spend over a lifetime.

Another important aspect of the life-cycle theory is a bit less obvious. Economists assume that all money is created equal. Whether it is take-home pay, savings, gifts, or retirement funds, money is interchangeable. The technical term is *fungible*.[4] Furthermore, if money is fungible, then we should spend on the basis of our total wealth regardless of how we think about it. Consider the case of your income tax refund. Many people deduct more money from their paychecks than is necessary to cover their federal income taxes each year. (Later on we consider whether this is a good idea or not.) As a result, in the spring these people receive an income tax refund from the government. What people do with this money once it arrives depends on how they think about it. For example, imagine that after a woman calculates her personal budget and estimates her probable lifetime earnings, she concludes that approximately 15 percent of her income can be spent on nonnecessities. The rest should go to savings, debt repayment, and normal expenses. But she also has a hankering for a vacation in Vermont, and she is expecting a $2,000 tax refund check. The rational economist adhering to the life-cycle theory would remind our taxpayer that the refund is a piece of her normal income and should be treated in exactly the same manner as her monthly paycheck. It is part of her lifetime earnings and does not alter the shape of her income curve. But for many people, the income tax refund is placed in a different mental account labeled "mad money," and according to several published studies, people tend to increase their spending right after getting a tax refund.[5] It is common to think of the refund as a bonus—separate from the normal budget—available for splurging. This kind of mental accounting is particularly dangerous if you are still encumbered with debt in the early part of the life cycle.

How we deal with windfalls—unexpected gains—is a topic that economists and psychologists have studied in depth. According to the life-cycle theory, if a windfall actually alters your potential lifetime earnings, it might afford you the opportunity to increase your level of spending; however, the increase should be spread out over time. For example, if you receive an inheritance of $25,000 at a point when you expect to live another fifty years, you could afford to increase your level of spending by $500 per year—or a bit more if you deposit the inheritance in an interest-bearing account. Given that we often do not think about windfalls with such clear-eyed foresight, the life-cycle theory provides a good guide to saving and spending.

But we face many challenges as we try to negotiate our individual life cycles. Despite the economist's claim that money is fungible, we think about it in many different ways, and simple changes in the language used to describe a sum of money can have dramatic effects on our behavior. For example, in September 2001, the US federal government returned $38 billion to its citizens in the form of a tax rebate. Depending on income, taxpayers received checks for $300, $500, or $600. One of the stated purposes of the 2001 tax rebate was to stimulate the economy by putting more spending money in the hands of the people, but the evidence suggests that the program would have been more effective if it had not been called a "rebate." In a series of experiments, psychologist Nicholas Epley and his colleagues have demonstrated that money described as a "bonus" is more likely to be spent than a similar amount of money identified as a "rebate." For example, Epley invited Harvard University students into the laboratory and informed them that they would each be receiving a check for $50. Half the students were told that the laboratory had acquired some excess funds and, as a result, this money was being offered as "tuition rebate." For the other students the money was described as "bonus income." As part of the experiment, the students were asked to fill out an accounting sheet reporting any use they made of the $50 in the following week. When the accounting sheets were returned, they revealed that the "bonus" group spent an average of $31 of the money and saved the rest, whereas the rebate group spent an average of only $7.[6] In another study, taxpayers were approached on a Boston street and asked about the 2001 federal income tax rebate six months after they had received it. Those who said they considered the rebate to be "extra income" remembered spending more of it than people who thought of it as "returned income." Despite the economist's claim that money is fungible, real people tend to put income from different sources into different mental accounts. By simply altering the language used to describe a sum of money, Epley and his colleagues demonstrated what psychologists call a *framing effect*. Whether they are about money or other things, the decisions and choices we make can be dramatically affected by subtle differences in the way they are described.

The classic example of a framing effect taught in many introductory psychology classes is the *Asian disease problem*. Participants are told that a new disease has surfaced that is expected to kill six hundred people, and they must choose between pairs of unpleasant options aimed at combating the disease. The first set of choices is as follows:

PROGRAM A: Two hundred people will be saved.
PROGRAM B: There is a one-third probability that all six hundred people will be saved, and a two-thirds probability that no one will be saved.

When I've presented these options in introductory psychology classes, most students choose program A. It is not a very good plan of action, but it guarantees that two hundred people live. Next, I present a second set of options.

PROGRAM C: Four hundred people will die.
PROGRAM D: There is a one-third probability that nobody will die and a two-thirds probability that six hundred people will die.

Given these options, most students now want to take a chance with program D. The one-third chance of avoiding all deaths seems more appealing than the four hundred certain deaths of program C. But the choices are exactly the same. The only difference between the first pair and the second is the way in which they are framed. Programs A and B are presented in terms of the number of people "saved," and programs C and D describe the number of deaths, but program A = program C, and program B = program D. So why do people prefer program A, the sure thing, in the first set of choices but switch to program D, the risky option, in the second?

This problem was first introduced by psychologists Amos Tversky and Daniel Kahneman. Together they conducted a long and distinguished research career articulating the many ways our everyday thinking goes astray. As Kahneman outlined in his bestselling book *Thinking, Fast and Slow*, the two used very simple examples such as the Asian disease problem, to demonstrate how things that should not influence our decisions—such as the way a problem is framed—nonetheless have powerful effects on how we choose. Because so many of their discoveries were important to the field of economics—and especially to the emerging field of behavioral economics—Kahneman was awarded the Nobel Prize in economics in 2002. At the time, he was only the second psychologist to receive this honor. (Tversky undoubtedly would have shared the prize with his close friend and collaborator, but the rules stipulate that the Nobel Prize be awarded to living recipients only. Unfortunately, Tversky succumbed to cancer in 1996.)

Kahneman and Tversky's work, and that of many other behavioral economists, has popularized the idea of *bounded rationality*, first introduced by Herbert Simon, the first psychologist to win the Nobel Prize.[7] Although economists have long assumed that humans are rational animals, making the best possible decisions as they maneuver their way around the marketplace, behavioral economic researchers have found that, contrary to this standard view, we use a number of mental shortcuts that often work quite well but sometimes fail us in important ways. Over the last forty years, researchers have uncovered many of the common pitfalls that plague us when we approach both economic and noneconomic decisions. In the specific case of the Asian disease problem, Kahneman and Tversky proposed an explanation they called *prospect theory*.

Prospect theory suggests that when we are presented with choices, we consider the effects of each option relative to our present circumstances. Will we gain or lose relative to our current status quo? Furthermore, as many experiments have demonstrated, we give different weights to options that enhance the status quo than to ones that diminish it. Of course, we prefer gains. It is always better to receive money than to lose it. It is always better to save lives than to lose them. But Kahneman and Tversky's crucial contribution was the recognition that losses and gains are not weighed equally: losses hurt more than gains feel good. The disappointment felt at the loss of $50 from our current level of wealth has greater pull than the happiness of a gain of $50 would have. This effect is illustrated in Figure 8.2, where the loss of $50 produces a much greater

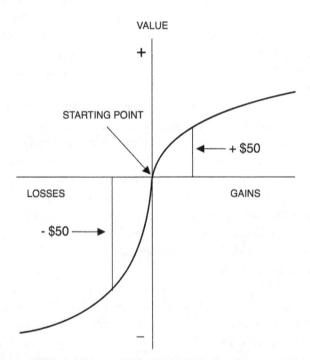

Figure 8.2 Prospect theory. Gains and losses relative to the current status quo are measured on the horizontal axis, and the perceived value of these gains and losses is presented on the vertical axis. As indicated, losses produce a greater change in value than equal-sized gains: losses hurt more than gains feel good.

decrease in value or happiness relative to the starting point than the upward shift produced by a gain of equal size.

This simple theory has several important implications. First, it suggests that we are more likely to be risk-seeking with respect to avoiding losses. Losses— such as four hundred deaths from a disease—carry substantial negative weight. If there is a chance to avoid this big hurt altogether, we are more inclined to take the risk. This was the case in the choice between program C and program D. These two options were stated in terms of deaths. They were, of course, the same two choices as those presented in programs A and B, but because they were described in terms of the number of lives lost, they emphasized a downward movement relative to the status quo. As a result, more people are willing to take the risky choice, program D, in an attempt to avoid the losses altogether. Gains have a more modest effect on the status quo, and so when confronted with programs A and B, many people find it more attractive to lock in the modest gain of two hundred lives saved. Although the prospect of six hundred lives saved is appealing, this larger gain is not so powerful an attraction as to make the gamble worthwhile.

Prospect theory helps to give an explanation for our inconsistent choices in the Asian disease problem, but this example's true punch comes from understanding that both pairs of options are the same. Our shifting choices are created not by real differences in gains and losses but by perceptions produced by the way each option is described. Similarly, simply framing a sum of money as a "bonus" rather than a "rebate" is enough to make it burn a hole in our pocket. Money that seems to raise us above the status quo is treated differently than money that merely restores the status quo. Framing effects also have important implications for advertising. For example, marketing research shows that customers prefer hamburger that is described as "more than 75 percent lean" rather than "less than 25 percent fat."[8]

MANAGING YOUR MENTAL ACCOUNTS

Although the life-cycle theory stands as an example of what many economists consider to be wise and rational behavior, it bears little resemblance to what people actually do. For example, most people are incapable of calculating the total value of their future earnings and, as a result, have no idea what portion of that total should be considered available for use today.[9] In addition, rather than drawing on savings in later life, as predicted by the model, many elderly people maintain their assets and, in some cases, even continue to save.[10] Finally, the fungibility assumption is in serious doubt. We often place money from different sources into different mental compartments, some of which are more accessible than others. These violations of the life-cycle theory should not trouble us, but they do have important implications for personal financial management. Some mental accounts encourage spending—even when it is not a good idea—and others discourage it.

Problems Connecting and Disconnecting

We seem to have an innate propensity to find relationships between objects and events. The many achievements of our species largely stem from our remarkable ability to learn from experience and adapt to changing demands, and this ability depends on finding reliable connections between events or between our actions and their effects on the world. Unfortunately, some of the connections we see are merely in the eye of the beholder, and when it comes to decisions about money, finding connections between events can sometimes be profitable and sometimes not.

A well-known example of unwise connection-making involves being swayed by what economists call *sunk costs*. To understand sunk costs, consider the following example. Imagine you planned to attend a play and you purchased a ticket for $20. When you arrive at the theater moments before the curtain is to go up, you discover that you have lost the ticket. Would you buy another ticket for $20 and attend the play? Now consider the following variation. Imagine you have planned to attend a play, but this time you did not purchase a ticket in advance. When you arrive at the theater moments before the curtain goes up, you discover that you have lost $20 out of your wallet. Assuming you still have enough money, would you buy a ticket and attend the play?[11]

Many people treat the two versions of this theater ticket scenario quite differently. In the second version of the story, most people say that of course they will go on and attend the play. It is frustrating to lose money, but it does not affect the attractiveness of the entertainment. However, many fewer people say that they will buy a second ticket in the lost ticket version of the scenario. These people tend to lump the two sums of money together and conclude that $40 is too much to pay. But as you undoubtedly recognize, the principle of fungibility suggests the two scenarios are exactly the same. The amount lost is the same whether it takes the form of a lost ticket or a lost $20 bill. Furthermore, the principle of sunk costs suggests that we should not be affected by money that has been spent in the past. The money spent on the ticket is "sunk"—gone, not recoverable. Therefore the only relevant question is whether the play is worth $20. If we still believe it is, then the correct choice is to buy another ticket. The decision to go to the play is clearer in the case of the lost $20 bill, because we put that financial loss in a different mental account.

The lost theater ticket case urges us to spend rather than withhold spending, and as a result, its message is not appropriate to the task of maintaining wealth and avoiding debt. However, an unwise concern for sunk costs can also prompt us to make the opposite kind of money mistake. One example of this kind of sunk-cost error involves throwing good money after bad. The following case, taken from a study by psychologists Hal Arkes and Catherine Blumer, demonstrates this problem:

> As the president of an airline company, you have invested 10 million dollars of the company's money into a research project. The purpose was to build a plane that would not be detected by conventional radar, in other words, a radar-blank plane. When the project is 90 percent completed, another firm begins marketing a plane that cannot be detected by radar. Also it is apparent that their plane is much faster and far more economical than the plane your company is building. The question is: should you invest the last 10 percent of the research funds to finish your radar-blank plane?[12]

Eighty-five percent of the participants in Arkes and Blumer's study said they would spend the additional money to complete the project. However, when presented with a version of the story that made no mention of the $10 million in sunk costs, only 17 percent said they would spend the money on the project. In this case, it would be best to cut your losses rather than throw good money after bad, but having invested heavily in the project already, there is a tendency to want to finish it—even if the plane is doomed to failure.

Sunk costs can also play a role in everyday financial management. Suppose you are a college student who is short on cash at the end of the month and needs approximately $50 to eat for the rest of the week. You know that you can get $4 each for some of your CDs down at the local used-record store, so you fill up a box with some of your older albums and head to the store. With luck, you will be able to trade twenty or so for enough cash to live on until your next paycheck. Someone might say, "Why would you sell $200 worth of CDs for $50?" Of course, the answer is that the $200 spent on the CDs is gone, never to be recovered. What matters now is the current value of the CDs (to you, as part of your collection) relative to $50 in cash and the food you could buy with it.

I came across a similar case years ago when I was looking for a house to buy. A realtor told me about a house that seemed right for my needs. She explained that the house had been on the market for over a year and had, in her opinion, been overpriced. Once I showed interest, the sellers finally lowered their price, and I bought the house. I later discovered that they had spent quite a bit of money in renovations to the home, and when it came time to sell, the memory of those expensive improvements had moved them to set an unrealistically high price. They failed to learn one of the basic rules of homeownership: the money you sink into home improvements is rarely earned back when you sell.

So hesitancy to sell an object based on the money we have paid for it—or put into it—in the unrecoverable past is a mistake. Those funds are gone, and under anything less than truly miraculous circumstances, you will never get them back. But, in a psychological sense, selling an object for much less than we paid for it makes it official that we have lost money, and as prospect theory suggests, we are particularly averse to losses. A similar phenomenon— also related to prospect theory—is demonstrated by the *endowment effect.* For many people, an object gains value once we own it. This situation creates the unusual circumstance that the owner would demand more in payment to sell the object than he or she would pay out to buy it. A friend of mine was forced to sell some valued furniture, a chair and wardrobe, before moving to a different city. She got a good price in return for these items, but she has always regretted having to give them up. Nevertheless, as she looks back on this episode, my friend also recognizes that she would not be willing to pay as much to have the items back as she received when she sold them. Prospect theory suggests that this endowment effect happens because the negative psychological impact of the loss of the furniture outweighs the potential positive effect of regaining it.

The endowment effect is a classic example of the central principle of prospect theory. Losses hurt more than gains feel good, and so if we are going to experience the loss of furniture, we must get more money to compensate for that loss. If, on the other hand, we don't own the furniture and are simply considering buying it, the value will be lower because gains have a more modest positive effect on the status quo. Sunk cost effects often seem to have a similar loss aversion aspect to them, but in this case the effect is connected to a past action. If I sell the CDs, the $200 that I paid for them will be lost. If I sell the house at the market price, I will lose the cost of those improvements. When we stumble in our consideration of sunk costs, it is because we fail to recognize that the money was gone long ago and our immediate decisions should not be affected by the past.

Other problems can result from connecting past events with present ones. If we have just gained or lost money, it can have a substantial effect on what we do next. Perhaps one of the clearest examples is found in the behavior of gamblers. If a blackjack player has just won a large sum of money, she may become a bit more risky in subsequent hands because she is "playing with the house money." Of course, it is really her money. It used to belong to the house, but once she won the hand, it became her money to have and to hold. But the gambler's theory of mental accounting seems to be consistent with prospect theory. Once a large win has been encountered, you are above your status quo—richer than your starting point at the beginning of the evening. As a result, any subsequent loss will be combined with this gain, diminishing its effect. In a series of experiments, economists Richard Thaler and Eric Johnson demonstrated that the house money effect was real. Participants in a two-stage question were first told that they had won $15.00. Next they were asked whether they would be willing to gamble $4.50 on a coin toss: heads you win $4.50 and tails you lose $4.50. Under this arrangement, 77 percent of people said they would take the bet. On the other hand, if presented with a choice between a sure thing, $15.00 with a 100 percent probability, and a one-stage gamble—tails you win $19.50 and heads you win 10.50 (exactly the same total winnings as in the previous case)—only 44 percent of participants were willing to take the bet. An early win is mentally combined with subsequent losses and takes away a little of the sting, resulting in reckless behavior.[13]

Risky betting can also result from a prior loss. Because the initial status quo point is given such psychological importance, people are more likely to take a chance on bets that provide the opportunity to break even. In a different case, Thaler and Johnson told participants that in the gamble just preceding they had lost $4.50. Then in a second stage they were given a choice between $5.00 for sure or a one-third chance to win $15.00 and a two-thirds chance to win nothing. In this case, 68 percent of participants chose the sure thing, which provided the chance to be whole again with a slight overall gain of $0.50, and 32 percent gambled. But in a second version of this choice the results were quite different. When the initial loss was $7.50 and the sure thing provided the opportunity to get back only $2.50—nowhere near the break-even point— Thaler and Johnson's participants were much more inclined to take a risk. This time, 29 percent of participants took the sure thing, and 71 percent chose to gamble on a one-third chance to win $7.50 (and break even) and a two-thirds chance to win nothing. When the sure thing in stage two did not afford the possibility to break even but gambling did, participants were willing to take a chance.[14]

The preceding problems involved poor decisions caused by connecting events occurring at different points in time: the original cost of CDs versus their current value, and the outcome of an earlier gamble versus the gamble we are considering right now. But sometimes we have problems with connections that are more spatial than temporal. As shown in the rebate-bonus example, the context of a decision can affect our choices. For example, when we are trying to decide whether to buy an item or not, the circumstances of the sale matter. The following example comes from a study published by Tversky and Kahneman in 1981:

> Imagine that you are about to purchase a jacket for $125, and a calculator for $15. The calculator salesman informs you that the calculator you wish to buy is on sale for $10 at the other branch of the store, located 20 minutes drive away. Would you take the trip to the other store?

Sixty-eight percent of Tversky and Kahneman's subjects said they would make the trip. (It is probably important to remember that $5 had much greater value in 1981 than it does today.) However, in a second version of the problem the authors reversed the prices of the items, making the jacket $15 and the calculator $125, and in this case the calculator was on sale for $120 at the other store. Now only 29 percent of participants said they would make the trip, even though the savings, $5, and the inconvenience, a twenty-minute drive, were exactly the same in both problems. If a twenty-minute drive is worth $5 in one instance, it should also be worth it in another. But Tversky and Kahneman's respondents were affected by the ratio of the savings to the price of the object. (Note that the total amount being spent on jacket and calculator together is the same in both versions of the problem; therefore what varies is the relationship of the savings not to the total amount spent but to the price of the specific object.) When the $5 savings represented one-third of the cost of the calculator, the trip to the other store was worth it, but when $5 off represented a relatively modest percentage savings on the more expensive $125 calculator, people were less likely to go to the other store. This kind of behavior is understandable but irrational. For the consumer hoping to save money, being swayed by the relative rather than absolute amount of money saved can be dangerous. For example, when making a large purchase such as a car, many people agree to also purchase expensive dealer add-ons, such as rustproofing. The $300 cost of rustproofing may seem negligible in comparison to the many thousands of dollars being spent on the car, but according to the life-cycle theory, money should always be weighed equally regardless of its source. Hence, this loss should be judged in isolation, rather than relative to the cost of the item. At some point in the future, you might wish you had $300 for some pressing need, and the relationship of this sum of money to an expensive car will have been forgotten.

So, as pattern-seeking creatures, we tend to draw connections between parts of a purchasing decision that should or should not be connected. Sometimes the current decision is affected by a previous event, as in the case of the house money and break-even effects. In other cases, we judge the value of money or things on the basis of extraneous factors. In both cases, behavioral economics helps us see how difficult it is to keep our eyes on the relevant factors of many financial decisions.

How Context Influences Prices

Being thrifty is often a challenge. The price of a product can vary considerably depending on where and how it is presented to us, and even when the price is very high, we are sometimes moved to pay it. Consider the following example:

> You are lying on the beach on a hot day. All you have to drink is ice water. For the last hour you have been thinking about how much you would enjoy a nice cold bottle of your favorite brand of beer. A companion gets up to go make a phone call and offers to bring back a beer from the only place where beer is sold, a fancy resort hotel. He says that the beer might be expensive and so asks how much you are willing to pay for the beer. He says that he will buy the beer if it costs as much or less than the price you state, but if it costs more than the price you state, he will not buy it. What price do you tell him?[15]

When Richard Thaler asked a group of first-year MBA students this question—in 1985, when beer was cheaper and cellular phones were not ubiquitous—the average price the students were willing to pay was $2.65. However, when another group was given the same scenario but with the hotel changed to a run-down grocery store, the average price they wanted to pay dropped to $1.50. The circumstances of their thirst had not changed, nor had their financial fortunes, but when the only beer available came from a fancy resort hotel, they were willing to pay more.

Popcorn is ridiculously expensive at the megaplex. A bottle of wine costs three times its liquor store price at the local French restaurant. Yet we pay. Under the right circumstances we can be coaxed into shelling out sums of money we would not normally consider paying. These cases have two things in common. First, they are environments where the seller has a virtual monopoly on the product being offered. At the restaurant or the movies, it would be difficult to obtain the same products from a competitor. To further discourage competition, some restaurants and most movie theaters have rules against bringing in items from outside. Second, in many of these cases we expect to pay more, and not just because the seller has a monopoly. A fancy resort hotel is assumed to be expensive, and as a result, experience tells us the price of a beer—or anything else—is likely to be higher than somewhere else.[16] Fancy restaurants are expensive, so we adjust the price of the wine upward.

We are willing to grant the owner a larger profit margin simply because their establishment conveys a sense of greater luxury. It is interesting to note that not all virtual monopolies result in elevated prices. Just as the run-down grocery store influenced purchasers' willingness to pay, at lower-status venues such as a minor-league baseball game prices are likely to be lower than at the higher-status major-league park or Broadway theater. The entertainment is geared toward a lower-income clientele and is expected to be lower in cost.

So a seller can increase costs—and convince us to pay more—simply by changing the atmosphere of the establishment to evoke a sense of luxury, but there are other ways to get us to pay more. For example, our understanding of the cost of an item is based on standard quantities. When we buy a candy bar at the grocery store, we know it will be of modest size and we will pay something more than a dollar but less than two dollars. Because we have these fairly specific expectations, a markedly higher cost would violate our trust and be likely to discourage the purchase. This system of expectations can be easily disrupted by offering the product in unusual sizes that are difficult to compare to the standard units. Thus, the candy offered at the megaplex comes in large boxes not sold anywhere else. Simply because we are at the theater, we expect to pay more, but by selling the product in quantities not available elsewhere, the amount of the premium we are paying is more difficult to calculate. Furthermore, if the size being offered is much larger than usual, we can rationalize that it is still a good value. This method of marketing products can easily lead us to buy more than we wanted to buy and pay more than we wanted to pay. And—in the case of candy and popcorn—eat more than we wanted to eat.[17]

More on Windfalls and Mental Accounting

As we have seen, it makes a big difference whether a sum of money is framed as a gain or a loss. All money may be created equal, but we certainly don't act as if it were. Even when we restrict ourselves to the happy topic of gains—money coming in—we discover that our attitude toward this good fortune is affected in unusual ways.

As discussed earlier, when we receive windfalls—unexpected or unusual infusions of money—we often fail to adhere to the dictates of the life-cycle theory. In fact, we sometimes do almost the exact opposite. Consider the following scenario: George was expecting a modest sum of money. He had been contracted to do some extra work, a one-time-only job, and a week or so later he was to get a check for $600. George had been wanting to buy a new stereo system to replace the older one he was using to play his tunes, and so he developed a plan to use the check for a new shelf-mounted system that would fit nicely in the living room of his apartment. Once the check was safely deposited in the bank, George headed to the electronics store. When he got there he found a very nice system that would cost approximately $600, but right next to it was one for $1,200 that looked even nicer and had much better speakers. Knowing that it was a bit of splurge, George bought the more expensive system.[18]

The exact details of this story may not match your own experience, but many of us can think of similar episodes in our own lives. An influx of money becomes the justification for spending more than we would otherwise and more than the amount of the influx itself. It is particularly interesting to note that $600 was apparently enough of an obstacle that, prior to the windfall, George would not just go out and buy the stereo, but once the check arrived and he was at the store he discovered he was willing to combine $600 of his current assets with the recent windfall in order to finance a more expensive sound system.

Windfalls are tricky. Often, like George, we fail to adhere to the wisdom of the life-cycle theory. According to the theory, at all times we should have a current "spend rate" in our heads: 70 percent of my income goes to current expenses and 30 percent goes to paying off debts or to savings. The actual percentages will vary from person to person depending on each individual's expected lifetime earnings and his or her current location in the life cycle, but the basic principle is the same. All income is equivalent. The spend rate can go up only if the windfall is big enough to alter your predicted lifetime earnings, and even then the increase in spending must be spread out across your entire remaining life. As a result, the life-cycle model leaves little room for financing a stereo system with a paycheck received for extra work, yet many of us have made purchases just like George's.[19]

Windfalls are often treated differently than other kinds of income, and a number of factors influence what accounting methods we apply. One important variable is what economists call *liquidity constraint*, a condition that is thought to affect 20 percent of American households. A liquidity-constrained household is one that has little cash on hand and little ability to obtain cash. For example, if you are of relatively low income, your credit cards are maxed out, and you have little or no money in your savings and checking accounts, your liquidity is substantially constrained. A number of studies have shown that households with tight, liquidity-constrained budgets are more likely to increase spending in response to an influx of money, such as a bonus, a tax rebate, or an income tax refund.[20] These are households like those where the members cannot come up with $400 to cover an emergency. The pent-up desire for cash and the things it can obtain is released by the appearance of a windfall. People whose budgets are less constrained also increase spending following a windfall, but they are more likely to purchase durable items—such as George's stereo system—than are constrained households. People who have little access to cash are more likely to spend a windfall, such as their annual tax refund, on nondurable items, such as food and entertainment.[21]

In addition, the size of the windfall appears to have an effect on how it is used. In a 1966 study of Israeli citizens who received restitution payments from the German government, economist Michael Landsberger found that families who received larger payments were more likely to save them, and those who received smaller ones tended to spend them.[22] Apparently larger sums of money were considered assets that should be preserved, whereas smaller sums were regarded as current income available for spending.[23] Indeed, Landsberger found that those Israelis who received the smallest payments actually reported spending twice as much as the amount received—just like George.

The Pain of Payment and the Pleasure of Consumption

It hurts to pay, and we would all love to avoid shelling out cash if we could. The free lunch is still an elusive dream, but in the modern world, there are many ways to handle the unpleasantness of paying. How we time and structure our payments affects our mental accounting system, which can have a powerful influence on whether we save or spend.

The basic dilemma is that we love to consume but we hate giving up our money to do so, and the experience of each is affected by the other. An expensive meal at a five-star restaurant is a great pleasure, but if the cost of the evening exceeds your budget, the pleasures of fine dining will be greatly diminished by the thought of how much you are paying for it. On the other hand, if your boss gives you a gift certificate for the restaurant as a reward for an excellent conclusion to a big project at work, the food is likely to taste better and the evening will be more relaxed. Furthermore, just as the act of consumption can be affected by thoughts of payment, the unpleasantness of paying can be affected by the manner in which it is done. For most people, paying for a vacation in advance is doubly advantageous. Each payment is made less onerous by the thought of the upcoming vacation, and once the vacation arrives, it can be more thoroughly enjoyed, knowing that it has already been paid for. It almost feels like it is free.[24]

The basic problem, as described by behavioral economists Drazen Prelec and George Loewenstein, is that the psychological coupling of payment and consumption can increase or decrease our enjoyment.[25] In the case of paying in advance for a vacation, thoughts of future enjoyment on the beach or at a resort help soften the blow of the payments we must make now. Later, the vacation—which has been decoupled from the act of payment—is also more enjoyable. In contrast, if we pay for the vacation after the fact, writing the check is a particularly painful task because we have nothing to look forward to. Being indebted to someone else is an unpleasant state of affairs, and most people would prefer to avoid it. Similarly, most people prefer to be paid after they complete their work. That way the employer is indebted to you and not the other way around.

In the vacation situation, some of the difficulty stems from the fact that the vacation is an experience—not an object—and it is consumed relatively quickly. It comes, we have a wonderful time, and then we go back to work. The purchase of durable goods is somewhat different. Many of the same people who would prefer to pay for a vacation in advance are just as content to pay for a washer and dryer over time, after the appliances have been delivered, or to rent them in a pay-as-you-go arrangement. Furthermore, most people find they have very little emotion wrapped up in the daily possession of a washer or dryer. Thus, there isn't much pleasure to be ruined by the thought of payment, and there is little anticipated enjoyment to offset the unpleasantness of the bill. So the usual power of the hyperbola is more likely to encourage us to stretch out payment over the life of the object.

When paying produces pain, Prelec and Loewenstein suggest, we—or those with whom we do business—often try to find ways to decouple the payment and consumption. One of the simplest examples is the use of chips or tokens. The chips used at casinos are a kind of "funny money" that is easier to spend because it has been separated in time from the act of forking over cold hard cash in exchange for plastic disks. Similarly, foreign money often feels unreal. But a more common form of decoupling is exemplified by the following true story told by Prelec and Loewenstein:

> A Manhattan newlywed couple were deciding whether to live on the East side (her preference, on account of the better restaurants) or the West side (his preference, on account of the cheaper rent). The clinching argument put forth in favor of the West side was that the rental savings would easily cover any reasonable number of taxi rides to the East side. However, having moved in, the couple soon realized that the cost of the round-trip taxi ride made the cost of eating out on the East side look too expensive. Their solution: On the first of the month they would set aside ("prepay") a certain amount just for the cab rides.

By earmarking a certain amount in advance as taxi money, the couple was able to separate the consideration of eating out on the East side from the associated transportation cost, and dining out at their favorite restaurants became much easier to accomplish.

Most of us use similar forms of decoupling in many areas of our lives. On occasion I have attended a monthly "wine dinner" at a local restaurant. The food is beautifully prepared and rich, and diners are given the opportunity to taste a number of wines. But I would probably never consider such an indulgence were it not offered prix fixe. Because the cost of the evening is contained and understood at the outset, the mental accounting is made easy. You can relax and enjoy the entire experience without having to consider the cost of each gourmet morsel. In much the same way, many people have a preference for all-inclusive vacation packages, flat rate Internet and cell phone plans, and automatic monthly billing for streaming video packages. It may seem like ancient history, but it really isn't so long ago that cell phone plans were based on a certain number of call minutes, and we had to be concerned about whether we had gone over our limit and whether we were "roaming" or not. Similarly, I remember a Thanksgiving when all the assembled went around the table and declared something they were thankful for. I have forgotten all of the testimonials offered on that day except for one teenage girl who said, "I am thankful for unlimited texting." Nobody liked those old plans because each time we used the phone we had to worry about the cost, and as a result, they have all but disappeared. Our enjoyment is greatly enhanced by disentangling our use of the service from the cost, a phenomenon is known as "flat-rate bias." But as we will see, this preference for disconnecting payment from consumption often leads us to pay more for a flat-rate plan than we would have paid on a per-use plan.[26]

Some very unusual forms of mental accounting occur when payments are separated by larger spans of time. For example, consider the following problem that Eldar Shafir and Richard Thaler posed to the recipients of a wine newsletter:

> Suppose you bought a case of good 1982 Bordeaux in the futures market for $20 a bottle. The wine now sells at auction for $75 a bottle. You have decided to drink a bottle of this wine with dinner. Which of the following best captures your feeling of the cost to you of drinking this bottle?[27]

Given a number of options to choose from, most of the newsletter subscribers—many of whom were economists—either said drinking the wine would feel like it did not cost them anything because the wine had been paid for long ago or drinking the wine would feel like they had saved $55, based on the difference between what they had originally paid and the current value. Both of these responses seem to ignore the concept of "opportunity costs," taught in many introductory economics classes. By drinking the wine, the subscribers would forgo the opportunity to sell the bottle for a $55 profit. Even if no money is lost by drinking the wine, the opportunity to make a profit is lost. Interestingly, when Eldar and Thaler asked the newsletter subscribers how they would feel if, instead of drinking the bottle, they had dropped the bottle and broken it, most said it would feel like they had lost $75. When there was just loss and no consumption, it was the full replacement cost of $75 that suddenly came to mind.

This wine example demonstrates an important effect of decoupling the original payment from consumption. When we pay long before we intend to use a good or service, the cost of the commodity loses some of its reality. For the individual who is trying to live a financially sound life, this means that sometimes keeping payment and consumption more closely connected is a better plan. For example, some kinds of purchases are commonly made in bulk at relatively long intervals and yet consumed on a discretionary basis day by day. Soda, chips, ice cream, and beer are all hedonic items that consumers often buy in bulk in order to save money. But, as the $20 Bordeaux example suggests, this pattern of buying is one that can produce higher levels of usage, and therefore might actually end up costing the consumer more rather than less money. Once payment is in the past, the commodity begins to look free. As a result, buying in bulk—a strategy often undertaken to save money—might be less frugal than a pattern of buying smaller amounts more frequently, only when the product is desired or needed. Utilitarian products such as light bulbs and toothpaste are a different case. These items tend to be consumed as a simple function of the passing of time, and we do not need to wrestle with the question of whether we should use another light bulb tonight or not. As a result, bulk purchases of utilitarian objects save both time and money. But when the act of consumption is a matter of choice, bulk purchases may not help us save. It is much easier to reach for another Dove Bar if we purchased our supply in bulk at the local BJ's Wholesale Club or Sam's Club two weeks ago. In turn, this greater consumption may lead to more purchases. Market researchers have suggested that retailers and manufacturers can increase profits by offering products in multiple unit bundles because, even when a volume discount is offered, the increased consumption of the product created by the decoupling of payment and use can lead to higher profits.

Part of the explanation for the increased consumption of bulk items is thought to be the work of *payment depreciation*.[28] There are many effects of making a payment for the purchase of a good or service, but some of these effects appear to fade with time—or depreciate. In one study, participants were asked to imagine whether they would lend their big-screen TV to a coworker who was planning a Super Bowl party. Half the participants were told they had paid for the TV at the time of purchase, two years earlier. The other half were told the TV was purchased two years ago but, thanks to the store's deferred payment plan, they had only paid the bill recently. Although in both versions of the scenario the television was of equal age and, presumably, value, having paid for it more recently led the second group to be significantly more reluctant to lend it out. They acted as if they valued the TV more simply because they had paid for it more recently.[29]

Payment depreciation also affects our thinking about sunk costs. When we prepay for membership in an athletic club, a shopping club such as BJ's or Sam's Club, or a subscription to a series of plays, the recency of the payment has a strong influence on our attendance. We are more likely to go to the play or the health club soon after paying the bill.

Drawing on this understanding of payment depreciation, marketing researchers have suggested that health club operators could minimize crowding of their facilities by having widely spaced membership payments that are staggered throughout the year. That way, at any given time during the year, a substantial portion of the membership would be experiencing payment depreciation and be considerably less likely to attend.[30] But the examples so far have involved a time-limited event that, once prepaid, must be consumed or lost. The effect of payment depreciation is thought to be in the opposite direction, encouraging consumption, when—as in the example of the $20 bottle of wine—the product remains available for use as the effect of payment is weakened. When we consume an item, the cost is often a deterrent to both purchasing and consumption. If the shirt is too expensive, we are less willing to buy it no matter how much we love it. Similarly, if the bottle of wine costs quite a bit of money, we are both less likely to buy it in the first place and—should we indulge in the purchase—more likely to hold off on opening the bottle until a suitable special occasion arrives. But as payment and consumption become decoupled, we act more freely. Once the big expense is safely in the distant past, its deterrent effect is diluted, and we feel freer to consume what we "paid for a long time ago."

Choosing with Plastic

Behavioral economists have spent some time studying how the use of credit cards affects our spending decisions. Several cleverly conducted experiments have shown that credit cards—in the endearing jargon of social science—are "spending facilitating stimuli."[31] For example, with the help of the staff at a local restaurant, Purdue University consumer researcher Richard Feinberg recorded the amount of the check, the size of the tip, and method of payment— credit card or cash—for 135 customers. He found that tips were significantly larger when people paid with a credit card rather than cash. Credit card tips averaged approximately 17 percent of the bill and cash tips were approximately 15 percent.[32] But this is a classic case of "correlation does not mean causation." It might simply be that Feinberg's credit card customers were wealthier than his cash customers and could afford to be more generous. So to follow up on this initial investigation, Feinberg went into the laboratory to see whether credit-card-related stimuli, such as MasterCard insignias and replicas of actual MasterCards, could act as "primes" to encourage spending. To test this idea, he had undergraduate students come into a laboratory room where they were shown pictures of various products and asked to indicate how much they were willing to pay for each one. For half of the students in the experiment, there were MasterCard-related materials left out on the table, and for the other half no credit-card-related materials were present. Remarkably, Feinberg found that the group of students who were exposed to the MasterCard symbols reported being willing to pay significantly more money for the same products than was the non-credit-card group. In addition, Feinberg found some evidence that the MasterCard group was also more motivated to buy these items.[33] Since the students were randomly assigned to the credit-card and no-credit-card groups, it is unlikely the differences were produced by their personalities, backgrounds, or financial circumstances.

Taken together, Feinberg's studies provide good evidence that credit cards—or simply credit-card-related symbols—can alter our judgments about the value of a product and make us more likely to buy. But his laboratory experiments did not involve people making decisions about actual purchases, so to follow up on his results, Drazen Prelec and Duncan Simester conducted another study, titled "Always Leave Home without It."[34] In this case, business students from the Massachusetts Institute of Technology were solicited to participate in two real auctions, one for a pair of tickets to a Boston Celtics game and one for tickets to a Boston Red Sox game. The Celtics tickets were for the last regular-season game with the Miami Heat, a game that Boston needed to win to clinch the division title, and like all Celtics games during that period, it was a sold-out event. The Red Sox tickets were for a game with the Toronto Blue Jays. The students who volunteered reported to a classroom at noontime and were handed a sheet of paper on which to report their bids for the Celtics tickets and for the Red Sox tickets. However, unbeknownst to the bidders, they were randomly handed one of two versions of the bidding sheet. Half the students were given a sheet that said payment had to be with a credit card and asked bidders to report what kind of card they intended to use. The other students were told payment needed to be in cash and were asked if they had ready access to a cash machine. When they were finished, the participants handed in their bidding sheets and were told that the winners would be announced at 5:00 P.M. that day.[35]

The results were striking. The credit card group was willing to pay *more than twice as much* on average for the Celtics tickets as the cash group. The outcome was similar for the Red Sox tickets, though not as dramatic, perhaps because these seats were not as rare and not for such a crucial game. But in this case people made real bids for real commodities. (Prelec and Simister did give the tickets to the winning bidders, but in the end, they chose to sell the tickets at face value.) So these results, and those of a second study by Prelec and Simister, provide strong evidence that people spend more if they are using plastic.[36]

These researchers have considerably less to say about *why* people spend more when paying with a credit card, perhaps because it is difficult to know the answer. Feinberg proposed that credit card symbols, such as the MasterCard paraphernalia used in his study, become associated with shopping and spending through a kind of conditioning process and that when credit card stimuli are present, it becomes easier to spend. There is undoubtedly some truth to this speculation, but it seems likely that at least two other aspects of credit card spending play a role. First, often—and particularly for Prelec and Semester's sports fans—there are limits on your use of cash that do not exist for credit cards. Plastic enhances your liquidity. As previously mentioned, for people without much savings, cash is available in rather small increments and must be reserved for those expenses that require it. Many of the business students may have had limits on their available cash that did not apply to what they could put on their credit cards. If this were the case, it would have inhibited the bidding of the students who received the cash version of the form. Second, as we learned in chapter 4, the hyperbola has a powerful effect on credit card spending. The loss of cash is an immediate and very concrete event, but placing additional debt on a credit card is a more delayed and diminished form of loss.

Up to now we have been discussing the immediate effects of using a credit card as your method of payment, but consumer researchers have also looked at the effect of plastic on future purchases. In general the answer is that when you have been paying for your recent purchases with a credit card, you are likely to spend more now than if your previous payments were with cash or checks. In this case, the explanation is quite simple: we forget. It is only natural that past spending should have an inhibitory effect on current purchases. If you know that money has been slipping through your fingers like water, you are likely to be somewhat hesitant about the next items that present themselves for purchase. But if this inhibitory effect is to work, you must remember your recent payment stream, and paying with a credit card makes it easier to forget. In one simple study, researchers stopped forty-one students as they emerged from a campus bookstore.[37] Each was asked how they had paid for their purchases and the exact amount paid. Sixty-seven percent of the students who paid cash accurately remembered the amount, but only 35 percent of the credit card customers could remember their outlay. Of those who used a credit card and did not remember the purchase amount, all of them either reported a lower figure or said they had no idea how much they had spent. Obviously, this is not a controlled experiment, and it could be that the more forgetful students tend to use plastic. But in subsequent laboratory-based studies, students were randomly assigned to separate credit card and check-writing groups and simulated the process of either writing out checks or signing credit card receipts to pay bills or make purchases. The results provided support for the idea that writing out checks helps us remember. The active practice involved in writing down the amount of purchase (twice on the check and once in the check register) helps us recall the amounts later.[38] In contrast, the quicker routine of signing for credit card purchases gives us limited exposure to the amount we are spending.

So paying with plastic makes it easier to spend more—both now and in the future—but recent research suggests the method of payment also affects how we feel about the thing we buy after we own it. Several classic psychological studies show that things that are painful to acquire often are valued more. Cash is thought to be the most painful way to pay, and the unreality of plastic—like chips at the casino—creates a kind of insolation from that pain. A group of researchers led by Avni Shah of the University of Toronto conducted a series of studies that showed this effect in action.[39] They offered students on a US campus a mug normally priced at $6.95 for just two dollars. Half the students were told they could only pay in cash, and the other half were told they had to pay with a credit card. Two hours after the purchase the researchers asked the new mug owners to fill out a questionnaire. The cash group reported that they had significantly greater psychological connection to their mugs than the credit card group, and when asked how much money they would need to receive to give up the mug, the results were striking. Both groups showed an endowment effect, wanting more money to sell the mug back than what they paid for it, but the cash group wanted an average of $6.71 for the mug—over three times what they paid. In comparison, the credit card group wanted an average of $3.83, less than twice their cost.

In a laboratory experiment, Shah and colleagues found that this effect of paying cash was felt even when you are spending someone else's money. Participants were asked to evaluate three charities and choose one to which they would contribute five dollars. None of the participants donated their own money. Instead, half were given a five-dollar bill to donate and half were given a five-dollar voucher. A week later the participants filled out a questionnaire about the charities, and those who donated cash showed a stronger psychological connection to their chosen charities than those who donated a voucher.

All of this points to the virtues of paying with cash—or methods closely related to cash, such as writing a check. Cash may be difficult to part with, but given the winds of the marketplace blow so strongly in favor of spending, perhaps that is a good thing. People who pay with cash are much more careful in their consideration of purchases, and after they have decided, they value their purchases more. There may be times when we have no alternative but to pay with plastic, but there is good evidence that we will be happier in the long run if we keep our cards in our wallets.

The Magic of Credit Limits

It is a wonderful feeling. You apply for your first MasterCard, hoping to be accepted. Finally it arrives in the mail, and you feel like a million bucks. It is shiny and new, and it comes with a letter that tells you your credit limit. In most cases, this happy event occurs when you are somewhere in your early twenties. As a result, the credit limit often seems like an amazingly large figure. Never before have you experienced this "superior purchasing power," and you are a bit dizzy thinking about the possibilities that lie before you.[40] If you wanted to, you could buy that new high-end computer that just came out, or you could take a vacation to Australia. Yesterday these were fantasies that you never would have thought possible, but with this little card in your hand, you could have them in an instant.

Most people experience their first credit limit as a kind of affirmation: "Gosh, that's a big number. They must think I am good for it." But how do the banks set your credit limit? Ideally the spending limit should be a measure of your future earning potential. Consistent with the life-cycle theory, banks should look at this young person and, based on the information available to them, make an educated judgment about your future income and ability to repay the debt. Large banks have tons of data available to them, including your entire credit history and their past experiences with people of your age, education, work status, and other characteristics. They should be able to create a very accurate statistical model that will separate those who are worthy of credit from those who are not.

At least that's what you'd think. But before the Great Recession of 2008 there was little evidence that banks engaged in such a rational process. Apparently, there were no formal guidelines for banks to use in setting credit limits, and *past* credit history—not future earning potential—was a much more common factor in setting limits. In addition, credit limits were commonly used as a marketing tool.[41] In an effort to entice you to apply for a new card, letters routinely arrived in the mail saying you had been "preapproved" for an intoxicatingly high credit limit. During the easy credit years, once your balance hit the credit limit, banks were very accommodating about raising it for customers who had a good payment record. Thus, the accumulation of debt continued uninterrupted.

Today things are a bit different. Although the number of credit cards offered has finally topped the prerecession peak, the amount of credit being offered is somewhat less for most people. Card holders with very high credit scores are now offered somewhat higher credit limits than before, but, on average, those in the middle range of good credit and below are being offered approximately one thousand dollars less than in the prerecession days.[42] In addition, the CARD act of 2009 introduced new standards that require lenders to consider cardholder's ability to pay. As a result, it is common to have to report your income, basic expenses, and other debts on your application.[43] But some things have not changed. Offers for preapproved credit cards still come in the mail, and for many people, the first glimpse of a credit limit is an intoxicating experience.

Whether it is or not, the evidence suggests that some people see the credit limit as the bank's prediction of their future earning potential, and as a result, a high credit limit can encourage spending. It is as if the consumer believes that everyone is operating according to the life-cycle theory. The bank has offered a certain amount of credit based on the consumer's worthiness, and believing this, the new holder of the credit card uses the credit limit as a guide for spending. This kind of thinking probably also contributed to the subprime mortgage bubble in the years prior to 2008. People who were offered mortgages for homes they never imagined they could afford probably saw the bank's approval of the loan as an expression of confidence in the borrower—a prediction of rising income—and as a result they signed papers. It is clear now that many subprime lenders were not really making that kind of judgment at all.

In our contemporary world, the distinction between borrowing for utilitarian purposes and borrowing for mere hedonic consumption have all but disappeared, resulting in many people finding it easy to see the credit card as a source of alternative income. In some cases, if the credit limit is large, the cardholder feels free to increase spending. Marketing researchers Dilip Soman and Amar Cheema did a series of studies that demonstrated some of the factors that determine whether your credit limit will fool you into spending.[44] For example, your beliefs about how your credit limit was set appear to matter. In one study, Soman and Cheema stopped people on a university campus and asked them to consider a hypothetical spending scenario in which they were deciding whether or not to purchase an expensive computer. If participants were told their available credit had been determined using a simple and convenient method based on limited information, the size of the credit limit did not affect the likelihood of saying they would spend. In addition, being older and wiser helps. Most people who have been out in the world for a while become skeptical of advertising claims, and a similar distrustfulness seems to apply to the marketing appeals of credit card companies. When you have been around the block a few times, the MasterCard pitch "You work hard for your success—let MasterCard reward you with unparalleled convenience and freedom" is taken with a grain of salt.[45] Soman and Cheema's older and more experienced participants were not influenced by the size of the credit limit they were given—even when they were told to imagine their credit limit had been decided using a very scientific method that accurately forecasted future earnings potential. But the same description *did* have a substantial effect on college students who participated in the study.[46] If these relatively naive consumers were told that the credit limit was a reliable indicator of the bank's faith in them, then a higher credit limit made them more likely to say they would purchase the computer.

Normally, of course, credit card companies don't tell us much about how they set credit limits. For the purposes of their research, Soman and Cheema provided their respondents with descriptions of the process used to determine the credit limit. But in real life, consumers are free to make their own inferences about what is going on behind the walls of the bank, and some give greater meaning to the credit limit than others. In a subsequent study, Soma and Cheema asked credit card users to consider a hypothetical purchase of a $1,200 piece of antique furniture. Participants who said they believed the limits on their credit cards were set based on an accurate prediction of their future earnings were more likely to say they would buy the furniture than those who did not.[47] How these consumers came to this belief is not clear, but this line of research suggests that people who read more significance into their credit limits have a greater tendency to spend.

Credit Cards and Purchases That Are Useful versus Those That Are Fun

As we have seen, economists and consumer researchers sometimes divide purchases into the categories of utilitarian versus hedonic. Often a single purchase can be a mix of these attributes. For example, if it is your primary means of getting to work, a car can be a very utilitarian purchase, but a Porsche Panamara 4S Sport Turismo with optional heated fourteen-way memory seats, LED headlights, and a surround sound audio system is much more than just a way to get to work. It is a hedonic machine. When considering purchases, shoppers are very aware of the mix of utilitarianism versus hedonism in the things they buy, and there is some evidence this distinction affects the way people choose to pay.

According to the life-cycle theory, consumers borrow early in life based on their predictions of future earnings and needs, and they get into trouble when they borrow too much in the present, which limits their options for spending in the future. The easy availability of credit makes it possible to get into this kind of trouble. According to some researchers, consumers worry about their ability to avoid becoming overextended, and this worry affects the way they approach hedonic and utilitarian purchases. Specifically, since borrowing money—by taking out a loan or paying with a credit card—creates an obligation that will limit future spending, many buyers are unwilling to pay for hedonic purchases on credit. If you want it just for fun, you ought to be able to pay for it up front so that it does not put a strain on your finances. Utilitarian purchases, on the other hand, are more justifiable and thus more likely to be financed.[48] For example, in one study, college students were presented with a hypothetical purchase of a new suit and were asked whether they would be more likely to pay with a check or credit card. Some of the students received a description that emphasized the suit's utilitarian value ("great for you to wear at work") and others received a description that stressed hedonic value ("great to wear when you go out at night"). This subtle difference in how the purchase was framed produced a substantial effect on the reported method of payment. The students were more likely to say they would pay with a check when the item was framed as a fun purchase rather than a useful one.

One interpretation of this reluctance to finance immediate pleasures with plastic suggests that in a small way we are trying to do what is best for ourselves. Paying for our splurges with cash both limits the amount of mad money we can draw on for these nonutilitarian things—just what we have on hand—and protects the future. If we use up our available credit today on discretionary purchases, then it won't be available tomorrow when we are confronted with true necessities. In contrast, when framed as work clothes, the purchase is considered more utilitarian and therefore closer to a need than a mere want. Obviously, people differ on their ability to exercise this method of self-control, but paying for pleasures with cash is a small commitment strategy that can be a hedge against ballooning debt.

Anchoring and Adjustment

Psychologists have been studying the importance of first things for a long time: first impressions, first words, first memories. Things that are first are special, and when we are confronted by more than one thing, the first one will often be treated differently. Behavioral economists have spent considerable time studying a particular kind of first thing—an "anchor"—on our judgments later on. An anchor is usually encountered as a quantitative estimate. How much do you think this house is worth? In the case of estimating the value of a piece of real estate, a figure given in advance can have a powerful effect on later estimates—even for experts. In one study, real estate agents toured houses in Tucson, Arizona. These agents were given a complete Multiple Listing Service report on the house as well as information about comparable homes recently sold in the area. All of the agents were shown the same information, except for the listed asking price. For some of the agents the asking price was listed 11 to 12 percent above the true assessed value and for others it was listed 11 to 12 percent below the assessed value.[49] The real estate agents were given some time to wander around the house in an effort to estimate its value. In the case of one house that had been assessed at $135,000, the average estimates of the agents were all substantially lower, but the estimates were strongly affected by the listing price. The average value assigned by the agents who saw the lower listing price was $114,204, whereas those who saw the higher price valued the same home at $128,754. All of these people were experts, all of them had lots of information about the house, and all of them were free to walk around and inspect the property. But the real estate agents' estimates were anchored to the listing price, and despite all the information available, they did not sufficiently adjust their estimates away from the anchor.[50]

The affects of anchoring and insufficient adjustment away from the anchor are often felt during shopping. In particular, different ways of presenting the price of an item or making purchase suggestions can have a powerful effect on the quantities purchased. For example, many of the things we see in the store are described as "two for $5" or "five for $1." This is known as multiple-unit pricing, and it can sometimes get us to buy more than we would otherwise. In many cases, when we go to the store, we are in the market for single units of the things we need: one box of detergent, one box of cookies, or one bottle of juice. Yet for both the retailer who is selling you the product and the product manufacturer, there are advantages to convincing you to buy more than a single unit. For the manufacturer, competing against many other brands, getting you to buy more Keebler Fudge Stripes cookies today is a hedge against some flashy new product that might be introduced between now and your next trip to the grocery store. If you just buy one package today, you may buy the flashy new product next week, but if you buy more than one package today, you may not need cookies next week. In addition, as discussed earlier, the consumer who stockpiles hedonic items at home is likely to consume more.

Although Tversky and Kahneman were the first to study anchoring and adjustment, consumer researchers soon recognized the importance of these concepts and have begun to reveal some interesting ways that advertising anchors affect our buying and consuming.[51] For example, multiple-unit pricing does produce the intended effect. There is some ambiguity produced by a sign that says "two for $10." If it does not also explicitly say "$5 each," then some consumers may believe that they must buy two items to get this price. In fact, the store must make it clear there is a higher individual price if multiple purchases are required. Finally, some consumers may be convinced that "two for $10" represents a sale price, simply because of the format of the pricing, even if $5 is the normal per-unit cost.[52]

As these examples show, it is not entirely clear whether anchoring alone gives multiple-unit pricing its power to make us buy more, but a clearer example of anchoring can be seen in "limited quantities" pricing. Imagine you are at the grocery store and you come across a soup display announcing that each can has been marked down by approximately 15 percent, but the sign also says "Limit four per customer" or "Limit twelve per customer." In one study, conducted in three supermarkets in Sioux City, Iowa, people who saw a sign showing a twelve-can limit bought significantly more cans of soup than those who were told there was either no limit or a four-can limit. Per-customer limits tend to suggest that the item in question is popular, a bargain, and/or in limited supply, but this research strongly suggests that the number of units allowed becomes a figure we focus on. When confronted with a sign that says "Limit X per customer," many people who intended to buy just a can or two of soup may be convinced to stockpile, and how much they buy will be affected by the value of X.

Clearer effects of anchoring can be seen in advertisements that suggest a quantity that consumers should purchase without tying this number to the price: "Buy three in case friends drop by." Here the anchor is thrown out on its own as a direct line to the quantity purchased and without any implication that buying more affects the deal consumers will get. In a study of this kind of anchoring, university students were asked to imagine a scenario in which they were confronted with an advertising appeal for Snickers bars. Half the students were urged to "buy eighteen for your freezer," and the others were simply told to "buy some for your freezer." The group who received the anchor of eighteen bars—undoubtedly a much higher number than the normal purchase quantity—expressed the intention to buy more Snickers bars than the group who had not received a numerical suggestion. It should be pointed out that on average students in the "buy eighteen" group said they would purchase between two and a half and four Snickers bars—well below eighteen—but these figures were significantly higher than for the group who received no specific suggestion about how many candy bars to buy.[53]

As shoppers doing our best to negotiate today's economic environment, it is clear we are influenced by a variety of subtle stimuli. In fact, the anchors that pull at us can be completely arbitrary—even meaningless—and yet they alter the decisions that we make. In a remarkably extreme example, a group of researchers gave university students a shopping scenario in which products were marked as having been "shipped to stores" in boxes of seven, fourteen, twenty-eight, or fifty-six. This is an entirely irrelevant anchor. What do we care how many widgets were in each box when they came to the store? Nonetheless, the number mattered. When asked how much of the product they would purchase, the students gave numbers that paralleled the "shipped to the store" numbers.[54] Similar advertising ploys, such as "101 uses," "Buy a month's worth," and "Buy for all your friends," undoubtedly have the effect of moving us in the direction of purchasing a larger quantity, but the news is not all bad. It appears that simply thinking of our normal level of purchase can insulate us against the effects of anchors presented in point of purchase advertisements. In a different study, university students who were asked to think about the normal quantity of gum they purchased were later unaffected by point-of-purchase appeals urging them to buy more.[55] Apparently, by thinking about their typical purchase the students set their own, internal anchor, which was more persuasive than the external anchor suggested in the point-of-purchase advertisement.

Additional evidence that simple mental strategies can help us avoid the pull of unrealistic anchors comes from studies of mail-in rebates. The evidence suggests that mail-in rebate offers tend to accentuate the effects of our underlying motivations. If we are inclined to purchase a new electric shaver, discovering that the model you want comes with a $10 rebate will further enhance your tendency to buy. On the other hand, if it is your spouse who wants the electric shaver and you would prefer to buy something else, you are likely to see the rebate on the shaver as a hassle and an argument against buying it.[56] But if you are leaning toward buying, incorporating a rebate into your decision-making represents a kind of gamble on your own future behavior because rebates typically involve work. The buyer must assemble the rebate form, the original cash register receipt, and a proof of purchase that you must cut off the packaging—all to be enclosed in an envelope that you supply, along with a stamp. Finally, the envelope must somehow make it into the mail. Online rebates are simpler, but they still require sitting down at the computer to type in a bunch of letters and numbers. Furthermore, in this digital age, the failure to benefit from a rebate can come later in the process. After the rebate is mailed in or entered online, often many weeks pass before the purchaser receives in the mail—not a check—but a prepaid debit card. The card must be activated before it can be used and is far less liquid than a check. I once tried to determine how to transfer the balance of a rebate card to my bank account and gave up in frustration. Finally, many of these cards have expiration dates, so if you fail to use them within six months, you lose the money entirely.[57] As a result many rebates are never redeemed—to the benefit of the merchant's bottom line—but when we are standing before the smartphone display, thinking about buying this new gadget, the rebate can be very persuasive.[58]

When it comes to rebates, we tend to be overly optimistic in our predictions about the outcome. If we are considering a purchase that we are inclined to make, we have a tendency to ignore the possibility that we will fail to complete the rebate process or that there will be other problems getting our money back. However, one line of research suggests a way to avoid being overly influenced by a mail-in rebate offer. Three groups of people were asked to imagine that they were considering the purchase of a large box of detergent that came with a mail-in rebate. One group was asked to think about and write down two or three reasons why they would redeem the rebate, and another group was asked to think about and write down two or three reasons why they might *fail* to redeem the rebate. A final group was not asked to think about the rebate at all.[59] Interestingly, this last group and the group asked to generate positive reasons why they would redeem the rebate expressed the same level of confidence that they would complete the task. This pattern of results suggests that under normal circumstances, when we are not asked to think about our future rebate-redeeming behavior, we are optimistic about our chances—equally as optimistic as people who were deliberately asked to think positive thoughts. But, as you might imagine, the group asked to think about reasons why they might not redeem the rebate were significantly less optimistic about their chances. In fact, they predicted an average success rate of only 42 percent, as compared to 61 percent for the other two groups.

Finally, research on bidders on eBay shows both the effects of anchors and at least one interesting contradiction of the usual anchoring effect. When an auction starts with a relatively low bid, we would expect the low number to serve as an anchor, making subsequent bids adjustments to that figure. As a result, based on the usual anchoring and adjustment effects, we would expect the winning bid also to be relatively low. But, as we have seen, an auction is a social environment, considerably different from a simple in-store shopping experience. In one study, researchers observed eBay auctions for 179 Tabriz Persian rugs and discovered that the lower the starting bid, the higher the winning bid.[60] Why? The higher winning bid is caused by a two-stage process. A lower starting bid draws more people into the auction, and then—the researchers surmise—the greater interest reflected by high traffic is interpreted by participants as a reflection of value. All these eBay bidders can't be wrong. The rug must be pretty good.

Lest you think anchoring effects are nonexistent in the special world of eBay, there is clear evidence that in circumstances more closely resembling two-for-$5 pricing, anchors have the usual effect. In their study of bidding for the board game Cashflow 101, Lee and Malmendier found that the final price was higher when the product description mentioned the considerably more expensive manufacturer's price of $195. Interestingly, it was the more experienced eBay bidders who were most affected by this advertising strategy, so among eBay users, wisdom does not always come from experience. The manufacturer's retail price was irrelevant to the eBay context, where the game could be had for much less—either at auction or through a Buy It Now purchase. Nonetheless, it served as an anchor, driving up the final price. Similarly, other studies show that bidders are more likely to overbid for a product if the seller offers free shipping. The special psychology of the eBay environment is such that the heat of competition and a number of other irrelevant factors can lead to overspending.[61]

Overconfidence

Optimistic thinking about mail-in rebates undoubtedly encourages us to buy the items we want, but economic wishful thinking is not limited to this example. It is a problem that can be very costly in a variety of situations. Psychologists have long understood that when we are asked to evaluate ourselves, we tend to put on rose-colored glasses. Suddenly we are all above average on every positive trait imaginable. We are overly optimistic about what we can accomplish, and we are very certain our judgments and opinions are correct, even when they are based on very limited knowledge. Overconfidence has been blamed for the disastrous decision to launch the US space shuttle *Challenger,* for the miscalculations of bank CEOs during the lead-up to the Great Recession, for politicians' erroneous belief that wars can be easily won, and for the wrongful executions of many people convicted of capital crimes on the basis of eyewitness testimony.[62] It turns out that how certain a witness feels about their identification of a suspect is a poor indicator of accuracy.[63] When asked what single human bias he would most like to eliminate, Nobel Prize winning behavioral economist Daniel Kahneman named overconfidence.[64]

But not everyone is overconfident all the time. Being in a situation that provides frequent feedback about accuracy helps. For example, weather forecasters are generally very good at matching the confidence of their predictions to their accuracy.[65] They find out whether they are right or not every day of the week in a very public way. But the tendency for most of us to cheerily assess our lives and the world we live in is sufficiently pervasive that a famous study of depression carried the whimsical subtitle "Sadder but Wiser?"—a suggestion that the difference between nondepressed people and those who are mildly depressed is that depressed people have a more realistic view of themselves and their place in the world.[66]

Without question, there are many benefits that come with being optimistic, and psychologists have spent considerable time looking for ways to help people build an upbeat approach to life.[67] But as consumers, overconfidence can often be a rather expensive trait. Overconfidence about the likelihood of follow-through on a mail-in rebate is one example of how optimism can cost us money, but many times a day we make small but important assessments of our economic circumstances both now and in the future. As a result, behavioral economists have given much attention to the pitfalls of undue optimism.[68] Sometimes our overconfidence is about our current financial situation.[69] We believe we are saving enough and that we are not overspending. If we are considering the purchase of a new car, we reason, "Even though it is rather expensive, I can afford it because my salary is big enough to cover the payments." But as we stand here in the present thinking about our current budget and dreaming about a new car—using Nora Ephron's system of amortization to translate the cost into cups of cappuccino—we tend to forget the many unanticipated expenses that can crop up. That's why we call them "unanticipated." We optimistically think that things will be just fine and that at no point in the life of the car will we come to regret the purchase we are about to make.

Similarly optimistic decisions are often made about investments and business ventures.[70] It is a sad fact that a large number of new businesses fail. This is a well-known truth, but every day—at considerable personal risk—people sink their savings into new business enterprises, confident that they are somehow different from the other guys. Unlike the losers, these self-assured entrepreneurs are convinced they have the key to success.[71] We all have a bit of hubris that leads us to ignore many important downsides of the options before us. As we think about the future, the many reasons why things will work out for us seem quite obvious. If, in addition, we were to deliberately consider the many ways we might fail—as painful as this kind of thinking might be—we might make better decisions.

But in our lives as consumers, often the kind of overconfidence that hurts our pocketbooks the most is overconfidence about ourselves—about our behavior in the future and our basic capabilities. When I go to the bookstore or browse the titles on Amazon.com, I am often tempted to buy. When I do buy a book, it is at a moment when I am truly interested and fully intend to read it. Usually I have some other book going at the time, so I buy this new book knowing that I will not be able get to it immediately. But I do intend to read it. Really. That said, if you were to come to my house today and take a book off my shelf at random, the chances would be very good that I bought the book in question but have not read it.

As consumers, we are remarkably bad at predicting our future behavior. Many of us have had the experience of buying all the parts and tools required to complete some craft, hobby, or home improvement project, only to have these items lie fallow for months or years. When it comes to the goal of improving health, we seem to be particularly prone to wishful thinking. Many people buy exercise equipment—often rather expensive exercise equipment—fully intending to use it. Yet barbells and stationary bicycles are some of the most common items found at yard sales. We also join health clubs and sign up for yoga and aerobics classes with the best of intentions. One study found that health club members substantially overestimated the number of times they would visit the gym each month.[72] This is perhaps not surprising, but when the researchers examined the attendance of thousands of subscribers to three large health clubs, they found that monthly subscribers paid an average of $17 per trip. Had these members gone to the gym the same number of times and paid on a per-trip basis, they would have saved $7 per visit and approximately $600 for the year. Those who signed up for annual contracts were only slightly better at predicting their behavior, paying an average of $15 per visit—$5 more than the per-visit cost. Of course, part of the appeal of paying gym memberships on monthly or annual basis stems from a desire to separate payment from the act of going. It is difficult enough to get yourself to the gym under normal circumstances, but having to shell out money each time would be an additional disincentive. Many of us are willing to pay a premium on our memberships to disentangle the pain of payment from the pain of squat thrusts. Nonetheless, overconfidence about the amount of time or energy we will have in the future often leads us to spend money now that we later wish we could have back.

A DIFFERENT PATH THROUGH THE LIFE CYCLE

As an alternative to the life-cycle theory, Richard Thaler and his colleague Hersh Shefrin have proposed the behavioral life-cycle theory, which provides a better description of our actual behavior and suggests methods to help people achieve the kind of balance hoped for in the original life-cycle theory.[73] As previously mentioned, one problem with the traditional theory is that we have very limited information about the future. What really is our earning potential? What kinds of expenses will we encounter around the next corner? These unknowns can have a profound effect on our ability to make wise choices in the present. But Shefrin and Thaler are even more concerned about problems of self-control such as those discussed in chapter 4. We have much difficulty avoiding spending today in favor of saving for tomorrow, and as a result, for many people the "in-the-red" section of the diagram at the beginning of this chapter extends throughout the entire life span. The call of the hyperbola is the obstacle to getting into the black.

The alternative approach taken by Shefrin and Thaler has a number of features. First, similar to Thomas Schelling's story of the reformed smoker who throws away his friend's forgotten pack of cigarettes, Shefrin and Thaler recognize that we are of two minds about the decisions we face—or, as they put it, we have two selves. They call these selves "the Doer," the person who wants to act now based on what seems best at the moment, and "the Planner," who takes the long view and wants to make sure things work out in the distant future. The conflict between these two selves is the primary challenge to the life-cycle theory.

The second important part of Shefrin and Thaler's behavioral life-cycle theory is the recognition that we put money into different mental accounts. As we have seen, rather than acting as though all money is the same, we often treat income from different sources differently. Some funds are more fungible than others. Specifically, Shefrin and Thaler divide money into three important categories. *Current income* is typically the salary or pay that we receive on a regular basis, and in most people's minds, this money is primarily for immediate use. We spend current income to pay the rent, buy our food, and fill the tank with gas. A second source of funds is *current assets*, such as money we have saved or the value of our home. These funds are less likely to be spent than current income and are often seen as a source of future income. Finally, Shefrin and Thaler also allow for the category of *future income*, funds that are expected but will not be received until long in the future, such as an inheritance or retirement savings that cannot be spent now.

The separation of money into these three categories follows naturally from the kinds of mental accounts consumers tend to apply. For example, one group of MBA students was asked how much more per month they would spend on current expenses if they received $2,400 distributed in three different ways. When the students were told they would be inheriting $2,400 from a relative in five years, they said they would not increase their spending at all.[74] In contrast, when these students were asked to imagine being given a $2,400 bonus in a lump sum, they said they would spend $400 more in the following month and approximately $785 more in total for the entire year. Finally, when these students imagined that their income for a year would be increased by $200 a month, they reported they would begin to spend $100 more per month, for a total of $1,200 in additional spending for the year. Contrary to the idea of fungibility, receiving $2,400 in these three different ways had very different effects on current spending. Shefrin and Thaler's three accounts make sense because future income is seen as having no effect on current spending, large lump sum bonuses have some effect on current spending, and increases to current income have a substantial effect on current spending.

When income is not spent, it is typically saved, and the tension between spending and saving—the battle between the Doer and the Planner—is the crux of our contemporary dilemma. If we are going to make it out of the red or remain in the black, windfalls should not be considered current income. Naturally, a small windfall, such as an unexpected bonus of $50 or $100, is likely to be absorbed quickly and spent. But to be prudent, large windfalls should be assigned partially or entirely to the current assets account: savings rather than current income. Finally, perhaps the most important struggle involves deciding how much current income should be saved. The Doer is strongly inclined to buy a new iPad if there is cash on hand, whereas the Planner is worried about being able to pay the rent when retirement age rolls around. This is the great hyperbola problem, and Shefrin and Thaler's behavioral life-cycle theory acknowledges the difficulty of self-control. How do we get people to distribute enough of their current income and windfalls to savings?

The solution to this basic problem is going to require the exertion of some kind of control, and Shefrin and Thaler suggest that the control can come from the outside (from institutions or governments) or from the inside (from the individual). For example, many pension plans apply external control by requiring that employees save a portion of their income and prohibiting the use of these funds before retirement except under the most dire of circumstances. What Shefrin and Thaler call internal control is the traditional notion of willpower. They quote the American psychologist William James, who said, "Effort of attention is thus the essential phenomenon of will."[75] If external control is insufficient to keep our impulses in check, we will need to make wise choices, and these choices will require effort. But some choices are easier than others. It is easier to avoid the peril of the Sirens if long before you approach them you commit yourself to a different course. Similarly, as we sail the contemporary economic ocean, there are ways we can construct our odyssey so as to avoid disaster. Thanks to recent developments in contemporary psychology and behavioral economics, we have discovered methods of achieving self-control that are more effective than efforts to summon raw willpower. In chapter 9, I draw on these new developments to suggest ways you can avoid debt and achieve financial stability. Finally, I suggest several institutional and policy reforms that would encourage solvency and savings for all Americans.

NEIL

I met Neil during visiting hours in prison. He was at a maximum-security facility, so I could not use a tape recorder and was prohibited from bringing anything into the room, including pencil and paper. For a convicted murderer, he was a surprisingly frail-looking man, with the pale, translucent skin of a person who never saw the sun.

Neil grew up in North Dakota, graduated at the top of his high school class, and got accepted to a prestigious engineering school on the East Coast. After graduation he worked for a small engineering firm in Massachusetts. He met his wife while in school, and after five years of marriage, she gave birth to a baby boy. By all reports, they lived modestly but happily. There was bickering from time to time, as is the case in many marriages, but there were never any reports of violence. Neil and his wife were active churchgoers, and Neil was a dependable and valued employee.

Eventually, however, Neil got the urge to do something different. He had always been concerned about social justice issues, and although he liked his work with the engineering firm, he wanted to make a greater contribution to society. With his wife's blessing, he began to attend law school at night with the goal of becoming a defense attorney, perhaps even a public defender or a public interest lawyer. It was difficult to straddle a full-time job and law school, but Neil had always been a good student. After only four years of part-time study, he finished law school and passed the bar exam. Feeling a deep commitment to his new path, Neil began to look for a job. Unfortunately, by now he was somewhat older than the typical law school graduate, and because he had been working full-time, he hadn't been able to take on the clerkships that might have helped him land a job. Eventually, he quit his engineering position and set up a solo practice. The couple had a small amount of savings to get him going, and based on his previous job and academic successes, he was confident things would work out.

A few clients came Neil's way, but it was difficult building a practice from scratch. He just wasn't making enough money for the family to get by. Before long Neil started taking money out of his practice—spending his clients' retainers before he had done the work—just to keep his household going. He felt intense guilt about this, and to make matters worse, his money problems were enough of a distraction that they affected his ability to concentrate on his cases.

In time, he had used up every retainer he had and had borrowed $15,000 against his credit card. He now had a mortgage and other bills to pay, and he could not see where he was going to get the money. Nor could he tell anyone, including his wife, about the extent of his financial problems. It did not occur to him, he told me, that he might try to get his old job back, despite some indication that, had he tried, he might have been able to do so. Instead, isolated and deeply depressed despite being on medication, he decided to end his current situation once and for all.

He called his wife and, claiming that he had gotten a big settlement, told her he wanted to take her and their son out for a celebratory dinner that evening. His original idea had been simply to commit suicide, but, recalling that both he and his wife had once said they would choose death over living without the other, he decided he should take both their lives. It never occurred to him that, with the help of her family and friends, she might be able to cope with his loss. Moreover, because he hated the state child welfare agency that he believed would get custody of their son after both parents were gone, he said, he would rather his child die than become a ward of the state. It never occurred to him that relatives might seek custody of their son. So, following this twisted logic, Neil came to the conclusion that he must kill them all, and he made plans to do so after they went out to dinner. However, after killing his wife and son, he appears to have lost the nerve to take his own life. Instead, he left the house, and after wandering around for more than a day, he went to a friend's house, where he soon confessed to the crimes. He subsequently was sentenced to life in prison without the possibility of parole. Ironically, the reports that appeared about the case often mentioned that he and his wife were up to date on their mortgage payments and car loans.

Neil's murders may have been the result of true mental illness. A forensic psychiatrist hired by the state prosecutor's office said that at the time of the murders, Neil suffered from "major depression, severe, recurrent, and was acutely suicidal," and that his depression "rendered him substantially incapable to appreciate the wrongfulness of his conduct." In the opinion of the psychiatrist, Neil thought that killing his family was a merciful act. What is impossible to know is how much of Neil's depression stemmed from his financial problems and how much of it was there to begin with. It appears that he took matters into his own hands at the moment he ran out of cash, but his money problems alone cannot account for what he did. Sadly, it is easy to see many points in the story where an action here or there might have helped him to consider other, less drastic alternatives and to avoid this deeply tragic outcome.

Neil was a failure in the old-fashioned sense of a person who goes out into world and loses everything. He was entrepreneurial, a quality our society values, but like many entrepreneurs, he was unsuccessful. His story—one of money problems, stress, and, ultimately, violence—may be an extreme case, one that is not representative of the majority of debt problems in this book, but there is little question that financial stress can be an enormous burden and can sometimes fuel desperate acts. Indeed, two of the seven people we have already encountered volunteered that, at the darkest moments of their private financial disasters, they considered taking their own lives.

How Not to Go Broke

It's a wonderful, wonderful gift to like cheap food. I mean, some people just happen to like expensive food and then they are unhappy most of the time, or else, they spend all their money on food. But if you just by chance are born loving cheap food, then you can eat everything that you love.

—ECONOMIST STEVEN LEVITT

So why are Americans going broke? Why are so many people carrying so much debt? Why don't more people save? As the last chapter suggests, part of the problem is simply a matter of how we think about money—the common mental errors that plague our everyday decisions. But these human quirks alone cannot explain the great expansion of indebtedness and financial strain beginning in the 1970s. Presumably the reasoning errors discovered by psychologists and behavioral economists have been there all along. It is impossible to know for certain what has caused our national pastime of spending more than we earn. There are no controlled experiments in the real world of the US economy, but there are a few things we can say for certain. Since the 1970s, technological advances in banking and our retail world have introduced many new challenges to our self-control. Credit is still fairly easy to come by and—perhaps even more important—exchangeable for almost anything. Cash is still the universal currency, completely liquid and acceptable in almost every circumstance, but credit cards have become very close rivals. In today's world, there are only a few cases where plastic will not do, and, in a pinch, credit cards can be used to get cash.

Since the 1970s, we have entered a twenty-four-hour world of material desire. Commercial messages come at us from all directions, and the branding process has turned every manufactured item into an advertisement for itself. As all the blank spaces in our world are filled in with commercial messages, there are fewer and fewer moments when we are free of the tug of advertising. Finally, new innovations quickly leapfrog from being mere desires to needs.

Since the 1970s, it has become possible to spend in many more places, times, and ways. Before the popularization of toll-free numbers and the Internet, most spending took place in conventional retail locations during business hours. Today, almost anything you can imagine can be purchased by anyone at almost any time.

Since the 1970s, many other things have happened that have made our economic lives more treacherous. Changes in the structure of the American economy have played an important role in our great indebtedness. In his 2006 book *The Great Risk Shift*, Yale University political scientist Jacob Hacker showed that despite the optimistic picture painted by many standard economic indicators even in those prerecession times, middle-class Americans were not feeling optimistic about their own circumstances.[1] As several authors have recently pointed out, income inequality in the United States is high and continuing to rise.[2] But even more troubling is an increase in income insecurity, which was dramatically demonstrated during the Great Recession. By 2015 the official US poverty rate had dropped to 13.5 percent, but during the postrecession period of 2009 to 2011, almost a third of the country, 31.6 percent, fell below the poverty level for at least two months.[3] In addition, retirement plans have moved from "defined benefit," which provides the retiree with an expected level of income in retirement, to "defined contribution," as with 401(k) plans, for which the income is uncertain. Finally, despite the improved rate of coverage under the Affordable Care Act, millions of Americans still are not covered by health insurance.

Hacker pointed out that in judging the value of a stock, securities analysts take note of its volatility—how much its price fluctuates. Greater volatility means greater risk for the investor, and as we have seen, the lives of many American families have increased in their volatility—their level of risk—since the 1970s. Add to this an economy built on easy credit and low levels of personal savings, and it is not difficult to understand why so many people are in debt. Several of the people profiled in this book faced income volatility or sudden changes in expenses and were unable to absorb these events because they had built up debt rather than savings. Susan lived with her mother in a condo, depending on this arrangement, and was caught short when her mother died. Kathy, Marcia, and Joel were all struggling to survive on somewhat variable income from low-paying jobs. According to the latest statistics, they are not alone. Americans are facing much greater economic risk than they were in the 1970s, and they are substantially less well prepared to take it on.

Of course, the problem is not limited to the United States. This is an affliction of the economically developed countries; however, levels of household debt are generally lower in Europe and Asia than they are in America. But, as we have seen, Canada is not far behind the United States, and according to recent reports, levels of personal indebtedness in England are quite high, with a 2016 survey indicating that the average British household owed a record £13,000 in unsecured debt.[4] Household debt is also a serious problem in Australia, where as of April of 2017, the National Debt Helpline was experiencing record numbers of calls and 22 percent of mortgage-holding households were in "mild mortgage stress."[5] So Americans are not alone in their sense of being chained to their bills.

Some of these problems are systemic and beyond the scope of this book. If you are living in poverty—as is the case for far too many people in a nation as wealthy as the United States—there are no easy budget plans that will produce a reasonable life. But for the rest of us, there is some good news: it is possible to live well in America. Given a reasonable level of income, you can save, avoid debt, and enjoy life. Today's world does not make the job very easy, but there are things we can do to make financial stability achievable—things we can do as individuals and things we can do together as citizens.

This is not primarily a self-help book. My first task was to answer the paradoxical question of why so many people in the richest nation on earth are having so much trouble with money, and in the foregoing chapters I presented a story of financial challenge that draws on an understanding of psychology and behavioral economics. This story also points to a number of ways to avoid going broke, and I outline some of these in the following pages. I have no suggestions about how to become wealthy through investing. For that kind of advice there is no shortage of books, tapes, and professionals who are waiting to give you their wisdom, but given our recent history, I recommend you mix a healthy dose of skepticism with any advice you receive.[6] Instead, the suggestions that follow are for the middle-class person who is having difficulty getting along month to month—for those of us who know we should be able to make ends meet but are having trouble doing so.

In some cases the advice I give will differ substantially from the standard view—and for good reason. The shelves of your local bookstore are filled with books aimed at bringing you financial stability and helping you get out of debt, but the majority of these books make the same mistake made by many generations of economists: they assume you are rational. They assume you always have your best interests at heart and that all you need is better information to get you there. Most get-out-of-debt books offer you budgets. They assume that if you carefully analyze your income and expenditures, you will be able to figure out where the money should or should not go: this much for rent, this much for bills, this much for food, etc. The problem is that you are not rational—none of us are—at least not in the sense that the classical economist Adam Smith assumed we were. Nor are most people rational about budgets. If everyone were able to achieve financial stability by simply following a budget, there would be no need for a book such as this one or most of the budget books in your local bookstore. In contrast, the approach I will take is far less rational. Recent research by behavioral scientists and economists points to a number of ways we can engineer our personal and commercial environments to better serve our needs. It is to these engineering ideas that we turn now.

HOW YOU CAN SAVE MORE

As we have seen, many of our problems with debt could be avoided by having cash on hand. When the brakes go out on the car and there's nothing in the bank, the person with credit available on a Visa card will be hard pressed to come up with a solution other than plastic. But add to this equation a modest rainy day fund, and the hapless driver has another, more appealing option. The situation is further improved if there is a steady stream of deposits going into the savings account. Even if an unexpected expense wipes out a big chunk of the cash on hand, you know that—unless you are hit with an unusual number of expensive disasters—it will just be a matter of time before the balance is restored. But what hurts about savings is the sense of loss. If we actually have to make payments to our savings account—deliberately depositing checks or cash—our loss aversion predicted by prospect theory kicks in and it may be difficult to avoid being distracted by some more immediate use for your cash.

Of course, sometimes there really is no cash to save. If your basic expenses are greater than your income, then saving will just push you more rapidly into debt. Furthermore, many people reach this point without actually realizing it. Particularly if you have experienced a recent decrease in income or if you have become confused about the extent of your financial obligations—which, in today's world, is remarkably easy to do—then cutting expenses may be a more pressing concern than saving. In a case such as this, constructing a budget can be a very useful exercise. Once you have a handle on your personal balance sheet, you may discover that the rent or mortgage exceeds your ability to pay, or that these or other expenses should be cut. But there is a difference between *constructing* a budget, as a means of assessing how much is coming in and going out, and *following* a budget on a daily basis. This is where it gets sticky. Most people—even those who would consider themselves lower-middle-class—should be able to save something, at least a little, each pay period, but for many people, the savings never seem to accumulate. Here is where behavioral economics provides some useful suggestions.

Know Your Balances

Most people who have ever had to work to maintain a healthy weight know that an important part of the process involves getting on the scale every day. Chances are if you asked them at random, they could tell you within a pound what they weigh that day. These people understand that if you don't weigh yourself, you will never know whether you are making progress or not. Similarly, sound financial management requires knowing your balances on your checking and savings accounts, as well as your credit cards and other loans. The busyness of our daily lives is such that we easily lose track. Thankfully, today's world makes it easy to check. Most banks now have sophisticated websites and apps that allow you to check your balances as often as you like. There are also a number of personal finance software programs that can pull all of your accounts together and put all your information in one place. You can set up a budget, monitor how you are doing on a daily basis, and watch the movement of your net worth. However you choose to do it, it is important to check your balances often. You can't make progress unless you know what direction you're moving.

Make Saving Automatic

When you put money away in a savings account you are showing a very obvious form of self-control. You are forgoing a smaller immediate reward in the interest of some larger, more distant reward. Furthermore, in many cases that future reward is somewhat abstract. If you are not saving "for" something, such as future college tuition, a car, or a down payment on a home, the object of your saving is rather vague: future financial security, whatever that is supposed to be. It is nowhere near as clear and appealing as the latest iPad, dinner at that new French restaurant, or any other impulsive urge that might be welling up inside you. This kind of deliberate savings, making deposits each week or each month, requires a tough fight against the hyperbola—what we commonly call willpower. The immediate use for money in hand is always going to have a stronger pull than an equally appealing item off in the future—simply because it is immediate and riding the high end of the hyperbola. Furthermore, because the contemporary world offers up so many temptations, there are endless opportunities to lose money earmarked for savings to an impulsive purchase.

Savings is an investment in, or for, the future, and the future is very uncertain. Contrary to the standard life-cycle theory, which calls for borrowing early in life and saving later on, most people should probably be saving in some manner throughout their lives. In order to make saving as painless as possible, there are a couple of basic principles from behavioral economics that we should apply. First, like Odysseus lashing himself to the mast, we should employ commitment devices to steel ourselves against weaknesses of self-control. To do this, if at all possible, we should make our decision to save when we are a safe distance away from the actual act of doing so. That way our long-term better judgment, the Planner half of our personality, is more likely to prevail, rather than the impulsive Doer. In addition, we should lock in this decision made at a distance. When our impulsive self is subdued and our wise, forward-thinking self is active, we should make a prudent commitment to lock in our good judgment.

Second, we need to make doing the right thing happen automatically. Behavioral economists have much to say about *default behavior*. Most default behavior is what happens when you do nothing. If your savings plan requires you to make regular deposits by going to the bank or pulling up your bank's website on your computer or your smartphone it will only work if you remember to take deliberate action. When it comes to many things—particularly things that we consider onerous, such as paying bills—the default behavior is to do nothing. So, for any saving program you set up, you should always ask yourself, "What happens if I do nothing?" If you arrange for savings to accumulate automatically, the answer to the question will be, "My savings will still grow whether I am paying attention or not." On the other hand, if you have to remember to make a savings deposit each month, then the default behavior of forgetting is likely to cause you problems.

The United States Internal Revenue Service (IRS) understands default behavior very well. Rather than leaving it up to workers to set aside money for their federal income taxes, most employers are required to withhold funds for taxes from each paycheck. Thus, the default behavior of doing nothing ensures that the IRS will get its money. Sometimes not quite enough has been withheld, but the guidelines for withholding based on employees' salaries and the size of their families make certain that the federal government gets the bulk of its money without having to depend on the employee remembering to pay. Payments to the federal government for Social Security and Medicare are also handled by payroll deduction. Furthermore, the evidence shows this strategy works. According to the IRS, underpayment of taxes is much more prevalent among the self-employed, who don't have payroll withholding and are required to make payments throughout the year.[7] Employee retirement plan contributions are often handled in a similar way. Automatic withholding means that if the employee does nothing, these important payments will still be made.

So how can we apply these two principles to our everyday lives? How can we (1) make our decision to save separated in time from the behavior of saving and (2) make saving the default action, not a deliberate action? As individuals, we do not have the clout or the administrative apparatus of our employers or the federal government, so we face additional challenges. But before we begin to think about a savings program for ourselves, we might first consider a system devised by economist Richard Thaler and his colleague Shlomo Benartzi to increase employee retirement contributions. Retirement savings is arguably the most important savings plan an individual can undertake. For most of us, a time will come when we either cannot work or prefer not to work. Social Security is good, but it will not provide enough income for us to live on. As retirement plans have shifted from defined benefit plans, where employees know how much income they will receive at retirement, to defined contribution plans, where they know how much they are paying into their IRA or 401(k) but not how much they will get out of it on retirement, employee contribution rates have declined. Unlike defined benefit plans—what we tend to think of as a true pension—defined contribution plans require that the employee opt in. Saving is not the default option, as it was for most defined benefit retirement plans. Employees must sign up, deliberately choosing to have money deducted from their paychecks, decide how much to contribute each pay period, and in some cases decide among several investment options.

Because the default behavior under defined contribution plans is not to enroll, the shift to this kind of pension system has led to many fewer employees saving for retirement.[8] Obviously, this failure to save for the future does not make sense on several levels. Most people would like to retire at some point, and in order to achieve a comfortable dotage, most will need to save throughout their earning years. By not enrolling in a pension plan, many workers are passively choosing to not retire at all. When they reach retirement age and find they haven't enough money to live on, many will choose—or be forced to choose—to continue working or be dependent on others. Furthermore, IRAs and 401(k)s involve substantial tax benefits designed to make it easier to save, so there are real financial rewards for enrolling in these programs. On the national level, encouraging people to save for retirement benefits us all. Without higher rates of saving, the shift to defined contribution plans will have created a new class of elderly poor who will be in greater need of social services.

Thaler and Benartzi devised a program they call Save More Tomorrow (also known as SMarT), which uses a few simple principles of behavioral economics to make it much easier for employees to contribute to their pension plans.[9] SMarT is now offered by over half the large retirement plans in the United

States, and it produces substantial improvement in pension plan participation and increased levels of saving.[10] The SMartT plan has three important features. First, knowing the power of the hyperbola, Thaler and Benartzi recommend that employees be asked to enroll in the program several months before they would begin having money deducted from their pay. Although retirement savings is not really a loss of money—rather a shift of assets from the present to the future—it feels like an immediate loss of funds, and under most circumstances saving more produces a reduction in take-home pay. As a result, the hyperbola's tendency to reverse our better judgment makes self-control—choosing to save rather than spend—much easier when the saving is a few months off in the future. So under the SMarT program, employees are asked to commit to a savings plan well in advance. In addition, Thaler and Benartzi employ a clever strategy to diminish the pain of saving. Prospect theory tells us that gains and losses are measured relative to the current status quo and that losses tend to hurt us more than an equivalent-sized gain. Therefore, to minimize the sting of savings, the Save More Tomorrow program times the beginning of retirement contributions to the same pay period in which employees receive their annual cost of living adjustment. Because most people adapt to their current level of income, timing the start of retirement savings in this way means the employee sees no reduction in pay. The amount of the increase is reduced, but relative to the status quo, the employee experiences a gain rather than a loss. In the most extreme case, if employees choose to contribute their entire salary increase to retirement savings, they see no change in current income. The status quo is maintained. Finally, the SMarT plan asks employees to commit a percentage of several subsequent pay increases to retirement savings, until the maximum allowed level of contribution is reached—typically within four years. Of course, employees have the choice to opt out at any time, but in Thaler and Benartzi's experience, once employees begin the program, very few drop out.

Like Odysseus's strategy of lashing himself to the mast, the Save More Tomorrow program is a commitment device designed to lock in prudent behavior well in advance of the moment of truth, and it has been extremely successful. If you would like to see such a program implemented at your place of business, contact your human resources office. But for those who are merely trying to save for a rainy day, there are a couple of hints you can take from the SMarT program. First, make it automatic. Today it is easy to have savings electronically deducted from your checking account on a regular schedule, thereby making saving the default option. Whether you are investing in mutual funds or merely depositing money in the savings account at your bank, the act of paying can be made automatic. There is no need to dirty your hands with the task of making savings deposits, nor do you have to strain your brain trying to remember to save each month. In most cases, your employer can deduct money directly from your paycheck, just like your income tax withholdings and Social Security and Medicare contributions. Payroll deductions make saving particularly painless because they are almost invisible; the money never hits your checking account. In contrast, when the savings contributions are taken from your checking account, the money spends a short time there before being automatically withdrawn, perhaps giving you the momentary impression you are wealthier than you have reason to believe. (There are ways to minimize the problem of money passing through your checking account, but I will save discussion of these techniques for the next section, on how to keep your money from leaking away.) Second, if the savings deposits will be large enough to make a noticeable dent in your current income, time them to begin at the same time as your next cost-of-living adjustment. Sometimes smaller savings deposits each pay period can be absorbed without much noticeable strain, but if you want to avoid the sense of moving the status quo downward, use the SMarT system of timing the additional withdrawals to the moment when you are due to get a raise.

Rethink the American Dream

One of the most popular formulations of the American Dream involves the promise of upward mobility and the good life.[11] Several generations of Americans have come to expect that, if they work hard, they can achieve a higher standard of living than their of parents; however, there is a growing recognition that for recent generations, the expectation of a better life is unjustified. A 2017 study based on an analysis of IRS data showed that thirty-year-olds in 1970 had a 90 percent chance of earning more than their parents, but that figure has been dropping precipitously for decades. By 2014, thirty-year-olds had only a 50 percent chance of earning more than their parents.[12] Another recent study looked at lifetime earnings of groups of workers who started their careers between 1957 and 1983.[13] Over that time period, the median lifetime earnings of male workers dropped between 10 and 19 percent. Women workers experienced steady and substantial gains in lifetime earnings over that same period, but women workers started at a very low earning level in 1957. Furthermore, the gains in lifetime earnings for women were not sufficient to compensate for the decline for men. Overall, the amount of money Americans can expect to earn in their lifetimes is on the decline.

These studies further solidify two main conclusions about incomes in the United States over the recent decades: (1) income inequality has increased substantially and (2) average incomes for middle-income and lower workers have remained flat or decreased. Inequality need not be inherently bad. Indeed, there is good evidence that people are more interested in rewards being fair than equal.[14] But when all the gains of the economy go to the wealthy, the exaggerated inequality of our economy begins to look very unfair to the rest of the workforce. At very least, from the 1970s through today—the years that are the focus of this book—the American Dream of upward mobility and a life better than our parents' has been gradually slipping away. As a result, it is important that we think differently about our life cycles and some of the basic assumptions of the American Dream.

Rethinking Home Ownership

Changes in the American economy have forced us reconsider core principles of The Dream. For example, home ownership is a classic part of The Dream, yet it is interesting to note that home ownership is substantially higher in many other countries. As noted in chapter 1, home ownership in the United States hit a fifty-year high of 69 percent in 2006, just before the bubble burst, and fell sharply after the recession. In contrast, as of 2014 Latvia, Norway, Poland, Hungary, Bulgaria, and Croatia all had home ownership rates in the 80-percent range. Romania had an astonishing home ownership rate of 96 percent.[15]

Home ownership is down in the United States, in part due to the foreclosure crisis. People walked out the front doors of their homes and didn't come back. But experience with the recession has also given us further reason to be suspicious of the advertised benefits of buying a home. Of course, if you are wealthy enough to buy a house with cash, then little of this applies to you. But for the great majority of prospective homeowners, buying a house means signing a mortgage—a loan that obligates the homeowner to pay a large sum of money over a period of (typically) thirty years. If the current market value of the home goes up, owning a home can be a good way to build your wealth, but sometimes the market goes down. Furthermore, houses are expensive to maintain. Even when prices are going up, it can be difficult to profit from real estate sales. Finally, buying a house brings additional risk because it represents an illiquid asset—it is difficult to sell and turn back into cash. Even a car is far easier to sell than a house. Thus if you get laid off at work or suffer some other financial hardship, it will be relatively difficult to lower your housing expenses by selling your home. In the case of a mortgaged home, your illiquid asset is encumbered by a very sticky form of debt. As a result, it is easy to fall prey to the romance of buying a big beautiful home, but in an uncertain economy, there are good reasons to think about avoiding this risky obligation and renting instead.[16]

RETHINKING COLLEGE

Another standard feature of the American Dream is education—higher education in particular. For many people, education offers the promise of upward mobility and the good life, but the cost of college has risen at rates that far exceed inflation during a period when salaries have declined or remained flat for most families. With the availability of grants and other forms of support on the decline, young people are taking on enormous amounts of debt. As we have seen, this form of borrowing now represents the second-largest source of household debt (after mortgages) and delinquencies are on the rise. The demand for college remains strong, but the financial system that supports it is unsustainable. The Great Recession taught us what a housing bubble looks like, but it is more difficult to predict what a bursting bubble in higher education would involve.

There is strong evidence that college increases earnings. Studies have consistently shown that college graduates earn substantially more than their high school graduate cohort, and the gap is widening. In a recent study, economist David Autor found that the wage gap between high school and college graduate men was $17,411 in 1979 and by 2012, after accounting for inflation, had risen to $34,969.[17] For women, the college advantage was smaller, but it too has almost doubled, going from $12,887 to $23,280 from 1979 to 2012. So there are benefits of having a college diploma.

For some young people (and their parents), the process of getting into college begins in the primary grades. By the time children hit middle school, every test is taken and every paper is written with the knowledge that grades are the ticket to a good college. Once the student has done all this work and the acceptance letters start rolling in, there is a strong temptation to choose the highest ranked, most prestigious school, regardless of price. The prospect of passing up enrollment at a favored school due to cost sets up a tremendous disappointment for the student who has dreamed about this for years. It is a kind of psychological trap that leads many eighteen-year-olds to take on debts that will dog them for decades. The hyperbola is strong in these young people. Their shiny new college is just a few weeks away, and the pain of payment is far off in the future. Until, of course, it isn't.

Americans are still reluctant to talk about money, but parents and children should have serious conversations about money beginning at an early age. If seventeen- or eighteen-year-olds are going to be responsible for deciding whether or not to assume tens of thousands of dollars in student loan debt, then their parents should make sure they know something about earning and saving money. As attractive as going to a top school might be, families should have frank discussions about whether it is wiser to go to an expensive private college or to avoid debt by choosing a less expensive institution. Community colleges and state colleges and universities often provide a very good education for a fraction of the cost of private institutions, and it is not clear the added costs of private institutions are worth it. From a straight economic perspective, some studies show that more selective colleges do produce higher-income graduates, but it is unclear how big a difference it makes and how general the outcome. For example, one study found that only low-income students benefited from attending selective colleges.[18] The choice of major is a much more powerful factor in future earnings.[19] Even if more expensive colleges result in higher incomes after graduation, it is not clear whether the difference is sufficient to compensate for decades of student loan payments. There is growing evidence that graduates with student loan debt are moving back home with their parents in larger numbers and delaying a number of life events, including getting married and buying homes and cars.[20] Part of the explanation for these delays may come from the fact that at ages twenty-five and thirty, student loan borrowers have substantially lower average credit scores than non-student-loan borrowers.[21] The decision-making that goes into choosing a college is never entirely economic. Students dream about having wonderful experiences in school and creating friendships and memories that will keep them company their entire lives. But once the loan payments come due, some students may wonder whether it all was worth it.

The discussion website Reddit.com has a number of student loan forums, and in December of 2016 a user posted the question "If you could go back and do it all over again, would you still take out student loans?" Of the twenty-nine people who responded in the following seven months, 45 percent said they would not. Their loans weren't worth it.[22] Of course, this is not a scientific poll, and it was clear from the comments that some of the unhappy borrowers had attended for-profit colleges, which have been the source of many complaints.[23] But it seems clear that the potential for student loan regret is very real. The following response from a Reddit user seems particularly wise:

> Absolutely not. I would go to a community college for the first two years then transfer to a state school. No private universities. I would also work harder to pay my way through school. For grad school I would work harder at getting a stipend or TA-ship and do everything I could to exit with little to no student loan debt.
>
> I'm 35, make a very good income, and paying $900 a month can still be very restricting. Changes the house you can live in, cars you drive, disposable income to have fun with, money you can share with others, etc.
>
> You might have to bust your ass during school but you'll be glad you did later.[24]

Owning a home and getting a good education are core features of the American Dream. At times the demand for these two commodities seems inelastic—all but impervious to soaring price increases. Unfortunately, for many Americans both these pieces of the Dream involve large piles of very risky debt. Mortgages are risky because they set in place a long sequence of payments that must be met regardless of loss of employment, divorce, or illness. Furthermore, getting out from under a mortgage is lengthy process that only works well in a favorable housing market. Student loan debt can also be substantial, and it hits us at the very beginning of our earning lives, often slowing progress toward other financial goals. Furthermore, as Sylvia, the struggling law student, learned, declaring bankruptcy does not provide relief from student loan debt. Whether you complete your degree or not, going to college on a loan is an inescapable commitment to pay.

HOW YOU CAN SPEND LESS

Much of this book has described the jungle of temptation we now inhabit, and in this section I suggest a few paths through that jungle. There are many financial advisors and home economists who can give you tips on how to trim expenses by bringing your lunch to work or remembering to turn off lights in your house.[25] These techniques can be very helpful, but my suggestions will be aimed at the problems of self-control and rational decision-making that have been subject of the previous chapters. Problems that cannot be solved by fewer trips to Starbucks. Today there are so many ways to be separated from your money that it takes a special level of vigilance to avoid emptying out your bank account and maxing out your credit cards. In one sense, this is not a fair fight. It is hard to listen to the angel on your right shoulder when there are so many devils fighting for a spot on your left. But there are several useful strategies that can help us resist the onslaught of commercial pressure.

Want Less by Limiting Your Exposure to Advertising

As we have seen, Americans come into contact with more advertising than ever before, and the invasion is not over. Much of this exposure is unavoidable. If you ride a bus or a commuter train to work, you cannot help seeing billboards and overhead ads. But some kinds of advertising come packaged with things we choose to bring into our lives, and these are choices we can reconsider. Here are just a few suggestions:

- *Clean Your Screens.* The mute button was once our only defense. You'd be watching a very exciting episode of *Law & Order* and, with frustrating regularity, loud attention-getting commercials would burst onto the screen with out warning, breaking the flow of the story. The best option to avoid the next few minutes of unwanted hucksterism was to hit the mute button. Unfortunately, this is still the circumstance whenever we watch the scheduled TV programming on cable, broadcast, or online TV services such as Sling, Direct TV Now, Hulu, or YouTube TV. In many cases, cutting the cord and buying your live TV from one of these Internet streaming services can produce substantial savings over cable, but generally speaking you still get commercials. Thankfully we now have other options.

  If you are willing to watch your shows after their original air dates, you can avoid commercials by watching streaming services or using cable on-demand. Amazon Prime and Netflix offer thousands of hours of commercial-free viewing. At the time of this writing, Hulu's base plan included limited commercials, but a commercial-free plan was available for slightly higher monthly fee. In addition, some online and physical DVR recorders allow you skip the commercials on playback. For now, if you want to watch news or weather programming, you will be forced to endure commercials, but for much of our TV watching there are very effective ways to push back the advertising assault.

  For the other screens in your life, ad-blocking software can make a dramatic difference. There are a number of free ad-blocking extensions that can be added to most Internet browsers. Instantly your online newspaper is presented as a clean, uncluttered page. Some ads still sneak through, but what was once a bewildering array of banners and pop-ups is greatly reduced. Some of the same blockers are available for your phone or tablet device. Ad blocking software makes reading your screen a much more pleasurable experience.

- *Opt out of direct mail advertising.* Although the Internet has dramatically changed the retail landscape, direct solicitations have not gone away. Spam e-mail is rampant, and catalogs and other appeals still fill our mailboxes. This is a rather frustrating battle, but there are a few ways to fight back. First is to diligently opt out of all offers to "keep you informed about future product announcements" by checking or unchecking the appropriate boxes when ordering on the Internet or registering at an Internet site. If e-mail ads sneak into your in-box, whenever possible you should use the unsubscribe option, which is often in very small letters at the bottom of the message. Junk mail and spam filters that come with most e-mail programs have improved in recent years, but lots of solicitations from retailers, social action groups, and nonprofits still make their way into your inbox. Being diligent about unsubscribing can make a big difference.

If you would like to make a systematic approach, the Federal Trade Commission's website (https://www.consumer.ftc.gov/) provides information about how to join the National Do Not Call Registry, which allows citizens to block most telemarketing calls. In addition, the Direct Marketing Association (DMA) operates a Mail Preference Service, which allows people to systematically reduce the amount of junk postal mail they receive.[26] People who register are added to a "delete" file, and companies who do direct mailings and do not want to waste postage on unreceptive customers will delete you from their mailing lists. The DMA also offers a similar service for junk e-mail. Both services are very inexpensive, and details can be found on the Federal Trade Commission website.

- *Go generic.* Once you realize the effect that brand competition and status spending have on our lives, there is a dual-edged benefit in turning away. You can save money on your purchases and reduce the subtle influence of advertising on your desires. One way to reduce the impact of fads and brand competition in our lives is to refuse to become a human billboard. Don't buy clothes or other items that display visible brand names or symbols. This can be difficult. As I mentioned, I wear jeans that have brand labels that would be difficult to remove without damaging the pants. But often there is a choice, and we can avoid becoming roving advertisements by seeking out products that are more generic in appearance.

  Second, we can buy fewer things that are new. Because children have the unfortunate habit of growing out of clothes very rapidly, consignment shops for the sale of previously owned children's clothes are quite common and do not carry the class stigma associated with thrift shops, but adults can also find great things inexpensively at thrift shops, consignment stores, and yard sales. Not too long ago, I bought an Italian-made suit for $10 at a local thrift shop. It needed some alteration, but it became a favorite outfit. Stores that feature off-price overstock merchandise often carry well-known designer and brand name labels, but more generic items are also sold. To the extent that buying clothes at these outlets keeps you away from the malls and out of competition for the latest trend, they are a step in the right direction.

Buying a previously owned lawn mower, dress suit, car, kitchen appliance, book, or computer has a number of positive effects. It keeps junk out of the landfill and diminishes the enormous waste created by a throwaway society in which people rarely repair or reuse the things they buy. In addition, advertising appeals often change rapidly in an effort to gain attention and stimulate interest, which quickly disconnects used items from the latest commercial pitch. As a result, your use of older durable goods diminishes the influence of advertising in your life. Finally, as previously mentioned, recycled items save you money and keep you off the commercial battlefield. You may not be seen as the hippest trendsetter on your block, but many people find great satisfaction from stepping out of the race for the latest fad.

- *Make special efforts for children.* Children are particularly vulnerable audience for advertising. Many marketing agencies now have a "tween" strategy aimed directly at the eight-to-twelve-year-old age group, but often commercial messages are directed at even younger children.[27]

There is no free lunch in children's television. Even public television, although free of traditional commercials, is replete with program tie-ins. When they were younger, my children were great fans of the Public Broadcasting Service shows *Barney* and *Thomas the Tank Engine,* and before long our house was filled with videos, Thomas collectible trains, and Barney plush toys. During those years, the kids did not watch any commercial stations, yet television still served as a subtle conduit for merchandise promotion. The Internet is also filled with advertising that many parents would rather their children not see. The good news is that parents now have much more control over the situation. The same streaming services that adults use to watch movies provide excellent commercial-free content for children. Browsers often have safe modes that can be set to keep children away from unwanted content, and the devices that children use can also be equipped with ad blocking software.

The passivity that screens produce is a source of inner conflict for many parents. Given the demands of child rearing, it is tempting to simply hand the kid an iPad so that you can do something else for a few minutes, but studies have shown a correlation between the hours of screen time and body weight.[28] It is probably unrealistic to eliminate screens from our children's lives entirely. For many of us, computers are now an integral part of life at work and at home. Parents regularly hear pleas to limit their children's screen time to promote a more healthy lifestyle at an early age. If we are more careful at monitoring and structuring what our kids see, we can also offer them a less commercial childhood.

Just like their parents, children and teens read magazines and other printed materials, and these media expose them to the entire panorama of the advertising world. Furthermore, subscriptions in a child's name inevitably put him or her on direct marketing mailing lists, opening up the world of junk mail for the younger set. At school, corporate sponsors often offer curriculum packages to teachers, and these printed materials sometimes contain both biased information and advertising.[29] Parents can diminish their children's exposure to advertising by monitoring Internet use, making careful choices about magazine subscriptions, and keeping an eye on the materials being used in schools. Commercial influence in schools goes well beyond curriculum material and is a larger community issue. We will return to the topic of commercialism in education later in this chapter.

Finally, parents need not be alone in this effort to protect their children from unwanted advertising; they can enlist their kids as collaborators. For example, the nonprofit NewDream.org (https://www.newdream.org/) is devoted to promoting a simpler, commercial-free lifestyle, and they offer a free guide for parents called "Kids Unbranded" filled with tips on how to limit screen time and exposure to commercial messages.[30] This and other websites and organizations can be a great help to parents who want to arm their children with the tools to avoid and evaluate the marketing messages they encounter.

Despite all these efforts, wanting will strike. When you least expect it and when you think you have protected yourself from advertising's pull, you will get a strong desire to buy some indulgence you know perfectly well you would be quite content to live without. But getting an urge is only the beginning, and not all urges will or should be satisfied. So here are some strategies for managing the hyperbola, holding on to your money, and sorting out the differences between needs and wants.

Make Nondiscretionary Spending Automatic and Invisible

Economists use the concept of *disposable income*, which is simply your after-tax income or what we think of as take-home pay. But much of what we get in our paychecks is spent before we even receive it on expenses we have no choice but to pay: mortgage or rent, insurance, utilities, car payments, phone, cable, and a host of other things. What is left after all these necessities are taken care of is called *discretionary income*.[31] Discretionary income is what is left over for the satisfaction of wants rather than needs, and poor people, by definition, have no discretionary income. If they are able to pay for their necessities, there is nothing left over for mere wants.

Most of us do have discretionary income, but if asked how much money we have to spend each month, many of us would be hard pressed to say. Furthermore, because—like the savings deposits mentioned above—the money that is earmarked for rent, utilities, and other necessities comes and goes from our account, it can give us the impression that we have more discretionary income than we actually have. Since you have no choice but to pay for your basic necessities, for two reasons it is better if your nondiscretionary expenses are paid automatically. First, if you are living close to the edge, having to write out the electric bill each month may give you the dangerous impression that this payment is discretionary. That—maybe just once—you could forgo paying the bill and deal with it next month. As my story at the beginning of the book suggests, I've been there before. Second, even under the best of circumstances, every bill you have is an opportunity for delinquency. Failure to pay on time can cost you in late fees and damage to your credit rating, so, in the case of bills that are never going to go away, you are better off paying them automatically out of your checking account. Nowadays, many employers can arrange for automatic deposit of your paycheck, and many mortgages, rents, and bills can be automatically withdrawn from your account, thereby making paying on time the default condition. Some people are incredibly diligent bill payers. They get a bill in the mail, and the check goes out the next day. For these well-disciplined individuals, payment on time is the default outcome. But for the rest of us, automatic bill paying is the answer.

Looking at every bill as an opportunity for delinquency also helps explain why it is best to keep your number of bills to a minimum—at least for those of us who are not prompt and diligent bill payers. Utilities and rent or mortgage are unavoidable, but if you have several credit card accounts with balances on them, you have greatly expanded your opportunities for a missed payment, which can cost you in exorbitant late fees and usurious penalty interest rates. Often you will go to a store and be offered instant credit and a discount on anything you buy with the first charge to your new store credit card. The clerk confirms that the approval process will be quick, and when you have an armful of clothes you are about to charge, the offer of a new credit card speaks to you on a couple of levels. First, there is the prospect of saving money through the markdown on this first-time introductory charge. In addition, there is the possibility of holding on to your cash as well as the available balances on your other credit cards. As it does in any credit card purchase, the hyperbola diminishes the sting of a distant payment and allows us to avoid an immediate loss of cash. But there are a couple of reasons why this offer is something to pass up. First, the interest rates on these store accounts can be very high, and in the rush of trying get through the checkout, this fact may escape you. Second, by charging your items on a new store card, you have increased your chances of missing a payment by one. Again, for people whose default behavior is to pay every bill promptly, this may not be a problem. But for many of us, it is a better practice to keep the number of bills down to a manageable minimum. Resist the temptation to acquire lots of cards, and where possible, consolidate debt in a single, low-interest account. In fact, if you must use credit, it is best if you restrict your charging to a single major credit card. By limiting yourself to one card, you keep the opportunity for delinquency to a minimum and you always have a clear measure of your indebtedness. When your debts are spread across several accounts it is much easier to lose track of where you stand, but if you use only one card, you simply need to look at the bill to know how deep into the red you have gone and whether the situation is getting better or worse.

By reducing the total number of bills and by making bill-paying automatic, we have eliminated a number of potential problems, but we still don't have a handle on our true level of discretionary income each month. If your whole paycheck is going into your checking account and then savings, rent, and bills are automatically withdrawn, you still must witness the ups and downs of your bank balance. When the balance is up, right after your paycheck is received, you may feel more powerful than is warranted because your bank account does not reflect your true discretionary income. So the next step is to separate out your nondiscretionary spending and forget about it. The best way to do this is to set up a completely separate checking account devoted to nondiscretionary spending. There are a number of ways to accomplish this. Many employers will allow you to split the automatic deposit of your paycheck between two different accounts. In this case, you can have a fixed amount of money deposited into the "bill-paying" account, and the rest into your "discretionary" checking account, which can be at a completely different bank. Alternatively, you can have your entire paycheck deposited in your bill-paying account, and use the bank's website to set up a regular payment into your discretionary checking account. Most banks now have online banking systems that make this kind of arrangement very easy to do. Finally, the ATM card you carry in your pocket should be for your discretionary checking account, and if possible, it should be a little inconvenient to get cash out of your bill-paying account. My own bill-paying account is at a local credit union. I have checks for this account, which I can use to make some nondiscretionary payments where automatic payment is not possible, but I do not have an ATM card for this account. In addition, the credit union has only a few offices, none of which is particularly convenient for me.

When setting up the bill-paying account, it is important to anticipate all the predictable expenses that come up throughout the year. Many people get into trouble because they fail to plan for important obligations that crop up at specific but widely spaced times: holiday gift giving, children's camps and lessons, vacations, and insurance, licenses, or membership payments. Many of these expenses will be paid with a check rather than by automatic withdrawal, but just like monthly bills, in many cases they are not really discretionary spending. These are predictable expenses that appear every year at some point in the annual cycle. If the bill-paying account is going to reflect your true level of nondiscretionary spending, the automatic deposits going in will need to be sufficiently large to cover these more irregular obligations. As part of your preliminary budgeting process, you will need to make a realistic estimate of the annual total of these expenses and then make certain that the deposits going into the account every pay cycle are sufficient to build up the necessary sum through the course of the year. That way, when it is time to buy holiday gifts or go on vacation, the money will be there automatically.

This may seem like a bit of game playing, an attempt to trick yourself into prudent financial management, but the goal of these strategies is to take the important decisions off the table and make staying within your budget much easier to do. If the only money you have any discretion over is, in fact, the discretionary portion of your income, then it will be much easier to stay on the straight and narrow path. Eventually, the "trick" will become a habit. In addition, if you use automatic saving as a commitment device, then savings will be the default option. You will tend to forget about the balance in your savings account and be concerned with it only when you have a real need to withdraw from it. Experts disagree about how much we need to contribute to our pension accounts to live comfortably in retirement, and I will not presume to give advice about this or about how much you should have on hand in your regular savings account. It will depend on the magnitude of the potential calamities that might befall your life. But having liquid assets on hand when the furnace quits or the muffler falls off your car will protect you from having to take on debt. To save money, you must forgo something now, but not having savings when life throws you a curve means that any expense that exceeds what you have in your discretionary account can only be covered by taking on debt. Furthermore, as we have seen, credit cards are not as universally acceptable as cash, and debt costs you money in interest charges. Finally, making savings relatively invisible, automatic, and ongoing will make it as painless as possible.

Don't Save to Consume

Some financial advisors recommend that, if you have difficulty saving, you should set a goal. Think of something you'd like to have: a new laptop, an island vacation, or a diamond tennis bracelet. Set yourself a goal, and then figure out how much you need to save per month for how many months to finance your purchase.[32]

This may work for some people, but it really doesn't address the problem. Once you meet your goal and obtain your reward you are right back where you started. In addition, the focus of this strategy is on the act of consumption. Saving is just a means to that end. A much better strategy is to psychologically disconnect the act of saving from consumption as much as possible.

Saving is something you should always be doing. Everyone should have a worst-case-scenario rainy day fund. Enough liquid funds available to get through losing your job, huge medical expenses beyond what your health insurance can handle, or totaling your car. How big your rainy day fund should be is a calculation you should make on your own, but once you have a number in mind, you have your goal. Savings goals should always be about your bank balance. Once you establish the habit of saving, new goals will emerge the minute you achieve the old one. If you focus on the act of accumulation, once you have worked hard to get two thousand, ten thousand, or fifty thousand dollars in a savings account, you are more likely to want to keep the ball rolling. By reversing the focus and keeping it on your bank balance, you will naturally think about your big purchases differently, too. When you think about going to Barbados, you will be asking yourself whether or not you are willing to take the hit to your savings account. That's the way we should think about all our spending decisions.

Build in Delays

The hyperbola's power comes from immediacy. Today, the tiniest momentary impulse to buy can be satisfied almost instantly. Short of unplugging from the Internet entirely, we cannot completely avoid the immediacy of Internet spending, and going offline forever is too high a price for many of us to pay for reduced temptation. But one simple method of self-management—for those who can do it—is to make yourself wait, whether online or at the store. Build in at least a small delay between impulse and response. If you are about to order something, ask yourself, "Do I need this right this minute? Will it matter if I order this a little later?" It may help to write out a list of the things you want, and make a rule that you will not order the item for a day or two. If, after a few days or a week, you still want the thing, you can go ahead and order it. But in many cases you will discover that the urgency is gone.

We have already discussed the difference between wants and needs. The ratcheting up of needs is an important factor in our unquenchable desire for stuff. But it is useful to recognize that there are many levels of want, and much money can be saved by learning to separate your real wants from momentary urges. Building in a delay is one way to help you distinguish between a real want—an enduring desire that has some true meaning—versus an ill-considered act of fancy.

Have Second Thoughts

A corollary of the principle of building in delays is the principle that you can reverse yourself. Ironically, when you make any purchase, particularly an avoidable purchase, you have entered into a commitment to a failure of self-control: you're going to listen to those Sirens come what may. It is as if you are promising to exchange funds for a good or service and to not reverse that commitment even if reversing it would be the wise thing to do. But buying and returning clothes is a time-honored technique among serious shoppers, particularly if there is a spouse or someone else at home whose opinion you value. Yes, returns are a hassle. They draw on the variables of time and effort and can often involve the upper levels of the large muscle hierarchy. Similarly, many online retailers have made it much easier to return items by providing preprinted mailing labels and free return postage, but there is still the work of repackaging and getting the item back to the post office. Nonetheless, if you have second thoughts about a purchase, you should return it.

Many people fail to recognize that they can have second thoughts even earlier in their commitment to buy. Orders—even orders made online or over the phone—can be canceled. In most cases, an order that has not shipped yet can be canceled very easily with a few clicks of the mouse or a quick call to a toll-free number. So if you failed to follow the principle of building in delays, but a day later—during what should have been the delay period—you recognize that you don't really need that vintage *Betty and Veronica* comic book, you can go online and cancel it. It should be mentioned, however, that the inability to cancel is part of eBay's evil genius. Once you have won an eBay auction, you are irreversibly committed to complete the deal. Second thoughts are not allowed, and any winning bidder who stiffs the seller risks getting negative feedback.

Interestingly, for all Internet shopping other than eBay, there is a relationship between your choice of shipping method and the window of opportunity for easy cancellation. If the hyperbola really has a grip on you and you are anxious to get the item as soon as possible, you may choose some form of expedited shipping. This decision costs you twice. First, it often adds significant expense to your purchase. The shipping charges on an Amazon.com book can easily exceed any discount you receive on the bestseller you are anxious to get your hands on. But the other, perhaps less often considered drawback of expedited shipping is that it gives you almost no time to change your mind. In the era of

Amazon Prime 2-day shipping, the time between the commitment to buy and the notice that the item has shipped is remarkably short, but if your second thoughts come quickly, you can save yourself some trouble by canceling.

So the additional rules of ordering that come out of this analysis are (1) try to avoid expedited shipping and (2) if you have any regrets about your purchase upon rising clear-eyed and sober the next day, cancel the order. Go back online and cancel. Your commitment to buy is not locked in, and most reputable merchants are more interested in your satisfaction with the company than with any individual purchase. If they treat you well today, you are much more likely to come back and buy in the future.

Warning: don't use the possibility of returns and cancellations as a rationalization for the initial purchase. Many a person who said, "I can always return it" has fallen victim to inertia. This imagined return is off at the distant, flat end of hyperbola. From your vantage point in the store or at your computer keyboard, it is easy to be overconfident about your future willingness to follow through, but when the prospect of actually returning the item arrives, the time and effort variables loom large.

Just-in-Time Shopping

If life at your house is anything like life at mine, food often spoils in the refrigerator before it gets eaten. This is where just-in-time shopping can make a difference.

In the world of manufacturing, there is a concept known as just-in-time inventory, which was introduced by Toyota.[33] Building a product that is made of many parts can involve a huge inventory problem. To feed the hungry assembly line, all the parts that go into making a Toyota Corolla must be available at the precise time they are needed. This once meant that parts were made in great quantities and stored and managed in large warehouses. Toyota's management discovered that costs could be lowered by warehousing many fewer parts and making the parts just in time to meet the manufacturing need.

A similar approach to shopping can help save money. Although this advice goes contrary to much common wisdom, I recommend that you always avoid buying hedonic items in bulk (see chapter 8), and if you find that you often throw away unused food, avoid buying perishable foods in bulk. The bulk purchase of nonperishable utilitarian items, such as toilet paper, soap, and pasta, is another matter. If you can save money by buying in bulk and have sufficient storage space for these kinds of needed items, buy in bulk. But for perishable foods and more hedonic items, just-in-time purchasing can be more economical. Fewer items get lost in the freezer or are thrown out unused at the end of the week.

Avoid Spending as a Leisure-Time Activity

We live in a society in which most everyone has leisure. But some forms of leisure are expensive and should be avoided. As the profiles of Frank and Caroline demonstrate, gambling is a losing game, and shopping is also a potentially very expensive activity. If your preferred form of leisure activity has you making regular exchanges of money, then unless you are so wealthy that these exchanges are harmless, you should find a less expensive way to amuse yourself. Shopping has been promoted as a leisure-time activity in many ways, both blatant and subtle. It might be better if we all saw the purchasing of goods and services as necessary means to other ends, not as ends in themselves. When purchasing becomes the point, then we are likely to get into trouble.

As part of this effort, it is a good idea to keep track of the hedonic aspects of shopping. If you find yourself shopping for someone else (without being asked, or when it is not a normal gift-giving time) or engaging in shopping as a competition, an adventure, or a way to ease daily stress and trepidation, it may be a signal that your buying is taking on more meaning. Although shopping can address these other goals, there are less expensive ways to do these things. Try substituting reading, visiting local museums, volunteering for a local civic group, sports, music, or binge-watching *The Sopranos* on Netflix for your more expensive leisure activities.

Finally, if you still want to shop as an entertainment or a pastime, separate out the leisure and utilitarian functions. Treat leisure shopping as pure leisure: window-shop and browse without buying. If a utilitarian purchase brings you to the store and you want to also do some browsing, make your utilitarian purchase first, then browse without buying for as long as you like. Try to keep the two functions of shopping separate, and if something appeals to you during your period of leisure shopping, employ one of the delaying tactics to help determine how important a purchase really is. Remember, too, that once you are in the store, all the momentum is in favor of buying. That's what stores are for. To determine how important a purchase really is, turn that momentum around. Ask yourself, "What would be the harm if I *don't* buy this?" Framed in this way, many urges lose their force.

Simple Living

The cheap food-loving Steven Levitt in the epigram to this chapter is an economist who, along with Stephen Dubner, is the coauthor of the popular *Freakonomics* books and podcast series. After reviewing the research showing that only very sophisticated wine connoisseurs—but not average people—can tell the difference between cheap and expensive wine, Levitt has developed an interesting approach to buying wine:

> My approach to buying wine for gifts is simple: I go in the store, and I look for the label that looks the most expensive of anything in the store. And I make sure it costs less than $15, and if it does, then I buy it.[34]

Despite having plenty of money, Levitt has been known to live in quite sparse surroundings and says that he has very little interest in stuff.[35]

Steven Levitt's ideas about buying food and wine, as well as many of the suggestions I've made—reduce screen time, build in delays, and avoid spending as leisure—can be rolled together into a larger lifestyle choice: simple living.[36] There is a certain irony in recommending simple living in an era when Americans have elected a billionaire president whose favorite color appears to be gold, but for over two thousand years, philosophers, religious figures, and other sages have advocated frugality and simple living—even poverty.[37] Setting aside the traditional—and rather dubious—claims that frugal people are more virtuous or more holy, there are many reasons to choose a simpler, less materialistic life. Many of those who have done so discover that they have greater happiness, more time, and less stress.

Although we live in a highly materialistic consumer-driven economy, there has long been a resistance movement aimed at decluttering, doing things yourself (DIY), and living more modestly. The economist Juliet Schor has written several very readable books that are classics of the simple living movement, including *The Overspent American, Born to Buy* (about the commercialization of childhood), and *True Wealth*. For those who are interested, there are many helpful websites and blogs online, but one of the best sources of information about living less materialistic and stressful life is the one I mentioned earlier, New Dream (formerly the Center for a New American Dream at https://www. newdream.org/), whose mission is "to empower individuals, communities, and organizations to transform their consumption habits to improve well-being for people and the planet."[38] In addition to their programs for children, New Dream provides resources for people wanting to consume less, live more sustainably, and promote community engagement.

Remember the Lessons of Behavioral Economics

In chapter 8 we encountered a number of examples of irrational thinking about money—common financial errors that move us toward rather than away from indebtedness. Now I will list a few suggestions based on these behavioral economic principles.

Beware of Overconfidence

Just-in-time food shopping is a way to avoid waste, but our problems with overconfidence are much larger than food. One of the universal principles I have tried very hard to live by and to pass on to my children is that things always take longer than you think they will. No matter what the project—a term paper, cooking a meal, or painting a room—more often than not, your initial estimate of the time required to complete the job will undershoot reality by an impressive margin. We tend to be overconfident about our abilities and about the smooth unfolding of events. If you are at all prone to unfinished projects, then just-in-time purchasing can be a help. Do not buy the materials to put in a new bathroom sink unless you know that you will have the time to work on this project in the next day or so.

The study of rebates from chapter 8 suggests that overconfidence can be checked by reminding yourself of the reasons things might not work out: it is a pain to have to cut off the UPC, fill out the form, and send it in; I might be too busy to mail in the rebate; Bill said he might drop by this weekend, and I know that if he does, I will probably play golf with him instead of working on the bathroom sink. If you are able to recognize those instances when your plans depend on you doing something in the future and consider a few reasons why you might not follow through, you may avoid some waste. Before you buy that expensive elliptical trainer, try to imagine all the excuses you might give in the future for keeping it at a safe distance.

Don't Be a Slave to Sunk Costs

When considering whether to sell something for much-needed cash, do not be influenced by the amount you paid for the item. The decision should be based on what it is worth to you now, not what it once cost. That amount is now irrelevant. The past is gone—along with the money you spent back then. You might consider how much you would pay now to buy it back. Once you own the item, the endowment effect tends make your selling price higher than your buy-it-back price. But if there is a pressing need for money, the buy-it-back price is not relevant. What matters is how much you can get for the CD or car or other possession you are considering selling and whether having that amount of cash is currently more important than having the possession. If the cash wins out in this equation, then you should sell, regardless of the amount of money you originally paid. The original payment price was lost long ago.

Beware the House Money Effect

I hope you avoid gambling altogether, unless you have sufficient income to make your (almost inevitable) losses a trivial disappointment or you gamble such small amounts of money as to make this a reasonable entertainment expense. But whether the money comes to you from gambling winnings, an unexpected bonus, a lucrative trade on the stock market, or an inheritance, do not take on additional risks because the sum you are putting up came to you without effort. The phrase "easy come, easy go" is a kind of justification for the house money effect. If you want to be financially stable, money that came to you easily should leave your wallet just as reluctantly as money you earned through the sweat of your labor.

Use Windfalls Wisely

The previous lesson, to beware the house money effect, is related to the larger question of what to do with windfalls. Be a Planner, not a Doer, when it comes to windfalls. Many people see windfalls as an opportunity to buy something they might not otherwise be able to afford, but this is hyperbolic thinking. It overvalues the nifty toy dangling in front of your eyes and tends to undervalue the many expenses that are likely to crop up down the line. For someone who recognizes the difficulties of preparing for the future and avoiding debt, there are really just three rules for windfalls.

Rule 1: If you have debt—particularly unsecured debt, such as credit card balances—use your windfall to pay it down. Mortgages and car loans that are backed up by assets are less of a concern, but credit cards or other forms of commercial debt should be paid off as quickly as possible. They are costly, and the balances threaten your ability to absorb future unexpected expenses.

If you have unsecured debts and little cash savings, it may be wise to put some of your windfall into a savings account, simply because some emergency expenses may require cash. But in general debts should be paid off as quickly as possible.

Rule 2: If you have no debt, save your windfalls. Which brings us to the question of tax refunds. The recommendations of financial advisors are so consistent on this point that the message takes on the air of received wisdom: don't let the government borrow your money interest-free. According to most personal finance experts, you should trim your payroll deductions down so that at the end of the year just enough has been withheld to cover your taxes and no more.[39] That way you will have more money in your paycheck each month to do with what you will. That's all well and good for supremely rational financial advisors who can be trusted to do just the right thing with their take-home pay each month, but what about the rest of us? According to the latest economic data, many of us are still having trouble trying to save money, and income tax refunds represent a very effective commitment device. Why? Because, just like your pension contributions, the money is taken out before you ever see it. It never shows up in your pay. True, we earn no interest on this little savings mechanism, but it is an excellent way to bolster your self-control. You set the level of your withholding by filling out a form at work; you do it once and forget about it. When tax time rolls around, it is much easier to approach the task of preparing your taxes if you know you have a healthy refund coming. In contrast, it is no fun to write out a check for unpaid taxes on April 15, and given the uncertainty of our financial lives, it is difficult to gauge precisely how much you should withhold to avoid both a tax bill and a refund. Refunds are better, and despite the received wisdom, they are an excellent way to save.

Rule 3: If you have no debt and plenty of savings, do whatever you want with your windfalls. We congratulate you on your financial wisdom and resolve.

Finally, beware of the way your windfall is framed. Remember that a sum of money described as extra income, a "bonus," will be a greater challenge to your self-control than money described as restored income, a "rebate." Rebates do not have the feeling of a true windfall. They seem to restore the status quo rather than move it upward. If you are going to manage your money well, rebates and bonuses should go into the same mental account. If they are not needed for immediate necessities, then the three rules above apply.

Don't Be Fooled by the Way Things Are Priced

It is easy to be distracted by irrelevant features of the way a product or service is priced, and these distractions can be expensive. For example, it is important not to be dragged down by an anchor. Instead, recognize the anchor when you see it and adjust away from it. If you see signs that say "Limit three per customer" or "two for $8," ask yourself, "When I came into this store, was I considering buying more than one?" If the answer is no, don't be tricked into buying multiple quantities.

Similarly, take note of whether costs are being lumped together, because prospect theory tells us that the way losses and gains are bundled affects on our judgment. Undercoating for a new car or a service contract on a new refrigerator may seem like a small additional charge in relation to the large expense of the car or the fridge, but ask yourself whether you would buy them if—a week after you got your new item home—someone came to the door and tried to sell you undercoating or a service contract as a separate purchase. The blending of losses together and the assessment of losses in relation to other losses are not good ways to make money decisions.

Finally, once you know that people generally have a bias in favor of flat-rate pricing, you can begin to evaluate whether your flat-rate contracts are worth it.

Flat-rate pricing often affects your behavior by decoupling the act of consumption from the act of paying. Consider following the example of the couple who lived on the West Side and liked to dine on the East Side. They found that setting aside an amount of money each month for cab fares diminished the sting of traveling to their favorite restaurants. When it came time to go out, they simply took some cash from their dine-out cab fare envelope and off they went. Health club goers could take a similar approach by joining the club on a pay-per-visit basis and paying themselves (or their workout cash account) a flat rate each month that is equivalent to the club's flat rate. The beauty of these self-service flat-rate systems is that any excess money goes to you, not the health club.

EVALUATE YOUR DEFAULT PAYMENTS

In today's world, it is common to have many prepaid subscriptions going all at the same time. The health club fee is automatically deducted from your checking account, and your Netflix, Amazon Prime, Hulu, and newspaper subscriptions are all charged to a credit card. Some are charged monthly, others are annual fees that come at odd times. Once these payments are set in place, they become defaults. If you do nothing, you continue to be charged, and often you don't notice them on your credit card and bank statements. There may have been a very good reason to start those subscriptions at the time you signed up, but your behavior is likely to drift. After a while, it may turn out that you are not really using Hulu very often and you are not going to the gym at all. Defaults are a powerful influence on our behavior. If you do nothing, you will continue to be charged. Just as eliminating spam e-mail may take a deliberate effort to unsubscribe, it is a good idea to make a periodic review of all your subscriptions and eliminate the ones that no longer make sense.

BEWARE THE PSYCHOLOGY OF SPENDING WITH PLASTIC

As Richard Feinberg's research shows (chapter 8), credit cards are spending facilitators. The unreality of spending with a card has led some people to eschew the use of credit and debit cards altogether. They carry cash and pay cash whenever possible, or alternatively, they write paper checks. (Most of us would prefer they not do this in the grocery store checkout line.) This may not be a practical solution for everyone in all situations, but for those who want greater control over their out-of-pocket expenses, there is much to recommend the return to a cash economy. Cards are convenient, but as we have seen, conveniences have their costs.

Finally, remember that your credit limit is not a measure of the bank's faith in you or of your financial prowess. Only you can judge what level of spending and indebtedness you can live with, and it is wise not to factor your credit limit into this equation. Just as many mortgage companies will approve people for mortgages that end up being too much for them to handle, credit card companies will often extend you more credit than it is wise to carry.

You and the ATM

A final note about cash. As mentioned earlier, since the 1970s, many of the barriers to obtaining cash have been eliminated. No longer do you need to wait until the bank is open, nor do you need to go to your own bank. Armed with an ATM card, you can get cash at one of the thousands of ATMs around the country, as well as in most grocery store checkout lines. For some people, managing the cash in their wallets is part of their overall problem with money. As we have seen, it is particularly difficult to remember how much you are spending when you pay with plastic, but some people have a similar problem with cash. Yes, you often need to retrieve and count out bills to make a purchase, and this should help you keep track of what you have been spending. Some people also choose to keep a list of all their expenditures throughout the day and hang on to all their receipts. But when it comes to spending, $20 bills all look alike. Furthermore, if you go to the ATM and get a larger amount of cash—say, $100 or $200—few of your typical daily purchases will require any budgeting on your part. At the beginning, the supply of bills is more than adequate, so it is easy to peel off as many as the current purchase requires. Just as payment depreciation makes ice cream bars bought in bulk feel like they are free, having a big wad of twenties in your wallet makes it much easier to peel off a few for whatever impulsive purchase you are currently considering.

A simple strategy for diminishing the leakage from your wallet is to restrict the amount of cash you carry to a modest sum. Make it a rule to only withdraw $40 or perhaps $60 from the cash machine on a routine visit. Limiting the amount of cash on hand puts a modest restraint on out-of-pocket expenses. If you are going to maintain enough cash on hand, you will need to keep track of what you have. Will there be enough for your food truck lunch tomorrow? Given that we are confronted with so many enticements to spend throughout the course of a typical day, it is useful to have some restrictions on our financial flexibility. If you have to do a little daily budgeting of cash simply to avoid additional trips to the ATM, you will spend less recklessly. Some will say that small withdrawals from the ATM don't make economic sense. Unless you are using one of the machines operated by your own bank, you are likely to be charged a transaction fee of three dollars at the foreign ATM and potentially another fee by your own bank. Because these fees are the same whether you take out $20 or $200, some people say you should take out larger sums to cut down on ATM fees. But this logic holds only if you spend your money in exactly the same way when you have $20 in your wallet as when you have $200.

It is best to avoid ATM fees altogether, but if you have to use a foreign ATM, don't let the fee affect the amount you withdraw. If you are likely to spend more freely with a large wad in your pocket, the restraint on spending provided by smaller amounts of cash will often save more money than the cost of the additional transaction fees.

WORKING FOR A BETTER ECONOMY

One answer to the question of why so many Americans are going broke might simply be that they are supposed to. The country seems to have endorsed the Keynesian view that thrift, though good for individual consumers, is not good for the economy as a whole. Spending—even spending until you are deeply in debt—is good for the country, good for the economy, good for business. Furthermore, as individual citizens at sea in the roiling waves of the market, we are easily overpowered by the forces aligned against us. Millions of families are up to their eyeballs in debt, and ten years after the Great Recession of 2008, over half a million people a year declare bankruptcy, mortgage foreclosures are still much higher than their prerecession levels, and millions of people are delinquent on their student loan payments. Of course, we can employ any number of personal strategies in an effort to bolster our self-control, and these will undoubtedly help. We can choose to take on the entire burden of our financial stability in this risky and rapidly changing economic environment, which will satisfy the politicians and business interests who have emphasized the need for greater personal responsibility. Personal responsibility is a virtue, and we must do what we can to encourage it. But despite the popular rhetoric, we seem to have created a world where it is very easy to get into trouble.

Much has happened since the 1970s. Despite the narrative I have developed in the preceding chapters, some may prefer to think the financial tragedies they see around them are a sign of diminished character, people who never learned the lessons of the Great Depression and are simply less prudent than their parents. But there is ample evidence that the demands on our self-control are much greater now than they ever were for previous generations. It is much more difficult to be good today than it was before the 1970s, and although some things have improved since the Great Recession, other things have gotten worse. As a result, it seems reasonable to ask whether it has to be this way. Is there anything we can do to reshape our economy so that it will encourage more responsible and farsighted behavior? Must the wind blow only in one direction, toward spending and debt? Isn't there a way we can build a more wholesome economic environment?

If we are going to reshape the American economic landscape, it will require an organized effort. As citizens, we can work for change in our local communities as well as on the state and federal level, but to accomplish this we will have to band together with others and work for community and legislative change. Many of the economic challenges we face have been put in place by powerful business and political interests, and the challenge is great. Following, the 2008 banking crisis, Elizabeth Warren, then a Harvard Law professor working on a congressional oversight committee, advocated for the creation of a government office that would fight to make sure individual citizens were treated fairly by lenders and banks. In 2011, the Consumer Financial Protection Bureau (CFPB) was launched as part of the Dodd–Frank Wall Street Reform and Consumer Protection Act. The CFPB's purpose is to "protect consumers from unfair, deceptive, or abusive practices and take action against companies that break the law."[40] In 2016, Wells Fargo Bank was discovered to have been scamming customers by creating over 1.5 million fake customer accounts, and the CFPB fined Wells Fargo $185 million. Furthermore, as of 2017, the bureau had recovered $12 billion in funds for consumers who had been scammed.[41] Although the CFPB is a good thing that came out of the Great Recession of 2008, since its inception the bureau has been challenged by Republican lawmakers and powerful banking lobbyist. As I write this in late 2017, the CFPB remains an embattled agency whose fate under the current Republican administration remains uncertain.[42]

As this episode suggests, the odds are against the consumer. Big banks have lawyers, lobbyists, and money for campaign contributions, and individual consumers, particularly those who are middle-income and lower, can't compete. That's why a government agency like the CFPB is needed. Furthermore, the effort to keep banks from bilking citizens addresses only one feature of a system designed to make it easy to get into debt. As the previous chapters have shown, the American economic marketplace has laid a bewildering number of traps for consumers. Fighting back against the interests of big business will always be a challenging task, but there are things we can do. In the following pages I list a few promising community-based programs and legislative proposals aimed at making it easier for consumers to achieve economic stability.

Before addressing more specific programs, it should be pointed out that simply increasing the economic and social security of average Americans would help many people stay out of debt. As individual consumers, we take on a stream of expenses—rent or mortgage, utilities, transportation, and food— and life proceeds apace as long as we can meet this stream of expenses with an equally steady stream of income. But in recent decades, many workers have lost well-paying jobs to downsizing or outsourcing, and when they are able to find employment again, too often it is in lower-paying service sector jobs.[43] The results of the 2016 election suggest that many citizens are worried about their jobs being taken by globalization and immigrants to the United States, but the evidence suggests that automation poses a much larger threat.[44] In addition, as we have seen, many more young people are beginning their lives handicapped by mountains of debt.

Finally, the United States is a country with a very leaky social safety net. Although the Affordable Care Act allowed many more people to obtain health insurance, there are still millions of uninsured Americans, and the current administration came into power on the promise of eliminating the Affordable Care Act altogether. As of this writing, that effort has not yet succeeded, but the fate of the American healthcare system is very uncertain. Whatever happens, it seems likely that the United States—unlike almost all the other developed countries of the world—will not reach the goal of universal healthcare any time soon. For over a decade, the country has been in the grip of a growing opioid addiction crisis, and in 2016, for the first time in over twenty years, overall life expectancy in the United States declined for both men and women.[45] Finally, we have a retirement system that places much of the burden and risk of saving and investment on the individual employee. All of this adds up to millions of Americans living lives that are far less secure than the ones their parents had and than those in many other developed countries.[46] It is not difficult to see why easy credit and a consumer economy, combined with this kind of economic and social uncertainty, can lead to debt, foreclosure, bankruptcy, and other forms of ruin.

Financial Literacy Programs

Today's economic world is more complicated than ever before. In addition to credit cards and conventional banking and lending practices, consumers are confronted with a daunting array of financial products, such as adjustable-rate and reverse mortgages; payday lending; and rent-to-own purchasing. Many people are inadequately equipped to evaluate these offers, and the financial risks involved are not always clear. A simple—and, today, much needed—protection against financial mishap is better education. Recent surveys of consumer literacy show that many high schoolers and adults often lack basic financial knowledge. For example, surveys of financial literacy have shown that only one-third of the population understands compound interest and how credit cards work. As one might expect, research shows that people who are lower on financial literacy are more likely to report carrying more debt than they would like.[47] According to a

2012 survey, in comparison to eighteen developed nations of the Organization for Economic Cooperation and Development (OECD), teenagers in the United States have an average level of financial literacy, just below that of Latvians and just above Russians. Teens from economical ascendant China had the highest financial literacy scores among OECD countries by a substantial margin.[48] Schools are an obvious place to introduce financial education, but today only seventeen states require high school students to take a financial literacy course. In addition to personal financial management, the best of these programs also cover consumer decision-making issues, such as how to distinguish needs from wants, how to critically evaluate advertising claims, and consumer rights and responsibilities.

There is some evidence these programs work. A study led by Stanford University economist Douglas Bernheim found that adults exposed to a state-mandated high school financial education curriculum saved significantly more money and had significantly greater net wealth than those who had not received this training.[49] Another study found that, in states where financial education courses were required, high school graduates had average credit scores that were between 15 and 19 points higher than nearby states without this requirement.[50] But much more financial education is needed. Jump$tart, a coalition of business and advocacy organizations, maintains a set of voluntary national standards for financial education for primary and secondary school students, and has worked with a number of state legislatures in support of mandated financial education programs.[51] At the moment, despite the efforts of groups such as the Consumer Federation of America, there is no standardized national campaign for consumer education.

In addition to school-based education programs, there is a growing recognition that financial education can and should be introduced in a wide variety of settings. For example, many consumers would benefit from financial training offered at work, at banks and credit unions, through mortgage lenders, through counseling agencies, and through the military.[52] Consumers make important financial decisions in a variety of settings (e.g., decisions about employee retirement plans), and educational programs geared toward the consumer's current needs could be very effective. Employers have a particular incentive to provide financial education programs for their workers because financial difficulties can create absenteeism, lowered productivity, and stress-related illness.[53] Finally, as we have seen, younger and younger children are being exposed to advertising and becoming tiny consumers. There is a clear need for consumer education well before the high school years. "Tweens" and younger children could benefit from age-appropriate instruction on consumer decision-making and the evaluation of advertising appeals. Rather than leaving this kind of education to parents alone, these important life skills should be implemented in our schools at the elementary level.

Programs to Promote Savings

Much of the heartbreak portrayed in these pages could be avoided by having adequate emergency savings on hand that could be put to use when the unexpected—which, of course, often *can* be expected—happens. Because the United States has had such a dismal record of personal savings, there have been a number of efforts aimed at stemming the tide. For example, America Saves (https://americasaves.org/) is a coalition of government, nonprofit, and corporate groups working together to encourage household savings. Consumers who enroll in America Saves set savings goals and receive information on savings accounts, e-mail or telephone advice from financial planners, and other forms of support—all free of charge.

But as we have seen, wanting to save—and even having support in your efforts to save—may not be as important as innovations that make use of behavioral economic concepts, and several of the ideas currently being promoted by advocacy organizations, think tanks, businesses, or legislators take advantage of what we know about default behavior, the hyperbola, and the effect of anchors. For example, a number of new initiatives are aimed at making it even easier to save all or part of your annual tax refund. For example, starting in 2007 the IRS began to allow electronic deposits of tax refunds to be split between up to three different accounts, even if they are in different banks.[54] As a result, people who are hesitant to put all of their refund into savings might be willing to save part of the refund and put the rest in their checking account for immediate use. In addition, taxpayers now have the option to use some or all of their refunds to buy US savings bonds.[55] Of course, decisions to save all or part of a tax return through bonds or some other savings mechanism are made easier by virtue of their distance in time from when the money will be received. Our best financial selves come out when we are looking out toward the far end of the hyperbola.

Other proposals attempt to make saving, either for retirement or for a rainy day, the default behavior. As we have seen, the Save More Tomorrow program can increase savings in defined contribution retirement plans. The decision to save is made well in advance of the time the plan kicks in, and the sting of loss is diminished by timing the increased savings to coincide with the annual raise. But an even more aggressive system makes retirement savings the default behavior rather than an opt-in choice. Knowing that employees often take the path of least resistance when making financial decisions, economists have begun to examine companies that implement systems in which new employees are automatically signed up to save some percentage of their pay in a 401(k) account. Workers always have the right to opt out of the plan, but research shows that few do. A test at a medium-sized chemical company in the United States showed that 95 percent of employees remained enrolled when automatically put into a plan to save 3 percent of their pay toward retirement. Furthermore, when the company increased the default savings to 6 percent of pay, there was little change. Participation rates remained 25 percent higher than in the prior opt-in system.[56] A similar proposal—but on a national scale— would encourage regular rainy day savings by automatically enrolling all workers in a payroll savings plan with a default 2 percent contribution rate.[57] Employees could choose from a variety of low-cost investment options, and the participants would always have the ability to withdraw funds or opt out of the system. Employers would facilitate the depositing of funds but would incur no additional costs. Based on what we have seen from the research on other kinds of savings, it is probably safe to say that the path of least resistance would lead to many employees saving 2 percent of their pay.

One of the potential problems of default systems is that they may produce less than optimal anchoring effects. Some of these experimental automatic retirement savings plans have used a default of 3 percent savings on the part of the employee—even when contributions up to 6 percent were matched or partially matched by employer contributions—based on the belief that a higher rate of contribution in an automatic opt-out system would be too onerous. But research shows the default rate of 3 percent has a powerful effect on the amounts contributed, even when employees are free to choose higher or lower rates of contribution at any time.[58] Employees who were started at 6 percent contributed at much higher rates, probably due to inertia, but probably also due to the anchoring effect of the automatic savings rate. Once the 3 percent amount was suggested, it was difficult for employees to adjust away from it. As a result, companies that use an automatic contribution retirement saving plan should choose the default level of contribution with care. It could have a powerful effect on the future retirement security of their employees.

In their bestselling book *Nudge: Improving Decisions about Health, Wealth, and Happiness*, economist Richard Thaler and law professor Cass Sunstein use the term "libertarian paternalism" to describe programs—such as the savings proposals just discussed—that make use of defaults and other principles of behavioral economics to promote desirable behavior.[59] These programs are libertarian because they preserve individual choice. The employee is always free to opt in or out of the savings plan at any time, and as a result, no particular behavior is regulated or mandated. Yet these programs are paternalistic because they are cleverly designed to promote behavior that is good for the employee. Despite the fact that these programs avoid the heavy-handed approach of regulating behavior, some conservative commentators have criticized them for diminishing the opportunities for reason, judgment, and will.[60] But Thaler and Sunstein point out that whether we think about it deliberately or not, there is always a default response. They give the hypothetical example of a cafeteria director who notices that the order in which foods are arranged on the buffet table influences the choices people make. Once she has observed this phenomenon, she has three choices. She can arrange the food in a way that she thinks would benefit the health and well-being of the customers, she can arrange the food randomly, or she can deliberately order the food in a way that will make the customers as obese as possible.[61] None of these arrangements alters the free choice of the diners, but would it be wrong for the cafeteria director to place the fruits before the desserts? Thaler and Sunstein argue that, given a clear understanding of people's long-term goals—health and fitness over obesity and illness—it is quite reasonable to arrange the environment in ways that will help them achieve these goals rather than hinder them. When it comes to helping Americans save, it is clear that libertarian paternalism could have a very positive effect on people's lives without forcing them to do anything. Given the many influences aligned to separate people from their money, it seems only fair to introduce behavioral economic principles aimed at nudging people in the other direction.

A variety of more aggressive programs to encourage saving have been suggested. For example, a number of proposals would set up government-funded savings accounts for each child at birth, to which the children or their families could add money. Another idea would provide tax-supported matching funds for low- and middle-income workers who deposit money in a Roth IRA through their place of employment. In addition, several ideas have been suggested to encourage saving for college and to further rejuvenate the US savings bond program.[62] These kinds of government programs require the social and political will to commit resources to the economic security of all Americans, but they are worth serious consideration. A country with a minimal savings rate is not strong, and its citizens are not adequately prepared to face the inevitable uncertainties of the future. We can just turn away and say, "It's your own fault," or we can recognize that we are all in this together and that with a little effort we can do better.

Reasonable Limits on Commercialism

Given what we have learned, there are two ways to curtail the pull of commercialism in our lives: limit our exposure to advertising, and turn the physics of spending on its head by reversing the effects of the five variables that control spending. We could reduce the availability of goods and services, make spending more time-consuming and more effortful, take away the financial wherewithal, and put up additional social barriers. The problem, of course, is that all of these approaches fly in the face of free enterprise.

The United States is committed to markets that are open and free, and many of the same changes that have led to our indebtedness over the last three decades have been the product of that commitment. Adam Smith's invisible hand of the marketplace was supposed to benefit us all, and in many ways it has. But innovations that are good for business often produce greater risk for individual consumers. When so many Americans are pulled down by so much personal debt, it may be time for a shift in the balance between business and consumer interests. In some cases, reasonable, limited regulation may be needed in order to push back the boundaries of commercialism in our lives. In other cases, it may be possible to use the techniques of behavioral economics and libertarian paternalism to make prudent behavior more likely without limiting choice.

In the case of advertising, both regulation and consumer choice could be strengthened. On the community level, there is much room for activism. Cities and towns can implement limits on outdoor advertising and branding in public locations. Especially in large cities, visual clutter and enjoyment of the environment could be improved by regulating the use of signs, stickers, leaflets, and placards. It is hard to imagine Times Square as anything but a blazing monument to commercialism, but many other city spaces could be preserved for the private enjoyment of the citizenry.

Of particular concern for many people is children's exposure to advertising. There are competing interests here, too, because candy sales and other product promotions are common fundraising vehicles for sports teams and other school groups. PTAs and other groups often encourage students and parents to sell products in return for money for trips, computers, or other projects. Similarly, products are often donated to schools in return for the display of advertising. Many public schools require that students put paper covers over their textbooks to preserve them for future use, and I have fond memories of carefully disassembling brown paper bags for this purpose. But today, paper textbook covers festooned with advertising are often given away free in schools. As we have seen, children are an important marketing demographic. A 2005 industry estimate suggested that 47 percent of US household spending was controlled or influenced by children under fourteen years of age.[63] As a result, marketers are invading the school day, changing what should be a protected academic environment into just one more commercial marketplace. Parents and others who become active in their communities can fight against Channel One and other advertising campaigns aimed at schoolchildren. These are areas where parents can have considerable influence, and those who want to stem the commercial tide can make measurable changes.[64]

Finally, those who strive to resist the increasing influence of commercialism in almost every corner of our lives may want to become involved in a larger advocacy organization. In particular, the Campaign for a Commercial-Free Childhood (CCFC) (http://www.commercialfreechildhood.org/) is a very active group making great strides on a variety of fronts. They have been a leader in the fight to remove Channel One from classrooms and branded fast foods from school cafeterias. As I write this they are working with the Federal Trade Commission in an effort to get Instagram to require the identification of all paid posts as advertising.[65] The CCFC website has a number of resources for parents who want to become advocates in their communities or to simply limit their children's exposure to commercial messages.[66] Finally, in May of each year CCFC sponsors a Screen-Free Week in coordination with Children's Book Week.[67]

Stemming the intrusion of the marketplace in our lives will be increasingly difficult. Efforts to limit the times and locations where commerce can take place are likely to fail. Some states and towns still have blue laws prohibiting the sale of alcohol on Sunday, a vestige of an era when drinking was considered a sin and many believed that sinners should be in church rather than a bar. But today, spending is a patriotic virtue, and efforts to curtail it are rare and unpopular. Most communities use zoning laws and other ordinances to put some boundaries on the places and times that business can be conducted, but it is unlikely that we can legislate a world in which the five variables that control spending have been reversed. As we have seen, much of our challenge with self-control has come with technological developments over the last three decades, and once the Pandora's box of progress has been opened, it is very difficult to repack it. So much of the challenge of financial stability will have to be approached through individual strategies aimed at promoting prudent behavior. Nonetheless, there are important things that governments and businesses could do to help citizens in their efforts to maintain balance.

Perhaps because people consider gambling to be a vice, there is some possibility of regulating it in ways that will bolster self-control. As we have seen, the trend is currently in favor of further expansion of casino gambling, so it is likely there will be even more access to this spending response in the future. But there are ways that gambling's more negative effects could be diminished. For example, the several states have implemented a system allowing problem gamblers to voluntarily ban themselves from casinos.[68] Once they sign up for the ban it can never be revoked, and those who defy their own voluntary exclusion face arrest and fines. The voluntary ban program provides more choice rather than less. Making this option available has no effect on people who are able to adequately control their gambling, and it provides problem gamblers with an additional choice: a powerful commitment device that they would never be able to implement on their own. Although there are ways the program could be improved, there is now research evidence that it works, and as a result, New Jersey, Maryland, Illinois, and a number of other states have introduced voluntary exclusion systems.[69] In addition, some casinos have taken the system a step further. For instance, once a player is banned in a state where Caesars Entertainment, Inc., operates a casino, Caesars bans the individual at all of its casinos worldwide.[70]

Voluntary exclusion programs are a helpful development, but because they apply only to people with serious gambling problems, such policies will have limited impact on the rest of us who just have trouble staying out of debt. Yet, building on the idea of libertarian paternalism—regulations and policies that preserve choice while promoting welfare—behavioral economists have suggested a number of promising new ideas that could be used to help control spending and debt. In each case, the goal has been to provide a system—such as voluntary exclusion from gambling—that will help those who need it without inconveniencing those who don't.

An approach called "asymmetric paternalism" has been proposed by a group led by economist Colin Camerer.[71] These programs are asymmetric because they are designed to have their greatest effect on those who would otherwise act against their own interests and have little effect on those who don't have this problem. But Camerer and his associates also recognize that many regulations reasonably do apply to us all because there are certain situations where even people who are of sound mind may stumble. Laws against selling your organs or selling yourself into servitude keep people who might be in desperate straits from doing things they would later regret, and prohibitions against narcotics are based on the idea that these substances can turn rational people into irrational people. Other kinds of regulation are not blanket prohibitions but are designed to encourage wisdom in the way default retirement savings plans make certain that, where there is a status quo bias, the outcome will benefit the individual.

Camerer suggests two other forms of regulatory programs that should help those who need help without overly taxing those who don't: requirements for additional information and cooling-off periods. One of the assumptions of classical economics is that individuals have full information when making decisions. If the marketplace is going to function smoothly, all the players must have adequate information. But, as we have seen, consumers often do not have a clear understanding of important financial issues. As a result, providing more information may sometimes lead to better decisions. Among the possibilities are prominently displaying the odds of winning a lottery prize, providing more information about the true cost of rent-to-own merchandise, and modifying credit card bills to display the effects of compound interest and the true cost of borrowing. This last suggestion became part of the 2009 CARD Act passed in the wake of the Great Recession. Since 2010, credit card bills are required to indicate how long it would take to pay off the balance if only minimum payments are made, as well as the payment amount required to pay off the balance in three years.[72]

In some cases, these regulations would likely be resisted by the affected industries. For example, providing gamblers with—or simply reminding them of—the odds of winning the lottery might decrease sales. Sales at rent-to-own stores might experience a similar slump if total purchasing costs were more prominently displayed. According to some findings, 66 percent of rent-to-own merchandise is eventually purchased by the customer, often at an exorbitant cost.[73] A 2014 *Washington Post* article documented customers of an Alabama rent-to-own store paying $4,150 over time for a couch valued at $1,500. For consumers without other resources available to them rent-to-own may represent a viable option, but it seems fair that customers—especially the low-income customers who are disproportionately affected—be as well informed as possible. As result, there is reason to implement regulations that require clearer disclosure of rent-to-own terms.[74]

Cooling-off periods are another kind of asymmetrical program designed to help people do what is in their long-term interests. Many important decisions are made under "hot" circumstances that promote impulsive decisions, and sometimes these impulsive contexts are not of our own creation. A classic case is door-to-door sales. When approached by a salesperson at the door, people often feel pressured to buy things they would otherwise not and later experience buyer's remorse. As a result, the Federal Trade Commission requires a mandatory cooling-off period for this kind of purchase. Most purchases of $26 or more made through a door-to-door salesperson can be canceled within three days, and the salespeople are required to tell their customers about the cooling-off period at the time of the sale.[75] In the state of California, there was sufficient concern about elderly people being pressured to buy home emergency notification systems—such as those promoted with the classic commercial line "I've fallen, and I can't get up!"—that a law was passed to make the cooling-off period seven days long. The FTC rules provide for cooling off periods for several other kinds of sales, but it is notable that online, telephone, and mail order sales are not subject to a cooling off period. In contrast, the European Union provides for a 2-week-long cooling off period for any sale not made at a retailer's shop.[76]

The potential benefits of cooling-off periods are obvious. The high end of the hyperbola speaks quite loudly when the salesperson is standing right in front of you going through their routine. This is a case where the social context strongly encourages spending, rather than being a barrier to it (variable five). But, in the United States, cooling-off periods apply in a limited number of situations. Furthermore, some of the most important kinds of purchases—cars, real estate, or insurance—are not covered by the FTC cooling-off rule. Finally, your home is not the only context in which unwise impulsive decisions might occur, and as a result, Camerer and colleagues suggest that cooling-off periods could also be helpful in other situations. As we have seen, online purchases often have the equivalent of a very short cooling-off period. Although consumers may not realize it, if the item has not yet shipped, they can often cancel the order.

Another group of behavioral economists has suggested somewhat more invasive programs that are designed to encourage foresight on the part of the consumer. These suggestions, which they call "early-decision" regulations, generally have the effect of making things a bit scarcer than they are right now, thereby forcing us to think ahead.[77] Consider, for example, the world before there were ATMs. Like today, live bank tellers dispensing cash were available only at certain times. Furthermore, back then paying with a credit card was slower and less common due to the absence of electronic point-of-sale devices, and checks were not always accepted, particularly when you were away from your local area. Many things required cash, and having cash on hand required planning. Once you were out in the world—regardless of how wealthy you were—the amount of money in your pocket was a limitation. It was a little harder to be impulsive about a purchase that presents itself while you are busy doing something else. If you gave in to temptation and bought something that was a mere "want," later in the day you might find you were unable to pay for a true necessity.

It is just this kind of budgeting and the positive effects it can bring that early-decision regulations are designed to promote. For example, if a society wanted to encourage people to smoke less without banning tobacco and e-cigarettes altogether, they might limit the sale of cigarettes and vaping supplies, either by time or by location. As it is now, there are few reasons to ration your use of these products. Tobacco and e-cigarettes can be purchased almost anywhere and at almost any time of day or night. Location-based early decision legislation might create a system where only one retail outlet in a particular area would be licensed to sell cigarettes. Potential vendors in each location might compete for the right to sell cigarettes and pay a licensing fee. Under this arrangement, it would require a little more thinking to make sure you always had smokes available. Going to the local vendor would be less convenient, and many people might ration their consumption to avoid the hassle of running out when the smoke shop is some distance away. A time-based early-decision program might limit sales to a single hour a day—for example, 8:00 to 9:00 A.M. Again, smokers would need to think ahead and make sure they had enough cigarettes.

This kind of early-decision regulation is perhaps easier to imagine in the context of cigarettes, a product that is considered a serious health risk and already has restrictions on advertising and sales to minors. But what about early-decision programs and spending? Once again, unless aimed at restricting products that have clear health risks or—like gambling—carry the taint of vice, regulations such as these are likely to be attacked on the basis of restraint of trade. Business interests will complain that they are trying to make a living, and regulations that make it more difficult for their customers to come up with the wherewithal or have access to the transaction are unfair and harmful to the economy. But it is obvious the current economic environment is harming many Americans. Debt is rampant and financial anxiety is at a fever pitch. So some kind of action is needed—if not outright regulation, then perhaps voluntary early-decision options. This kind of program increases consumer choice rather than decreasing it.

Voluntary early-decision programs for consumers would be akin to the voluntary exclusion programs for gamblers. Furthermore, in a modest strike back at the effects of modern technology on spending, these interventions might use technology to the consumer's benefit and encourage planning ahead and budgeting rather than discouraging them. For example, consumers might opt to limit the time of day or days of the week when their credit cards are effective. Of course, we all have the ability to cut up our cards or cancel our accounts. But modern technology offers the possibility of much more systematic commitment devices. Furthermore, the early decision approach simply puts controls on spending that would introduce a hedge against impulsivity without being as drastic as cutting up cards. For example, with the help of a centrally controlled system, consumers could voluntarily request that all their credit cards be operational only on Saturday. Or only from 9:00 A.M. to 6:00 P.M., or only from 6:00 P.M. to midnight. Purchases attempted outside the approved time period simply would be declined. Given our current electronic banking network, such a system should be possible, and it could have very positive effects.

The simple act of limiting credit card purchases to a particular block of time can break up the rhythm of shopping and help separate true needs from fleeting wants. I once interviewed a problem gambler who had been convicted of stealing money to support her obsession with slot machines. Following her sentencing, she was banned from the local casinos by court order, but, determined to continue playing, she drove to a dog-racing track in a neighboring state where she could play video poker. The only problem was that, unlike the casinos she was used to, the dog track closed for a few hours each night. This simple interruption in the availability of the spending response had a profound effect. As she put it, "It was the first time I ever left with money in my pocket." In her previous life as a gambler, even on a night when she had been lucky and hit the jackpot, she would turn around and put her winnings into the machine. The great constant in her life was gambling, and this behavior stopped only when it could no longer continue due to a lack of wherewithal. Of course, the odds are inexorably against the player, and if you play enough, all the money ends up in the house's account. But given a forced interruption in play, this gambler sometimes left the dog track with money in her pocket.

Without question this woman had a serious gambling problem that is not comparable to the average person's difficulty sticking to a sound budget. But many consumers can improve their position by interrupting the flow of transactions. Designating particular days or times as shopping periods would be a useful way to increase self-control. Some of the burden of building in delays to purchases can be eliminated by concentrating your transactions at particular times. Of course, the system could be designed to make exceptions for emergencies. For example, charges made at automobile service stations and medical facilities could be exempted from time limitations. These transactions are clear necessities. But by creating some temporary barriers, this kind of voluntary early decision mechanism could be very useful.

Reasonable Regulation of Lending

Modest levels of regulation can be useful when it is important to maintain consumer choice. Voluntary exclusion from gambling and early decision programs are moderately intrusive forms of regulation, but because they are asymmetric in their influence—affecting only those who choose to enroll—they are more likely to be found to be acceptable. However, sometimes the full force of regulation is justified. As mentioned above, there are some situations where even people of sound mind might stumble. But if we believe it is important to remove the option of selling your organs for profit, why shouldn't there be limits on borrowing, too? Selling an eye or a hand to an organ broker is an irreversible decision that will have permanent negative implications. The problem is that in a desperate circumstance—for example, faced with losing the family home— there are people who might choose to sell off pieces of their body. Why? Because the loss of the home looms large at the immediate end of the hyperbola, and the loss of body function—while also immediate—is somewhat more abstract. You will still have another eye and another arm, and it may not be until sometime later that you understand the implications of this choice or recognize the other options that were available.

Obviously, borrowing cannot and should not be made altogether illegal, but as we saw in chapter 2, even the great founding father of free market capitalism, Adam Smith, believed that lending was one industry that should be regulated. Our economy and financial growth depend on the ability to borrow money, but many of the kinds of lending common today bear a sad resemblance to the moneylender Shylock's demand for a pound of flesh in Shakespeare's *Merchant of Venice*. At this point in our history, the goal is as much to maintain the regulatory progress we have achieved as it is to introduce new protections.

The financial collapse of 2008 was a tragedy of substantial proportions, and ten years later, many of the people left in its wake have yet to get their lives back. Some who lost jobs and homes never will. But if there is an upside to the Great Recession it is that, in the wake of the crisis, Congress passed a number of very valuable and long-overdue banking rules. The CFPB established as part of the Dodd-Frank banking reforms law, introduced a number of protections to help consumers from getting into trouble. In the area of mortgage lending, the CFPB has implemented new rules governing the approval of loans and the information provided to borrowers. Lenders must make greater efforts to determine whether potential homebuyers will be able to pay, and they must do a better job of informing borrowers about the contingencies of the loan. As previously mentioned, the CARD Act requires that credit card bills provide more information about the cost of revolving credit, and other CARD Act reforms include requirements that banks give forty-five days notice before an interest rate change, allow a minimum of twenty-one days between the bill being sent to you and the payment due date, and apply payments to balances with the highest interest rates first. Importantly, as part of its oversight function, the CFPB has the power to fine financial institutions that don't follow the rules.[78]

As of this writing the CFPB has operated quite effectively for seven years, but as mentioned above, its future is in doubt. The current Republican administration has proposed to eliminate many of the regulatory protections of Dodd-Frank in ways that would benefit the banking industry. Congress, rather than the Federal Reserve, would approve funding for the CFPB, and the president would have the power to fire the director of the CFPB for any reason. These changes would politicize this important agency and put its fate in the hands of politicians who receive large campaign contributions from the banking industry.[79]

A New Kind of Leadership

Finally, as the previous section suggests, we are sorely in need of a different kind of leadership. People who use the power of their positions to promote economic security for all of us. Take the simple issue of saving. I am old enough to remember public service announcements about payroll savings plans from the 1970s. A series of people from different walks of life would come on the TV screen and talk about how little they had saved. "I make nine bucks an hour, and last year that's about what I saved. Nine bucks!" The commercial would go on to promote investment in US Savings Bonds through the payroll deposit program at work. Ironically, these commercials ran during a period when the personal savings rate was four times as high as it is now.

Today things are very different. I cannot remember a time in the last two decades when a public service announcement, the president, or a business leader promoted personal savings. There are plenty of commercials for apps to help you keep track of your credit score and for companies that want to help to consolidate your debt or to negotiate on your behalf with the IRS to get a better deal on the back taxes you owe. But there are no speeches about how to avoid these problems in the first place. About the virtues of having money in the bank. Instead, spending is presented as a patriotic act. After the events of September 11, 2001, stopped the nation in its tracks, President George W. Bush urged people to go out and shop and "Get down to Disney World in Florida."[80] The stock market had crashed, the dollar had lost value, and the president proposed that spending money was the best way for Americans to pull themselves out of devastating national tragedy. No wonder we get ourselves into trouble. If we hope to avoid the financial hardships that have marked these early years of the twenty-first century, we will need to find leaders who are looking out for us. Leaders who have consumers in mind and not just the stock market.

THE NEW TRAGEDY OF THE COMMONS

The modern world presents problems of financial self-control that have never before been encountered. The physics of spending has been employed to create an environment where our desires can be satisfied at any time and in any location. The expansion of easy credit and even easier spending opportunities has challenged many whose lives are less stable than our own and, perhaps, less stable than those of a generation ago. In recent decades, the United States has experienced tremendous economic growth, but at the expense of millions of bankruptcies and foreclosures. Many more families struggle to carry a debt burden that seems to have no end.

Still, even in today's risky environment, there is much we can do to resist the call of the hyperbola. The field of behavioral economics has emerged just when we seem to need it most, and we can use our new understanding of commitment strategies, prospect theory, payment depreciation, and many other behavioral economic concepts to take control of our financial lives. But as encouraging as these developments are, it is not entirely fair to make our new, perilous economic environment the exclusive responsibility of the consumer. Great fortunes are being made by the manipulation of our self-control. So if the American economy is to show a better balance between the interests of business and the consumer, we are going to need some regulatory reform. Less intrusive interventions, such as asymmetrical regulations and early decision programs, are best, but sometimes—as in the case of the banking and credit card industries—the full force of law is needed.

The tragedy of the commons is a well-known moral tale in economics whose message is drawn from a conflict between individual and community interests. If you are a cattle rancher and your animals graze in a common field, you and your fellow farmers have an interest in avoiding overgrazing. If too many cattle eat the grass in the field, this essential resource will be depleted and none of the farmers will be able to feed their animals. The problem arises when each farmer thinks like an individual—precisely in the way that Adam Smith's free enterprise system would have him or her think. For this self-interested farmer, the benefits of adding another steer to the herd will often outweigh the small additional cost in diminished grass. But tragedy results when this kind of self-interested decision-making is employed by all the farmers using the common field. The multiplicity of self-interested decisions destroys the resource, and all are harmed. A similar desire to avoid a tragedy of the commons is the motivation behind fishing regulations that impose limits on the size of a boat's catch so that the fishing beds will continue to be available for all.[81]

In today's world a different kind of tragedy of the commons is unfolding. In a consumer economy built increasingly on the exchange of goods and services rather than manufacturing, consumers are an important collective resource. As spenders, we all provide income for an increasingly service-oriented economy. But, like the cattle farmers, we must not deplete this important resource— we must not turn on ourselves. Increasingly, the United States economy has sacrificed the physical, psychological, and financial health of its citizens in the interests of a relatively few wealthy businesses. High-calorie fatty foods are produced cheaply with the help of government subsidies, and unchecked business practices have produced enormous wealth for a small group at the expense of great hardship for millions more. The results have been profitable businesses, obesity, and debt. We can respond to this condition by simply accepting the prevailing view that people get what they deserve, that the system is fair and efficient and metes out rewards and punishments in equal measure, and that as individuals, it is our responsibility to muddle through as best we can. Or we can adopt a more community-minded attitude, acknowledging that some of us have a better starting point than others, that our choices are not all equally free, and that if we want to live in a world that honors not just the lucky among us but also the unlucky, we must make it harder for the strong to prey on the weak. We must recognize that we are all part of one great collective resource, and if this is to be a community of which we all can be proud, we must work together to avoid the tragedies we see around us.

CHAPTER 1

1. I used several documents to recreate this financial history, including a credit report I obtained from Experian in 1999 and another that I got from www.experian.com in 2004. For simplicity, when referring to either one of these reports I have used the phrase "my credit report," but, in fact, two reports, showing slightly different information, were used. In addition, I have used my Social Security statement, which provided my taxed Social Security earnings beginning in 1967, my junior year in high school. As anyone who has seen his or her Social Security statement can attest, this is a rather humbling document, laying out in simple numbers one's entire earning history, year by year.

2. S. Chan, "An Outcry Rises as Debt Collectors Play Rough," *New York Times*, July 5, 2006, A1, A17; Lucy Lazarony, "Debt Collector Horror Stories," *Bankrate.com*, April 15, 2004, www.bankrate.com/brm/news/cc/20030519a1.asp; C. E. Mayer, "As Debt Collectors Multiply, So Do Consumer Complaints," *Washington Post*, July 28, 2005, A1; J. Pavini, "Millions of American Consumers Are Complaining to the FTC," *MarketWatch.com*, December 8, 2016, http://www.marketwatch.com/story/millions-of-american-consumers-are-complaining-to-the-ftc-2016-12-08; Federal Trade Commission, *Consumer Sentinel Network: Databook for January–December 2016*, 2017, https://www.ftc.gov/reports/consumer-sentinel-network-data-book-january-december-2016. Further information about consumers' rights with regard to debt collection can be found at the Federal Trade Commission website, https://www.ftc.gov/.

3. Threatening to sue for a debt is an illegal collection tactic, because agencies can mention the possibility of a lawsuit only if they actually intend to take the debtor to court.

4. "Personal Saving Rate," Federal Reserve Bank of St. Louis, December 28, 2017, https://fred.stlouisfed.org/series/PSAVERT.

5. Errin El Issa, "NerdWallet's 2016 Household Debt Study," *NerdWallet*, accessed August 20, 2017, https://www.nerdwallet.com/blog/average-credit-card-debt-household.

6. Errin El Issa, "NerdWallet's 2016"; D. DeSilver, "For Most Workers, Real Wages Have Barely Budged for Decades," *Pew Research Center*, October 9, 2014, http://

www.pewresearch.org/fact-tank/2014/10/09/for-most-workers-real-wages-have-barely-budged-for-decades/.

7. G. Campbell, A. Haughwout, D. Lee, J. Scally, and W. van der Klaauw, "Recent Developments in Consumer Credit Card Borrowing," *Liberty Street Economics blog*, August 6, 2016, http://libertystreeteconomics.newyorkfed.org/2016/08/just-released-recent-developments-in-consumer-credit-card-borrowing.html.

8. Organisation for Economic Co-operation and Development (OECD), "Household Accounts—Household Savings—OECD Data," https://data.oecd.org/hha/household-savings.htm; OECD, "Health at a Glance 2015: OECD Indicators," doi: http://dx.doi.org/10.1787/health_glance-2015-en; D. U. Himmelstein, D. Thorne, E. Warren, and S. Woolhandler, "Medical Bankruptcy in the United States, 2007: Results of a National Study," *American Journal of Medicine* 122, no. 8 (2009): 741–46; U.S. National Center for Health Statistics, "National Health Interview Survey, 1997–June 2016, Family Core Component," https://www.cdc.gov/nchs/data/nhis/earlyrelease/earlyrelease201611_01.pdf.

9. Liz Hamel, Mira Norton, Karen Pollitz, Larry Levitt, Gary Claxton, and Mollyann Brodie, "The Burden of Medical Debt: January 2016 Results from the Kaiser Family Foundation/New York Times Medical Bills Survey," http://kff.org/report-section/the-burden-of-medical-debt-introduction/.

10. Bureau of Labor Statistics, "13 Percent of Private Industry Workers Had Access to Paid Family Leave," *Economics Daily*, November 4, 2016, https://www.bls.gov/opub/ted/2016/13-percent-of-private-industry-workers-had-access-to-paid-family-leave-in-march-2016.htm; International Labor Organization, "Maternity and Paternity at Work: Law and Practice across the World," 2014, http://www.ilo.org/wcmsp5/groups/public/---dgreports/---dcomm/---publ/documents/publication/wcms_242615.pdf.

11. The Editorial Board, "The Gig Economy's False Promise," *New York Times*, April 10, 2017, https://nyti.ms/2oQBA0M.

12. Bloom, Ester, "Here's How Many Americans Have Nothing at All Saved for Retirement," CNBC, October 24, 2017, accessed December 29, 2017, https://www.cnbc.com/2017/06/13/heres-how-many-americans-have-nothing-at-all-saved-for-retirement.html.

13. US Bureau of the Census, "Homeownership Rate for the United States [RHORUSQ156N]," retrieved from FRED, Federal Reserve Bank of St. Louis, https://fred.stlouisfed.org/series/RHORUSQ156N; ; R. Lightner, "Home Values Rebound, But Not for Everyone," *Wall Street Journal*, December 27, 2016, http://graphics.wsj.com/housing-market-recovery/.

14. Z. Bleemer, M. Brown, D. Lee, and W. van der Klaauw, "Debt, Jobs, or Housing: What's Keeping Millennials at Home?" Staff Report No. 700, *Federal Reserve Bank of New York*, 2015, https://www.newyorkfed.org/medialibrary/media/research/staff_reports/sr700.pdf; Meta Brown, Andrew Haughwout, Donghoon Lee, Joelle Scally, and Wilbert van der Klaauw, "The Student Loan Landscape," *Liberty Street Economics blog*, February 18, 2015, http://libertystreeteconomics.newyorkfed.org/2015/02/the_student_loan-landscape.html; Alvaro Mezza, Daniel Ringo, Shane Sherlund, and Kamila Sommer, "On the Effect of Student Loans on Access to Homeownership," working paper, Board of Governors of the Federal

Reserve, March 1, 2016, https://www.federalreserve.gov/econresdata/feds/2016/files/2016010pap.pdf.

15. Andrew Haughwout, Donghoon Lee, Joelle Scally, and Wilbert van der Klaauw, "Subprime Auto Debt Grows Despite Rising Delinquencies," *Liberty Street Economics blog*, November 30, 2016, http://libertystreeteconomics.newyorkfed.org/2016/11/just-released-subprime-auto-debt-grows-despite-rising-delinquencies.html.

16. P. LeBeau, "New Car, New Reality: Auto Loan Borrowing Hits Fresh Highs," cnbc.com, June 02, 2016, http://www.cnbc.com/2016/06/02/us-borrowers-are-paying-more-and-for-longer-on-their-auto-loans.html.

17. Annamaria Lusardi, Daniel J. Schneider, and Peter Tufano, "Financially Fragile Households: Evidence and Implications," *National Bureau of Economic Research*, 2011, http://www.nber.org/papers/w17072.

18. Board of Governors of the Federal Reserve System, "Report on the Economic Well-Being of U.S. Households in 2015," May 2016, https://www.federalreserve.gov/2015-report-economic-well-being-us-households-201605.pdf; Neal Gabler, "The Secret Shame of Middle-Class Americans," *The Atlantic*, May 2016, https://www.theatlantic.com/magazine/archive/2016/05/my-secret-shame/476415/.

19. World's richest, at least as measured by GDP. See Prableen Bajpai, CFA (ICFAI), "The World's Top 10 Economies," *Investopedia*, August 23, 2017, http://www.investopedia.com/articles/investing/022415/worlds-top-10-economies.asp. However, according to data from the World Bank, in 2016, the United States was eighth in per capita gross domestic product (GDP), with Luxembourg at number one, http://data.worldbank.org/indicator/NY.GDP.PCAP.CD?year_high_desc=true.

20. It is not clear to me how I ended up with this Sears MasterCard account, but in the early years of this decade, the company began aggressively marketing the card to its customers. I subsequently closed this account. See R. Berner and H. Timmons, "Sears: A Slippery Slope Made of Plastic," *Business Week*, May 6, 2002, www.businessweek.com/magazine/content/02_18/b3781075.htm.

21. Claire Tsosie, "The Credit Card Act of 2009: What It Does and Doesn't Do," *NerdWallet.com*, June 22, 2017, https://www.nerdwallet.com/blog/credit-cards/credit-card-act/.

22. Matti, Dominique, "We're Worth More Than What We Don't Have—Dominique Matti—Medium," *Medium.com*, August 5, 2017, https://medium.com/@DominiqueMatti/were-worth-more-than-what-we-don-t-have-2ab813ce315f.

23. P. Hannaord-Agor, S. Graves, and S. Spacek-Miller, "The Landscape of Civil Litigation in State Courts," *National Center for State Courts*, 2015, https://www.ncsc.org/~/media/Files/PDF/Research/CivilJusticeReport-2015.ashx.

24. C. Flango, C. Smith, C. Campbell, and N. Kauder, eds., "Trends in State Courts: Special Focus on Family Law and Court Communications," *National Center for State Courts*, 2016, 91, http://www.ncsc.org/~/media/microsites/files/trends%202016/trends-2016-low.ashx.

25. Federal Reserve Bank of New York, "Quarterly Report on Household Debt and Credit," May 2017, https://www.newyorkfed.org/medialibrary/interactives/householdcredit/data/pdf/HHDC_2017Q1.pdf.

26. Chapter 12 is a form of bankruptcy that is specifically designed for family farmers, and some individuals may choose to file under the Chapter 11 reorganization that

is usually used by commercial business, but the Chapter 12 and Chapter 11 cases represent a tiny fraction of all individual bankruptcies.

27. Five states (Florida, Iowa, Kansas, South Dakota, and Texas) and the District of Colombia have unlimited homestead exemptions, which has resulted in some remarkable inequities of the bankruptcy process. For example, the state of Florida has had several cases of individuals filing for bankruptcy while retaining multimillion-dollar homes. M. Reutter, "Bankruptcy Loophole Lets Debtors Keep Mansions While Others Suffer," University of Illinois News Bureau, April 1, 2001, https://www.newswise.com/ articles/bankruptcy-loophole-lets-debtors-keep-mansions-while-others-suffer.

28. T. H. Holmes and R. H. Rahe, "The Social Readjustment Rating Scale," *Journal of Psychosomatic Research* 11 (1967): 213–18.

29. R. J. Bruss, "How to Profit from Foreclosure Sales," *Tribunedigital-chicagotribune*, May 12, 1994, http://articles.chicagotribune.com/1994-05-12/business/ 9405120008_1_second-mortgage-mortgage-defaults-foreclosure-auction.

30. Frank James, "Nearly One in Four U.S. Homes with Mortgages 'Underwater,' " NPR, November 24, 2009, http://www.npr.org/sections/thetwo-way/2009/11/one_ in_four_us_homes_underwate.html.

31. K. E. Case and R. J. Shiller, "Mortgage Default Risk and Real Estate Prices: The Use of Index-Based Futures and Options in Real Estate," *Journal of Housing Research* 7 (1996): 243–58.

32. Matthew Desmond, "No Place Like Home: America's Eviction Epidemic," *The Observer*, February 12, 2017, https://www.theguardian.com/society/2017/feb/12/ americas-eviction-epidemic-matthew-desmond-housing-crisis.

33. Jake Blumgart, "Evictions Used to Be Rare and Scandalous. Now They're an Epidemic," *Slate Magazine*, March 17, 2016, http://www.slate.com/articles/ business/metropolis/2016/03/an_interview_with_matthew_desmond_on_ evicted_his_book_about_the_eviction.html; Matthew Desmond, *Evicted: Poverty and Profit in the American City* (New York: Broadway Books, 2016).

34. Cox Automotive Solutions, "2017 Used Car Market Report," https://publish. manheim.com/content/dam/consulting/2017-Manheim-Used-Car-Market-Report.pdf; S. Pyles, "Garnishment: What It Is, What You Can Do about It," *Nerdwallet.com*, August 18, 2016, https://www.nerdwallet.com/blog/finance/wage-garnishment/.

35. ADP Research Institute, "Garnishment: The Untold Story," 2014, https://www. adp.com/tools-and-resources/adp-research-institute/insights/~/media/RI/pdf/ Garnishment-whitepaper.ashx.

36. Jessica Silver-Greenberg, Stacy Cowley, and Natalie Kitroeff, "When Unpaid Student Loan Bills Mean You Can No Longer Work," *New York Times*, November 18, 2017, www.nytimes.com/2017/11/18/business/student-loans-licenses.html.

37. A. D. Vinokur, R. H. Price, and R. D. Caplan, "Hard Times and Hurtful Partners: How Financial Strain Affects Depression and Relationship Satisfaction of Unemployed Persons and Their Spouses," *Journal of Personality and Social Psychology* 71, no. 1 (1996): 166–79; F. L. Williams, V. Haldeman, and S. Cramer, "Financial Concerns and Productivity," *Financial Counseling and Planning* 7 (1996): 147–55.

38. R. C. Brown, "Financially-Troubled Employees and Threats of Violence Impact the Workplace," *Personal Finances and Worker Productivity* 3, no. 1 (1999): 38–47.

39. US Bureau of the Census, "Real Median Household Income in the United States," *Federal Reserve Bank of St. Louis*, https://fred.stlouisfed.org/series/MEHOINUSA672N.

CHAPTER 2

1. Neal Gabler, "The Secret Shame of Middle-Class Americans," *The Atlantic*, April 26, 2016, https://www.theatlantic.com/magazine/archive/2016/05/my-secret-shame/476415/.

2. D. Mechanic and D. A. Rocheforte, "Deinstitutionalization: An Appraisal of Reform," *Annual Review of Sociology* 16 (1990): 301–27.

3. E. F. Torrey and M. T. Zdanowicz, "Deinstitutionalization Hasn't Worked," *Washington Post*, July 9, 1999.

4. American Psychiatric Association, *Diagnostic and Statistical Manual of Mental Disorders*, 5th ed. (DSM-5) (Washington, DC: American Psychiatric Association, 2013).

5. Constance Holden, "Psychiatry: Behavioral Addictions Debut in Proposed DSM-V," *Science* 327, no. 5968 (February 5, 2010): 935, doi:10.1126/science.327.5968.935.

6. Marcelo Piquet-Pessôa, Gabriela Ferreira, Isabela Melca, and Leonardo Fontenelle, "DSM-5 and the Decision Not to Include Sex, Shopping or Stealing as Addictions," *Current Addiction Reports* 1, no. 3 (2014): 172–76, doi:10.1007/s40429-014-0027-6.

7. Ellen Frank, Holly Swartz, and David Kupfer, "Interpersonal and Social Rhythm Therapy: Managing the Chaos of Bipolar Disorder," *Biological Psychiatry* 48, no. 6 (2000): 593–604, doi:10.1016/S0006-3223(00)00969-0.

8. Debtors Anonymous, *A Currency of Hope* (Needham, MA: Debtors Anonymous, 1999); Donald Black, "A Review of Compulsive Buying Disorder," *World Psychiatry: Official Journal of the World Psychiatric Association (WPA)* 6, no. 1 (2007): 14–18.

9. C. Han, M. K. McCue, and W. G. Iacono, "Lifetime Tobacco, Alcohol and Other Substance Use in Adolescent Minnesota Twins: Univariate and Multivariate Behavioral Genetic Analyses," *Addiction* 94 (1999): 981–93; Kenneth Kendler, Eric Schmitt, Steven Aggen, and Carol Prescott, "Genetic and Environmental Influences on Alcohol, Caffeine, Cannabis, and Nicotine Use from Early Adolescence to Middle Adulthood," *Archives of General Psychiatry* 65, no. 6 (2008): 674–82, doi:10.1001/archpsyc.65.6.674; Nikkil Sudharsanan, Jere Behrman, and Hans-Peter Kohler, "Limited Common Origins of Multiple Adult Health-Related Behaviors: Evidence from U.S. Twins," *Social Science and Medicine* 171 (2016): 67–83, doi:10.1016/j.socscimed.2016.11.002.

10. Marie Ng, Michael Freeman, Thomas Fleming, Margaret Robinson, Laura Dwyer-Lindgren, Blake Thomson, Alexandra Wollum, et al., "Smoking Prevalence and Cigarette Consumption in 187 Countries, 1980–2012," *JAMA* 311, no. 2 (2014): 183–92, doi:10.1001/jama.2013.284692.

11. Michael R. Nadorff, Karen K. Lambdin, and Anne Germain, "Pharmacological and Non-Pharmacological Treatments for Nightmare Disorder," *International Review of Psychology* 26, no. 2 (2014): 225–36, doi:10.3109/09540261.2014.888989.

12. Pfizer pharmaceuticals markets, Chantix® for smoking cessation, http://www.chantix.com/. Nardorff et al., "Pharmacological"; Black "A Review of Compulsive."

13. M. E. Seligman, "Positive Psychology, Positive Prevention, and Positive Therapy," in *Handbook of Positive Psychology*, ed. C. S. Snyder and S. J. Lopez (New York: Oxford University Press, 2005), 3–9.

14. Most of the history that follows is drawn from R. Gelpi and F. Julien-Labruyere, *The History of Consumer Credit* (New York: St. Martin's, 2000).

15. Gelpi and Julien-Labruyere, *The History of Consumer Credit*; O. Langholm, *The Aristotelian Analysis of Usury* (Bergen: Universitetsforlaget AS, 1984).

16. W. A. M. Visser and A. McIntosh, "A Short Review of the Historical Critique of Usury," *Accounting, Business, and Financial History* 8, no. 2 (1998): 175–89.

17. Adam Smith, *An Inquiry into the Nature and Causes of the Wealth of Nations* (Chicago: University of Chicago Press, 1976 [1776]), 372.

18. J. M. Jadlow, "Adam Smith on Usury Laws," *Journal of Finance* 32, no. 4 (1977): 1195–200.

19. M. K. Lewis and L. M. Algaoud, *Islamic Banking* (Cheltenham, UK: Edward Elgar, 2001).

20. Riyadh Mohammed, "Hot Trend in 2017: Rise of Islamic Banks on Main St. USA," CNBC.com, December 2, 2016, http://www.cnbc.com/2016/12/02/under-the-radar-islamic-banks-rise-in-th.html.

21. Quoted in S. A. Sandage, *Born Losers: A History of Failure in America* (Cambridge, MA: Harvard University Press, 2005), 46.

22. Sandage, *Born Losers*.

23. The following history of consumer credit is drawn from L. Calder, *Financing the American Dream: A Cultural History of Consumer Credit* (Princeton, NJ: Princeton University Press, 1999).

24. Calder, *Financing the American Dream*.

25. Bethany McLean, "Payday Lending: Will Anything Better Replace It?" *The Atlantic*, May, 2016, accessed March 3, 2017, https://www.theatlantic.com/magazine/archive/2016/05/payday-lending/476403/; M. Flannery and K. Samolyk, "Payday Lending: Do the Costs Justify the Price?," working paper presented at Federal Reserve System Community Affairs Research Conference, Washington, DC, April 2005. See also https://www.advanceamerica.net/ .and https://www.consumer.ftc.gov/articles/0097-payday-loans.

26. For example, see Sandage, *Born Losers*, 55.

27. Internet commenter accessed on March 3, 2017, https://www.theatlantic.com/business/archive/2016/04/the-costs-of-financial-isolation/478830/#article-comments.

28. R. J. Herrnstein and C. Murray, *The Bell Curve: Intelligence and Class Structure in American Life* (New York: Free Press, 1994); S. J. Gould, *The Mismeasure of Man* (New York: W. W. Norton, 1981); J. Diamond, *Guns, Germs, and Steel: The Fates of Human Societies* (New York: W. W. Norton, 1998).

29. R. E. Guiley, *Harper's Encyclopedia of Mystical and Paranormal Experience* (San Francisco: HarperCollins, 1991).

30. L. Ross, "The Intuitive Psychologist and His Shortcomings: Distortions in the Attribution Process," in *Advances in Experimental Social Psychology*, ed. L. Berkowitz, (Orlando, FL: Academic Press, 1977), 10: 173–240.

31. Claudia Dalbert, Isaac M. Lipkus, Hedvig Sallay, and Irene Goch, "A Just and Unjust World: Structure and Validity of Different World Beliefs," *Personality and Individual Differences* 30 (2001): 561–77.

32. Calder, *Financing the American Dream.*

33. In fact, many psychologists and philosophers believe in a deterministic universe in which we have no free will. Our choices are determined by our environment and heredity, and the feelings of free will that we experience are an illusion. This is another ancient chestnut of philosophy and psychology related to the mind-body problem. Determinists argue that if free will exists, where is it? We must have a soul or some other nonphysical force that drives our choices, a mind distinct from our physical bodies that, unlike the rest of us, is free to make whimsical and unpredictable decisions. At the same time, a completely deterministic world, in which we are mere biological machines bouncing up against the world around us, is too bitter a pill for most to swallow. Freedom of will is a basic assumption of Aristotle's philosophy, and it is the foundation on which many of our social institutions rest. For our current purposes, we need not fight this fight again. I am merely pointing to something many of us can agree on: some choices are much easier than others.

Chapter 3

1. George W. Bush, "President Bush's Speech to the Nation on the Economic Crisis," transcript, September 28, 2008, http://www.nytimes.com/2008/09/24/business/economy/24text-bush.html.

2. Daren Blomquist, "Seriously Underwater Properties Decrease by 2.2 Million in 2014, Down 5.8 Million from Peak Negative Equity in Q2 2012," *RealtyTrac.com*, January 12, 2015, http://www.realtytrac.com/news/mortgage-and-finance/year-end-2014-underwater-home-equity-report/.

3. For an example of the conservative commentary, see Peter Wallison, *Hidden in Plain Sight: What Really Caused the World's Worst Financial Crisis and Why It Could Happen Again* (New York: Encounter Books, 2015).

4. For a liberal account, see Joseph E. Stiglitz, *Freefall: America, Free Markets, and the Sinking of the World Economy* (New York: W. W. Norton, 2010).

5. From www.opensecrets.com.

6. "President Signs Bankruptcy Abuse Prevention, Consumer Protection Act," press release, March 20, 2005, www.whitehouse.gov/news/releases/2005/04/20050420-5.html.

7. A good example of a Version One account is an article published by the Cato Institute, a libertarian think tank: V. McKinley, "Ballooning Bankruptcies: Issuing Blame for the Explosive Growth," *Regulation* 20 (1997): 33–40.

8. For example, see T. L. O'Brien, "Fortune's Fools: Why the Rich Go Broke," *New York Times*, September 17, 2006, sec. 3, 1.

9. D. A. Skeel, *Debt's Dominion: A History of Bankruptcy Law in America* (Princeton, NJ: Princeton University Press, 2001); McKinley, "Ballooning Bankruptcies"; Erica

Sandberg, "Why Bankruptcy of the Rich and Famous Is Nothing Like Yours," Nasdaq.com, September 28, 2015, http://www.nasdaq.com/article/why-bankruptcy-of-the-rich-and-famous-is-nothing-like-yours-cm525079#ixzz4cdsixK17.

10. Fred O. Williams, "Fed: Credit Card Banking Remains Highly Profitable," *CreditCard.com*, June 13, 2016, http://www.creditcards.com/credit-card-news/card-issuer-bank-profit.php.

11. R. D. Manning, *Credit Card Nation: The Consequences of America's Addiction to Credit* (New York: Basic Books, 2000). This is a good example of a Version Two account, and much of the history recounted here is drawn from *Credit Card Nation*.

12. Manning, *Credit Card Nation*.

13. J. S. Hacker, *The Great Risk Shift: The Assault on American Jobs, Families, Health Care, and Retirement and How You Can Fight Back* (New York: Oxford University Press, 2006).

14. Lawrence Mishel, Elise Gould, and Josh Bivens, "Wage Stagnation in Nine Charts," *Economic Policy Institute*, January 6, 2015, http://www.epi.org/files/2013/wage-stagnation-in-nine-charts.pdf

15. D. M. Cutler, "Employee Costs and the Decline of Health Insurance Coverage," working Paper 9036, National Bureau of Economic Research, www.nber.org/papers/w9036.

16. M. B. Jacoby, T. A. Sullivan, and E. Warren, "Rethinking the Debates over Health Care Financing: Evidence from the Bankruptcy Courts," *New York University Law Review* 76 (2001): 375–418.

17. Of course, many economists also attempt to create reasonable models for various phenomena—including consumer indebtedness and bankruptcy—and test those models with the available data. Like correlational studies, however, the results of these tests need to be taken with a grain of salt. Often the findings depend heavily on the premises adopted by the researchers, and given different premises, the tests would produce different results.

18. D. Ellis, "The Effect of Consumer Interest Rate Deregulation on Credit Card Volumes, Charge-offs, and the Personal Bankruptcy Rate," *Bank Trends*, 98-05, March 1998, www.fdic.gov/bank/analytical/bank/bt_9805.html; Igor Livshits, James MacGee, and Michele Tertilt, "Accounting for the Rise in Consumer Bankruptcies," *American Economic Journal: Macroeconomics* 2, no. 2 (2010): 165–93, http://economics.uwo.ca/people/livshits_docs/AccountingForRise_AEJM.pdf.

19. J. McConville, "New Law Cuts Bankruptcies," *NJBIZ*, February 12, 2007, www.njbiz.com/weekly_article_reg.asp?aID=1990679.1107077.908531.6121329.7108236.043&aID2=69878.

20. Ellis, "The Effect of Consumer Interest Rate Deregulation."

21. Studies implicating decreases in stigma include D. B. Gross and N. S. Souleles, "An Empirical Analysis of Personal Bankruptcy and Delinquency," *Review of Financial Studies* 15 (2002): 319–47, and Livshits, MacGee, and Tertilt, "Accounting for the Rise in Consumer Bankruptcies." Studies finding no decrease in stigma include K. Athreya, "Shame as It Ever Was: Stigma and Personal Bankruptcy," *Economic Quarterly* 90 (2004): 1–19, and Congressional Budget Office, *Personal Bankruptcy*.

22. Phil LeBeau, "New Car, New Reality: Auto Loan Borrowing Hits Fresh Highs," Cnbc.com, June 2, 2016, http://www.cnbc.com/2016/06/02/us-borrowers-are-paying-more-and-for-longer-on-their-auto-loans.html.

23. Michael Lazar, "Why You Should Never Do a Cash-Out Auto Refinance," *Huffington Post*, November 20, 2016, http://www.huffingtonpost.com/michael-lazar/why-you-should-never-do-a_b_8609028.html

24. Federal Reserve Bank of New York, "Quarterly Report on Household Debt and Credit," May 2017, https://www.newyorkfed.org/medialibrary/interactives/householdcredit/data/pdf/HHDC_2017Q1.pdf

25. # Occupy Wall Street "Declaration of the Occupation of New York City," https://archive.org/details/DeclarationOfTheOccupationOfNewYorkCity

26. Andrew Josuweit, "Where the Candidates Stand on Student-Loan Debt," Cnbc.com, April 4, 2016, http://www.cnbc.com/2016/04/04/where-the-candidates-stand-on-student-loan-debt-commentary.html.

27. For examples of the ongoing student loan rebellion, see https://debtcollective.org/ and http://debtfair.org/.

28. Thomas Heath, "People Are Starting to Default on Their Risky Auto Loans, but This Isn't the Next Housing Bubble," *Washington Post*, March 29, 2016, https://www.washingtonpost.com/business/economy/people-are-starting-to-default-on-their-risky-auto-loans-but-this-isnt-the-next-housing-bubble/2017/03/29/3ff055e4-1498-11e7-9e4f-09aa75d3ec57_story.html?utm_term=.dfb024379f6b

29. Stefania Albanesi and Jaromir B. Nosal, "Insolvency after the 2005 Bankruptcy Reform," staff report, Federal Reserve Bank of New York, No. 725, 2015, https://www.econstor.eu/bitstream/10419/120789/1/822062429.pdf; Wenli Li, Michelle J. White, and Ning Zhua, "Did Bankruptcy Reform Cause Mortgage Defaults to Rise?," *American Economic Journal: Economic Policy* 3, no. 4 (2011): 123–47; https://philadelphiafed.org/-/media/research-and-data/publications/working-papers/2010/wp10-16.pdf; Donald P. Morgan, Benjamin Charles Iverson, and Matthew J. Botsch, "Subprime Foreclosures and the 2005 Bankruptcy Reform," *Economic Policy Review*, 18, no. 1 (March 2012): 47–57, http://www.newyorkfed.org/research/economists/medialibrary/media/research/epr/forthcoming/1102morg.pdf.

CHAPTER 4

1. However, there is evidence the decreased value is not a function of the additional risk that a delayed reward will not be received. See K. N. Kirby and M. Santiesteban, "Concave Utility, Transaction Costs, and Risk in Measuring Discounting of Delayed Rewards," *Journal of Experimental Psychology: Learning, Memory, and Cognition* 29 (2003): 66–79.

2. For a more detailed explanation of exponential equations and compound interest, see Howard Rachlin, *The Science of Self-Control* (Cambridge, MA: Harvard University Press, 2000).

3. Rachlin, *The Science of Self-Control*.

4. R. Strotz, "Myopia and Inconsistency in Dynamic Utility Maximization," *Review of Economic Studies* 23 (1955–56): 165–80.

5. The exact shape of the discounting curve is still a matter of debate. A hyperbola-like curve that tends to be even more angular than the standard hyperbola may be a slightly superior candidate. For a review, see L. Green and J. Myerson, "A Discounting Framework for Choice with Delayed and Probabilistic Rewards," *Psychological Bulletin* 130 (2004): 769–92.

6. As a practical matter, there are some problems with this example. Issues of status and social comparison often complicate a simple evaluation of the values of these two cars. Some people are so enamored of the image provided by a luxury car that they will not switch to the Corolla no matter how old the Lexus. It is these kinds of difficulties that make money such a popular commodity in research.

7. A. W. Logue, *Self-Control: Waiting until Tomorrow for What You Want Today* (Englewood Cliffs, NJ: Prentice Hall, 1995).

8. R. J. Herrnstein and W. Vaughan, "Melioration and Behavioral Allocation," in *Limits to Action*, ed. J. E. R. Staddon (New York: Academic Press, 1980), 143–76.

9. Heyman, "Resolving the Contradictions of Addiction."

10. L. N. Robins, "Vietnam Veterans' Rapid Recovery from Heroin Addiction: A Fluke or Normal Expectation?" *Addiction* 88 (1993): 1041–54.

11. Anne Case and Angus Deaton, "Rising Morbidity and Mortality in Midlife among White Non-Hispanic Americans in the 21st Century," *Proceedings of the National Academy of Sciences* 112, no. 49 (2015): 15078–83; Anne Case and Angus Deaton, "Mortality and Morbidity in the 21st Century," 2017, https://law.yale.edu/system/files/area/workshop/leo/leo17_case.pdf

12. William James, *The Principles of Psychology* (Cambridge, MA: Harvard University Press, 1981), 125.

13. A. Smith, *Theory of Moral Sentiments* (Albany, NY: Prometheus Books, 2000 [1759]).

14. T. C. Schelling, "Coping Rationally with Lapses from Rationality," *Eastern Economic Journal* 22 (1996): 251–69 (used with permission).

15. The term "precommitment" is used by many authors, but I have chosen to use the simpler phrase, following the lead of Rachlin in *The Science of Self-Control*.

16. H. Rachlin and L. Green, "Commitment, Choice and Self-Control," *Journal of the Experimental Analysis of Behavior* 17 (1972): 15–22.

17. Barry Schwartz, *The Paradox of Choice: Why More Is Less* (New York: Ecco, 2004).

18. W. Du, L. Green, and J. Myerson, "Cross-Cultural Comparisons of Discounting Delayed and Probabilistic Rewards," *Psychological Record* 52 (2002): 479–92.

19. Walter Mischel *The Marshmallow Test: Mastering Self-Control* (New York: Little Brown, 2014).

20. Green and Myerson, "A Discounting Framework"; Scott F. Coffey, Gregory Gudleski, Michael E. Saladin, and Kathleen T. Brady, "Impulsivity and Rapid Discounting of Delayed Hypothetical Rewards in Cocaine-Dependent Individuals," *Experimental and Clinical Psychopharmacology* 11 (2003): 18–25; Nancy M. Petry, "Delay Discounting of Money and Alcohol in Actively Using Alcoholics, Currently Abstinent Alcoholics, and Controls," *Psychopharmacology* 154 (2001): 243–50; Nancy M. Petry, "Pathological Gamblers, with and without Substance Abuse

Disorders, Discount Delayed Rewards at High Rates," *Journal of Abnormal Psychology* 110 (2001): 482–87.

21. Meier, Stephan, and Charles D. Sprenger, "Time Discounting Predicts Creditworthiness," *Psychological Science* 23, no. 1 (2012): 56–58.

22. Green and Myerson, "A Discounting Framework."

CHAPTER 5

1. J. Schultz, "The Merchants That Don't Take Cash," *New York Times*, June 8, 2010, https://bucks.blogs.nytimes.com/2010/06/08/sorry-no-cash-please/?_r=0

2. Irina A. Telyukova, "Household Need for Liquidity and the Credit Card Debt Puzzle," 2006, https://escholarship.org/uc/item/4c67r71r; Irina A. Telyukova and R. Wright, "A Model of Money and Credit, with Application to the Credit Card Debt Puzzle," 2005, http://citeseerx.ist.psu.edu/viewdoc/download?doi=10.1.1.467 .4551&rep=rep1&type=pdf.

3. B. F. Skinner, *The Behavior of Organisms* (Acton, MA: Copley Publishing Group, 1938).

4. L. Calder, *Financing the American Dream: A Cultural History of Consumer Credit* (Princeton, NJ: Princeton University Press, 1999).

5. This story of the beginnings of Diners Club comes from L. Mandell, *The Credit Card Industry: A History* (Boston: Twayne, 1990).

6. Calder, *Financing the American Dream.*

7. R. D. Manning, *Credit Card Nation: The Consequences of America's Addiction to Credit* (New York: Basic Books, 2000).

8. Mandell, *The Credit Card Industry.*

9. Manning, *Credit Card Nation.*

10. Manning, *Credit Card Nation.*

11. R. E. Litan, *A Prudent Approach to Preventing "Predatory" Lending* (Washington, DC: Brookings Institution, 2001, www.aba.com/NR/rdonlyres/D881716A-1C75–11D5-AB7B-00508B95258D/13716/LitanReport993.pdf.

12. Public Broadcasting Service, *Frontline,* "Secret History of the Credit Card," 2004.

13. "S.2753 - Credit Card Reform Act of 2008," https://www.congress.gov/bill/110th-congress/senate-bill/2753.

14. "Nielsen Estimates 118.4 Million TV Homes in the U.S. for the 2016–17 TV Season," Nielsen.com, August 26, 2016, http://www.nielsen.com/us/en/insights/news/2016/nielsen-estimates-118-4-million-tv-homes-in-the-us--for-the-2016-17-season.html.

15. R. Bly, *Complete Idiot's Guide to Direct Marketing* (Indianapolis, IN: Alpha Books, 2001).

16. N. Ross, *A History of Direct Marketing* (New York: Direct Marketing Association, 2000).

17. US Census Bureau, www.census.gov/hhes/www/housing/census/historic/phone.html.

18. D. Bianco, "Direct Marketing," in *Encyclopedia of Business,* 2nd ed., ed. J. A. Malonis (Farmington Hills, MI: Thomson Gale, 2006), www.referenceforbusiness.com/encyclopedia/Dev-Eco/Direct-Marketing.html.

19. See https://www.llbean.com/customerService/aboutLLBean/company_history.html?nav=ln. It should be noted that L.L. Bean did not introduce a toll-free number

until 1985, but the company continued to show rapid growth through the 1980s and 1990s. In 1975, L.L. Bean reported sales of $60 million. By 1990, sales had risen to $600 million. In 2005, L.L. Bean sales were $1.5 billion. Ross, *A History of Direct Marketing.*

20. Mandell, *The Credit Card Industry.*

21. J. Nocera, *A Piece of the Action: How the Middle Class Joined the Money Class* (New York: Simon and Schuster, 1994).

22. Nocera, *A Piece of the Action.*

23. EVM Connections, "Optimizing Transaction Speed at the Point of Sale," February 2017, http://www.emv-connection.com/optimizing-transaction-speed-at-the-point-of-sale/; S. Kossman, "8 FAQs about EMV Cards," creditcard.com, March 22, 2017, http://www.creditcards.com/credit-card-news/emv-faq-chip-cards-answers-1264.php.

24. Smart Card Alliance, "MasterCard *PayPass,*" 2005, www.smartcardalliance.org/newsletter/june_04/feature_0604.html.

25. Brian McKenzie, "Who Drives to Work? Commuting by Automobile in the United States: 2013," *American Community Survey Reports,* 2015, https://www.census.gov/hhes/commuting/files/2014/acs-32.pdf; Transportation Research Board, *Making Transit Work,* Special Report No. 257 (Washington, DC: National Academy of Sciences and Federal Highway Association, 2001); Federal Highway Administration, US Department of Transportation, *Our National Highways 2000* (Washington, DC: Federal Highway Administration, 2000), www.fhwa.dot.gov/ohim/onh00/our_ntns_hwys.pdf.

26. Calder, *Financing the American Dream.*

27. Most of this history of urban sprawl comes from A. Duany, E. Plater-Zyberk, and J. Speck, *Suburban Nation: The Rise of Sprawl and the Decline of the American Dream* (New York: North Point Press, 2000). It should be noted that what is presented here is a common account of the history of sprawl, but it is not universally accepted. For a contrasting view, see R. Bruegmann, *Sprawl: A Compact History* (Chicago: University of Chicago Press, 2005).

28. Jane Jacobs, *The Death and Life of Great American Cities* (New York: Random House, 1961).

29. R. Longstreth, *City Center to Regional Mall: Architecture, the Automobile, and Retailing in Los Angeles, 1920–1950* (Cambridge, MA: MIT Press, 1997).

30. L. Cohen, "From Town Center to Shopping Center," *American Historical Review* 101 (1996): 1050–81; J. Green, "Is Urban Revitalization without Gentrification Possible?," *The Dirt,* September 26, 2014, https://dirt.asla.org/2014/09/26/is-urban-revitalization-without-gentrification-possible/.

31. J. Anderson-Maples, "Experts Discuss New Trend of Eating Out vs. Eating at Home," MedicalXpress.com, May 25, 2015, https://medicalxpress.com/news/2015-05-experts-discuss-trend-home.html.

32. United States Department of Agriculture Economic Research Service, "Food-Away-from-Home," December 28, 2016, https://web.archive.org/web/20161228042542/https://www.ers.usda.gov/topics/food-choices-health/food-consumption-demand/food-away-from-home.aspx.

33. "Personal Saving Rate," FRED. August 01, 2017, accessed August 24, 2017, https://fred.stlouisfed.org/series/PSAVERT.

34. For example, Paul B. Farrell of *Foxnews.com*. See www.foxnews.com/story/0,2933,192192,00.html. Also, Neil Murray; see http://money.canoe.ca/Columnists/Murray/2006/01/09/1385731.html.

35. A. Samuelson, *Economics*, 8th ed. (New York: McGraw-Hill, 1970); J. M. Keynes, *The General Theory of Employment, Interest, and Money* (New York: Harcourt, Brace and Co., 1935).

36. See http://en.wikipedia.org/wiki/Economy_of_the_United_States.

37. Atif Mian and Amir Sufi, *House of Debt: How They (and You) Caused the Great Recession, and How We Can Prevent It from Happening Again* (Chicago: University of Chicago Press, 2015); Anthony Pennington-Cross and Souphala Chomsisengphet, "Subprime Refinancing: Equity Extraction and Mortgage Termination," *Real Estate Economics* 35, no. 2 (2007): 233–63.

38. D. Papadimitriou, E. Chilcote, and G. Zezza, *Are Housing Prices, Household Debt, and Growth Sustainable?* (Annandale-on-Hudson, NY: Levy Economics Institute, 2006); C. E. Weller, *For Middle-Class Families, Dream of Own House Drowns in Sea of Debt* (Washington, DC: Center for American Progress, 2005).

CHAPTER 6

1. E. Hoffman, "Abraham Maslow: Father of Enlightened Management," *Training Magazine*, September 1988, 79–82, http://pws.cablespeed.com/~htstein/hoff2.htm.

2. B. Cooke, A. J. Mills, and E. S. Kelley, "Situating Maslow in Cold War America: A Recontextualization of Management Theory," *Group and Organization Management* 30 (2005): 129–52; E. Hoffman, *The Right to Be Human: A Biography of Abraham Maslow* (Los Angeles: Jeremy Tarcher, 1988).

3. A. Maslow, "A Theory of Human Motivation," *Psychological Review* 50 (1943): 370–96.

4. Martin E. P. Seligman, Tracy A. Steen, Nansook Park, and Christopher Peterson, "Positive Psychology Progress: Empirical Validation of Interventions," *American Psychologist* 60 (2005): 210–21.

5. A. Maslow, *Motivation and Personality* (New York: Harper and Brothers, 1954), 354.

6. A. Maslow, *The Maslow Business Reader*, ed. D. E. Stephens (New York: Wiley, 2001); Hoffman, "Abraham Maslow: Father of Enlightened Management."

7. D. I. Hawkins, D. L. Mothersbaugh, and R. J. Best, *Consumer Behavior: Building Market Strategy*, 10th ed. (New York: McGraw-Hill, 2007).

8. Hawkins, Mothersbaugh, and Best, *Consumer Behavior*.

9. M. J. Arnold and K. E. Reynolds, "Hedonic Shopping Motivations," *Journal of Retailing* 79 (2003): 77–95; Hawkins, Mothersbaugh, and Best, *Consumer Behavior*.

10. Arnold and Reynolds, "Hedonic Shopping Motivations"; Terry L. Childers, Christopher L. Carr, Joann Peck, and Stephen Carson, "Hedonic and Utilitarian Motivations for Online Shopping Behavior," *Journal of Retailing* 77 (2001): 511–35.

11. Stefano DellaVigna and Matthew Gentzkow, "Persuasion: Empirical Evidence," *Annual Review of Economics* 2, no. 1 (2010): 643–69; G. S. Becker and K. M.

Murphy, "A Simple Theory of Advertising as Good or Bad," *Quarterly Journal of Economics* 108 (1993): 941–64.

12. P. Nelson, "Advertising as Information," *Journal of Political Economy* 82 (1974): 729–54.

13. Nelson's theory (in "Advertising as Information") has also been extended to include the concept of a *credence good*. In the case of a credence good, the consumer lacks information to evaluate the good either before or after purchase. Credence goods are often ones for which the consumer must rely almost entirely on the claims made by the seller or judgments of experts. Typical credence goods include car repairs, medical treatments, and education. Although many of the debtors in this book point to unexpected medical expenses and car repairs as contributors to their indebtedness, the credence good aspect of these purchases was not relevant. Credence goods are not presented in this section of the book because, whatever role these kinds of purchases may play in the current debt crisis, the information deficits involved do not appear to be related to problems of self-control and indebtedness. If anything, the lack of information and concerns about the trustworthiness of sellers and other experts is a deterrent to spending. R. Milgrom and J. Roberts, "Relying on the Information of Interested Parties," *RAND Journal of Economics* 17 (1986): 18–32.

14. Nelson, "Advertising as Information." Consistent with this view, newspaper advertisements are much more likely to feature advertising for locally available search goods than either television or radio.

15. W. E. Baker, H. Honea, and C. A. Russell, "Do Not Wait to Reveal the Brand Name: The Effect of Brand-Name Placement on Television Advertising Effectiveness," *Journal of Advertising* 33 (2004): 77–85.

16. B. D. Till and D. W. Baack, "Recall and Persuasion: Does Creative Advertising Matter?" *Journal of Advertising* 34 (2005): 47–57.

17. W. D. Hoyer and S. Brown, "Effects of Brand Awareness on Choice for a Common, Repeated-Purchase Product," *Journal of Consumer Research* 17 (2006): 141–48.

18. There is some debate—both in the field of consumer behavior and in psychology generally—about how much influence attitudes have on actual overt behavior. Although much time has been spent researching how to build positive attitudes toward various products and services, Foxall argues that the role of positive attitude may be much smaller than other factors. See G. R. Foxall, *Consumer Psychology in Behavioral Perspective* (New York: Routledge, 1990).

19. P. Gray, *Psychology*, 4th ed. (New York: Worth, 2002).

20. M. J. Rosenberg et al., *Attitude Organization and Change: An Analysis of Consistency among Attitude Components* (New Haven, CT: Yale University Press, 1960); Hawkins, Mothersbaugh, and Best, *Consumer Behavior*.

21. C. Janiszewski, "Preattentive Mere Exposure Effects," *Journal of Consumer Research* 20 (1993): 376–92.

22. Hawkins, Mothersbaugh, and Best, *Consumer Behavior*.

23. This paragraph reports a version of the elaboration likelihood model. See Hawkins, Mothersbaugh, and Best, *Consumer Behavior*, 409–11.

24. Nielsen Company, *Nielsen Total Audience Report Q1 2016*, http://www.nielsen. com/content/dam/corporate/us/en/reports-downloads/2016-reports/total-audience-report-q1-2016.pdf.

25. Caroline Crosson Gilpin, "How Much of Your Day Is Voluntarily Spent Screen-Free?," *New York Times*, March 08, 2017, https://www.nytimes.com/2017/03/ 08/learning/how-much-of-your-day-is-voluntarily-spent-screen-free.html; Kelly Wallace, "Urging Companies to Crack Down on Distracted Driving," CNN. com, April 4, 2017, http://www.cnn.com/2017/04/04/health/distracted-driving-company-cell-phone-bans-impact/.

26. "Advertising Spending in the U.S. by Medium 2016 | Statistic," *Statista.com*, 2017, https://www.statista.com/statistics/272315/advertising-spending-in-the-us-by-medium/.

27. Alex Chris, "Top 10 Search Engines in the World," *Reliablesoft.net*, February 23, 2017, https://www.reliablesoft.net/top-10-search-engines-in-the-world/; Samuel Gibbs, "Gmail Does Scan All Emails, New Google Terms Clarify," *The Guardian*, April 15, 2014, https://www.theguardian.com/technology/2014/apr/15/gmail-scans-all-emails-new-google-terms-clarify; Trevor Mogg, "Gmail Joins the Billion Users Club," *Digital Trends*, February 2, 2016, https://www.digitaltrends.com/web/ gmail-joins-the-billion-users-club/.

28. Harper Neidig, "New GOP Bill May Revive Internet Privacy Fight," *The Hill*, May 26, 2017, http://thehill.com/policy/technology/335194-new-gop-bill-may-revive-internet-privacy-fight.

29. Elizabeth Dwoskin and Craig Timberg., "Google Now Knows When Its Users Go to the Store and Buy Stuff," *Washington Post*, May 23, 2017, https://www. washingtonpost.com/news/the-switch/wp/2017/05/23/google-now-knows-when-you-are-at-a-cash-register-and-how-much-you-are-spending/

30. Seth Fiegerman, "Facebook Tops 1.9 Billion Monthly Users," *CNNMoney.com*, May 3, 2017, http://money.cnn.com/2017/05/03/technology/facebook-earnings/; Mathew Ingram, "Here's How Google and Facebook Have Taken Over the Digital Ad Industry," *Fortune.com*, January 4, 2017, http://fortune.com/2017/01/04/google-facebook-ad-industry/; Ellen McGirt, "Facebook's Mark Zuckerberg: Hacker. Dropout. CEO," *Fast Company*, February 4, 2014, https://www.fastcompany.com/ 59441/facebooks-mark-zuckerberg-hacker-dropout-ceo.

31. Molly Wood, "Media Consolidation and What That Means for You and Me," *Marketplace*, October 28, 2016, https://www.marketplace.org/2016/10/28/ business/media-consolidation-and-what-means-you-and-me; P. Wellstone, "Growing Media Consolidation Must Be Examined to Preserve Our Democracy," *Federal Communications Law Journal* 52 (2000): 551–54, http://www.repository. law.indiana.edu/cgi/viewcontent.cgi?article=1240&context=fclj.

32. IHeartMedia, "Advertise with Us," IHeartMedia, http://www.iheartmedia.com/ iheartmedia/index.

33. David Wright, "White House Overtaken by Russian Onion Domes on New Time Cover," CNN.com, May 18, 2017, http://www.cnn.com/2017/05/18/politics/white-house-russia-time-cover/; G. Goodale, "Now for a Word from Our Sponsors," *Christian Science Monitor*, August 27, 2004, www.csmonitor.com/2004/0827/p12s02-altv.html.

34. Goodale, "Now for a Word."

35. Larry Kelley, Kim Sheehan, and Donald W. Jugenheimer, *Advertising Media Planning: A Brand Management Approach* (New York: Routledge, 2015).

36. "Advertising Spending in the U.S. by Medium 2016 | Statistic."

37. "The 80's Were the Decade of the Cable Guy," *TV by the Numbers by zap2it. com*, July 26, 2009, http://tvbythenumbers.zap2it.com/reference/the-80s-were-the-decade-of-the-cable-guy/; Stanley M. Besen, and Robert W. Crandall, "The Deregulation of Cable Television," *Law and Contemporary Problems* 44, no. 1 (1981): 77–124.

38. "Advertising Spending in the U.S. by Medium 2016 | Statistic."

39. J. Turow, *Breaking Up America: Advertisers and the New Media World* (Chicago: University of Chicago Press, 1997).

40. J. A. Karrh, K. B. McKee, and C. J. Pardon, "Practitioners' Evolving Views on Product Placement Effectiveness," *Journal of Advertising Research* 43 (2003): 138–49.

41. Karrh, McKee, and Pardon, "Practitioners.'"

42. S. K. Goo, "Apple Gets a Big Slice of the Product Placement Pie," *Washington Post*, April 15, 2006, D1, www.washingtonpost.com/wp-dyn/content/article/2006/04/14/AR2006041401670.html.

43. Mindi Chahal, "Is Product Placement out of Control?" *Marketing Week*, November 25, 2015, https://www.marketingweek.com/2015/06/23/cover-has-product-placement-gone-too-far/; Jon Nathanson, "The Economics of Product Placements;" *Priceonomics*; December 4, 2013; https://priceonomics.com/the-economics-of-product-placements/.

44. Karrh, McKee, and Pardun; "Practitioners.'"; L. Petrecca, "Junk Mail Still Going Strong as Spending Forecast Sees 7.5% Increase," *USA Today*, December 4, 2006, www.usatoday.com/money/advertising/2006-12-04-junk-mail-forecast_x.htm.

45. Matthew Rocco, "Inside MLB's Virtual Ads at the World Series," *Fox Business*, October 26, 2016, http://www.foxbusiness.com/features/2016/10/26/inside-mlbs-virtual-ads-at-world-series.html.

46. Kate Bulkley, "New Technology Could Add Product Placement to Old TV Programmes," *The Guardian*, June 22, 2016, https://www.theguardian.com/media/2016/jun/22/new-technology-could-add-product-placement-to-old-tv-programmes.

47. Lindsay Bennett, "Netflix Slammed for 'Worst Product Placement Ever'" *AdNews*, May 3, 2017, http://www.adnews.com.au/netflix-slammed-for-product-placement; Nathanson, "The Economics of Product Placements." James D. Sargent, Jennifer J. Tickled, Michael L. Beach, Madeline A. Dalton, M. Bridget Ahrens, and Todd F. Heatherton, "Brand Appearances in Contemporary Cinema Films and Contribution to Global Marketing of Cigarettes," *Lancet* 357 (2001): 29–32. According to this study, brands of cigarettes appeared in 28 percent of the 250 top-grossing films of 1988–1997, and brands of cigarettes were as common in films intended for adolescent audiences as in films for adults.

48. L. Petrecca, "Authors Strike Deals to Squeeze in a Few Brand Names," *USA Today*, September 10, 2006, www.usatoday.com/money/advertising/2006-09-10-books-product-placement_x.htm.

49. G. M. Lamb, "Product Placement Pushes into Print," *Christian Science Monitor*, September 29, 2005, www.csmonitor.com/2005/0929/p12s02-wmgn.html.

50. James Rainey, "On the Media: A Plea for Honesty in Paid TV Pitches," *Los Angeles Times*, December 22, 2010, http://articles.latimes.com/2010/dec/22/entertainment/la-et-onthemedia-20101222.

51. This quote and the other material in this section come from L. Story, "Anywhere the Eye Can See, It's Now Likely to See an Ad," *New York Times*, January 15, 2007, A1, A14.

52. S. Zukin, *Point of Purchase: How Shopping Changed American Culture* (New York: Routledge, 2004).

53. R. Bowlby, *Carried Away: The Invention of Modern Shopping* (New York: Columbia University Press, 2001).

54. Hayley Peterson, "Dying Shopping Malls Are Wreaking Havoc on Suburban America," *Business Insider*, March 5, 2017, http://www.businessinsider.com/dying-shopping-malls-are-wreaking-havoc-on-suburban-america-2017-2.

55. V. Gruen and L. Smith, *Shopping Towns USA: The Planning of Shopping Centers* (New York: Reinhold Publishing, 1960), 24.

56. Reema Khrais, "Showing Off Shopping Sprees, Fashion 'Haulers' Cash In Online," NPR, March 14, 2013, http://www.npr.org/2013/03/14/174305909/showing-off-shopping-sprees-fashion-haulers-cash-in-online.

57. Shan Li, "Watch How These YouTube Stars Make Money Unboxing Toys," *Los Angeles Times*, December 24, 2015, http://www.latimes.com/business/la-fi-toy-unboxing-boom-20151224-story.html.

58. Jasonrobertkeef, "2017 Barbie Wonder Woman—Barbie Collector Black Label Doll Review," *YouTube.com*, May 23, 2017, https://www.youtube.com/watch?v=d6iWc2efi_E.

59. Zaful, "For Online Retailers, 'Net Stars' Are the Next Big Thing in Advertising," *PR Newswire: News Distribution, Targeting and Monitoring*, May 4, 2017, http://www.prnewswire.com/news-releases/for-online-retailers-net-stars-are-the-next-big-thing-in-advertising-300451352.html.

60. Alexandra Ma, "How to Make Money on Instagram," *Huffington Post*, December 29, 2016, http://www.huffingtonpost.com/entry/make-money-on-instagram_us_55ad3ad6e4b0caf721b3624c.

61. W. Hooper, "The Tudor Sumptuary Laws," *English Historical Review* 30 (1915): 433–49. I thank Candace Howes for alerting me to sumptuary laws.

62. Hooper, "The Tudor."

63. H. Dittmar, *The Social Psychology of Material Possessions: To Have Is to Be* (New York: St. Martin's Press, 1992), 62.

64. H. W. Marsh, C. Kong, and K. Hau, "Longitudinal Multi-Level Models of the Big-Fish-Little-Pond Effect on Academic Self-Concept: Counterbalancing Contrast and Reflected-Glory Effects in Hong Kong Schools," *Journal of Personality and Social Psychology* 78 (2000): 337–49.

65. J. Sullivan, *Jeans: A Cultural History of an American Icon* (New York: Gotham Books, 2006).

66. Gerard Tellis, "Toyota's Gamble on the Prius," *Financial Times*, March 4, 2014, https://www.ft.com/content/146ad23c-7230-11e2-89fb-00144feab49a.

67. J. B. Schor, *The Overspent American: Why We Want What We Don't Need* (New York: Basic Books, 1998): J. B. Schor, *Born to Buy: The Commercialized Child and the New Consumer Society* (New York: Scribner, 2004). Other examples include N. Klein, *No Logo: Taking Aim at the Brand Bullies* (New York: Picador, 2000), and A. Quart, *Branded: The Buying and Selling of Teenagers* (New York: Perseus, 2003).

68. "About Us," *Channelone.com*, https://www.channelone.com/about-us/.

69. L. A. Maxwell, "School Bus Radio Venture Raising Concerns," *Education Week*, September 27, 2006, 5, 16; Zach Miners, "School Bus Radio Program Plays Its Last Tune," *U.S. News and World Report*, September 29, 2009, https://www.usnews.com/education/blogs/on-education/2009/09/29/school-bus-radio-program-plays-its-last-tune.

70. P. Taylor, C. Funk, and A. Clark, *Luxury or Necessity? Things We Can't Live Without: The List Has Grown in the Past Decade* (Washington, DC: Pew Research Center, 2006), http://www.pewsocialtrends.org/files/2010/10/Luxury.pdf; Paul Taylor and Wendy Wang, "The Fading Glory of the Television and Telephone," *Pew Research Center's Social and Demographic Trends Project*, August 19, 2010, http://www.pewsocialtrends.org/2010/08/19/the-fading-glory-of-the-television-and-telephone/.

71. "Bureau of Labor Statistics Data," US Bureau of Labor Statistics, accessed June 12, 2017, https://data.bls.gov/timeseries/LNS14000000.

72. Taylor and Wang, "The Fading Glory."

73. Taylor, Funk, and Clark, *Luxury or Necessity?*, 3.

74. John B. Horrigan, and Maeve Duggan, "Home Broadband 2015," *Pew Research Center: Internet, Science and Tech*, December 21, 2015, http://www.pewinternet.org/2015/12/21/home-broadband-2015/. Aaron Smith, "U.S. Smartphone Use in 2015," Pew Research Center: Internet, Science & Tech, April 1, 2015, accessed June 12, 2017, http://www.pewinternet.org/2015/04/01/us-smartphone-use-in-2015/.

75. Alex Philippidis, "The Top 15 Best-Selling Drugs of 2016," *GEN*, March 6, 2017, http://www.genengnews.com/the-lists/the-top-15-best-selling-drugs-of-2016/77900868.

76. "Humira," Abbott 2006 Annual Report: Humira, https://web.archive.org/web/20080113230332/http://www.abbott.com:80/static/content/microsite/annual_report/2006/humira.html.

77. Kathleen Doheny, "The Real Monthly Cost of Arthritis Medication," *EverydayHealth.com*, October 30, 2015, http://www.everydayhealth.com/news/real-monthly-cost-arthritis-medication/.

78. Bruce Horovitz and Julie Appleby Kaiser, "Prescription Drug Costs Are Up; So Are TV Ads Promoting Them," *USA Today*, March 16, 2017, https://www.usatoday.com/story/money/2017/03/16/prescription-drug-costs-up-tv-ads/99203878/; John Marshall, "Why You See Such Weird Drug Commercials on TV All the Time," *Thrillist*, March 23, 2016, https://www.thrillist.com/health/nation/why-are-prescription-drug-advertisements-legal-in-america.

79. David Lazarus, "Sick: The Biggest Increase in Healthcare Costs in 32 Years," *Los Angeles Times*, September 20, 2016, http://www.latimes.com/business/lazarus/la-fi-lazarus-rising-healthcare-costs-20160920-snap-story.html.

80. Philippidis, "The Top 15 Best-Selling."

81. Indeed, a widely cited study conducted in 1999 found that approximately as many as 40 percent of those filing for personal bankruptcy cited an illness or injury as a reason for filing. M. B. Jacoby, T. A. Sullivan, and E. Warren, "Medical Problems and Bankruptcy Filings," *Norton's Bankruptcy Adviser*, May 2000, 1–12.

82. Federal Reserve Bank of St. Louis, "U.S. All Grades All Formulations Retail Gasoline Prices (Dollars per Gallon)," https://www.eia.gov/dnav/pet/hist/LeafHandler. ashx?n=pet&s=emm_epm0_pte_nus_dpg&f=a; Federal Reserve Bank of St. Louis, "Total Vehicle Sales," https://fred.stlouisfed.org/series/TOTALSA.

83. "One-in-Three U.S. Drivers Cannot Pay for an Unexpected Car Repair Bill," *AAA NewsRoom*, April 4, 2017, http://newsroom.aaa.com/2017/04/one-three-u-s-drivers-cannot-pay-unexpected-car-repair-bill/.

CHAPTER 7

1. This portrait of Igor Ansoff is drawn from his obituary, "Igor Ansoff, the Father of Strategic Management," *Strategic Change* 11 (2002): 437–38.

2. A. Lowry and P. Hood, *The Power of the 2×2 Matrix* (San Francisco: Jossey-Bass, 2004).

3. Jethro Nededog, "The Number of US Homes without a TV Doubled in Just 6 Years," *Business Insider*, March 1, 2017, http://www.businessinsider.com/how-many-tvs-in-american-homes-number-us-department-energy-2017-3.

4. S. Zukin, *Point of Purchase: How Shopping Changed American Culture* (New York: Routledge, 2004).

5. J. M. Mayo, *The American Grocery Store: A Business Evolution of an Architectural Space* (Westport, CT: Greenwood Press, 1993).

6. Mayo, *The American Grocery Store*.

7. This branding example comes from S. Strasser, "Woolworth to Wal-Mart: Mass Merchandising and the Changing Culture of Consumption," in *Wal-Mart: The Face of Twenty-First-Century Capitalism*, ed. N. Lichtenstein (New York: New Press, 2006), 31–56.

8. See chapter 5 in R. Bowlby, *Carried Away: The Invention of Modern Shopping* (New York: Columbia University Press, 2001).

9. In fact, Polk Bros., a legendary discount appliance dealer who my father suggested may have supplied the television, advertised next-day delivery and Monday delivery for sales made on Saturday. See A. Paden, *I Bought It at Polk Bros: The Story of an American Retailing Phenomenon* (Chicago: Bonus Books, 1996).

10. Rachel Gillett, "The Largest Employers in Each US State," *Business Insider*, June 11, 2017, http://www.businessinsider.com/largest-employers-each-us-state-2017-6.

11. Zukin, *Point of Purchase*.

12. R. Spector, *Category Killers: The Retail Revolution and Its Impact on Consumer Culture* (Boston: Harvard Business School Press, 2005).

13. M. Petrovic and G. G. Hamilton, "Making Global Markets: Wal-Mart and Its Suppliers," in *Wal-Mart: The Face of Twenty-First-Century Capitalism*, ed. N. Lichtenstein (New York: New Press, 2006), 107–41.

14. Deborah Weinswig, "Walmart and Target Are Set To Be The Big Winners From Toys "R" Us Closures," *Forbes*, March 26, 2018, https://www.forbes.com/sites/deborahweinswig/2018/03/26/walmart-and-target-are-set-to-be-the-big-winners-from-toysrus-closures/#3402139199df; Matthew Hudson, "What Is a Category

Killer?," *The Balance*, September, 30 2016, https://www.thebalance.com/category-killer-2890178; Spector, *Category Killers*.

15. David Carrig, "Sears, J.C. Penney, Kmart, Macy's: These Retailers Are Closing Stores in 2017," *USA Today*, June 1, 2017, https://www.usatoday.com/story/money/2017/03/22/retailers-closing-stores-sears-kmart-jcpenney-macys-mcsports-gandermountian/99492180/.

16. Population Reference Bureau, "Traditional Families Account for Only 7 Percent of U.S. Households," 2003, www.prb.org.

17. Jonathan Vespa, Jamie M. Lewis, and Rose M. Kreider, "America's Families and Living Arrangements: 2012," US Census Bureau, 2013, https://www.census.gov/prod/2013pubs/p20-570.pdf

18. "Productivity and Real Median Family Income Growth, 1947–2013," *State of Working America.org*, http://stateofworkingamerica.org/charts/productivity-and-real-median-family-income-growth-1947-2009/.

19. D. Levinson and A. Kumar, "Temporal Variations on the Allocation of Time," *Transportation Research Record*, no. 1493, 1995, 118–27, http://rational.ce.umn.edu/Papers/Temporal.html.

20. N. Lichtenstein, "Wal-Mart: A Template for Twenty-First-Century Capitalism," in *Wal-Mart: The Face of Twenty-First-Century Capitalism*, ed. N. Lichtenstein (New York: New Press, 2006).

21. B. Olsen and D. Lyons, *Station Wagons* (Osceola, WI: MBI Publishing, 2000).

22. Olsen and Lyons, *Station Wagons*.

23. Brent D. Yacobucci, "Sport Utility Vehicles, Mini-Vans and Light Trucks: An Overview of Fuel Economy and Emissions Standards," *Congressional Research Service, Library of Congress*, 2003, https://digital.library.unt.edu/ark:/67531/metacrs5621/m1/1/high_res_d/RS20298_2003Apr17.pdf. Subsequently SUVs, Minivans, and light trucks were all required to adhere to the same standards as passenger vehicles. See Alan Neuhauser, "Feds Tighten Fuel and Car Emissions Standards," *U.S. News and World Report*, March 3, 2014, https://www.usnews.com/news/articles/2014/03/03/feds-tighten-fuel-and-car-emissions-standards.

24. S. O. Company and M. E. Personick, "Profiles in Safety and Health: Retail Grocery Stores," *Monthly Labor Review* 115 (1992): 9–17.

25. T. Wilson, *The Cart That Changed the World: The Career of Sylvan N. Goldman* (Norman: University of Oklahoma Press, 1978).

26. S. Nickles, "'Preserving Women': Refrigerator Design as Social Process in the 1930s," *Technology and Culture* 43 (2002): 693–727.

27. P. Underhill, *The Call of the Mall* (New York: Simon and Schuster, 2004).

28. I have this on the authority of a Best Buy sales clerk.

29. Finn Arne Jørgensen, "A Pocket History of Bottle Recycling," *The Atlantic*, February 27, 2013, https://www.theatlantic.com/technology/archive/2013/02/a-pocket-history-of-bottle-recycling/273575/; Tom Vanderbilt, "The Brilliant Redesign of the Soda Can Tab," *Slate*, September 23, 2012, http://www.slate.com/articles/life/design/2012/09/can_tabs_how_aluminum_pop_tabs_were_redesigned_to_make_drinking_soda_safer_and_the_world_a_cleaner_place_.html.

30. Todd Johnson, "What Makes PET Plastics Advantageous over Other Plastics?" *ThoughtCo*, November 24, 2014, https://www.thoughtco.com/what-are-pet-plastics-820361.

31. "Our History," PepsiCo, accessed June 27, 2017, http://www.pepsico.com/company/Our-History.d.

32. S. Zukin, *Point of Purchase: How Shopping Changed American Culture* (New York: Routledge, 2004).

33. "Food Expenditures," US Department of Agriculture, https://www.ers.usda.gov/data-products/food-expenditures/.

34. "How Drive-Thru Windows Changed the Way America Orders Food," McDonald's—Official Global Corporate website, July 25, 2016, http://news.mcdonalds.com/Corporate/Feature-Stories-Articles/2016/How-Drive-Thru-Windows-Changed-the-Way-America-Ord.

35. "STORES Top Retailers 2017," *STORES: NRF's Magazine*, http://stores.org/stores-top-retailers-2017/; Berta, Dina, "Drive-Thru of the Future," Restaurant Business, February 7, 2017, accessed July 10, 2017, http://www.restaurantbusinessonline.com/operations/sales-finance/drive-thru-future#page=0.

36. Mindi Cherry, "Why You Need to Stop Wearing Pajama Pants in Public," *Moms Need To Know*™, March 7, 2015, http://momsneedtoknow.com/need-stop-wearing-pajama-pants-public/.

37. Lauren Gensler, "The World's Largest Retailers 2017: Amazon & Alibaba Are Closing In on Wal-Mart," *Forbes*, May 24, 2017, https://www.forbes.com/sites/laurengensler/2017/05/24/the-worlds-largest-retailers-2017-walmart-cvs-amazon/#327ca73820b5.

38. J. McMillen, "Understanding Gambling: History, Concepts and Theories," in *Gambling Cultures: Studies in History and Interpretation*, ed. J. McMillen, (London: Routledge, 1996), 6–42.

39. McMillen, "Understanding Gambling."

40. McCown and Chamberlain, *Best Possible Odds*; C. T. Clotfelter and J. Cook, *Selling Hope: State Lotteries in America* (Cambridge, MA: Harvard University Press, 1989).

41. Clotfelter and Cook, *Selling Hope*.

42. Clotfelter and Cook, *Selling Hope*.

43. Clotfelter and Cook, *Selling Hope*.

44. T. L. O'Brien, *Bad Bet: The Inside Story of the Glamour, Glitz, and Danger of America's Gambling Industry* (New York: Times Books, 1998).

45. Clotfelter and Cook, *Selling Hope*.

46. Zac Auter, "About Half of Americans Play State Lotteries," *Gallup.com*, July 22, 2016, http://www.gallup.com/poll/193874/half-americans-play-state-lotteries.aspx; US Census Bureau, "Income and Apportionment of State-Administered Lottery Funds: 2015," https://www.census.gov/govs/state/.

47. Per capita sales calculated from sales figures provided by the North American Association of State and Provincial Lotteries, www.naspl.org. See also Derek Thompson, "Lotteries: America's $70 Billion Shame," *The Atlantic*, May 11, 2015, https://www.theatlantic.com/business/archive/2015/05/lotteries-americas-70-billion-shame/392870/.

48. Thompson, "Lotteries."

49. RubinBrown LLP, "Gaming Statistics '17," 2017, http://www.rubinbrown.com/Gaming_Stats.pdf.

50. Auter, "About Half of Americans Play."

51. In its final report in June 1999, the National Gambling Impact Study Commission said, "Over the past 25 years, the United States has been transformed from a nation in which legalized gambling was a limited and a relatively rare phenomenon into one in which such activity is common and growing," *Final Report of the National Gambling Impact Study Commission*, 1–1.

52. In gaming industry reports, such as RubinBrown LLP, "Gaming Statistics '17," a distinction is made between tribal gambling and commercial gambling. For simplicity, I have lumped these together under the label commercial gambling, which is distinct from state-operated lotteries.

53. John W. Welte, Marie-Cecile O. Tidwell, Grace M. Barnes, Joseph H. Hoffman, and William F. Wieczorek, "The Relationship between the Number of Types of Legal Gambling and the Rates of Gambling Behaviors and Problems across US States," *Journal of Gambling Studies* 32, no. 2 (2016): 379–90.

54. Bogdan Daraban and Clifford F. Thies, "Estimating the Effects of Casinos and of Lotteries on Bankruptcy: A Panel Data Set Approach," *Journal of Gambling Studies* 27, no. 1 (2011): 145–54; S. A. Feldstein, *The Rise in Personal Bankruptcy: Causes and Impact* (Hackettstown, NJ: SMR Research Corp., 1998).

55. McCown and Chamberlain, *Best Possible Odds*.

56. "Gambling: As the Take Rises, So Does Public Concern," *Pew Research Center's Social and Demographic Trends Project*, May 22, 2006, http://www.pewsocialtrends. org/2006/05/23/gambling-as-the-take-rises-so-does-public-concern/;. Art Swift, "Birth Control, Divorce Top List of Morally Acceptable Issues," *Gallup.com*, June 08, 2016, http://www.gallup.com/poll/192404/birth-control-divorce-top-list-morally-acceptable-issues.aspx.

57. State of Connecticut Division of Special Revenue, "Agency History," www.ct.gov/ dosr/cwp/view.asp?a=3&q=290518.

58. Rich Donaldson, personal communication, November 21, 2006.

59. Rebecca R. Ruiz, "Catalogs, after Years of Decline, Are Revamped for Changing Times," *New York Times*, January 25, 2015, https://www.nytimes.com/2015/01/ 26/business/media/catalogs-after-years-of-decline-are-revamped-for-changing-times.html.

60. Eloise Parker, "There's No Place Like Home Shopping," *NY Daily News*, June 27, 2007, http://www.nydailynews.com/entertainment/tv-movies/no-place-home-shopping-article-1.221220.

61. "QVC Milestones," *QVC.com*, http://corporate.qvc.com/documents/20536/ 164719/QVC+Milestones+3-3-17.pdf/3bf3e38a-29cd-4cbb-9fd9-8da91f82bc36.

62. Tony Moore, "Joy Mangano," *Biography.com*, August 17, 2016, https://www. biography.com/people/joy-mangano-05202015.

63. Sami Main, "QVC Has Quietly Become Successful with Streaming Audiences, and Nearly Half Its Revenue Is from Ecommerce," Adweek, June 28, 2017, accessed June 30, 2017, http://www.adweek.com/tv-video/qvc-has-quietly-become-successful-with-streaming-audiences-and-nearly-half-its-revenue-is-from-ecommerce/.

64. CBS News, "Porn in the U.S.A.," *60 Minutes*, September 5, 2004, www.cbsnews. com/stories/2003/11/21/60minutes/main585049.shtml.

65. Tom Gara, "What Adults Do in Hotel Rooms Takes Its Toll on LodgeNet," *Wall Street Journal*, January 28, 2013, https://blogs.wsj.com/corporate-intelligence/

2013/01/28/what-adults-do-in-hotel-rooms-takes-its-toll-on-lodgenet/; E. Schlosser, *Reefer Madness: Sex, Drugs, and Cheap Labor in the American Black Market* (Boston: Houghton Mifflin, 2003); CBS News, "Porn in the U.S.A."

66. F. Wasser, *Veni, Vidi, Video* (Austin: University of Texas Press, 2002).

67. CBS News, "Porn in the U.S.A."

68. Wasser, *Veni, Vidi, Video.*

69. Discount Store News, "VCRs to Find Growth in Trade-Up Market," August 21, 1989, http://findarticles.com/p/articles/mi_m3092/is_n16_v28/ai_7906611/pg_1.

70. Wasser, *Veni, Vidi, Video.*

71. F. S. Lane, *Obscene Profits: The Entrepreneurs of Pornography in the Cyber Age* (New York: Routledge, 2000).

72. Amazon.com's patent on one-click ordering was to expire in 2017. Business Insider Intelligence, "Amazon's Patent on one-Click Payments to Expire," Business Insider, January 5, 2017, accessed July 3, 2017, http://www.businessinsider.com/amazons-patent-on-one-click-payments-to-expire-2017-1.

73. "EBay Inc. Reports Fourth Quarter and Full Year 2016 Results - eBay Inc," Investor Relations—eBay Inc., January 25, 2017, accessed July 3, 2017, https://investors.ebayinc.com/releasedetail.cfm?ReleaseID=1009166.

74. "The World's Biggest Public Companies," *Forbes*, accessed July 3, 2017, https://www.forbes.com/global2000/list/#industry:Internet%20%26%20Catalog%20Retail.

75. "Our History," EBay Inc News, accessed July 3, 2017, https://www.ebayinc.com/our-company/our-history/.

76. "Amazon.com," *Encyclopædia Britannica*, accessed July 3, 2017, https://www.britannica.com/topic/Amazoncom.

77. "How Yelp Is Weeding out Fake Reviews," *CBS News*, May 3, 2016, http://www.cbsnews.com/news/yelp-behind-the-scenes-consumer-protections-eliminate-fake-reviews/.

78. Aaron Smith and Monica Anderson, "Online Shopping and E-Commerce," *Pew Research Center*, December 19, 2016, http://www.pewinternet.org/2016/12/19/online-shopping-and-e-commerce/.

79. Lauren Gensler, "The World's Largest Retailers 2017."

CHAPTER 8

This chapter has benefited from much that has gone before, in particular, S. Plous, *The Psychology of Judgment and Decision Making* (New York: McGraw-Hill, 1993), and G. Belsky and T. Gilovich, *Why Smart People Make Big Money Mistakes* (New York: Simon and Schuster, 1999).

1. F. Modigliani, "Life Cycle, Individual Thrift, and the Wealth of Nations," *American Economic Review* 76 (1986): 297–313. The life-cycle theory is roughly equivalent to Milton Friedman's concept of the Permanent Income Hypothesis, which he introduced in M. Friedman, *A Theory of the Consumption Function* (Princeton, NJ: Princeton University Press, 1957).

2. For wages data, see L. Mishel, J. Bernstein, and S. Allegretto, *The State of Working America 2004/2005* (Ithaca, NY: Cornell University Press, 2005), figure 2B, p. 125;

J. Hacker, *The Great Risk Shift: The Assault on American Jobs, Families, Health Care, and Retirement and How You Can Fight Back* (New York: Oxford University Press, 2006).

3. R. H. Frank, *Microeconomics and Behavior* (New York: McGraw-Hill, 1991).

4. Frank, *Microeconomics.*

5. N. S. Souleles, "The Response of Household Consumption to Income Tax Refunds," *American Economic Review* 89 (1999): 947–58.

6. N. Epley, D. Mak, and L. C. Idson, "Bonus or Rebate? The Impact of Income Framing on Spending and Saving," *Journal of Behavioral Decision Making* 19 (2006): 1–15. The difference in the amount reportedly spent was statistically significant.

7. R. Mccoun, "Why a Psychologist Won the Nobel Prize in Economics," *APS Observer*, December 2002.

8. I. P. Levin and G. J. Gaeth, "How Consumers Are Affected by the Framing of Attribute Information, before and after Consuming the Product," *Journal of Consumer Research* 15 (1988): 374–78. Prospect theory was originally designed to describe our behavior with uncertain choices—gambles—but framing effects have been applied more generally to choices between two certain options.

9. H. M. Shefrin and R. H. Thaler, "Mental Accounting, Saving, and Self-Control," in *Choice over Time*, ed. G. Loewenstein and J. Elster (New York: Russell Sage, 1992), 287–330.

10. J. B. Davies, "Uncertain Lifetime, Consumption, and Dissaving in Retirement," *Journal of Political Economy* 89 (1981): 561–77.

11. This example and the results reported for it are based on D. Kahneman and A. Tversky, "Choices, Values, and Frames," *American Psychologist* 39 (1984): 341–50.

12. H. R. Arkes and C. Blumer, "The Psychology of Sunk Cost," *Organizational Behavior and Human Decision Processes* 35 (1985): 124–40.

13. R. H. Thaler and E. J. Johnson, "Gambling with the House Money and Trying to Break Even: The Effects of Prior Outcomes on Risky Choice," *Management Science* 36 (1990): 643–60. I have slightly altered the description of this research, but the essential features and results are accurate.

14. It should be mentioned that for both of the problems from Thaler and Johnson, "Gambling with the House Money," reported in this paragraph, the sure thing and the gamble have the same expected value. For example, the expected value of a one-third chance to win $15 and a two-thirds chance to win nothing is calculated by multiplying the value of each outcome by the probability and summing these values for each potential outcome. So the expected value of this example would be $(1/3 \times \$15) + (2/3 \times \$0) = \$5$. Therefore the expected value of the two options are equal, and we would expect participants to be indifferent—split evenly—on the choice of sure thing versus gamble.

15. This is a slightly edited version of the scenario presented in R. Thaler, "Mental Accounting and Consumer Choice," *Marketing Science* 4 (1985): 199–214. The next section, on methods of increasing the cost of a product, is drawn from this article.

16. This is the concept of a "reference price," See Thaler, "Mental Accounting and Consumer Choice."

17. Thaler, "Mental Accounting and Consumer Choice."

18. For similar scenarios see Thaler, "Mental Accounting and Consumer Choice."

19. Thaler and Johnson, "Gambling with the House Money."
20. Souleles, "The Response of Household Consumption"; David S. Johnson, Jonathan A. Parker, and Nicholas S. Souleles, "Household Expenditure and the Income Tax Rebates of 2001," Discussion Papers in Economics, No. 231, Princeton University, Woodrow Wilson School of Public and International Affairs, 2004, https://www.econstor.eu/bitstream/10419/23458/1/dp231.pdf.
21. Souleles, "The Response of Household Consumption."
22. M. Landsberger, "Windfall Income and Consumption: Comment," *American Economic Review* 56 (1966): 534–39.
23. Thaler and Johnson, "Gambling with the House Money."
24. Much of this section is drawn from D. Prelec and G. Loewenstein, "The Red and the Black: Mental Accounting of Savings and Debt," *Management Science* 17 (1998): 4–28.
25. Prelec and Loewenstein, "The Res and the Black." See also R. Kivetz, "Advances in Research on Mental Accounting and Reason-Based Choice," *Marketing Letters* 10 (1999): 249–66.
26. Prelec and Loewenstein, "The Red and the Black."
27. Eldar Shafir and Richard H. Thaler, "Invest Now, Drink Later, Spend Never: On the Mental Accounting of Delayed Consumption," *Journal of Economic Psychology* 27, no. 5 (2006): 694–712.
28. J. T. Gourville and D. Soman, "Payment Depreciation: Effects of Temporally Separating Payments from Consumption," *Journal of Consumer Research* 25 (1998): 160–74.
29. Gourville and Soman, "Payment Depreciation," study 1.
30. Gourville and Soman, "Payment Depreciation"; D. Soman and J. T. Gourville, "Transaction Decoupling: How Price Binding Affects the Decision to Consume," *Journal of Marketing Research*, February 2001, 30–44.
31. R. A. Feinberg, "Credit Cards as Spending Facilitating Stimuli: A Conditioning Interpretation," *Journal of Consumer Research* 13 (1986): 348–56.
32. Feinberg, "Credit Cards," experiment 1.
33. Feinberg, "Credit Cards," experiments 1 and 2.
34. D. Prelec and D. Simester, "Always Leave Home without It: A Further Investigation of the Credit-Card Effect on Willingness to Pay," *Marketing Letters* 12 (2001): 5–12.
35. I have glossed over some details of the bidding procedure used, but the basic description is accurate.
36. Study 2 from Prelec and Simester, "Always Leave Home without It."
37. D. Soman, "Effects of Payment Mechanism on Spending Behavior: The Role of Rehearsal and Immediacy of Payments," *Journal of Consumer Research* 27 (2001): 460–74.
38. Soman, "Effects of Payment Mechanism," experiments 1 and 2.
39. Avni M. Shah, Noah Eisenkraft, James R. Bettman, and Tanya L. Chartrand, " 'Paper or Plastic?': How We Pay Influences Post-Transaction Connection," *Journal of Consumer Research* 42, no. 5 (2015): 688–708, doi:10.1093/jcr/ucv056.
40. See https://www.mastercard.com/ca/personal/en/findacard/premium_list.html.
41. D. Soman and A. Cheema, "The Effect of Credit on Spending Decisions: The Role of Credit Limit and Credibility," *Market Science* 24 (2002): 32–53.

42. Melissa Lambarena, "Credit Card Limits Rise at the Top, Fall at the Bottom," *NerdWallet*, May 17, 2017, https://www.nerdwallet.com/blog/credit-cards/post-recession-credit-limits-arent-created-equal/.

43. Lindsay Konsko, "How Does My Credit Card Issuer Determine My Credit Limit?" *NerdWallet*, May 4, 2016, https://www.nerdwallet.com/blog/credit-cards/credit-card-issuer-determine-limit-how/.

44. Soman and Cheema, "The Effect of Credit."

45. See www.mastercard.com/us/personal/en/aboutourcards/credit/index.html.

46. Study 2 from Soman and Cheema, "The Effect of Credit on Spending Decisions."

47. Soman and Cheema, "The Effect of Credit on Spending Decisions."

48. This section is based on K. Werenbroch, D. Soman, and J. Nunes, "Debt Aversion as Self-Control: Consumer Self-Management of Liquidity Constraints," working paper, Rotman School of Management, University of Toronto, 2001, https://flora.insead.edu/fichiersti_wp/inseadwp2001/2001-08.pdf.

49. Plous, *The Psychology of Judgment and Decision Making*. This account is a simplified description of G. B. Northcraft and M. A. Neale, "Experts, Amateurs, and Real Estate: An Anchoring-and-Adjustment Perspective on Property Pricing Decisions," *Organizational Behavior and Human Decision Processes* 39 (1987): 84–97.

50. Plous, *The Psychology of Judgment and Decision Making*.

51. A. Tversky and D. Kahneman, "Judgment under Uncertainty: Heuristics and Biases," *Science* 185 (1974): 1124–30.

52. Study 1 from B. Wansink, R. J. Kent, and S. J. Hoch, "An Anchoring and Adjustment Model of Purchase Quantity Decisions," *Journal of Marketing Research* 35 (1998): 71–81.

53. Study 3 from Wansink, Kent, and Hoch, "An Anchoring and Adjustment Model."

54. B. Wansink, R. J. Kent, and S. J. Hoch, "Point-of-Purchase Promotions That Sell More Units," Working Paper Series MSI-97-120, Marketing Science Institute, Cambridge, MA, 1997, cited in Wansink, Kent, and Hoch, "An Anchoring and Adjustment Model." It should be noted that there seemed to be an overload effect for the last condition ("shipped to the store in boxes of 56"). Participants in the 56 condition said they would not purchase quite as many as those in the "boxes of 28" group, but the other three groups expressed intentions to buy larger quantities in a pattern that was proportional to the irrelevant "shipped to the store" anchor.

55. Study 4 from Wansink, Kent, and Hoch, "An Anchoring and Adjustment Model."

56. D. Soman and J. T. Gourville, "The Consumer Psychology of Mail-in Rebates: A Model of Anchoring and Adjustment," December 10, 2005, http://ssrn.com/abstract=875658.

57. Tony Mecia, "Beware: Rebate and Promotional Cards Can Expire Quickly," CreditCards.com, February 2, 2016, http://www.creditcards.com/credit-card-news/rebate-promotional-card-expire-quickly-1264.php.

58. B. Grow, "The Great Rebate Runaround," *Business Week*, November 23, 2005, www.businessweek.com/bwdaily/dnflash/nov2005/nf20051123_4158_db016.htm; Dan Horne, "Unredeemed Gift Cards and the Problem of Not Providing Customers with Value," *Journal of Consumer Marketing* 24, no. 4 (2007): 192–93. Concerns about rebates were such that the state of Connecticut passed a law preventing

the advertising of the net, after-rebate price of product unless the retailer credits the amount of the rebate at the time of purchase. See Department of Consumer Protection, "DCP: Rebates," http://www.ct.gov/dcp/cwp/view.asp?q=430768.

59. Study 1 from Soman and Gourville, "The Consumer Psychology of Mail-in Rebates." This study also included a group who were asked to think of both reasons they would redeem and reasons they would not, but discussion of this group is omitted for simplicity.

60. Gillian Ku, Adam D. Galinsky, and J. Keith Murnighan, "Starting Low but Ending High: A Reversal of the Anchoring Effect in Auctions," *Journal of Personality and social Psychology* 90, no. 6 (2006): 975.

61. Cong Feng, Scott Fay, and K. Sivakumar, "Overbidding in Electronic Auctions: Factors Influencing the Propensity to Overbid and the Magnitude of Overbidding," *Journal of the Academy of Marketing Science* 44, no. 2 (2016): 241–60.

62. Po-Hsin Ho, Chia-Wei Huang, Chih-Yung Lin, and Ju-Fang Yen, "CEO Overconfidence and Financial Crisis: Evidence from Bank Lending and Leverage," *Journal of Financial Economics* 120, no. 1 (2016): 194–209; H. A. Bedau and M. Radelet, "Miscarriages of Justice in Potentially Capital Cases," *Stanford Law Review* 40 (1987): 21–179.

63. G. L. Wells and E. A. Olson, "Eyewitness Testimony," *Annual Review of Psychology,* 54 (2003): 277–95. The correlation between confidence and accuracy was estimated to be .37.

64. David Shariatmadari, "Daniel Kahneman: 'What would I eliminate if I had a magic wand? Overconfidence,'" The Guardian, July 18, 2015, https://www.theguardian.com/books/2015/jul/18/daniel-kahneman-books-interview.

65. Plous, *The Psychology of Judgment and Decision Making*. This account is a simplified description of Northcraft and Neale, "Experts, Amateurs, and Real Estate." See also A. H. Murphy and R. L. Winkler, "Probability Forecasting in Meteorology," *Journal of the American Statistical Association* 79 (1984): 489–500.

66. L. B. Alloy and L. Y. Abramson, "Judgment of Contingency in Depressed and Nondepressed Students: Sadder but Wiser?" *Journal of Experimental Psychology: General* 108 (1979): 441–85.

67. On the benefits of being optimistic, see, for example, Sangy Srivastava, Kelly M. McGonigal, Jane M. Richards, Emily A. Butler, and James J. Gross, "Optimism in Close Relationships: How Seeing Things in a Positive Light Makes Them So," *Journal of Personality and Social Psychology* 91, 1 (2006): 143–53. On ways of building an upbeat life, see, for example, S. E. Taylor, *Positive Illusions: Creative Self-Deception and the Healthy Mind* (New York: Basic Books, 1989).

68. Most of the behavioral economic research in this area has not examined overconfidence about one's actions in the future, which is the primary concern here. Instead, these studies have been typically designed to measure overconfidence about the accuracy of various judgments, such as the participants' answers on a quiz (Plous, *The Psychology of Judgment and Decision Making*; J. E. Russo and J. H. Shoemaker, *Decision Traps: Ten Barriers to Brilliant Decision Making and How to Overcome Them* [New York: Simon and Schuster, 1989]), but the results of these studies have been used to interpret many common examples of consumer overconfidence (e.g., J. W. Alba and J. W. Hutchinson, "Knowledge

Calibration: What Consumers Know and What They Think They Know," *Journal of Consumer Research* 27 [2000], 123–56; Belsky and Gilovich, *Why Smart People Make Big Money Mistakes*).

69. Belsky and Gilovich, *Why Smart People Make Big Money Mistakes.*

70. Belsky and Gilovich, *Why Smart People Make Big Money Mistakes.*

71. C. Camerer and D. Lovallo, "Overconfidence and Excess Entry: An Experimental Approach," *American Economic Review* 89 (1999): 306–18.

72. S. Della Vigna and U. Malmendier, "Paying Not to Go to the Gym," *American Economic Review* 96 (2006): 694–719.

73. H. M. Shefrin and R. H. Thaler, "The Behavioral Life-Cycle Hypothesis," *Economic Inquiry* 26 (1988): 609–43.

74. These survey results are from Shefrin and Thaler, "The Behavioral Life-Cycle Hypothesis."

75. W. James, *The Principles of Psychology* (New York: Holt, 1981 [1890]), 1167.

CHAPTER 9

1. J. S. Hacker, *The Great Risk Shift: The Assault on American Jobs, Families, Health Care, and Retirement and How You Can Fight Back* (New York: Oxford University Press, 2006).

2. Thomas Piketty, *Capital in the Twenty-First Century* (Cambridge, MA: Harvard University Press, 2014); Joseph E. Stiglitz, *The Great Divide* (New York: Penguin Books, 2016); Jim Tankersley, "American Dream Collapsing for Young Adults, Study Says, as Odds Plunge That Children Will Earn More Than Their Parents," *Washington Post*, December 8, 2016, https://www.washingtonpost.com/news/wonk/wp/2016/12/08/american-dream-collapsing-for-young-americans-study-says-finding-plunging-odds-that-children-earn-more-than-their-parents/?utm_term=.e4f4cb4293da.

3. Jonathan Capehart, "The War on Economic Insecurity," *Washington Post*, January 14, 2014, https://www.washingtonpost.com/blogs/post-partisan/wp/2014/01/14/the-war-on-economic-insecurity/?utm_term=.951b17cf878e; Proctor, Bernadette D., Jessica L. Semega, and Melissa A. Kollar, "Income and Poverty in the United States: 2015," United States Census Bureau, September 13, 2016, accessed August 19, 2017, https://www.census.gov/library/publications/2016/demo/p60-256.html.

4. Brian Milligan, "UK Household Debt Now a Record £13,000, Says TUC," *BBC News*, January 8, 2017, http://www.bbc.com/news/business-38534238.

5. David Taylor, "Australia's Household Debt Crisis Is Worse Than Ever," *ABC News*, April 4, 2017, http://www.abc.net.au/news/2017-04-05/australias-household-debt-crisis-is-worse-than-ever/8413612.

6. I recommend G. Belsky and T. Gilovich, *Why Smart People Make Big Money Mistakes* (New York: Simon and Schuster, 1999).

7. Ann D. Witte and Diane F. Woodbury, "The Effect of Tax Laws and Tax Administration on Tax Compliance: The Case of the US Individual Income Tax," *National Tax Journal* (1985): 1–13.

8. Hacker, *The Great Risk Shift.*

9. R. H. Thaler and S. Benartzi, "Save More Tomorrow: Using Behavioral Economics to Increase Employee Savings," *Journal of Political Economy* 112, no. 1 pt. 2 (2004): S164–87.

10. This is according to Shlomo Benartzi's website at the UCLA Anderson School of management: "Shlomo Benartzi," UCLA Anderson, http://www.anderson.ucla.edu/faculty-and-research/behavioral-decision-making/faculty/benartzi.

11. Jim Cullen, *The American Dream: A Short History of an Idea That Shaped A Nation* (New York: Oxford University Press, 2004).

12. Lawrence F. Katz and Alan B. Krueger, "Documenting Decline in US Economic Mobility," *Science* 356, no. 6336 (2017): 382–83; Raj Chetty, David Grusky, Maximilian Hell, Nathaniel Hendren, Robert Manduca, and Jimmy Narang, "The Fading American Dream: Trends in Absolute Income Mobility since 1940," *Science* 356, no. 6336 (2017): 398–406.

13. Fatih Guvenen, Greg Kaplan, Jae Song, and Justin Weidner, *Lifetime Incomes in the United States over Six Decades*, National Bureau of Economic Research, No. w23371, 2017, doi: 10.3386/w23371.

14. Christina Starmans, Mark Sheskin, and Paul Bloom, "Why People Prefer Unequal Societies," *Nature Human Behaviour* 1 (2017): 82.

15. "Your Key to European Statistics," Home—Eurostat, accessed July 24, 2017, http://ec.europa.eu/eurostat.

16. Kelly Phillips Erb, "11 Reasons Why I Never Want to Own a House Again," Forbes, October 24, 2013, https://www.forbes.com/sites/kellyphillipserb/2013/09/27/11-reasons-why-i-never-want-to-own-a-house-again/#3f10565042fa.

17. David H. Autor, "Skills, Education, and the Rise of Earnings Inequality among 'the other 99 percent,'" *Science*, May 23, 2014, http://science.sciencemag.org/content/344/6186/843.full.

18. Dan A. Black, and Jeffrey A. Smith, "Estimating the Returns to College Quality with Multiple Proxies for Quality," *Journal of Labor Economics* 24, no. 3 (2006): 701–28; Stacy Berg Dale and Alan B. Krueger, "Estimating the Payoff to Attending a More Selective College: An Application of Selection on Observables and Unobservables," *Quarterly Journal of Economics* 117, no. 4 (2002): 1491–527; Lars J. Kirkeboen, Edwin Leuven, and Magne Mogstad, "Field of Study, Earnings, and Self-Selection," *Quarterly Journal of Economics* 131, no. 3 (2016): 1057–111; W. Bentley MacLeod, Evan Riehl, Juan E. Saavedra, and Miguel Urquiola. *The Big Sort: College Reputation and Labor Market Outcomes*, National Bureau of Economic Research, No. w21230, 2015.

19. Christopher Avery and Sarah Turner, "Student Loans: Do College Students Borrow Too Much—Or Not Enough?" *Journal of Economic Perspectives* 26, no. 1 (2012): 165–92.

20. Zachary Bleemer, Meta Brown, Donghoon Lee, and Wilbert van der Klaauw, *Debt, Jobs, or Housing: What's Keeping Millennials at Home?*, Staff Report No. 700, Federal Reserve Bank of New York, 2014; Meta Brown, "Young Student Loan Borrowers Retreat from Housing and Auto Markets," *Liberty Street Economics*, April 17, 2013, http://libertystreeteconomics.newyorkfed.org/2013/04/young-student-loan-borrowers-retreat-from-housing-and-auto-markets.html; Zachary Bleemer, Meta

Brown, Donghoon Lee, Katherine Strair, and Wilbert van der Klaauw, *Echoes of Rising Tuition in Students' Borrowing, Educational Attainment, and Homeownership in Post-Recession America*, Federal Reserve Bank of New York, No. 820, 2017. Dora Gicheva, "Student Loans or Marriage? A Look at the Highly Educated," *Economics of Education Review* 53 (2016): 207–16, doi:10.1016/j.econedurev.2016.04.006.

21. Brown, "Young Student Loan Borrowers."

22. "Were Your Loans Worth It? • r/StudentLoans," *Reddit*, https://www.reddit.com/r/StudentLoans/comments/5jtcs9/were_you_loans_worth_it/?st=j5mi1nrn&sh=819ce421.

23. Elizabeth A. Harris, "New York City Consumer Agency Investigating Four For-Profit Colleges," *New York Times*, April 2, 2015, https://www.nytimes.com/2015/04/03/nyregion/new-york-city-consumer-agency-investigating-four-for-profit-colleges.html.

24. Reddit user TheeHamSandwich.

25. Here is an example of this kind of budget trimming advice: http://www.lifehack.org/articles/money/30-ways-cut-your-monthly-expenses.html.

26. "Stopping Unsolicited Mail, Phone Calls, and Email," Consumer Information, United States Federal Trade Commission, June 9, 2017, https://www.consumer.ftc.gov/articles/0262-stopping-unsolicited-mail-phone-calls-and-email.

27. J. B. Schor, *Born to Buy: The Commercialized Child and the New Consumer Culture* (New York: Scribner, 2004).

28. Jonathan A. Mitchell, Daniel Rodriguez, Kathryn H. Schmitz, and Janet Audrain-McGovern, "Greater Screen Time Is Associated with Adolescent Obesity: A Longitudinal Study of the BMI Distribution from Ages 14 to 18," *Obesity*, April 16, 2013, http://onlinelibrary.wiley.com/doi/10.1002/oby.20157/full.

29. Center for a New American Dream, *Tips for Parenting in a Commercial Culture*, April 2006, www.newdream.org.

30. "Kids Unbranded," *The Center for a New American Dream*, https://www.newdream.org/resources/publications/kids-unbranded.

31. A. S. Campagna, *Macroeconomics* (New York: St. Martin's Press, 1981).

32. "How to Set a Savings Goal," Money Advice Service, https://www.moneyadviceservice.org.uk/en/articles/how-to-set-a-savings-goal.

33. James P. Womack, Daniel T. Jones, and Daniel Roos, *The Machine That Changed the World* (New York: HarperPerennial, 1990).

34. "Freakonomics: Do Wine Experts or Prices Matter?" *Marketplace*, https://www.marketplace.org/2010/11/30/life/freakonomics-radio/freakonomics-do-wine-experts-or-prices-matter.

35. Christopher Kompanek, "'Freakonomics' Co-Author Steven Levitt Talks Data—and Dieting," Financial Times, May 9, 2014, accessed July 29, 2017, https://www.ft.com/content/1b96cfdc-d13b-11e3-9f90-00144feabdc0; "How to Think about Money, Choose Your Hometown, and Buy an Electric Toothbrush: A New Freakonomics Radio Podcast Full Transcript," Freakonomics, October 3, 2013, http://freakonomics.com/2013/10/03/how-to-think-about-money-choose-your-hometown-and-buy-an-electric-toothbrush-a-new-freakonomics-radio-podcast-full-transcript/. Although it appears that Levitt is fairly frugal and nonmaterialistic

in his own life, he does not really advocate simple living as a lifestyle. In this October 3, 2013, podcast, he subscribes to a typical life-cycle view and argues that many young people do not spend enough.

36. For simplicity's sake, I am using the single term "simple living" to stand in for several different but related cultural movements: frugal living, simple living, plentitude (a term introduced by Juliet Schor), and other varieties of antimaterialistic lifestyles.

37. According to this 2015 interview, Donald Trump's favorite color is "whatever I am wearing," and his second favorite color is gold, "because it comes in gold." Given these somewhat inscrutable responses, I think it is safe to say that gold is President Trump's favorite color. Brian Frazer, "21 Fantastic, Unbelievable Questions for Donald Trump," *Esquire*, September 17, 2015, http://www.esquire.com/news-politics/q-and-a/a37998/donald-trump-questions/REFC; REFO:BKEmrys Westacott, *The Wisdom of Frugality: Why Less Is More—More or Less* (Princeton, NJ: Princeton University Press, 2016).

38. "Mission," New Dream.org, https://www.newdream.org/about/mission.

39. Here is an excellent example of the classic tax refund advice: M. Dalrymple, "Reclaiming Your Money," October 9, 2006, www.fool.com/personal-finance/taxes/2006/10/09/reclaiming-your-money.aspx.

40. "The Bureau," *Consumer Financial Protection Bureau*, https://www.consumerfinance.gov/about-us/the-bureau/.

41. Matt Egan, "5,300 Wells Fargo Employees Fired over 2 Million Phony Accounts," *CNNMoney*, September 9, 2016, http://money.cnn.com/2016/09/08/investing/wells-fargo-created-phony-accounts-bank-fees/index.html. Elizabeth Warren, *This Fight Is Our Fight: The Battle to Save America's Middle Class* (New York: Picador, 2018):189–91.

42. Joseph Lawler, "Hensarling to Cordray: Commit to Serving Out Term as CFPB Head or Resign," *Washington Examiner*, July 14, 2017, http://www.washingtonexaminer.com/hensarling-to-cordray-commit-to-serving-out-term-as-cfpb-head-or-resign/article/2628727.

43. Hacker, *The Great Risk Shift*.

44. Claire Cain Miller, "The Long-Term Jobs Killer Is Not China. It's Automation," *New York Times*, December 21, 2016, https://www.nytimes.com/2016/12/21/upshot/the-long-term-jobs-killer-is-not-china-its-automation.html.

45. Rob Stein, "Life Expectancy in U.S. Drops for First Time in Decades, Report Finds," NPR, December 08, 2016, accessed July 31, 2017, http://www.npr.org/sections/health-shots/2016/12/08/504667607/life-expectancy-in-u-s-drops-for-first-time-in-decades-report-finds.

46. Hacker, *The Great Risk Shift*.

47. Annamaria Lusardi and Peter Tufano. *Debt Literacy, Financial Experiences, and Overindebtedness*, National Bureau of Economic Research, No. w14808, 2009, https://www.econstor.eu/bitstream/10419/43242/1/606213376.pdf.

48. OECD, "PISA 2012 Results: Students and Money: Financial Literacy Skills for the 21st Century," Volume 6, PISA, OECD Publishing, 2014, http://dx.doi.org/10.1787/9789264208094-en.

49. B. D. Bernheim, D. M. Garrett, and D. M. Maki, "Education and Saving: The Long-Term Effects of High School Financial Curriculum Mandates," *Journal of Public Economics* 80 (2001): 435–65.

50. Carly Urban, Maximilian Schmeiser, J. Michael Collins, and Alexandra Brown, "The Effects of State Policies Requiring High School Personal Finance Education on Credit Scores," working paper 2016-002, Madison: University of Wisconsin, Robert M. La Follette School of Public Affairs, 2016.

51. Jump$tart Coalition for Personal Financial Literacy, www.jumpstart.org.

52. See Stephen Brobeck, executive director of the Consumer Federation of America, "The Role and Limits of Financial Education," testimony before the Committee on Banking, Housing, and Urban Affairs of the US Senate, May 23, 2006, www.consumerfed.org/pdfs/Financial_Literacy_Hearing_2006_SB_Testimony052426.pdf.

53. Ray Boshara, Reid Cramer, Leslie Parrish, and Anne Stuhldreher, *The Assets Agenda 2006: Policy Options to Broaden Savings and Ownership by Low- and Moderate-Income Americans* (Washington, DC: New America Foundation, 2006), available at https://static.newamerica.org/attachments/3736-the-assets-agenda-2006/Doc_File_3006_1.b10b742cd5de45948888c99150e8260e.pdf.

54. Reid Cramer, "Splitting Refunds: A Proposal to Leverage the Tax Filing Process to Promote Savings and Asset Building," *New America Foundation Asset Building Program*, Washington, DC, 2005, https://pdfs.semanticscholar.org/ed20/1cea3d6a478c3489a203157a643f2c076789.pdf.

55. "Frequently Asked Questions about Splitting Federal Income Tax Refunds," accessed August 1, 2017, https://www.irs.gov/individuals/frequently-asked-questions-about-splitting-federal-income-tax-refunds.

56. John Beshears, James J. Choi, David Laibson, and Brigitte C. Madrian. "The importance of default options for retirement saving outcomes: Evidence from the United States." In Jeffrey R. Brown, Jeffrey B. Liebman, and David A. Wise, *Social security policy in a changing environment*, pp. 167–195. (University of Chicago Press, 2009).

57. David W. Rothwell, and Anna Goren, "Exploring the Relationship between Asset Holding and Family Economic Strain," *Journal of Health and Social Behavior* 40, no. 1 (2011): 1–16.

58. B. C. Madrian and D. F. Shea, "The Power of Suggestion: Inertia in 401(k) Saving Participation and Saving Behavior," *Quarterly Journal of Economics* 116 (2001): 1149–87.

59. C. R. Sunstein and R. H. Thaler, "Libertarian Paternalism Is Not an Oxymoron," *University of Chicago Law Review* 70 (2003): 1159–202; R. H. Thaler and C. R. Sunstein, "Libertarian Paternalism," *American Economic Review* 93 (2003): 175–79; Richard H. Thaler, and Cass R. Sunstein, *Nudge: Improving Decisions about Health, Wealth, and Happiness* (New Haven, CT: Yale University Press, 2008).

60. See, for example, the *Economist* magazine cover story, "The Avuncular State," April 6, 2006.

61. Thaler and Sunstein, "Libertarian Paternalism."

62. Boshara et al., *The Assets Agenda* 2006; Ray Boshara, "Every Baby a Trust Fund Baby," *Ten Big Ideas for a New America* (2007): 1–4, https://static.newamerica.org/attachments/3717-every-baby-a-trust-fund-baby/NAF_10big_Ideas_1.418d0bbc5b454b3b8ed467d62c3375cd.pdf

63. McNeal and Kids (College Station, Texas), cited in *Harper's* magazine, March 2007, 13.

64. Some valuable resources include the September 2000 US General Accounting Office report "Commercial Activities in Schools," www.gao.gov/archive/2000/he00156.pdf, and the Commercialism in Education Research Unit at Arizona State University, http://epsl.asu.edu/ceru/index.htm.

65. "Investigation Shows That FTC's Reminder Letters Are Ineffective at Disclosing Paid Posts on Instagram," Campaign for a Commercial-Free Childhood, June 26, 2017, accessed August 1, 2017, http://www.commercialfreechildhood.org/investigation-shows-ftcs-reminder-letters-are-ineffective-disclosing-paid-posts-instagram.

66. Mission statement: www.commercialalert.org.

67. "Screen-Free Week Organizer's Kit," Campaign for a Commercial-Free Childhood, accessed March 28, 2018, http://www.commercialfreechildhood.org/resource/screen-free-week-organizers-kit

68. New Jersey State Casino Control Commission Self Exclusion List, http://www.nj.gov/oag/ge/selfexclusion_bet.html; Illinois Gaming Board Self-Exclusion Program for Problem Gamblers https://www.igb.illinois.gov/RiverboatSEP.aspx;

69. S. M. Gainsbury, "Review of Self-Exclusion from Gambling Venues as an Intervention for Problem Gambling," *Journal of Gambling Studies* (2014) 30: 229–51, https://doi.org/10.1007/s10899-013-9362-0

70. "Caesars Entertainment Responsible Gaming Program," accessed on March 28, 2018, https://totalrewards.custhelp.com/app/answers/detail/a_id/650/~/caesars-entertainment---responsible-gaming-exclusion

71. Colin Camerer, Samuel Issacharoff, George Loewenstein, Ted O'Donoghue, and Matthew Rabin, "Regulation for Conservatives: Behavioral Economics and the Case for 'Asymmetric Paternalism,'" *University of Pennsylvania Law Review* 151 (2003): 1211–54.

72. Jennifer Saranow Schultz, "What the Credit Card Act Means for You," *New York Times*, February 22, 2010, https://bucks.blogs.nytimes.com/2010/02/22/what-the-credit-card-act-means-for-you/?_r=0.

73. James M. Lacko, Signe-Mary McKernan, and Manoj Hastak, "Customer Experience with Rent-to-Own Transactions," *Journal of Public Policy and Marketing* 21, no. 1 (2002): 126–38, https://www.researchgate.net/profile/Manoj_Hastak/publication/247837382_Customer_Experience_with_Rent-to-Own_Transactions/links/553031cf0cf27acb0de85573.pdf

74. Chico Harlan, "Rental America: Why the Poor Pay $4,150 for a $1,500 Sofa," *Washington Post*, October 16, 2014, https://www.washingtonpost.com/news/storyline/wp/2014/10/16/she-bought-a-sofa-on-installment-payments-now-its-straining-her-life/?utm_term=.14e8b4b2a7ca; "Rent-to-Own: Costly Convenience," Consumer Information, September 1, 2016, https://www.consumer.ftc.gov/articles/0524-rent-own-costly-convenience.

75. "Buyer's Remorse: When the FTC's Cooling-Off Rule May Help," Consumer Information, September 1, 2016, https://www.consumer.ftc.gov/articles/0176-buyers-remorse-when-ftcs-cooling-rule-may-help; "Guarantees: Repairs, Replacements, Refunds," Your Europe—Citizens, http://europa.eu/youreurope/citizens/consumers/shopping/guarantees-returns/index_en.htm.

76. Camerer et al., "Regulation for Conservatives."

77. John Beshears, James J. Choi, David Laibson, and Brigitte Madrian, "Early Decisions: A Regulatory Framework," National Bureau of Economic Research, No. w11920, 2006, https://www.researchgate.net/profile/David_ Laibson/publication/5186701_Early_Decisions_A_Regulatory_Framework/ links/02bfe511131b151801000000.pdf.

78. Kimberly Amadeo, "Ways the CFSB Protects You and You Don't Even Know It," *The Balance*, June 27, 2017, https://www.thebalance.com/consumer-financial-protection-bureau-3305629.

79. Amadeo, "Ways the CFSB Protects You."

80. "Bush Shopping Quote," C-SPAN.org, https://www.c-span.org/video/?c4552776% 2Fbush-shopping-quote; Robert Shiller, "Spend, Spend, Spend. It's the American Way," *New York Times*, January 14, 2012, http://www.nytimes.com/2012/01/15/ business/consumer-spending-as-an-american-virtue.html?mcubz=0.

81. R. H. Frank, *Microeconomics and Behavior* (New York: McGraw-Hill, 1991).

Further Reading

Belskey, G., and T. Gilovich. 1999. *Why Smart People Make Big Money Mistakes— and How to Correct Them: Lessons from the New Science of Behavioral Economics.* New York: Simon and Schuster.

Desmond, Matthew. 2016. *Evicted: Poverty and Profit in the American City.* New York: Broadway Books.

Dominguez, J., and V. Robin. 1992. *Your Money or Your Life: Transforming Your Relationship with Money and Achieving Financial Independence.* New York: Penguin.

Draut, T. 2005. *Strapped: Why America's 20- and 30-Somethings Can't Get Ahead.* New York: Doubleday.

Hacker, J. S. 2006. *The Great Risk Shift: The Assault on American Jobs, Families, Health Care, and Retirement, and How You Can Fight Back.* New York: Oxford University Press.

Kahneman, Daniel. 2013. *Thinking, Fast and Slow.* New York: Farrar, Straus and Giroux.

Kamenetz, A. 2006. *Generation Debt: Why Now Is a Terrible Time to Be Young.* New York: Riverhead Books.

Mian, Atif, and Amir Sufi. 2014. *House of Debt: How They (and You) Caused the Great Recession, and How We Can Prevent It from Happening Again.* Chicago: University of Chicago Press.

Manning, R. D. 2000. *Credit Card Nation: The Consequences of America's Addiction to Credit.* New York: Basic Books.

Plous, S. 1993. *The Psychology of Judgment and Decision Making.* New York: McGraw-Hill.

Rachlin, H. 2000. *The Science of Self-Control.* Cambridge, MA: Harvard University Press.

Schor, J. B. 1998. *The Overspent American: Why We Want What We Don't Need.* New York: HarperPerennial.

———. 2005. *Born to Buy: The Commercialized Child and the New Consumer Culture.* New York: Scribner.

———. 2011. *True Wealth: How and Why Millions of Americans Are Creating a Time-Rich, Ecologically Light, Small-Scale, High-Satisfaction Economy.* New York: Penguin.

Schwartz, B. 2004. *The Paradox of Choice: Why More Is Less.* New York: Ecco.

Thaler, Richard, and Cass Sunstein. 2009. *Nudge: Improving Decisions about Health, Wealth, and Happiness.* New York: Penguin.

Warren, E., and A. W. Tyagi. 2003. *The Two-Income Trap: Why Middle-Class Mothers and Fathers Are Going Broke.* New York: Basic Books.

———. 2005. *All Your Worth: The Ultimate Lifetime Money Plan.* New York: Free Press.

HELPFUL ORGANIZATIONS

Americans for Fairness in Lending

www.affil.org

Devoted to raising awareness of abusive credit and lending practices and to calling for regulation of the industry.

Center for Responsible Lending

www.responsiblelending.org

A nonprofit, nonpartisan research and policy organization dedicated to protecting homeownership and family wealth by working to eliminate abusive financial practices.

Commercial Alert

www.commercialalert.org

Working to "keep the commercial culture within its proper sphere, and to prevent it from exploiting children and subverting the higher values of family, community, environmental integrity and democracy."

Consumer Federation of America

www.consumerfed.org

An advocacy, research, education, and service organization working to advance proconsumer policy on a variety of issues before Congress, the White House, federal and state regulatory agencies, state legislatures, and the courts.

Consumer Finance Protection Bureau

www.consumerfinance.gov

US government bureau created to make sure consumer financial markets work for consumers, responsible providers, and the economy as a whole. The bureau provides information to consumers and has the power to take action against companies that break the law.

Debtors Anonymous

debtorsanonymous.org

Demos

www.demos.org

A nonpartisan public policy research and advocacy organization committed to building an America that achieves its highest democratic ideals and an economy where prosperity and opportunity are broadly shared and disparity is reduced.

The Jump$tart Coalition for Personal Financial Literacy

www.jumpstart.org

A national coalition of organizations dedicated to improving the financial literacy of kindergarten through college-age youth by providing advocacy, research, standards and educational resources.

Downshifting and Simplifying

Financial Integrity

www.financialintegrity.org

Offers tools for a healthy relationship with money with the goal of providing a sense of satisfaction and fulfillment from engagement with family, community, and the planet.

New Dream

www.newdream.org

Helping people consume responsibly to protect the environment, enhance quality of life, and promote social justice.

Simplicity Collective

simplicitycollective.com

An online gathering place and forum "dedicated to creatively exploring, promoting, and celebrating a materially simple but inwardly rich life."

For Kids

Media Smarts

mediasmarts.ca

A nonprofit organization promoting media and Internet education with the goal of giving children the critical thinking skills to engage with media as active and informed digital citizens.

A NOTE ABOUT THE INTERVIEWS

Of the eight cases presented in this book, five were contacted through the US courts' listings of personal bankruptcy cases. I mailed approximately 150 letters to people who had gone through this process, and I heard back from seven individuals or couples who were willing to talk to me. Response rates are typically quite low for mail surveys, but a response rate of 5 percent is unusually low, undoubtedly a reflection of many people's reluctance to revisit an unpleasant period of their lives. Frank and Caroline were referred to me by the coordinators of support groups they attended, and I approached Neil by mail after reading newspaper accounts of his case. All of the profiles except Neil's are based on a single audiotaped interview. In Neil's case, I conducted several interviews without the aid of a tape recorder, corresponded with him by mail, and, with his permission, obtained a number of court documents. In each case, the participant signed an informed-consent form, and the methods used to conduct the interviews were approved by the Connecticut College Institutional Review Board. The participants' names and some of the details of their cases have been changed to protect their anonymity, but the essential features of the situations they faced have been preserved. These profiles should not be taken as a representative sample of those who experience debt problems. Instead, they are presented here to show the range of paths to indebtedness and to put a human face on an otherwise hidden problem.

ACKNOWLEDGMENTS

I am particularly grateful to the debtors who agreed to be interviewed. Even under the protection of anonymity, it was difficult for these people to come forward and revisit very unpleasant periods of their lives, and I thank them for being willing to share their stories.

Connecticut College supported the first edition of this book in many ways, but I am particularly grateful for two sabbatical leaves that allowed me the time to think and write. In addition, I thank my colleagues in the Psychology Department for their support and encouragement. Ann Sloan Devlin, Jefferson Singer, Joan Chrisler, and our department administrator, Nancy MacLeod, deserve special mention.

The Psychology Department of the University of Rhode Island provided me with an office to conduct some of the interviews, and in particular I thank Jean Maher and my former student Dustin Wielt for their help in arranging for this space.

Much of what I know about philosophy—some of which appears in these pages—I have learned from my very generous colleagues Alan Bradford, Simon Feldman, Dirk Held, Derek Turner, and Larry Vogel. My meager study of philosophy has given me great pleasure, much of which I owe to these friends.

In my pursuit of data for this book I received substantial assistance from Meta Brown and Joelle Scally of the Federal Reserve Bank of New York; Ed Flynn, Executive Office for United States Trustees; Thomas Webb of Cox Automotive; and Christian E. Weller, senior economist, Center for American Progress.

Megan Patty, copyright assistant, National Gallery of Victoria, Melbourne, Australia, provided able assistance in connection with the use of John William Waterhouse's painting *Ulysses and the Sirens*. Special thanks to Darren Fleeger for providing the photograph of the Wellsville, New York, grocery store.

A number of people suggested or helped me obtain material and are gratefully acknowledged: William Hargreaves, Candace Howes, Spencer Pack, Herbert Sloan, Abigail Van Slyck, Keith Vyse, and Norma Vyse.

Many colleagues, relatives, and friends read sections of the manuscript and provided valuable commentary: George Ainslie, Lori Blinderman, Ann Sloan Devlin, Mitch Favreau, Marc Forster, Leonard Green, Gary Greenberg, Candace Howes, Stephen Loomis, Spencer Pack, Nancy Petry, Howard Rachlin, Hank Schlinger, Jefferson Singer, Abigail Van Slyck, Keith Vyse, and Norma Vyse.

I also thank Will Vaughan Jr., the wag of Chebeague Island, Maine, whom I got to know the way you do when you encounter people over beers at professional meetings. On the strength of this loose acquaintanceship, Will went to bat for me when, as a young assistant professor with deplorably inadequate preparation in mathematics and economics, I expressed interest in spending a pretenure sabbatical with him in Richard Herrnstein's pigeon laboratory at Harvard University. My time in Cambridge—where I had the great good fortune to meet Terry Belke, now of Mount Allison University—was a pivotal episode in my professional life, and this book is the most significant outgrowth of that experience.

I am very grateful for the support of Susan Lescher, my literary agent for the first edition of this book, and Jessica Papin, my agent for the second. At Oxford University Press, I begin my thanks with Joan Bossert, who gave me my first chance and has been loyal ever since. It was Joan who first suggested a book on debt, and in time I realized how good an idea it was. My editor for the first edition, Marion Osmun, was strongly committed to this project from the beginning and wise and wonderful throughout. The first edition also benefited from the editorial assistance of Steve Holtje and Sarah Harrington and was copyedited by Sue Warga. The second edition would not have come into the world without the great support and guidance of my editor at Oxford, Sarah Harrington. This edition benefitted from editorial assistance by Shelli Stevens, production editing by Devasena Vedamurthi, and expert copyediting by Sylvia Cannizzaro.

Chapter 9 was substantially improved by a number of suggestions made by Kevin Plummer, an extremely talented psychologist and oney manager who is also a very dear friend.

I am grateful to Marc Forster for many "writers' lunches" held during our sabbatical leaves.

I acknowledge the following friends and family members for their support of me in general and this project in particular: Gabby Arenge, Steven Colucci, Alexis Dudden, Mitch Favreau, Marc Forster, Robert Gay, Alex Hybel, Ross Morin, Kevin Plummer, Hank Schlinger, Abigail Van Slyck, Robert Whitcomb, Lisa Wilson, Norma Vyse, Arthur F. Vyse III, Keith Vyse, Emily Vyse, and Graham Vyse.

No one helped me more with the first edition of this book than Candace Howes. She read and commented on much of the manuscript, for which I am very grateful.